National Identity and Political Thought in Germany

*Wilhelmine Depictions of the
French Third Republic,
1890–1914*

MARK HEWITSON

CLARENDON PRESS • OXFORD

*This book has been printed digitally and produced in a standard specification
in order to ensure its continuing availability*

OXFORD
UNIVERSITY PRESS

Great Clarendon Street, Oxford OX2 6DP

Oxford University Press is a department of the University of Oxford.
It furthers the University's objective of excellence in research, scholarship,
and education by publishing worldwide in

Oxford New York

Auckland Bangkok Buenos Aires Cape Town Chennai
Dar es Salaam Delhi Hong Kong Istanbul Karachi Kolkata
Kuala Lumpur Madrid Melbourne Mexico City Mumbai Nairobi
São Paulo Shanghai Taipei Tokyo Toronto

Oxford is a registered trade mark of Oxford University Press
in the UK and in certain other countries

Published in the United States
by Oxford University Press Inc., New York

© Dr. Mark Hewitson 2000

The moral rights of the author have been asserted

Database right Oxford University Press (maker)

Reprinted 2003

ISBN 0-19-820858-8

ACKNOWLEDGEMENTS

I have become indebted to many people in the course of writing this book. Scholarships awarded by the Stiftung F.V.S., Hamburg, and the British Academy allowed me to carry out my research and complete most of the writing. Michael John, Heinz-Otto Sieburg, and Wolfgang Kruse kindly provided published and unpublished materials without which sections of the original thesis could not have been written. The French and German History Seminars at Oxford University were invaluable sources of discussion and reflection, encouraging me to consider new arguments and reconsider old ones during early drafts of the study. Many other friends, students, and colleagues have provided encouragement, ideas, and criticism at different stages. I especially wish to thank Leslie Mitchell and Rainer Liedtke, who read parts or all of the manuscript and offered much-appreciated comments and corrections. My examiners, Tony Nicholls and Michael John, were extremely kind, as well as perspicacious and influential, and have continued to give help and advice as the thesis has been turned into a book. Much of the groundwork of that thesis, and many of its ideas, I owe to Hartmut Pogge, whose enthusiasm and support went well beyond his duties as supervisor. Above all, I owe debts of gratitude, and much else, to Cécile Laborde and to my family, without whose patience, tolerance, and common sense this book would never have been finished.

Barnsley   M.H.
April 1998

CONTENTS

I

Introduction
Germany and the French Nation

1. National Comparison in the Modern Age

On 25 January 1914 a cartoon, entitled 'Zabern after the Judgment: A Neo-Futurist-Cubist Picture of the Times', appeared in the liberal satirical journal, *Kladderadatsch*.[1] It referred to the dismissal of charges against Prussian officers who, it was believed in most of the press, had run amok in the Alsatian town of Zabern, imprisoning large numbers of local inhabitants. When the majority of parties in the Reichstag had protested, Chancellor Theobald von Bethmann Hollweg, under pressure from Wilhelm II and the General Staff, had felt obliged to retort that the army had acted constitutionally. The War Minister had refused outright to answer deputies' questions about the affair, claiming that it was a matter which fell within the royal power of command (*Kommandogewalt*), not the jurisdiction of parliament. The most obvious allusion in the *Kladderadatsch* cartoonist's interpretation of these events was to political chaos in the Reich and to the damage which this occasioned: a tumultuous crowd of soldiers, judges, citizens, and officials were shown trampling underfoot a lachrymose Michel, the commonest national personification of Germany. In the background, a tangle of telegraph wires filled the sky. What was less obvious, perhaps, was that the nation-state itself, in the form of Michel and Marianne, was still not overtly challenged by the caricaturist. Home affairs were in complete disarray but national characterizations persisted. Whereas Michel was the innocent victim of political disorder, with whom the reader was meant to sympathize, the other figures in the cartoon were shown to be destructive, each following his own interest to the detriment of

[1] *Kladderadatsch*, no. 4, 25 Jan. 1914.

Germany—hence Marianne's barely concealed smirk. On the one hand, implied the caricaturist, there was the despised disorder of domestic politics and, on the other, the near-sanctity of the nation.

The cartoon hinted, in satirical form, at the connection between politics, the nation, and perceptions of abroad in the frenetic decades before 1914. For most German subjects, the world appeared to be in unusual flux, with individual consciousness threatening to fragment under the pressure of change. It was as if the heavy, ordered figures of a realist painter such as Wilhelm Leibl had been disarranged, their various planes and perspectives juxtaposed according to the relativist precepts of cubism.[2] In such a cubist world, nothing was fixed, everything had more than one meaning, just as objects appeared to change shape from different angles and in different lights. The same seemed to be true of German politics. Government, parties, intellectuals, newspapers, and magazines all proffered their conflicting views and interpretations to a bemused public. Amidst such confusion, a shared sense of national identity became politically important. Traditionally, politics was a negotiation over the legitimate exercise of power, in other words, over the relationships between institutions. Political stability depended on widespread acceptance of a particular institutional configuration. Yet it appeared to many Wilhelmine Germans that such acceptance was lacking. There were, at various times, rumours of a *coup d'état* from the right and socialist revolution from the left. The *Freisinnige*, it was said, favoured a republic and the Catholic Centre Party's loyalty to the political order was, in some quarters, still open to question. It seemed that traditional politics had not achieved consensus. By contrast, national identity existed above and beyond politics and enjoyed considerable protection from political criticism.[3] The reason was paradoxical, for national identity—that is, national indivisibility—constituted the very vessel of politics, the line which divided similar from dissimilar. If individuals were not similar in any respect, how could they organize themselves politically?

[2] C. Derouet, 'Als der Kubismus noch "deutscher Besitz" war', in W. Spies (ed.), *Paris–Berlin 1900–1933. Übereinstimmungen und Gegensätze Frankreich–Deutschland* (Munich, 1979), 42–6. See also cartoons such as 'Wieder daheim!', *Kladderadatsch*, no. 2, 11 Jan. 1914, which poked fun at cubism and futurism, evidently presuming that readers knew of the two movements.

[3] This was implicit in the charges levelled by the main Wilhelmine scholars of the nation-state against party appropriation of national symbols and labels. F. Meinecke, *Weltbürgertum und Nationalstaat*, 7th edn. (Berlin, 1927), 18; A. Kirchhoff, *Was ist national?* (Halle, 1902), 41.

They would have no common principles and no mutual interests. The national vessel would have disappeared, allowing its political contents to escape.[4]

There are three possible parts to national identity: political, cultural, and genetic. Whereas a political nation is a voluntary collective of individuals, which can change at will—a daily plebiscite in the overworked words of Ernest Renan—the genetic nation is a determined, barely changing group, in which identity is branded, not chosen. Between these poles of political advantage and genetic material lie various cultural definitions of the nation, where belonging is dictated by history and habit, language and religion. Generally, historians have emphasized the depth of cultural and genetic notions of nationhood, which established themselves in the absence of the nation-state before 1871, and the shallowness of German political tradition, which is usually portrayed as unstable and contradictory, much as contemporaries described it.[5]

I shall argue here, however, that a unifying political component was added to German national identity, betraying an often unspoken satisfaction with the performance of the Reich's institutions, compared with their French, British, Russian, and American equivalents. The facts were well known. Käthe Schirmacher, a regular correspondent of *Der Tag* and by no means uncritical of the German Reich, was one of many to rehearse them, in a book published in 1906, summarizing the reversed fortunes of France and Germany in the preceding thirty-five years. 'Germany', she wrote, 'is a flourishing land.'[6] In 1870 it had merely established itself as continental Europe's principal military power but today, she continued, the 'German Reich is one of the world's biggest and most rapidly expanding industrial export states in the world.'[7] Unlike France, it had an advanced social insurance system, a net annual population

---

[4] The fact that the nation, even if undefined, constituted the basis of political, legal, and economic decisions was noted at the time by Friedrich Neumann, *Volk und Nation* (Leipzig, 1888), pp. vii–xv. Also M. Weber, 'Der Nationalstaat und die Volkswirtschaftspolitik' (1895), in *Gesammelte politische Schriften*, 2nd revised edn. (Tübingen, 1958), 13.

[5] This assumption has characterized much of the debate over the continuities (Fischer) and peculiarities (Wehler) of German history, in particular the weaknesses of German liberalism (Dahrendorf). For revision of these views, see R. J. Evans, *Rethinking German History* (London, 1987); D. Blackbourn and G. Eley, *The Peculiarities of German History* (Oxford, 1984).

[6] K. Schirmacher, *Deutschland und Frankreich seit 35 Jahren* (Berlin, 1906), 67.

[7] Ibid. 23.

increase of 800,000, and a modern, enterprising, and scientific industrial sector.[8] National administration inevitably profited by association from such a perceived turn for the better.

Yet German institutions were not only compared favourably with
foreign counterparts, they were also pitted against them in a believ-
able political typology, which distinguished above all between a constitutional system of government in Germany and a parliamentary
system in France and Britain. Because such definition and evaluation
took place within the inner sanctum of national identity, which was
unofficially excluded from political controversy, it was barely
noticed. What Germany was and how it compared with other states
were matters discussed at length in the foreign affairs sections of
national newspapers and in case-studies of academic treatises, not in
Reichstag debates.[9] Nevertheless, these were issues on which most
Germans had an opinion and often one supportive of the Reich, even
among those who were otherwise sceptical of politics and government. Thus, the rise of a political component to national identity had
a stabilizing political effect, despite the apparent turbulence of party
life. A degree of political legitimacy had been granted to German
institutions through the back door, for the results of national comparison were usually quietly accepted rather than ostentatiously discussed. In the same way that the unuttered assumptions of national
identity prevented challenges to the idea of *Kleindeutschland* after
1871, so the assumptions of a German political identity, although
neither uniform nor consensual, were consolidated and helped to
protect the reputation of constitutional monarchy.

Implied in the rise of a political component to national identity
was the role of national comparison in political thought. Germans
required points of reference both to convince themselves that the
Reich was performing better than other nation-states and to distinguish how it differed from them. One reason that national comparison assumed such an important part in political thought in Germany
was the unsteady foundation of politics as a field of study.[10] In the
absence of any faculty of political science, the subject was taught by

[8] Schirmacher, *Deutschland und Frankreich seit 35 Jahren*, 23–4, 34, 66, 81–2, 84–6, 101.

[9] There were many comparative references made to foreign nation-states in Reichstag
debates, but these were made in passing. See, for instance, J. Penzler (ed.), *Fürst Bülows
Reden* (3 vols.; Berlin, 1907), i. 391–2, and ii. 108, 134, 238, 242–3, 246, 248, 270–1, 274–5,
289–90, 307–9, 311, 342–3, 352, 419, and iii. 22, 28, 145–53.

[10] H. Maier, *Politische Wissenschaft in Deutschland* (Munich, 1969), 15–52, 69–88.

historians such as Heinrich von Treitschke, whose lectures were published posthumously as *Politik* in 1898, lawyers like Georg Jellinek, who attempted to break away from the confines of legal positivism and provide a social explanation of state law, and historical economists such as Wilhelm Roscher, whose *Politik: Eine geschichtliche Naturlehre der Monarchie, Aristokratie und Demokratie* appeared in 1892.[11] The diverse disciplinary background of such academics was combined with a disinclination to follow classical dialectic or liberal theory, based on an a priori state of nature. Roscher, for example, despite the title of his book, in fact transformed the usual trinity of monarchy, aristocracy, and democracy, which he attributed to Socrates, Cicero, and Montesquieu, predicting instead a series of stages from ancient monarchy, via aristocracy, absolute monarchy, democracy, and oligarchy, eventually culminating in dictatorship. Similarly, although he was often criticized as an old-school liberal— he was born in 1817—his own theory of political types ran a long way off the course prescribed by either liberal economics or liberal politics, foreseeing neither a shrinking state nor a progressive movement towards political rights or democracy within Europe. Devoting two full chapters to the avoidance of the worst effects of democracy and plutocracy, Roscher forwarded an uncertain theory of political development, riddled with exceptions, precisely because he wished to escape his own worst premonitions of democratization. In the universities, as in the political parties, it seemed that the certainties of liberalism and classical antiquity had been exploded by modern political practice. Working political models such as foreign nation-states were influential in the absence of any widely acknowledged theoretical orthodoxy.

Specialization and empiricism in German social sciences tended to work against great schemes. For instance, Gustav Schmoller, the co-founder of the *Verein für Sozialpolitik*, initially envisaged the gathering of information on a vast scale, with careful studies of all areas in every epoch, before a generalizing historical theory could be formulated.[12] Yet this should not obscure the fact that more and more researchers investigated the connections between politics, society,

---

[11] H. v. Treitschke, *Politik* (Leipzig, 1898); G. Jellinek, *Allgemeine Staatslehre* (Berlin, 1900); W. Roscher, *Politik* (Stuttgart, 1892). G. Hübinger, 'Staatstheorie und Politik als Wissenschaft im Kaiserreich', in H. Maier, U. Matz, K. Sontheimer, and P.-L. Weinacht (eds.), *Politik, Philosophie, Praxis* (Stuttgart, 1988), 143–61.

[12] H. Winkel, *Die deutsche Nationalökonomie im 19. Jahrhundert* (Darmstadt, 1977), 102.

and economy within the nation, linking them in more sophisticated ways. True, academics were cautious about schematizing, but the sum of their knowledge of institutional relations within society had increased. They were more likely to see polity, society, economy, and culture as a complex, interdependent system, even if they were unsure how the various parts affected each other. Schmoller was a case in point. In his two-volume, 1,100-page *Grundriß der allgemeinen Volkswirtschaftslehre*, published in 1904, he included sections on the state, class conflict, races, peoples, and climates, as well as more traditional subjects such as trade and taxes.[13] Most important of all, the work began with an examination of what was termed the 'psychological and moral foundation' of economics, in which market decisions and practices were seen to depend on a wider moral system and were thereby tied to state and society. A sub-title of chapter 7, volume 1, read: 'The methods of moral education: social scorn, state penalties, religious ideas'. Moreover, since the most obvious bounds to such morality were national—Schmoller devoted two chapters to language and peoples—economy, society, state, and religion were usually analysed within a national frame, hence the conscious opposition of *Nationalökonomen* to the universality of classical liberalism.[14] In short, political institutions had been fitted into a national system by academics at the same time as politicians and officials had been forced to come to terms with economic intervention, social insurance, and policies which appealed to the nation. The state had not merely grown, by extending its jurisdiction, it had also changed its character, in becoming a nation-state. Only under such conditions did national comparison necessarily have implications for political thought.

Changes in perceived relations between political and cultural spheres were accompanied by a slow transformation of the means of political perception and participation. The nature of political discourse had altered. Broadly, power had shifted from municipal élites to national party caucuses and public debate had moved away from

---

[13] G. Schmoller, *Grundriß der allgemeinen Volkswirtschaftslehre* (2 vols.; Leipzig, 1900–4).

[14] W. Hennis, 'A Science of Man: Max Weber and the Political Economy of the German Historical School', in W. J. Mommsen and J. Osterhammel (eds.), *Max Weber and his Contemporaries* (London, 1987), 32–8; Karl Knies, *Die politische Oekonomie vom geschichtlichen Standpuncte*, 2nd revised edn. (Brunswick, 1883), 73; G. Cohn, *System der Nationalökonomie* (3 vols.; Stuttgart, 1885–98), i. 444–52; and K. Bücher, *Die Entstehung der Volkswirtschaft*, 7th edn. (Tübingen, 1910), i. 135–42.

political clubs and local broadsheets to mass-circulation newspapers and numerous, small-circulation journals.[15] Expansion, from 150 million newspapers and journals posted in 1868 to 1,200 million in 1900, combined with differentiation, from 3,300 journals in 1900 to 6,500 in 1914, to ensure that more people received more opinions through the press.[16] The fact that a greater part of political experience was thus mediated in turn lent greater weight to foreign examples, which were almost entirely mediated. Paul Stoklossa, who conducted one of the first content analyses of Berlin and provincial newspapers in 1910, found that foreign affairs accounted for a surprisingly high percentage of newspaper space: 6.05 per cent, compared with 11.15 per cent on domestic affairs.[17] Advertisements accounted for 34.38 per cent. Equivalent figures for France showed a much greater discrepancy between foreign and domestic reportage, with 7.85 per cent of space devoted to the former and 22.8 per cent to the latter.[18] What was more, news from abroad, which had dominated German political columns in the years before unification, when the reporting of German politics was censored, found itself eclipsed by home news in the 1870s and 1880s, but then regained public attention in the 1890s and 1900s. Otto Groth, later author of a seminal work on the press in Germany, demonstrated in 1913, for example, that foreign coverage in the *Frankfurter Zeitung* for the preceding twenty-five years had, as a percentage, doubled.[19] At the same time as political debate in general had switched to the national press, reporting of foreign news had increased. This could only accentuate the part played by national comparison in German political thought.

Statistically, France and Britain seemed to be Germany's main points of political comparison in the early twentieth century. In the

---

[15] This is not to deny the continuing significance of local politics, but rather to describe an ongoing shift in the processes of political socialization and perception. Even the liberal parties felt the need to create national party organizations—D. Langewiesche, *Liberalismus in Deutschland* (Frankfurt a.M., 1988), 211; D. S. White, *The Splintered Party* (Cambridge, Mass., 1976), 159—although they never overcame regional divisions. Whatever modifications have subsequently been made, Geoff Eley's thesis in *Reshaping the German Right* (New Haven, 1980), which describes a movement towards national, mass political leagues, still retains much of its original force.

[16] T. Nipperdey, *Deutsche Geschichte 1866–1918* (2 vols.; Munich, 1993), i. 809.

[17] P. Stoklossa, 'Der Inhalt der Zeitung. Eine statistische Untersuchung', *Zeitschrift für die gesamte Staatswissenschaft*, 66 (1910), 555–65.

[18] H. de Noussanne, 'Was ist die französische Tagespresse wert?' (1901), in W. Schulz (ed.), *Der Inhalt der Zeitungen* (Düsseldorf, 1970), 87.

[19] O. Groth, 'Der Stoff der Zeitungen, seine Einteilung und Verteilung', ibid. 115–17.

four major party newspapers, *Neue Preußische Zeitung*, *Germania*, *Freisinnige Zeitung*, and *Vorwärts*, 35.5 per cent of articles for the years 1900, 1906, and 1912 were on France, 30.4 per cent on Britain, 23.75 per cent on Russia, and 10.35 per cent on the United States.[20] Of these reports on France 30.8 per cent, the largest single category, were political in content.[21] Similar, although less differentiated, results were obtained from a survey of journals.[22] Overall, it appeared that France received more attention from newspapers than Britain, with more coverage in *Germania* for fourteen of the seventeen years between 1898 and 1914 and with more articles in the *Neue Preußische Zeitung*, *Freisinnige Zeitung*, and *Vorwärts* for the years 1900, 1906, and 1912. In a year-by-year analysis of journals, Britain gained marginally more attention, with nine out of seventeen years, compared with eight out of seventeen years for France. The relatively high number of journal articles on Russia was attributable in large part to the 1905 revolution: 74 of 217 articles were written in 1905 or 1906.

In addition to these quantitative proofs, there was considerable qualitative evidence, which hinted at the continuing importance of France as a point of political reference. Whereas Britain and the United States, given their geographical isolation, small standing armies, social cohesion, and political self-help,[23] were frequently detached by German scholars from continental tradition, France seemed in many ways either to have presaged or to have exemplified political development in Europe: 'The basic ideas of absolutism, revolution, and socialism certainly do not come from France, but nowhere have they become so real as in the Kingdom of the Sun, the events of 1789 and in all that is happening before our very eyes in France at the moment.... Whatever occurs in France always concerns humanity as a whole and the newspapers of all countries are well informed of what is happening there,' wrote Oskar Schmitz, one

[20] Table 1. On the choice of party newspapers, see K. Koszyk, *Deutsche Presse im 19. Jahrhundert* (Berlin, 1966), 138, 154–5, 176, 181, 197. The National Liberals have been omitted because they had no equivalent party organ. The *National-Zeitung*, which was perhaps closest to the party, experienced financial difficulties throughout the 1900s and changed its name and direction in 1910, becoming the *8 Uhr-Abendblatt* (ibid. 152).

[21] Table 3. A similar percentage of articles were devoted to foreign policy.

[22] Table 2.

[23] W. Schenk, *Die deutsch-englische Rivalität vor dem Ersten Weltkrieg in der Sicht deutscher Historiker*, D.Phil. thesis (Zürich; published Aarau, 1967), 51, cites Erich Marcks.

TABLE 1. *Articles in principal party newspapers* (%)

	France	Britain	US	Russia
(a) *Neue Preußische Zeitung*				
1900	31.1	39.9	2.2	26.8
1906	39.0	15.4	6.9	38.8
1912	40.5	30.6	14.6	14.3
TOTAL	36.9	28.6	7.9	26.6
(b) *Germania*				
1900	30.2	50.7	9.3	9.8
1906	37.1	18.7	9.5	34.7
1912	39.9	23.9	16.0	20.2
TOTAL	35.7	31.1	11.6	21.6
(c) *Freisinnige Zeitung*				
1900	23.3	50.0	11.5	15.2
1906	30.5	16.1	8.9	44.5
1912	43.1	28.6	14.1	14.2
TOTAL	32.3	31.6	11.5	24.6
(d) *Vorwärts*				
1900	37.3	34.9	10.6	17.1
1906	35.4	20.0	9.6	35.0
1912	38.4	36.2	10.7	14.7
TOTAL	37.0	30.4	10.3	22.3
JOINT TOTAL	35.5	30.4	10.3	23.8

Source: Calculated from newspaper articles of eight lines or more.

of a handful of German specialists on contemporary France.[24] If absolutism, revolution, democracy, and dictatorship were the great themes in the political works of Wilhelm Roscher, Heinrich von Treitschke, and Otto Hintze, then the sub-plot read: Bourbon absolutism, French revolution, republican democracy, and Napoleonic

---

[24] O. A. H. Schmitz, *Das Land der Wirklichkeit*, 5th edn. (Munich, 1914), 43–4. Such ideas had a long and illustrious pedigree. For instance, Leopold von Ranke, cited in H.-O. Sieburg, *Deutschland und Frankreich in der Geschichtsschreibung des 19. Jahrhunderts, 1848–1871* (Wiesbaden, 1958), ii. 262–3.

TABLE 2. *Major articles in political journals*

	France[a]	Britain[b]	US[c]	Russia[d]
1898	16	8	5	1
1899	17	6	7	4
1900	22	17	12	5
1901	8	14	6	9
1902	5	11	6	13
1903	13	8	2	10
1904	16	14	6	14
1905	14	18	4	39
1906	30	26	4	35
1907	15	13	12	14
1908	7	15	7	13
1909	7	16	6	10
1910	23	22	9	18
1911	15	19	4	5
1912	9	19	10	11
1913	8	14	2	9
1914	7	4	1	7
TOTAL	232	244	103	217

[a] Including articles on Paris and Dreyfus.
[b] Including articles on London.
[c] Including articles on New York and Washington.
[d] Including articles on Moscow and St Petersburg.

Source: *Internationale Bibliographie der Zeitschriftenliteratur* (Diedrich). Journals were taken from across the political spectrum: *Historisch-politische Blätter*, *Grenzboten*, *Hilfe*, *Hochland*, *Preußische Jahrbücher*, *Sozialistische Monatshefte*, *Nation*, *Stimmen aus Maria Laach*, *Christliche Welt*, *Neue Zeit*, and *Zukunft*. The category 'major article' comes from the *IBZ*.

dictatorship.[25] Similarly, in newspapers, the publicity given to French events such as the Dreyfus case appeared, to many journalists, to be an indication of German fascination with French politics.[26] But what if such treatment of French affairs was predicated on assumptions of race or culture? References to politics in France would, consequently,

[25] Roscher, *Politik*, for instance, devoted a full chapter to France in each of his sections on absolute monarchy, democracy, and Caesarism. The work ends with a chapter on Napoleon.
[26] *Neue Preußische Zeitung*, 10 Aug. 1899; *Germania*, 15 Feb. 1898; E. Henrici, *Dreißig Jahre nachher. Betrachtungen über das Verhältnis zwischen Deutschland und Frankreich* (Berlin, 1901), 45.

TABLE 3. *Articles on France in principal party newspapers*

	f.p.[a]	pol	soc	econ	mil	church	total	pol%
(a) *Neue Preußische Zeitung*								
1900	74	74	11	14	20	9	202	36.6
1906	44	180	45	27	50	104	450	40.0
1912	524	144	119	31	190	10	1108	13.0
(b) *Germania*								
1900	50	67	16	17	23	15	188	35.6
1906	55	117	27	23	39	134	375	31.2
1912	95	77	28	14	59	55	328	23.5
(c) *Freisinnige Zeitung*								
1900	73	70	5	4	26	6	164	42.7
1906	122	168	109	14	42	86	541	31.1
1912	261	84	58	16	90	4	513	16.4
(d) *Vorwärts*								
1900	27	70	27	5	18	8	155	45.2
1906	17	66	68	6	24	37	218	30.3
1912	84	46	36	4	23	1	194	23.7
TOTAL								30.8

[a] Categories: foreign policy (f.p.); politics (pol); social question (soc); economy (econ); military (mil); church; politics as percentage of total (pol%).

Source: Calculated from newspaper articles of eight lines or more. The category 'politics' is defined negatively to signify any article on politics which did not have a significant diplomatic, social, economic, military, or confessional component. In general, it denotes party wrangling, ministerial crises, and structural political problems.

be of little significance for German political thought, since the two nation-states would not be treated as fully comparable entities. French political institutions and practices could be acknowledged as being suited to a specific French race or culture at the same time as being deemed inapplicable in Germany. Obviously, the less racial and cultural assumptions interfered with political assessment—because of their implausibility or because of a separation of discourses—the more significant France was likely to be as an object of national political comparison. The following section examines genetic, cultural, and political versions of the French nation.

2. Three Types of French Nation

The first of the three types of nation—genetic—found virtually no
advocates so far as France was concerned. This is not to suggest that
racial theories fell on deaf ears in Germany—there is compelling
evidence that notions of race were widely believed in Europe when
they were framed against black Africans and Jews, for example[27]—but
it is to suggest that such theories did not coincide with a specifically
national identity.[28] Many philologists, anthropologists, and physical
anthropologists had spent the latter part of the nineteenth century
testing the Aryan or Indo-European hypothesis, which posited that
grammatical similarities between Sanskrit and the Romance and
Germanic languages were best explained by the migration of so-called
Aryans from India to Europe. By the 1900s, however, research in various disciplines appeared to have added little flesh to the bones of the
Indo-European argument. There had indeed been a dispute over race
in the 1870s and 1880s, after Armand de Quatrefages, one of the most
prominent French anthropologists, contended that Prussians were in
fact Finnish in origin, and not Aryan, as had been supposed. The main
riposte came from Rudolf Virchow, the founder of German anthropology, who was provoked into examining fifteen million German,
Austrian, Swiss, and Belgian schoolchildren for traits such as blond
hair and blue eyes. Yet, although they proved that such characteristics
were preponderant in North Germany, the enquiry's findings undermined the dominant theory at the time, floated by André Retzius, that
superior long-heads had settled in Scandinavia, Germany, England,
and France, pushing indigenous broad-heads to European outposts
such as Finland and Brittany. In fact, Virchow demonstrated that the
Finns were on the whole blond, and that south and west Germans
were typically brown-eyed and dark-haired, as might have been
expected for broad-heads. Confronted with such evidence, it was difficult for scientists to formulate racial theories of the nation.[29]

---

[27] G. L. Mosse, *Die Geschichte des Rassismus in Europa* (Frankfurt a.M., 1990) and
I. Geiss, *Geschichte des Rassismus* (Frankfurt a.M., 1988).

[28] Mosse, *Die Geschichte des Rassismus in Europa*, 101–5. Alfred Ploetz's *Archiv für
Rasse- und Gesellschaftsbiologie*, founded in 1904, contained articles which advocated inter-
marriage between Germans and French for their mutual genetic advantage. On the
inward-looking nature of German eugenics, see S. F. Weiss, *Race Hygiene and National
Efficiency* (Los Angeles, 1987), 103–4, 147–51.

[29] Mosse, *Die Geschichte des Rassismus in Europa*, 112–15. L. Poliakov, *Le Mythe aryen*,
2nd edn. (Brussels, 1987), 288–321. P. Weindling, *Health, Race and German Politics between
National Unification and Nazism, 1870–1945* (Cambridge, 1989), 48–9.

At the same time as many academics were questioning their earlier hypotheses, the general public became more interested in the Aryan myth. Yet here too there were few attempts to distinguish between France and Germany.[30] The most popular proselytizer of race in Germany was undoubtedly Houston Stewart Chamberlain, the son of a British diplomat, who joined the Bayreuth circle and married one of Richard Wagner's daughters. In his most famous book, *Die Grundlagen des neunzehnten Jahrhunderts*, which was already in its tenth edition by 1912, Chamberlain traced the origins of the word 'Germane' back to Tacitus, who used it to denote Celts, Teutons, and Slavs.[31] It was impossible to separate the three groups racially. The Germanen were compared to a breed of dogs, in which good genetic material had been refined by inbreeding and infrequent and selective cross-breeding within Europe, where blood-types were similar.[32] Chamberlain's aim was to demonstrate that the scientific, artistic, and religious basis of Western civilization was racial. He did not distinguish between French, British, German, and Italian contributions to that civilization. Thus, in the chapter on science, called 'Wissenschaft (von Roger Bacon bis Lavoisier)', Chamberlain cited the cases of amateur scientists such as Voltaire (astronomy) and Rousseau (botany) as well as academics like Bernard and Antoine Laurent de Jussieu (botanical classification) to prove that Germanic methodology was founded on exact observation and inductive reasoning, rather than on perfect mathematical form, as had been common in ancient Greece.[33] In the chapter on politics, he postulated that the Reformation had been the central event in European history between 1200 and 1800, expressing as it did the emancipation of the

---

[30] Both Arthur de Gobineau and Georges Vacher de Lapouge stressed that Aryans or long-heads had previously dominated France and that Europe in general was afflicted by racial degeneration. On Gobineau, see L. Poliakov, C. Delacampagne, and P. Girard, *Über den Rassismus* (Stuttgart, 1979), 100, and G. Mann, 'Rassenhygiene—Sozialdarwinismus', in G. Mann (ed.), *Biologismus im 19. Jahrhundert* (Stuttgart, 1973), 73–93; G. V. de Lapouge, 'Die Rassengeschichte der französischen Nation', *Politisch-anthropologische Revue*, 1 (1905), 29. Ludwig Woltmann's, *Die Germanen und die Renaissance in Italien* and *Die Germanen in Frankreich*, which were published in 1905 and 1907, respectively, classed Napoleon and Renan as Nordic. On degeneration, P. Weingart, J. Kroll, and K. Bayertz, *Rasse, Blut und Gene* (Frankfurt a.M., 1988), 58–66. The two main German-speaking apostles of decadence were Friedrich Nietzsche and Max Nordau. Both admired many aspects of French life.

[31] H. S. Chamberlain, *Die Grundlagen des neunzehnten Jahrhunderts*, 10th edn. (Munich, 1912), i. 466–7.

[32] Ibid. 277–87.   [33] Ibid. ii. 778–91.

Germanic soul. 1789 was then explicable as a reaction of free-spirited Germanen—in this instance, Frenchmen—against the narrowness and restriction of Catholicism. The Germanic blood of Frenchmen had finally overcome a political Catholic settlement. To Chamberlain, the revolution—so often a point of difference in other accounts— revealed Franco-German similarity and common blood.[34]

The absence of a convincing racial theory on France did not undermine the popularity of cultural characterizations of the French nation. Four out of nine of the general works on contemporary France published between 1890 and 1914 made extended references to a French national character.[35] The assumption behind such references was that habits of thought and behaviour had been developed and transferred through generations and that they were, as a result, difficult to alter. In one of the main works on contemporary France, *Die dritte französische Republik bis 1895*, Karl Vogel listed many of the traits often ascribed to Frenchmen:

Courageous is the Frenchman...he is, so long as passion does not come into play, sociable, friendly, polite and helpful in the highest degree, only occasionally pushy. Extremely talented and inventive, full of spirit and fantasy, often however too impatient, he gives his all in everything he undertakes....He loves to joke, sometimes playfully, sometimes gushingly, at other times bitingly, but he often also uses witticisms to deceive, occasionally successfully, when they end as paradoxes, but more often annoyingly confusing and missing the target....No people invests form and external appearances with such importance...its mastery [in questions of taste] does not just manifest itself in clothing and jewellery, in artificial decoration and ornament, but also, with some reservations, in manners, conversational tone and literature....By the same token, however, the Frenchman's greatest failing is vanity and an insatiable longing for fame....His preference [is] for blunting, smoothing generalization, which makes many things easier, but often in appearance only...so that he is not always able to escape reproaches of superficiality and one-sidedness....Always striving for change and novelty, the French today are just as unsteady, fickle, and vacillating as their ancestors.[36]

[34] Chamberlain, *Die Grundlagen des neunzehnten Jahrhunderts*, 838–54.

[35] K. Hillebrand, *Frankreich und die Franzosen*, 4th edn. (Strasbourg, 1898); H. N. Kuhn, *Frankreich an der Zeitwende* (Hamburg, 1895); Schmitz, *Das Land der Wirklichkeit*; and K. Vogel, *Die dritte französische Republik bis 1895* (Berlin, 1895), did use stereotypes extensively. H. Fernau, *Die französische Demokratie* (Munich, 1914); J. Haas, *Frankreich. Land und Staat* (Heidelberg, 1910); R. Mahrenholtz, *Frankreich. Seine Geschichte, Verfassung und staatliche Einrichtungen* (Leipzig, 1897); Schirmacher, *Deutschland und Frankreich seit 35 Jahren*; and K. E. Schmidt, *Im Lande der Freiheit, Gleichheit und Brüderlichkeit* (Berlin, 1908), did not.

[36] Vogel, *Die dritte französische Republik bis 1895*, 61–73.

Such characterizations were detailed, widespread, and more or less consistent. At their most extreme, they verged on assumptions of race, as in the historian Karl Hillebrand's would-be aphorism that when one scratched a Frenchman, an Irish Celt was exposed.[37] On the whole, however, allusions to national character rarely precluded political explanations of French events, practices, and institutions. One reason was that many of the stereotypes of France had their origins in political events, most notably the French Revolution. Thus, when Vogel labelled Frenchmen brave and warlike, he was in part prompted by the need to explain French military successes in the past: 'No state has...undertaken so many wars,' he added.[38] Likewise, imputations of instability and nervousness were often explicitly tied to France's history of revolution and political experimentation. Cause and effect were therefore never clear: did an unstable French character tend in itself to revolt, or did political revolution merely give the impression that Frenchmen were fickle? Moreover, even the most enthusiastic proponents of stereotypes simultaneously enlisted political analysis to their cause. Vogel, for example, depicted the ephemerality of political forms in France in terms of unrealizable republican ideals, deep-rooted support for the monarchy, and the collapse of state authority: 'As a result of the cluelessness and indecision, of the rudderless vacillation of a collegiate parliamentary regime...there has been a continuous undermining of government, administrative, judicial, and police authority.'[39] References to national character, then, were not employed to explain events, but rather filled gaps which other theories had failed to reach. In his study of German attitudes to French nationality, the young historian August Raif noted that stereotypes had changed little since the French Revolution.[40] Yet in that time evaluations of French political systems had fluctuated dramatically, from qualified admiration during the July revolution to disenchantment during the Second Empire. It was tempting to assume that stereotypes remained unchanged because they had little explanatory power. This could only increase the significance of political assessments of the French nation, which will be examined in the next section.

[37] Hillebrand, *Frankreich und die Franzosen*, 62.
[38] Vogel, *Die dritte französische Republik bis 1895*, 61.
[39] Ibid. 78.
[40] A. F. Raif, *Die Urteile der Deutschen über die französische Nationalität im Zeitalter der Revolution und der deutschen Erhebung* (Berlin, 1911), 2–3.

3. German Depictions of France

To Raif, and to many historians since, it appeared that citizens' conscious attachment to the nation-state encouraged cultural characterization, rather than political assessment, of foreign systems of government.[41] Germans' attitudes towards Frenchmen, rather than their opinions on French society and polity, were considered significant in the elaboration of a German national identity: 'Through debates about French national character, the German got to know his own national character more intimately and deeply; study, or even self-satisfied observation of foreign national character is a lever for the development of one's own nationality [*Volkstum*].'[42] What was more, such national self-definition was necessarily associated with heightened consciousness of national interest, in opposition to the foreign policies of other nation-states. In Germany, continued Raif, this opposition had occurred in 1813, as Germans had risen against Napoleon: 'German judgements of the French altered considerably in the relatively short time from the days of the revolution until the fall of Napoleon.'[43] Interpretation of foreign nation-states, according to this line of argument, was likely to be vitiated by national stereotypes and the perceived imperatives of foreign policy. Thus, critical reassessment of French history during the second half of the nineteenth century by historians such as Leopold von Ranke, Heinrich von Sybel, Ludwig Häusser, Heinrich von Treitschke, Wilhelm Oncken, and Adalbert Wahl has been seen as indicative of a shift from cosmopolitan impartiality to national bias.[44]

---

[41] R. Buchner, *Die deutsch-französische Tragödie 1848–1864. Politische Beziehungen und psychologisches Verhältnis* (Würzburg, 1965), 107, 119. Like Raif, M. Jeismann, *Das Vaterland der Feinde. Studien zum nationalen Feindbegriff und Selbstverständnis in Deutschland und Frankreich 1792–1918* (Stuttgart, 1992), postulates that German national identity was founded on French *Feindbilder* from the era of the Napoleonic wars onwards. H.-O. Sieburg, *Deutschland und Frankreich in der Geschichtsschreibung des 19. Jahrhunderts, 1848–1871* (Wiesbaden, 1958), ii. 225, 319, although more cautious, observes that, after 1815 and from the late 1850s onwards, even German historians were influenced in their work by national feeling. On the cosmopolitanism of Germans vis-à-vis France, see K. Kautz, *Das deutsche Frankreichbild im ersten Hälfte des 19. Jahrhunderts*, D.Phil. thesis (Cologne, 1957).

[42] Raif, *Die Urteile der Deutsche über die französische Nationalität*, 6.

[43] Ibid.

[44] Heinrich von Sybel, whose five-volume work, *Geschichte der Revolutionszeit von 1789–1800*, 4th edn. (Frankfurt a.M., 1882), was begun in 1851 but not completed until 1879, was certainly the most important figure in this German revision of the history of the French Revolution. K. Malettke, 'La Révolution française dans l'historiographie allemande du XIX siècle: Le Cas de Heinrich von Sybel', *Francia*, 16 (1989), 100–19;

It is not intended here to challenge the notion that Germans were swayed in their assessment of France by national sentiment, nor that German accounts of French history became more critical after 1848. Rather, it is proposed that criticism and national consciousness did not reduce the political comparison of nation-states to the level of demonic national stereotypes. Such argument turns on a false and anachronistic dichotomy between cosmopolitanism and nationhood. In *Weltbürgertum und Nationalstaat*, which was first published in 1908, Friedrich Meinecke's conclusion, whatever the subtlety of his analysis, amounted to little more than a Wilhelmine commonplace: genuine cosmopolitanism was only to be achieved through the nation-state: 'A more sophisticated view, which has always been maintained by educated Germans, is that the true, the best German national feelings also include the cosmopolitan ideal of a supra-national humanity, that it "is un-German, simply to be German".'[45] From the coexistence of national and universal Christian churches to the emergence of German national identity within the Holy Roman Empire, it seemed to Meinecke that there was a historical affinity between particular forms and universal ideas.[46] Modern nation-states did not, after all, exist in international anarchy but had joined together voluntarily, if always conditionally, in order to keep the peace.[47] They had been formed, like an individual in society, in a wider community of ideas, alliances, and conflicts, which, in turn, facilitated subsequent communication between nation-states: 'their essence is constructed in the same way as individual personality, through friction and exchange with neighbours.'[48] France, for all its claims to universality, was no different from other nation-states in this respect. It had the capacity to interpret and assimilate other cultures without losing its own identity: 'For culture, which emanates from these state structures, can also assimilate former members of other cultures and nations (in this sense). Such strength is not, of

---

H.-O. Sieburg, 'Aspects de l'historiographie allemande sur la France entre 1871 et 1914', *Francia*, 13 (1986), 561–9.

[45] Meinecke, *Weltbürgertum und Nationalstaat*, 17, citing J. E. Erdmann. Also H. Delbrück, 'Was ist national?' (1913), in *Vor und nach dem Weltkrieg. Historische und politische Aufsätze, 1902–1925* (Berlin, 1926), 380.

[46] Meinecke, *Weltbürgertum und Nationalstaat*, 23.

[47] Ibid. 21, refers to 'höheren, mehrere Nationen und Staaten vereinigenden Gemeinschaften'.

[48] Ibid.

course, victorious everywhere. But it is present and effective over the long run. It was this that Napoleon had in mind when he coined the phrase, which was later often cited: "Les français n'ont point de nationalité."[49] In order to survive and prosper, it appeared that nation-states had to remain open to foreign ideas.[50]

To Meinecke, the French Revolution, which has frequently been depicted as the apogee of a universal age, constituted one of the conclusive proofs of the link between nationhood and cosmopolitanism: 'Was not the very first nation-state [*Nationalstaat*] in Europe to be founded, quite self-consciously, on the autonomy of the nation the France of the revolution, emerging from the cradle of the eighteenth century, from ground which was thoroughly fertilized with universal and cosmopolitan ideas?'[51] By the late nineteenth century, even left-wing authors of works on France like Hermann Fernau could be found reiterating the verdict of leading, mid-century historians, such as Ranke, Sybel, and Burckhardt, that the French Revolution had sanctioned the idea of the nation-state, first in France, then in Germany.[52] Since there was virtual consensus in the Reich over the necessity of the *Nationalstaat*,[53] many authors, including conservatives, continued to depict the events of 1789 as an inevitable and beneficial conclusion to the corrupt court politics of the eighteenth century. Thus, for instance, a popular right-wing publicist like Oskar Schmitz agreed with a monarchist academic such as Hans Delbrück:

One can think what one likes of the enormities of 1789, it must be conceded however that absolutism was a spent force at the end of the eighteenth century. It was necessary in order to create, from the small states of the Middle Ages, large state structures, which pursued important ends. The unification of France

---

[49] Neumann, *Volk und Nation*, 131; A. Kirchhoff, *Was ist national?* (Halle, 1902), 21; L. Gumplowicz, *Nationalismus und Internationalismus im 19. Jahrhundert* (Berlin, 1902), 31–2.

[50] Vogel, *Die dritte französische Republik bis 1895*, 76.

[51] Meinecke, *Weltbürgertum und Nationalstaat*, 23.

[52] Fernau, *Die französische Demokratie*, 281. On Sybel, see Malettke, 'La Révolution française dans l'historiographie allemande du XIX siècle', 111. On Ranke, see Sieburg, *Deutschland und Frankreich in der Geschichtsschreibung des 19. Jahrhunderts*, ii. 274–5. On Burckhardt, see Sieburg, 'Die französische Revolution in der deutschen Geschichtsschreibung'. On neo-Rankeans, such as Max Lenz, see H.-H. Krill, *Die Rankerenaissance. Max Lenz und Erich Marcks* (Berlin, 1962), 67.

[53] Mommsen, *Arbeiterbewegung und nationale Frage*, 73; H.-U. Wehler, *Sozialdemokratie und Nationalstaat* (Würzburg, 1962), 70; James, *A German Identity*, 86; R. Fletcher, *Revisionism and Empire: Socialist Imperialism in Germany, 1897–1914* (London, 1984); W. Conze and D. Groh, *Die Arbeiterbewegung in der nationalen Bewegung* (Stuttgart, 1966), 126.

by Richelieu and Mazarin, and the formation of Prussia by Friedrich Wilhelm I and Friedrich II was only possible through the exercise of a single will, unconstrained by any kind of constitution. Now that the great machinery of state was in place, it became necessary to employ the forces of society in the service of the state and this was only possible by making those forces nationally conscious by giving them a share in government.[54]

Textbooks, too, articulated similar arguments: neither in its administration, education, finances nor its judicial system had eighteenth-century France managed to use the nation to the advantage of the state. The French Revolution had been provoked, it was said, by a rotten regime, which had prevented peaceable reform.[55]

The conviction of many German observers that the French Revolution had replaced an atrophied absolutist state with a modern nation-state tempered criticism of 1789. In the same way, German admiration of France as an archetypal *Nationalstaat* worked against national stereotypes and *Feindbilder*. After the French Revolution, it was evident to historians like Max Lenz that nation-building and national self-determination had become the leitmotif of the nineteenth century: 'If one wanted to search for a predominant formulation, a headline, which characterizes the full panoply of struggles that have shaken the world since the French Revolution, one would scarcely find a better, more pregnant one than the idea of the nation-state.'[56] From such a standpoint, it was tempting to try to discover the origins of the nation-state and, thereby, those of the modern era, for, although the French Revolution appeared to have sanctioned the principle of nationality, few German commentators doubted that the history of the *Nationalstaat* extended back far beyond 1789. France was, according to Meinecke's classification, a model *Staatsnation*, or a nation which rested 'primarily on the unifying force of a common political history and constitution'.[57] Typically, such nations, in which a more or less uniform culture was created by a dynastic state, managed to unite power and populace before *Kulturnationen*, such as Germany and Italy, in which a common culture antedated political

---

[54] Schmitz, *Land der Wirklichkeit*, 103. H. Delbrück, *Regierung und Volkswille* (Berlin, 1914), 122–5; Vogel, *Die dritte französische Republik*, 77.

[55] Haas, *Frankreich*, 64.

[56] M. Lenz, 'Nationalität und Religion' (1907), in *Kleine historische Schriften* (Munich, 1910), 234.

[57] Meinecke, *Weltbürgertum und Nationalstaat*, 10. Haas, *Frankreich*, 1; Vogel, *Die dritte französische Republik*, 31.

unification.[58] As early as 1100, recorded German historians, the Capetians had transformed a small kingdom in the Île-de-France by adding territories from other regions and establishing a state bureaucracy, 200 years before anything similar appeared in Germany.[59] By 1500, after a series of wars against English kings during the previous three centuries, a recognizable French culture and nation already existed, if Burckhardt and Ranke were to be believed.[60] Louis XIV and Napoleon I had then turned that inchoate *Staatsnation* into the most powerful *Nationalstaat* in the world. There was a sense in Wilhelmine historical literature that Germany owed its present position to this French and English precedent of nation-building.[61] As a result, the esteem which many Germans harboured for both nation-states never disappeared completely: although German territories had developed eventually 'into the great, national state of the present day', wrote the historical economist, Gustav Cohn, they were, 'when compared to the devlopment of England or France, far behind and only laboriously catching up with what these had already achieved'.[62]

This recognition of France as a forerunner of the German *Nationalstaat* prevented most Germans from demonizing the neighbouring state. Thus, although it was accepted in Wilhelmine diplomatic histories that France had used its preponderant power to prevent German national unification and maintain what was termed 'the break-up of Germany' through the Treaty of Westphalia, imposed in 1648, judgements of French foreign policy were still mixed, despite established 'facts' such as the seizure of Alsace-Lorraine under Louis XIV, the imposition of the continental system under Napoleon I, the threat to the Rhine in 1840, and the declaration of war on Prussia in 1870.[63] Arguably, the most sensitive period

[58] Meinecke, *Weltbürgertum und Nationalstaat*, 12.

[59] O. Hintze, 'Der Beamtenstand' (1911), in *Soziologie und Geschichte*, 2nd revised edn. (Göttingen, 1964), 82. Delbrück, *Regierung und Volkswille*, 119–22.

[60] Sieburg, *Deutschland und Frankreich in der Geschichtsschreibung*, ii. 263, 265, 303.

[61] Neumann, *Volk und Nation*, 149; H. v. Treitschke, 'Die Freiheit' (1861), in *Historische und politische Aufsätze*, 6th edn. (Leipzig, 1903), iii. 15.

[62] Cohn, *System der Nationalökonomie*, i. 445. Delbrück, 'Was ist national?' (1913), in *Vor und nach dem Weltkrieg*, 379–80; K. Schirmacher, *Was ist national?* (Posen, 1912), 5.

[63] Sieburg, *Deutschland und Frankreich in der Geschichtsschreibung*, ii. 283, 285, 287–8; id., 'Aspects de l'historiographie allemande sur la France entre 1871 et 1914', *Francia*, 13 (1986), 574–5; Buchner, *Die deutsch-französische Tragödie*, 113, 117. Even Max Weber, S. N. Eisenstadt (ed.), *Max Weber on Charisma and Institution Building* (Chicago, 1968), 183, and Adolf Wagner, *Vom Territorialstaat zur Weltmacht* (Berlin, 1900), 6, did not escape the historical legend that the 17th and 18th cents. had been a time of uninterrupted material poverty, political helplessness, and foreign domination for Germany.

of such Franco-German history was the Napoleonic occupation and the so-called 'wars of liberation', which culminated in the defeat of French forces at the battle of Leipzig in 1813. It was, as Hermann Oncken, Max Lehmann, and many others who gave centenary speeches in 1913 testified, generally agreed that the will to form a German political nation dated back to this time: 'the nation-state of today...has its deepest roots in those heroic and moving events of 1813.'[64] Given that this will to form a nation-state was also perceived to have arisen because of the injustices of French *Fremdherrschaft*, it was to be expected that images of Napoleon I would be diabolical.[65] Yet, notwithstanding occasional menacing allusions, the French Emperor was usually portrayed as a hero or as a clown in Wilhelmine political caricature:[66] examples of the latter, which were less common, tended to emphasize his small stature, bombastic gait, and penguin-like apparel;[67] instances of the former sometimes equated him with either Bismarck or Wilhelm II.[68] Bonaparte, who was the subject of at least nine plays between 1888 and 1912, all of which explored the theme of the great man in history, had even become more popular in Germany than in France, it seemed to some caricaturists.[69] One cartoon in *Simplicissimus* showed a famous Napoleon-actor reviewing French soldiers on the battlefield: 'Ernst von Possart has been hired by the French republic in order, as Napoleon I, to enthuse the troops,' ran the caption.[70]

---

[64] H. Oncken, *Der Kaiser und die Nation* (Heidelberg, 1913), 3. Delbrück, 'Was ist national?', in *Vor und nach dem Weltkrieg*, 381.

[65] Gumplowicz, *Nationalismus und Internationalismus im 19. Jahrhundert*, 32; K. Sturmhoefel, *Deutsches Nationalgefühl und Einheitsstreben im 19. Jahrhundert* (Leipzig, 1904), 3.

[66] Sieburg, 'Aspects de l'historiographie allemande sur la France', 576. H.-G. Haupt's study of reviews in the *Historische Zeitschrift*, 'Die Aufnahme Frankreichs in der deutschen Geschichtswissenschaft zwischen 1871 and 1914', in M. Nerlich (ed.), *Kritik der Frankreichforschung, 1871–1975* (Berlin, 1977), 57–8, which not only concludes that studies of Napoleon were still popular in German historiography, but also that verdicts were kind. H. Schmidt, 'Napoleon in der deutschen Geschichtsschreibung', *Francia*, 14 (1986), 546, confirms that 'Napoleoneuphorie' dominated German histories between 1900 and 1920.

[67] 'Einen Königreich für einen Mann', *Simplicissimus*, no date, vol. 4, no. 1; 'Der große Kladderadatsch', *Kladderadatsch*, 19 Oct. 1913, no. 42.

[68] 'Napoleon und Bismarck', *Simplicissimus*, 1 Aug. 1905, vol. 10, no. 18; 'Clemenceau vor dem Spiegel', ibid., 19 Nov. 1906, vol. 11, no. 34; ' "Le Kaiser" – oder der "Napoleon des Friedens" ', *Kladderadatsch*, 19 Mar. 1911, no. 12.

[69] H. Hirschstein, *Die französische Revolution im deutschen Drama und Epos nach 1815* (Stuttgart, 1912), 225–80. To Ferdinand Unruh, *Das patriotische Drama im heutigen Frankreich* (Königsberg, 1891), 1, it was remarkable that modern Frenchmen were blind to 'die Kolossalgestalt des ersten Napoleon'.

[70] *Simplicissimus*, 1 July 1907, vol. 12, no. 14.

Still more revealing were Wilhelmine descriptions of the
Napoleonic wars, with satirists, including those from the National
Liberal journal *Kladderadatsch*, concentrating on the unpatriotic
venality of German princes rather than on French aggression.[71] The
most widely read socialist publication, *Der wahre Jacob*, envisaged
Bonaparte riding through the debris of war ahead of the German
princes—'Napoleon and his fat German friends a hundred years
ago'—in a cartoon called 'Zur Stärkung des Patriotismus von heute'.
In an accompanying quotation by Fichte, it was made clear to readers
that German patriotism should be directed less against external
rivals like France than against internal enemies such as the avaricious
and cosmopolitan dynasties: 'The German princes grovelled before
foreigners; they opened up the lap of the fatherland to them...if
only they could thereby receive the title of king.'[72] A strip cartoon in
Simplicissimus carried a similar message.[73] Of course, conservatives
and nationalists were more likely to look for enemies abroad in 1913
than were socialists and left liberals: nevertheless, it did not escape
the attention of journalists that France's ally, Russia, was to be represented at the festival of the battle of Leipzig, and that the French
company, Pathé, was granted the exclusive right to film the
occasion.[74] Obviously, this did not mean that anti-French sentiment
had been banished from the historical memory of Wilhelmine
Germans, but it did suggest that that sentiment was mingled with
respect for a once-powerful nation-state and with confidence vis-à-
vis a weaker rival: 'They will perhaps never again, let us say hopefully,' recorded one travel writer, with a note of relief, 'regain their
former, general ascendancy, which was created for them by political
predominance, the precocious unification of the country under a
state, their great, thousand-year-old history of poetry and science,
industry and commercial wealth, and cosmopolitan education.'[75]

Like its foreign policy, France's culture constituted an inexpun-
gible part of German history. This, undoubtedly, made cultural
stereotypes of French character more popular, yet these did
not interfere significantly with political accounts of the French

[71] *Kladderadatsch*, 19 Oct. 1913, no. 42.
[72] *Der wahre Jacob*, no. 698, Apr. 1913.
[73] 'Im großen Jubiläumsjahre 1806–1906', *Simplicissimus*, 22 Jan. 1906, vol. 10, no. 43.
[74] 'Der ungebetene Gast in Leipzig', *Kladderadatsch*, 19 Oct. 1913, no. 42; 'Die
geschäftskundigen Patrioten von Leipzig', ibid., 2 Nov. 1913, no. 44.
[75] J. E. Schermann, *Von Paris zurück* (Ravensburg, 1901), 126.

nation-state during the pre-war period. First, as has already been seen, many cultural stereotypes in fact had a political pedigree.[76] Second, many educated Germans' knowledge of French culture was too deep and too varied to lend itself to crude stereotyping: as one history of Franco-German relations, which was published in 1901, remarked, French literature, art, and fashion remained popular under the *Kaiserreich*, well beyond the confines of the avant-garde and the *Bildungsbürgertum*: 'Very many Germans have a pronounced preference for this country—the educated part of the people for centuries already.'[77] As was to be expected, such knowledge and preference were most conspicuous amongst artists themselves, some of whom espoused internationalism as part of their attack on bourgeois society. Thus, when the landscape artist Carl Vinnen published his *Protest deutscher Künstler*, which criticized the francophilia of the German art world, seventy-five artists, art dealers, museum directors, and critics, including Max Liebermann, Wassily Kandinsky, Franz Marc, Max Pechstein, Otto Modersohn, and Max Slevogt, contributed to a rebuttal, entitled *Deutsche und französische Kunst*, which derided the protest's narrow-minded nationalism: 'national particularity in art!?...The great sons of the nations, whether it is Rembrandt, Velasquez, Rubens, or Dürer, are simply the great painters of humanity, are sons of art. And such are, in an uninterrupted series, the great painters of France.'[78] Given that many artists and writers had lived in Paris,[79] and that avant-garde publications such as *Der Sturm* and *Der blaue Reiter* contained numerous French articles and paintings,[80] it was not surprising that, on the whole, German artistic elites were well versed in French works and that they were rarely given to francophobia.

---

[76] See above.

[77] Henrici, *Dreißig Jahre nachher*, 54–5.

[78] Max Slevogt in anon., *Deutsche und französische Kunst*, 2nd edn. (Munich, 1912), 30–1, 62. P. Paret, *Die Berliner Secession* (Frankfurt a.M., 1983), 261–85.

[79] Spies (ed.), *Paris–Berlin 1900–1933*, 16–117; W. Hausenstein, 'Kulturelle Beziehungen zwischen Frankreich und Deutschland', in Deutsch-französisches Institut, Ludwigsburg, *Deutschland–Frankreich* (Stuttgart, 1954–66), i. 105–6; E. Bisdorff, *Thomas Mann und Frankreich* (Luxemburg, 1980), 9; K. H. Kiefer, 'Carl Einstein und die literarischen Avantgarden Frankreichs', in H.-J. Lüsebrink and J. Riesz (eds.), *Feindbild und Faszination* (Frankfurt a.M., 1984), 97–101; L. Reynaud, *Histoire générale de l'influence française en Allemagne* (Paris, 1914), 478–85.

[80] L. Jordan, '"A travers l'Europe". Französische Literatur in der Zeitschrift "Der Sturm" 1910–1920', in L. Jordan (ed.), *Interferenzen. Deutschland und Frankreich* (Düsseldorf, 1983), 104–10; H. C. v. Tavel (ed.), *Le Cavalier bleu* (Berne, 1986), 9–11.

The exposure of wider society to French culture was more haphazard, but nevertheless significant, with a magazine like *Der Türmer* devoting between 1 and 5 per cent of its space to France, its history, literature, and fashion.[81] French painting continued to figure so prominently in German art histories, journals, and exhibitions,[82] that Guillaume Apollinaire, who wrote for *Sturm*, felt obliged to admit, in July 1914, that Germany, not France, had become the main forum for French painters.[83] Not only did Berlin display more French works than Paris, provincial galleries had followed the capital's example, with a museum like Bremen purchasing thirteen French paintings, compared with eighty-four German ones, between 1899 and 1910.[84] At the same time, French literature reached ever-wider German audiences. According to one estimate, the nineteenth century accounted for 56.7 per cent of German translations of French works published during the period 1700–1950.[85] Modern poets such as Baudelaire, Verlaine, Mallarmé, and Claudel were all translated during the Wilhelmine period, together with authors of different schools, such as Flaubert, Daudet, Villiers de L'Isle-Adam, Huysmans, Loti, and Bourget.[86] By 1892, it was calculated that 100,000 books by Zola had already been sold in Germany.[87] One cartoon in *Kladderadatsch* showed the fortunes of the mass-market publisher, August Scherl, resting on Dumas and Maupassant, alongside popular German authors like Fontane and Freytag.[88] When such exposure to French culture was added to long-standing preferences for French words, manners, and fashions, then consistent, negative

[81] D. Goubard, *Das Frankreichbild in der Zeitschrift 'der Türmer', 1898–1920*, D.Phil. thesis (Aachen, 1977), 207–9; S. Fauchereau, 'Literarischer Austausch zwischen Frankreich und Deutschland von 1900 bis 1930', in Spies (ed.), *Paris–Berlin 1900–1933*, 437.

[82] W. Lübke, *Grundriss der Kunstgeschichte*, 14th edn. (Esslingen a.N., 1909), v. 319; A. Springer, *Handbuch der Kunstgeschichte*, 5th revised edn. (Leipzig, 1909), 272–417; R. Muther, *Geschichte der Malerei*, 4th edn. (Berlin, 1922), iii. 214–54; the first edition appeared before the First World War.

[83] Spies (ed.), *Paris–Berlin 1900–1933*, 20.

[84] Ibid. On Bremen, see Gustav Pauli in anon., *Deutsche und Französische Kunst*, 4–5.

[85] F. Nies, 'Spitzenautoren französischer Literatur im deutschen Sprachraum', in B. Kortländer and F. Nies (eds.), *Französische Literatur in deutscher Sprache* (Düsseldorf, 1986), 142.

[86] Ibid. 30–1, 62–75; R. Bauer, 'Französisches in der deutschen Literatur', in H. Loebel (ed.), *Frankreich und Deutschland* (Bonn, 1986), 106–7.

[87] F. Mauthner's calculation, in Yves Chevrel, 'Le Naturalisme français en Allemagne: L'Année 1892', in Lüsebrink and Riesz (eds.), *Feindbild und Faszination*, 91.

[88] *Kladderadatsch*, 24 May 1908, no. 21.

national stereotypes became more difficult to sustain.[89] There was always a countervailing pressure of cultural preference, even amongst those whose knowledge of France was superficial. As *Simplicissimus* put it, in a cartoon which showed a garishly dressed threesome 'Im Cabaret': 'It's best with these French chansons to laugh discreetly. Understanding them is another matter.'[90]

A third reason why cultural stereotyping did not invalidate political assessment of France—in addition to admiration of French culture and patriotism—was the perceived connection in Germany between a coherent culture and a strong nation-state. This was the central argument of Oskar Schmitz, who was probably the best-selling German writer on contemporary France.[91] Unitary and sophisticated foreign cultures were worthy of respect, rather than resentment, he claimed, because they strengthened the state by enlisting the support of the nation. France was termed 'wirklich' in the title of Schmitz's book, since its culture was able to transform the environment into a form acceptable to the nation: 'Of all peoples, the French have the greatest capacity to make what they want become real.'[92] Whereas, in Germany, general ideas had no effect because of the division between political, cultural, and professional strata— 'Germany splinters into sixty million camps, i.e. into just as many as it has inhabitants'[93]—in France everyone recognized and defended national culture, even if they did not participate in it.[94] Moreover, Frenchmen were joined by accepted conventions and a national social life, which was centred on Paris: 'Private life has thus been much less highly valued in Paris than in Germany, which has never

---

[89] L. Leibrich, 'Französische Wirklichkeit im Werke Thomas Manns', in Deutsch–französisches Institut, Ludwigsburg, *Deutschland–Frankreich*, iii. 168–86. 'Française', *Simplicissimus*, 5 Mar. 1906, vol. 10, nos. 48 and 49; 'Deutsche in Paris', vol. 14, no. 5; 'In Paris', vol. 5, no. 39; 'Palais de Glace in Paris', vol. 7, no. 47; '"Der lustige Witwe" in Paris', 14 Feb. 1910, vol. 14, no. 46. The *Berliner Illustrirte Zeitung* showed strips of 'Pariser Schönheiten', 23 July 1899, no. 30; fashions from Paris, 9 June 1901, no. 23; and news of the French stage—for instance, on Yvette Guilbert, 5 Feb. 1899, no. 6. The French actress Sarah Bernhardt was known simply as 'Sarah'; *Kladderadatsch*, 23 Sept. 1906, no. 38, and 13 July 1913, no. 28.

[90] *Simplicissimus*, 30 Dec. 1907, vol. 12, no. 40.

[91] On Schmitz, see G. Bott, *Deutsche Frankreichkunde 1900–1933* (Rheinfelden, 1982), 163–5. The coherence of French culture was also an important argument of Hillebrand, *Frankreich und die Franzosen*. Most authors assumed the coherence of a French national culture. See, for instance, Fernau, *Die französische Demokratie*, 1–2, and Max Weber, in Eisenstadt (ed.), *Max Weber on Charisma and Institution Building*, 215–16.

[92] Schmitz, *Das Land der Wirklichkeit*, 43.

[93] Ibid. 110.   [94] Ibid. 19.

had a public life to tempt fertile minds.'[95] The result was that France was able to withstand the centrifugal forces of modernity, reformulating the ideas of other nations to its own advantage, whilst Germany threatened to disintegrate.[96] This, in turn, had the double effect of securing France's international moral authority—'The French always had the ability to shape their ideas so that other peoples could do something with them'[97]—and of justifying its foreign policy: 'since Louis XIV, French national consciousness has... become so clear, thick, pure and tough, that, in terms of clarity, it can only be compared to Jewish and Greek consciousness. Even the net of English culture, however wide it is, is thinner and more broadly meshed.'[98] It was evident to Schmitz that so coherent a culture deserved its place in the sun. As far as cultural unity and foreign policy were concerned, France should be imitated, not execrated.

Paradoxically, the fact that French history was seen through a national looking-glass attracted Germans to France at the same time as it repelled them. The neighbouring state was venerated as an archetypal *Nationalstaat*, conducting a successful foreign policy and dominating the cultures of continental Europe, but it was also criticized as Germany's historical enemy, which had imposed its manners on German territories and prevented national unification. It is not my intention here to deny the continuing existence of traditional *Feindbilder* under the *Kaiserreich*, but rather to demonstrate that such stereotypes did not exclude the possibility of comparative political analysis. As the danger of French hegemony in Europe receded, it was easier for Wilhelmine Germans to stress France's pioneering, nation-building role, which the Reich could be seen to have continued and improved after 1871, rather than a domineering and oppressive role in international politics, which no longer seemed to pertain.[99] Given that France could be viewed by Germans as a paradigmatic nation-state, and not just as an enemy, the question arose in Germany whether that French nation-state had been strengthened or weakened by the republican form of government. Indeed, when it was placed in the context of a widespread belief in assimilation, which made national survival dependent on the successful adaptation of universal ideas, the issue of French success or failure under the Third Republic appeared to be a pressing one, for the latter was not

[95] Schmitz, *Das Land der Wirklichkeit*, 116, 162.
[96] Ibid. 38.   [97] Ibid. 112.   [98] Ibid. 85.
[99] See below, Ch. 6, sect. 1.

only 'the single great republic in Europe', in Karl Vogel's words,[100] it was also, in Otto Hintze's opinion, the heir of the French Revolution: 'The parliamentary republic of today is not the continuation of the liberal-constitutional institutions of this regime [Louis Philippe], from which it differs not only through its republican form, but still more through its universal suffrage; rather, it is to be seen as the continuation of the liberal-constitutional institutions of the Second Empire.... at bottom, though, it is the first complete embodiment of the principles of 1789.'[101] Authors from both left and right agreed with Hintze, as did caricaturists, who invariably portrayed the Third Republic in a revolutionary *bonnet rouge*.[102] Most of them also admitted that the French Revolution had posed unanswered questions, which had transformed the nature of political debate in modern Europe.[103] German observers were interested to find out, therefore, whether French republicans could fit the solutions of 1789 to the changed circumstances of industrial society.

4. Plan of the Book

The distinction between stereotyping and analysis, which has been assumed until now, is only one of degree. Crude analysis eventually becomes indistinguishable from sophisticated stereotyping. All descriptions of the French Third Republic were more or less mythical, since they were reduced inevitably to linguistic conventions, repeated categories, and simplified relations. This study seeks to identify such conventions, categories, and relations in order to reconstruct the images and arguments which were associated with the

---

[100] *Frankfurter Zeitung*, 23 July 1909; *Leipziger Volkszeitung*, 27 May 1908.

[101] Hintze, 'Das monarchische Prinzip und die konstitutionelle Verfassung', in *Staat und Verfassung*, 361.

[102] On the left, for example, Fernau, *Die französische Demokratie*, 1–3, 16–17, 37. On the right, Vogel, *Die dritte französische Republik bis 1895*, 329, or Kuhn, *Frankreich an der Zeitwende*, 21. This was also implicit in the frequent association of the Third Republic with the slogan 'liberté, égalité, fraternité', most conspicuously in Schmidt's book, *Im Lande der Freiheit, Gleichheit und Brüderlichkeit*.

[103] M. Spahn, *Der Kampf um die Schule in Frankreich und Deutschland* (Kempten and Munich, 1907), 4; Vogel, *Die dritte französische Republik bis 1895*, p. x; Schmitz, *Das Land der Wirklichkeit*, 305; Fernau, *Die französische Demokratie*, 1–2; E. Schomann, *Französische Utopisten und ihr Frauenideal* (Berlin, 1911), 171. Between 1871 and 1912, no less than 123 plays and novels on 1789 and Napoleon I appeared in German. See Hirschstein, *Die französische Revolution im deutschen Drama und Epos nach 1815*, 378–81.

republican regime in France. Its aim has been to discover common elements in Wilhelmine perceptions of the French polity and to trace the connections made between such elements. To this end, it was necessary to establish whether different political groupings in Germany emphasized different elements of the French republic, and whether they connected them in different ways. Regional and confessional variations were found to be subordinate to political affiliations. By contrast, government could not be equated with party, since politicians were virtually excluded from holding office. Thus, it was decided to use diplomatic correspondence, on the one hand, and conservative, liberal, socialist, and Centre Party newspapers and journals, on the other. Since such newspaper articles and official correspondence were frequently allusive, however, the sources were extended in scope to include monographs on France and academic treatises, which referred to French politics and society, in an attempt to explore the premisses and implications of journalists' and diplomats' allusions. In general, it was possible to discern broad arguments, rather than stereotypes, which crossed party lines. Nevertheless, alternative explanations and parallel political discourses continued to exist: Chapter 5 examines their relation to general arguments concerning the Third Republic and shows how they changed during the late Wilhelmine era.

The principal chapters commence with the public dénouement of the Dreyfus case. With hindsight, the affair was seen in Germany as a watershed for the French republic: most German political parties altered their view of the republican regime in France after 1898. Chapter 2 starts with the Dreyfus affair and the questions which it raised for German observers, including the fundamental relationship between law and the state. In many instances, this relationship defined the nature and extent of politics, often by excluding political parties from state affairs. Chapter 3 goes on to investigate the parliamentary basis of the Third Republic, which was seen by many Germans as the essence of the French political system. It concentrates above all on divergent conceptions in France and Germany of government functions and competencies. Chapter 4 looks at the connection between parliamentarism and universal suffrage, and the alleged consequences of that connection. The difficulty of checking popularly elected and legitimized ministries, together with associated dangers such as corruption, demagogy, and dictatorship, forms the core of this section. Chapter 5 shows how both government and political parties in Germany came to reject the French parliamentary republic as a political paradigm which was worthy of imitation. The study concludes, in Chapter 6, with an assessment of the Third Republic's position and role in common political typologies of the Wilhelmine period.

2

The German Rechtsstaat *and the French* Political State

1. Politics and the State

> What sort of people were they? What were they talking about?
> Which authority did they belong to? K. lived in a *Rechtsstaat* after
> all; peace existed everywhere; all laws were still in force; who dared
> to attack him in his own apartment?
>
> (Franz Kafka, 1914)[1]

The modern state both protected and threatened its citizens. It provided them with shelter from the tumult of international politics, it
maintained order and promised legal redress, it underwrote social
insurance and public education. But it also monitored and punished. It
levied money and conscripted men. It intervened and, consequently, it
grew. Josef K., Kafka's protagonist in *Der Prozeß*, trusted routinely in
the authorities and the law, until he was arraigned one day and warned
of an impending trial. Suddenly, the state became impenetrable
and omnipotent, a maze of rooms and corridors, unknown bureaucrats, and unexplained decisions. To the isolated clerk, the authorities
now appeared incomprehensible and dangerous, although they had
previously seemed necessary and beneficent. The modern European
political conundrum was: how was the state to extend its functions and
how, under certain circumstances, was it to be controlled?

Both France and Germany had long-standing state traditions,
which were seen to rest, above all, on culture, power, and law.[2] The
historical outlook of most Wilhelmine commentators, who wrote, like

---

[1] F. Kafka, *Der Prozeß* (Berlin, 1935), 3; written in 1914.
[2] K. H. F. Dyson, *The State Tradition in Western Europe* (Oxford, 1980), 101–85;
G. Poggi, *The Development of the Modern State* (London, 1978), 60–149; B. Chapman,
Police State (London, 1970), 33–49; A. Vincent, *Theories of the State* (Oxford, 1987),
45–118.

Dilthey,[3] as if philosophy had been superseded by history, ensured that there was a surprising amount of agreement about the origins of the modern state. Thus, although Gustav Cohn, an economist, Heinrich von Treitschke, an historian of the Prussian school, and Max Weber, a legally-trained sociologist, worked with different definitions of the state and had different views about its relation to civil society, all depicted the genesis of the *Staat* in similar terms. First, authority had had to be established, usually through a long period of coercion. For Cohn, it was evident 'that the advancing culture of peoples had been preoccupied initially, and for many centuries, with the securing of *domination* and *order*'.[4] Treitschke was more forthright. Authority depended ultimately and originally on force, and enforced order alone allowed the growth of complex and stable empires:

the state protects and surrounds the life of a people, ordering it externally from all sides. It does not ask on principle about beliefs, it demands obedience.... If the silent obedience of inhabitants becomes a reasonable, inner consent, then this constitutes a step forward, but such consent is not absolutely necessary. Empires have survived for centuries as powerful, highly-developed states without this inner consent from their subjects.[5]

Weber concurred. The defining feature of the state was its monopoly of violence over a given territory:

[the state is], in its fully-developed form, thoroughly modern.... The following features are formally characteristic of the present-day state: an administrative and legal order,... which claims to be valid not only for those who, largely through birth, are members of the same group, but also for all actions, broadly defined, taking place on subject territory.... Further, however: 'legitimate' violence only exists today to the extent that the state order allows or prescribes it.[6]

Law, claimed Weber, Cohn, and Treitschke, only emerged late in the history of states, after social order had been created by the exercise of power, sometimes in conjunction with a common set of cultural assumptions and beliefs. Nevertheless, once it had appeared, a legal framework became an integral part of advanced societies. The modern state rarely had to coerce, it was held, because its

[3] W. Dilthey, *Einleitung in die Geisteswissenschaften* (Leipzig and Berlin, 1922). The work was first published in 1883.

[4] G. Cohn, *System der Nationalökonomie* (3 vols.; Stuttgart, 1885–98), ii. 50.

[5] Treitschke, *Politik*, i. 32.

[6] Weber, *Wirtschaft und Gesellschaft*, 30. This section was compiled 1911–13.

government was predominantly rational and, therefore, consensual. The form of what Weber called 'rationale Herrschaft' was law. It alone defined competencies, offences and punishments in a predictable way, acceptable to rational individuals.[7] Although Treitschke was impressed by the power of government and by the limits of individual rationality, he conceded all the same that the state existed to increase individual liberty, within carefully described boundaries, and that, consequently, its most basic function was the provision of scientific law, which guaranteed internal order and, thereby, freedom: 'Every extension of state activity is a blessing and is reasonable, if it awakes, fosters and purifies the independence of free and reasonable people'.[8] Cohn agreed. The *Rechtsstaat* underpinned the *Kulturstaat* and even the well-governed *Polizeistaat* of the late nineteenth century rather than hindering them. Only narrow, liberal definitions of a nightwatchman state, as it had been recently termed, prevented the latter from assuming other social and cultural functions:

The much-used concept of the 'law-governed state' [*Rechtsstaat*], which is sometimes seen to oppose the other concepts of the 'police state' [*Polizeistaat*], 'welfare state' [*Wohlfahrtsstaat*] or even 'cultural state' [*Kulturstaat*], betrays by the very transformations of these oppositions the manifold nature of its content. One meaning, passed on to us by the philosophy of the previous century, coincides with that fundamental achievement of state institutions which aims to protect the rights of each member of the state association [*Staatsverband*]. The other meaning of the 'Rechtsstaat', which our age has pushed into the foreground, aims by contrast to accommodate the extended content of state activity, and consequently not to stand in opposition to the 'welfare' or 'cultural state', conflicting instead merely with the 'police state', and only with this in its worst sense, namely that state which rules arbitrarily, in contradistinction to the state which rules by means of law.[9]

In short, the *Rechtsstaat* ensured internal order by consent, which in turn permitted the state to acquire new responsibilities without public disquiet. Law, because it imposed limits on state and subject, constituted a platform for later disputes about forms of government. If particular political systems undermined the legal basis of society, with its guarantees of predictability and free spheres of action, then

[7] Weber, *Wirtschaft und Gesellschaft*, 125.   [8] Treitschke, *Politik*, i. 44, 70–2, 83.
[9] Cohn, *System der Nationalökonomie*, ii. 50–1.

there would be no medium for the negotiation of consensus, or at least compromise. Historically, the rule of law appeared to precede political debate in Germany: it had to be preserved, if that debate were to have any sense.

In both France and Germany, the institutions and the idea of the state, according to Otto Hintze and others, owed much to the legal traditions of absolute monarchies during the seventeenth and eighteenth centuries. In the course of the following century, these legal conceptions of the state were joined by newer discourses about national culture and politics, nation-states and political regimes. On the whole, the national idea was integrated successfully into French and German state traditions. Certainly, by 1900, no commentator in either country referred to contradictions between the *Rechtsstaat*, on the one hand, and the *Nationalstaat*, on the other. As has been shown, many Germans came to see France as a model nation-state during the nineteenth century. By contrast, the notion of a political regime, in which all aspects of the state were subject to party discussions about the distribution and exercise of power, met with considerable resistance in Germany. In this respect, it appeared that France, which had adopted a rights-based, political definition of the nation-state after 1789, was not regarded by many nineteenth-century Germans to be worthy of imitation. *Staat* and *Recht*, it was implied, were to be kept separate from politics and the compromises of sectional interests. Even a moderate liberal and later advocate of a parliamentary regime like Georg Jellinek, who scandalized legal faculties by admitting that the state could be examined politically, nonetheless maintained in his work a distinction between political and legal *Staaten*: 'Scientifically, there are two main ways to regard the state ... One is the legal, the other the political way of understanding the human collectivity.'[10] With the exception of socialists, few Germans argued that all parts of the state should be open to party-political scrutiny and reform. For most of the nineteenth century, it seemed, German states stood above politics.

Amongst academics, the putative opposition between politics and the state became more pronounced after 1848 and 1871, partly because of the increasing sacrosanctity of the national idea in Germany. Despite the esoteric nature of controversies within disciplines, it is

---

[10] G. Jellinek, 'Eine Naturlehre des Staates', in id., *Ausgewählte Schriften und Reden* (Berlin, 1911), ii. 320.

possible to discern a broad movement away from critical study of the *Staat*. Lawyers, who had dominated the old subject of *Politik*,[11] adopted the methods of legal positivism from the 1850s onwards, concentrating exclusively on the immanent qualities of law itself. As one leading exponent, Paul Laband, put it: 'all historical, political and philosophical observations are without importance for the dogmatics of concrete legal material.'[12] The effect of positivists' work, which provided rational principles to fill the lacunae between positive laws and granted a juridical personality to the *Staat*, was to deflect attention from the origins and rectitude of state authority and preclude investigation of the various organs of state.[13] Historians, although abhorring positivism, similarly avoided a critique of the German Empire. Like lawyers, they assumed the legitimacy of the state, although from opposing intuitive, rather than rational premisses.[14] The *Staat* was believed to be the largest and most important type of 'individuality', different to the sum of its parts and with its own morality, just as the human organism was superior to its organs.[15] It was partly because historicists attempted to understand the state intuitively, as a distinct individuality, that they ignored its relationship with society and its own internal contradictions. The further historical research strayed from the state, wrote Heinrich von Treitschke on becoming editor of the *Historische Zeitschrift* in 1896, 'the less it belongs to history'.[16] In their biographies of Luther, Freiherr vom Stein, Bismarck, and Wilhelm I, neo-Rankean historians like Max Lehmann, Erich Marcks, Max Lenz, and Erich Brandenburg consolidated the idea of an historically justified, if not

[11] H. Maier, *Politische Wissenschaft in Deutschland* (Munich, 1969), 45.

[12] Cited in Böckenförde, *Gesetz und gesetzgebende Gewalt*, 216; see also 211–20. Further, M. Stolleis, 'Verwaltungsrechtswissenschaft und Verwaltungslehre 1866–1914', *Die Verwaltung*, 15 (1982), 48–52.

[13] V. Hartmann, *Repräsentation in der politischen Theorie und Staatslehre in Deutschland* (Berlin, 1979), 136, 143, 167–71.

[14] H.-H. Krill, *Die Rankerenaissance. Max Lenz und Erich Marcks. Ein Beitrag zum historisch-politischen Denken in Deutschland 1880–1935* (Berlin, 1962), 80–138. E. Fehrenbach, 'Rankerenaissance und Imperialismus in der wilhelminischen Zeit', in B. Faulenbach (ed.), *Geschichtswissenschaft in Deutschland* (Munich, 1974), 54–7.

[15] G. G. Iggers, *The German Conception of History: The National Tradition of Historical Thought from Herder to the Present* (Hanover, NH, 1983), 7–12; W. Hofer, *Geschichtsschreibung und Weltanschauung* (Munich, 1950), 146; T. Kornbichler, *Deutsche Geschichtsschreibung im 19. Jahrhundert. Wilhelm Dilthey und die Begründung der modernen Geschichtswissenschaft* (Pfaffenweiler, 1984), 266–87.

[16] H. v. Treitschke, 'Die Aufgabe des Geschichtsschreibers', *Historische Zeitschrift*, 76 (1896). See also Treitschke, *Politik*, i. 63–4.

inevitable, Prussian-German Empire, characterized by Protestantism and the Hohenzollern dynasty.[17] Economists and sociologists were influenced by many of the same arguments and analogies. Historical economics, which gave rise to the new discipline of sociology in the early twentieth century, was based on a reaction in Germany from the 1840s onwards to the universal precepts of British and French economic theory. The German state, it was argued in the *Verein für Sozialpolitik*, which was set up to advise government, should intervene to protect, regulate and stimulate a national economy. Although economists and sociologists, unlike most historians, continued to investigate economy, society, and culture, they tended, as Max Weber pointed out in an attack on Gustav Schmoller, to assume a dichotomy between a scientific, neutral state and the divisive interest groups of politics.[18] To academics of the late nineteenth century, the *Staat* was at once unpolitical and the central organization of power in society.

German parties, too, had acknowledged the unique position and function of the state, particularly after 1871, and had refrained, sometimes because of government repression, from criticizing certain parts of it. This caution had been symbolized by Karl Kautsky's complete omission of the word 'Staat' from the SPD's Erfurt programme in 1891.[19] Nevertheless, party politicians, who were effectively barred from holding state office, remained less sceptical than academics, who were civil servants, about politics, the Reichstag, and social and economic interest groups. Consequently, they were more likely to bring the *Staat* under political scrutiny, discussing its strengths and weaknesses. After 1890, as anxiety over the separatism of Guelphs, Bavarians, Catholics, and even Alsatians, Danes, and Poles diminished, criticism of the political system became less

---

[17] See e.g. M. Lenz, *Martin Luther* (Berlin, 1883); E. Brandenburg, *Martin Luther's Anschauung vom Staate und der Gesellschaft* (Halle, 1901); M. Lehmann, *Freiherr vom Stein* (Leipzig, 1903); E. Marcks, *Kaiser Wilhelm I* (Berlin, 1897); M. Lenz, *Geschichte Bismarcks*, 4th revised edn. (Leipzig, 1913).

[18] M. Weber, in *Verhandlungen des Vereins für Sozialpolitik in Wien, 1909* (Leipzig, 1910), 286–7; D. Krüger, 'Max Weber and the Younger Generation in the Verein für Sozialpolitik', in W. J. Mommsen and J. Osterhammel (eds.), *Max Weber and his Contemporaries* (London, 1987), 76–8, and id., *Nationalökonomen im wilhelminischen Deutschland* (Göttingen, 1983); I. Gorges, *Sozialforschung in Deutschland 1872–1914. Gesellschaftliche Einflüsse auf Themen- und Methodenwahl des Vereins für Sozialpolitik* (Königstein, 1980), 118, 190; H. Winkel, *Die deutsche Nationalökonomie im 19. Jahrhundert* (Darmstadt, 1977).

[19] I. Gilcher-Holtey, *Das Mandat des Intellektuellen. Karl Kautsky und die Sozialdemokratie* (Berlin, 1986), 88.

circumspect and well-known treatises on government appeared on both left and right, from Friedrich Naumann's *Demokratie und Kaisertum* in 1900, which had sold 25,000 copies by 1905,[20] to Heinrich Claß's *Wenn ich der Kaiser wär* in 1912, which had exceeded 20,000 by August 1914.[21] By the 1900s, as important technical failings of government were exposed, especially in the conduct of foreign policy, German parties were ready to air their grievances in public and treat issues such as the constitution, military affairs and diplomacy, which had enjoyed considerable protection from party interference after 1871, like any other political question. Between 1908 and 1914, during the pre-war constitutional crisis of the *Kaiserreich*, many politicians, and a much smaller number of academics, were even willing to admit that the German state was a particular type of political regime, which could, if necessary, be replaced.

The French Third Republic constituted the most obvious European example of a regime which had attempted to politicize the state. In France, despite a strong tradition of the *État*, all aspects of the state were seen to be political and were therefore objects of party discussion and reform. By the early twentieth century, many German politicians were coming, much more slowly, to similar conclusions and, as a result, were prepared to consider France's political state on its merits, not least because the Third Republic was the first such European regime to have lasted more than a generation. German parties' new-found willingness to assess the French political state as a model for Germany did not imply a renunciation of the legal tradition of the *Staat*, however. Rather, Wilhelmine observers looked towards France to discover how justice, accountability, efficiency, and a strong state could be combined. In Germany, where legal conceptions of the state were deeply ingrained, foreign regimes would still be judged by the tenets of the *Rechtsstaat*.

2. Law, Legality, and Justice

The law had two main sources of legitimacy in late nineteenth-century Germany: rationality and tradition. The former constituted

[20] P. Gilg, *Die Erneuerung des demokratischen Denkens im wilhelminischen Deutschland* (Wiesbaden, 1965), 191. P. Theiner, *Sozialer Liberalismus und deutsche Weltpolitik. Friedrich Naumann im wilhelminischen Deutschland 1860–1919* (Baden-Baden, 1983), 63, notes that this was Naumann's most popular pre-war pamphlet.

[21] R. Chickering, *'We Men Who Feel Most German': A Cultural Study of the Pan-German League, 1886–1914* (London, 1984), 286.

one of the core elements of Max Weber's theory of capitalism and of his legal sociology. The West, he postulated, had overseen the growth of a rational legal system, with fixed rules and foreseeable outcomes, which permitted the systematic accumulation of capital.[22] The emergence of natural law, espousing reason as a touchstone of legitimacy rather than the authority of the law-giver, marked the separation of Europe from the rest of the world:

> only the Occident knew ... 'natural law'; only it has known the complete removal of the personal basis of law and the saying 'arbitrariness breaks the law of the land'; only it has seen the creation of an edifice from the unique foundations of Roman law and experienced an event like the reception of Roman law. All these events have, to a very considerable extent, political causes, with only rather distant analogies in the whole of the rest of the world.[23]

Weber's hierarchy and chronology were clear. Natural law had prepared the way in the eighteenth and nineteenth centuries for the refinement of Roman law. This, in turn, was associated with France. 'The classical inheritance was bestowed on France', wrote one commentator: 'Other peoples only received individual bequests. Roman law and Graeco-Roman thought were forced on them.'[24] Even the constitutional lawyer Otto von Gierke, despite eschewing Weberian rationality as the desirable kernel of law, nevertheless admitted that *Romanismus*, often imported from France, had become dominant in Germany under the historical school because its sources were both more plentiful and more reliable than those of its German counterparts.[25] With hindsight, Otto Hintze went further back in time in order to make the same case: the most significant turning-points in the legal history of the bureaucracy had been the introduction of Roman law in the sixteenth century and the emergence of the *Rechtsstaat* in the nineteenth century: the former, it was implied, informed the latter.[26]

For Weber, the commonality of German and French legal traditions manifested itself above all when compared to those of Britain. The anomalous social integrity of British ruling-elites allowed them to retain a two-tier system of justice by peers for the elites

[22] Weber, *The Protestant Ethic*, 25–6.
[23] Weber, *Wirtschaft und Gesellschaft*, 505. See also Eisenstadt (ed.), *Max Weber on Charisma and Institution Building*, 96, 102.
[24] Schmitz, *Im Lande der Wirklichkeit*, 76; Haas, *Frankreich*, 425.
[25] Gierke, *Die historische Rechtschule und die Germanisten*, 12–15.
[26] Hintze, 'Der Beamtenstand' (1911), in *Soziologie und Geschichte*, 103.

themselves and a type of informal 'khadi-justice' by magistrates for the people. By contrast, the relative disunity of continental elites obliged them to institute formal legal codes and adjudication: 'by allowing the legal system to function like a technically rational machine, specific legal formalism guarantees to individual litigants relative maximum scope to manoeuvre freely and, in particular, to calculate rationally the legal consequences and opportunities of their purposive actions.'[27] Democracies, however, were likely to override such formal rules:

The creation of informal law is encouraged, on the one hand, by authoritarian powers, which rest on *piety*, whether theocratic or patrimonial. On the other hand, certain forms of democracy can also have very similar formal effects. This is because all these cases concern powers whose holders—the head of a hierarchy, the despot..., the demagogue—...do not wish to be *bound* by any formal restrictions, not even by regulations which they themselves have imposed. All of them are obstructed by the unavoidable contradiction between the abstract formalism of legal logic and the need to fulfil material demands through law.[28]

Unable to rely on shared social assumptions, continental states were forced to link justice to formal, rational legal process, without reference to individuals. Whereas in Britain a sense of justice depended on partiality and personal ties, or trial by peers, in France and Germany it rested on strict impartiality, formality, and anonymity. Yet democracy not only ignored formal procedure in its eagerness to achieve quick results, it could also lead to a reassertion of individuality, as demagogues created the impression of individual affinities with their electors, which, unlike laws, were not subjected to concrete testing. Formal law could then be ignored with impunity, in the name of the majority.

Democracy, or at least the French version of it, likewise appeared to endanger the other main source of legal legitimacy: tradition. Obviously, there were in any case potential contradictions between rational law and traditional law, which were mitigated but not removed by the 'German' notion of reason working backwards, seeking to expound and to utilize the cumulative and superior reason of the past.[29] Reference to history rather than rationality, even if historical

---

[27] Weber, *Wirtschaft und Gesellschaft*, 469, 509–10. On English law, see Eisenstadt (ed.), *Max Weber on Charisma and Institution Building*, 84, 89.

[28] Weber, *Wirtschaft und Gesellschaft*, 469, 509–10.

[29] L. Krieger, *The German Idea of Freedom* (Boston, 1957), 129–38; P. Singer, *Hegel* (Oxford, 1983), 34–44. By the Wilhelmine period, the concept had been vulgarized, distinguishing between 'French' a priori rationality and 'German' historical reason. See, for instance, Schirmacher, *Deutschland und Frankreich seit 35 Jahren*, 106, and Schmitz, *Das Land der Wirklichkeit*, 72.

rationality, presupposed acceptance of extant law, or once-extant law, irrespective of its rational content. For this reason, *Germanisten* such as Gierke were criticized by Weber for having created a 'Naturrecht des historisch Gewordenen':

> But also all those less extreme, half-historical, half-naturalistic theories of a 'Volksgeist'—as the unique natural and therefore legitimate source from which law and culture emanate—and especially of that 'organic' growth of all supposedly genuine law, which is said to rest on a direct 'feeling for justice' [*Rechtsgefühl*] rather than on 'artificial' or rational statutes, ... contain the same premiss, which serves to downgrade enacted law to something 'merely' positive.[30]

The idea that law had evolved naturally, or organically, and that its legitimacy was derived above all from its status as a product of such evolution, was popular beyond narrow circles of *Germanisten*. Historians, economists, lawyers of the historical school, and publicists of all kinds bore witness to the enduring significance of tradition as a source of legal authority. To these observers, France had broken with tradition, and therefore with the traditional authority of law, in 1789 or, as Hans Delbrück more accurately recorded, in 1792, with the declaring of the First Republic: 'Louis XVI was taken prisoner, the republic declared, the king sent to the scaffold and the link with the past in France was severed.'[31] For Treitschke, the revolutionary act required to install a republican regime was itself an assault on the authority of law: 'The French have, in their time, spoken of the holy revolution...[Yet] in itself a revolution is always wrong; a violent disruption to the legal order contradicts the inner equilibrium of the state.'[32] Roscher not only reiterated this view in his exposition of the conditions favouring socialism and communism—one of which was a 'violent upheaval, indeed *confusion of public legality and justice through revolutions*'—but also pointed to the dangers of constantly altering and abolishing laws, giving the impression that the political state was completely unconstrained: 'Even without revolution proper, nothing encourages communism more than feverishly active,

---

[30] Weber, *Wirtschaft und Gesellschaft*, 497.
[31] Delbrück, *Regierung und Volkswille*, 123; J. Reber, *Ein Blick auf Frankreichs Schulwesen* (Aschaffenburg, 1897), 4.
[32] Treitschke, *Politik*, i. 131–2.

light-headedly changeable legislation, which not only damages respect for all that exists and has been passed on, but at the same time gives rise to the credulous idea among uneducated people that the state is able to do all that it wishes.'[33] Since they owed their existence to a revolutionary rejection of legal tradition, it could be argued, republics were less likely to recognize law as a permanent constraint on government activity. Rather, they tended to assume a popular legitimacy, which allowed them to enact, amend, and repeal laws at will.

In France, the political state appeared to have eclipsed the legal state. In his study of the *Rechtsstaat*, the revised edition of which was published in 1894, the old-school liberal Rudolf von Gneist traced the progress of the law-governed state, from its origins in Britain, via Germany, to its disappearance in eighteenth and nineteenth-century France, which was described in the title of chapter 7 as 'The Negation of the *Rechtsstaat*'. Gneist agreed with Hintze that state and society in France had merged, with the latter clearly ascendant:

As a rule, we speak of state and society as two powers, which oppose and supplement each other, whereas the Englishman fuses them both in the concept of the political society. In France, too, they like to use the expression société politique, the translation of which into German sounds completely foreign to us. This is because in France as well, since the great revolution, social interests have, with time, eclipsed state interests.[34]

There were, in Gneist's opinion, inevitable oppositions between and within state and society, which the 'brilliant one-sidedness' of the French political system ignored, but which the German *Rechtsstaat* countered, protecting the individual by law from a splintered and partial society: 'It can be construed as a favourable portent that, at the time when French social theory exercised a monopoly, the term "Rechtsstaat" appeared in Germany, as the expression of an organism which undertook to give back and maintain civic freedom to the fragmented life of society.'[35]

Historically, Gneist proposed, France had taken the wrong course. Its orders and corporations had been corrupted during the *ancien*

---

[33] Roscher, *Politik*, 536.

[34] Hintze, 'Das monarchische Prinzip und die konstitutionelle Verfassung', in *Staat und Verfassung*, 365–6.

[35] R. v. Gneist, *Der Rechtsstaat und die Verwaltungsgerichte in Deutschland*, 3rd edn. (Darmstadt, 1966), 7.

régime, insisting on their rights and neglecting their responsibilities. As a result, kings had circumvented laws, liberties, and privileges in order to maintain administration, but at the expense of law, legal jurisdiction, and continuity:

Nowhere did the separation of estates become so sharp and injurious for the middle and lower classes as in France.... This is precisely why the *monarchy*, its army and its bureaucracy was able, by violent means, to overcome such orders. It was always more a question of positions of power during this long, drawn-out struggle than the higher duty of the monarchy to administer law evenly. Such was the case during the violent suppression of the spiritual stirrings of the Reformation, which also brought losses to France's classical jurisprudence.[36]

Law remained in vestigial form, little more than a collection of individual and corporate rights and privileges. Further, since state and people were barely connected by law, with neither looking to legal forms of redress and restraint, the two parts briefly separated, only to be reunited after 1789 under the terms of popular sovereignty.

It was in the nature of *Volkssouveränität*, as a political construct, that it looked to rhetorical devices such as the rights of man rather than to binding and enforceable laws: 'Scholarly abstractions...are now put forward as the original, innate, and inalienable rights of every man, which only require "declaration" in order immediately to become valid.... The thought that such basic rights need to be administered through laws and a system of justice remains foreign to society, however.'[37] French democracy refused to compromise the political state by sanctioning the principle of constitutional safeguards and legal continuity, above and beyond the existing regime. Since politicians in France were legitimized solely by the populace, continued Gneist, there was no reason for them to seek the sanction of an external authority such as the Bundesrat in Germany: 'The idea of a permanent council of state [*Reichsrat*], both to represent the *existing legal basis* of state and society and to secure the organic grafting of new laws on to the existing constitution, remains so alien to democracy that it sees in all other "parts of the law-making process" only artificial obstacles to its own will.'[38]

It was no surprise, therefore, that the political masters of the Third Republic had sought to regulate most affairs by ordinary statute. Although constitutional law retained a special status, since it

---

[36] Ibid. 159–60.   [37] Ibid. 163.   [38] Ibid. 168–9.

could only be amended by the Senate and Assembly in joint session, the movement in recent French history appeared to be towards 'Deconstitutionalisationen'. According to Siegfried Brie, who was a professor of law at Breslau university and the author of the first German study of the Third Republic's constitution, this had occurred in 1875, after reference to an annual budget, the authorization of taxes and independence of the courts had been omitted from the constitutional laws, and in 1879 and 1884, after stipulations concerning the location of the assemblies and the election of the Senate had been removed from the constitution: 'In these acts of "deconstitutionalization", one can witness an attempt, which has also affected other countries recently, to give more of a role to ordinary legislation vis-à-vis the constitution than has previously been the case.'[39] Since the constitutional laws of previous regimes had been more difficult to alter than other statutes, which required a simple majority, the power of the political chambers to decide their own fate was rightly perceived to have increased.

It seemed essential to uphold the law against the incursions of the political state. France's failure to defend the former and its championing of the latter rested in part, it was contended, on an illusory conception of freedom. German writers from across the political and academic spectrum never tired of remarking the disjunction between noisy, public celebrations of *liberté* and unseen contraventions of real freedoms.[40] In a chapter entitled 'German and French Freedom', Oskar Schmitz contrasted the two ideas. Drawing on Max Lehmann's work on the Prussian reform period, he demonstrated how Freiherr vom Stein had acted according to a specifically 'Germanic' notion of freedom, granting liberties to groups, or orders, as they proved themselves worthy: 'Thus, it is no longer a question of the rights of man, but the privileges [*Vorrechte*] of men with different histories.'[41] Such particular, historically proven freedoms were enacted gradually and peacefully, becoming the core of an organic legal corpus, whose

[39] S. Brie, *Die gegenwärtige Verfassung Frankreichs. Staatsrechtliche Erörterungen* (Breslau, 1888), 19.
[40] Schmidt, *Im Lande der Freiheit, Gleichheit und Brüderlichkeit*, 2; Gneist, *Der Rechtsstaat*, 178; H. Semmig, *Czar, Empereur und Republik, oder Frankreich vor dem Richterstuhl des gesunden Menschenverstandes* (Leipzig, 1894), 70; M. Andler, *Die Städteschulden in Frankreich und Preußen und ihre wirtschaftliche Bedeutung* (Stuttgart, 1911), 19.
[41] Schmitz, *Das Land der Wirklichkeit*, 102.

authority then served to guarantee the liberties themselves. Britain, until the mid-nineteenth century, when it was corrupted by French ideas, had constituted the best example of this practice:[42]

Stein also likes to refer to England, where the old Germanic representation of estates has lasted longest, for the 'Commons' were originally estates. Only after the July revolution were French theories introduced into England, only then was the old organic system ruined by an abstract conception of freedom and England served up for the domination of the masses for ever. . . . Disraeli . . . drafted the electoral law, which he gave to workers in 1867, expressly not as a right of man, but as a privilege, of which a great part of the respectable working population had shown itself worthy.[43]

Whereas German freedom was historical, legal, and *ad personam*, French liberty was a priori, political, and universal. Starting from a study of the individual, with its common traits and qualities, French thinkers, it was held, had constructed a theory of political freedom based on the equitable distribution of power amongst rational, social, and virtuous equals: 'Precisely described, freedom in France consists in every citizen casting his vote in the election of deputies to the National Assembly', wrote Sybel.[44] The significance of law was diminished in two ways, it was believed. First, it was assumed that a society of equals required only minimal legislation to regulate its conduct. A harmony founded on reason, embodied in Rousseau's social contract, was expected to prevail. The rights of man were therefore more to remind citizens than to be enforced.[45] Second, law was seen merely as the creation of the legislature rather than as the historical wisdom of society. If relations of power were correctly ordered within a new *polis*, then it was understood that just and workable law would be passed automatically. Old law was thus redundant and, since it constituted an obstacle to the new political order, was revoked. The result, however, in Schmitz's opinion, as in that of many of his compatriots, was not a less regulated, more

---

[42] See also Gneist, *Der Rechtsstaat*, 38–64, who starts with Britain as the archetypal *Rechtsstaat*.

[43] Schmitz, *Im Land der Wirklichkeit*, 102.

[44] H. v. Sybel, *Was wir von Frankreich lernen können* (Bonn, 1872), 13. For Catholic authors, Spahn, *Der Kampf um die Schule in Frankreich und Deutschland*, 5, and A. Steinhauser, *Neustes aus Frankreich. Christliche Demokratie* (Cologne, 1899), 47.

[45] Gneist, *Der Rechtsstaat*, 163.

harmonious society, but a violent, extreme, and tyrannical anarchy: 'Famously, the Jacobins tried in 1789 to rebuild the state on the foundation of the rights of man; these rights are called liberty, equality and fraternity. Yet it is just as well-known that there has never been a time when so much human blood was spilled or when so many original human rights were trampled underfoot as in the period immediately after 1789 in the name of freedom.'[46]

To Treitschke, the bloodshed of the French revolutions and the ultimate failure of subsequent French regimes derived from a misconceived notion of political liberty. Individuals and groups were neither virtuous nor equal: 'All civil society is...a natural aristocracy.'[47] Consequently, it had taken centuries of struggle and conflict to describe the boundaries, perpetuated in law, within which humans were free. Law safeguarded the personal freedom of the individual against empty political definitions of liberty: 'We Teutons stick too stubbornly to the absolute right of the individual that we could find freedom in universal suffrage.'[48] Law ascribed limits to behaviour and bound society together by historical consent and coercion. There was no consensus over political forms. Thus, it was foolish, Treitschke continued, to suggest that individuals, emancipated from unequal laws, would obey political instructions because of their social rationale alone and not because they were backed by force:

Political freedom is optically limited freedom—this statement...is today acknowledged by everyone who is capable of political judgment....Notions of freedom, which were predominant during the French revolution, were an unclear mixture of the ideas of Montesquieu and the half-classical concepts of Rousseau...and what was achieved? The most abhorrent despotism that Europe has ever seen....The conclusion in Rousseau's phrase, which is false, seems all too obvious: where all are equal, each obeys himself.[49]

Individuals would only consent to a legal state whose sanctions were coercive.

Law underwrote personal freedom and thereby attached individuals to the legal guarantor, or *Rechtsstaat*. In the same way, it protected

[46] Schmitz, *Das Land der Wirklichkeit*, 100.

[47] Treitschke, *Politik*, i. 61.

[48] Treitschke, 'Die Freiheit' (1861), in *Historische und politische Aufsätze*, 6th edn. (Leipzig, 1903), iii. 3, 10; T. Süpfle, *Geschichte des deutschen Kultureinflusses auf Frankreich mit besonderer Berücksichtigung der literarischen Einwirkung* (2 vols.; Gotha, 1886–90), i. 4.

[49] Treitschke, 'Die Freiheit' (1861), in *Historische und politische Aufsätze*, 9.

corporations and simultaneously tied them to the state. Associations, churches, independent institutions, and local governments benefited from an historical conception of law because, without it, they were likely to be disbanded, as rival centres of power to the political state. Authors of textbooks such as Joseph Haas, a professor of philology at Tübingen, agreed with more audacious, and more subjective, publicists like Schmitz, that revolutionary and Napoleonic governments had destroyed the laws of the *ancien régime* and the corporations, regional and municipal administrations, which those laws had authorized: 'Soon after [the French Revolution] there followed the most ruthless tyranny of the sword that recent, and perhaps all history has known. Napoléon tore down numerous tiers between himself and the masses, both the rights of the old regime of estates and the parliamentary bodies of the revolution.... There was no more talk of freedom.... There was no longer any individualized communal and provincial life.'[50] Catholic writers like the historian Martin Spahn coincided in such matters with liberal academics such as Gneist, who demonstrated how the legal independence and, in some cases, actual autonomy of six areas of administration—*Polizei*, military, finances, towns, church, and education—had been undermined.[51] Moreover, this inadequacy of French self-government, which was so manifest in its legal upper branches, found confirmation from researchers investigating the roots of administration:

Whoever goes to France without knowledge of administrative law, would expect in this democratic republic, whose election slogan 'liberty, equality, fraternity' is posted on every street corner, to find the most thorough-going communal freedom. It would seem to him to be the logical consequence of this type of state. Remarkably, however, we find precisely in that country, which allows itself to be called the birthplace of freedom and in which the idea of freedom has developed the greatest imaginable wealth of forms—in theory—in France, we find precisely in that place—where an opportunity should be given for the wise use of freedom: in the communes—as good as nothing of it.[52]

A narrowly political idea of freedom had crushed individual and corporate initiative and independence, which, as shall be seen later,

[50] Schmitz, *Das Land der Wirklichkeit*, 100. Haas, *Frankreich*, 135.
[51] Gneist, *Der Rechtsstaat*, 178–88.
[52] Andler, *Die Städteschulden in Frankreich und Preußen*, 19.

virtually all German commentators acknowledged as a necessary part of a strong state.[53]

Instead, political liberty encouraged revolt. Since the state was the creature of society rather than the custodian of historical, legal wisdom, citizens insisted on their right to replace it, if necessary by revolution, as soon as they felt that it did not serve their interests: 'No generation in France to date', wrote Gneist, 'has been able to forget that the current powers of the state, which were established by the early strength of *society*, must again cede to society's forceful decree, if they no longer suffice to serve the purposes of the majority.'[54] A tradition of revolt against the state had passed unseen into French life. Max Nordau, one of the best-selling authors in Germany and French correspondent of the liberal *Vossische Zeitung*, noted how revolutionaries such as Papa Grégoire of the *quartier latin*, who had participated in uprisings in 1834, 1848, 1851, 1870, and 1871, were deified in their communities.[55] Even supporters of the republic such as Hermann Fernau admitted that 'the authority of the state in France since the revolution had never so absolute and acknowledged a power as, for example, in Germany, given the nervous, spontaneous, and undisciplined character of our neighbours.'[56] Further, when this tradition of revolt was added to the rhetoric of rights, individuals began to demand liberty without responsibility, ignoring the fact that the exercise of their own freedoms impinged on those of others. According to another author of popular books about contemporary France, Hermann Kuhn, political rebellion had, by the *fin de siècle*, come to characterize French social mores as well. Revolution, suitably trivialized, had become a daily habit: 'The new age means the translation of the revolution out of the political and into social and family life. The republic is, in the same way as the revolution, seen as a blank cheque for everything. "Why are we a republic then, if I must keep to the old rules, and cannot do whatever I like"; that is a manner of speaking which is commonplace.'[57]

[53] See below, Ch. 5, sect. 1. Treitschke, *Politik*, i. 44; Roscher, *Politik*, 610; Vogel, *Die dritte französische Republik*, 585; Andler, *Die Städteschulden in Frankreich und Preußen*, 41; Spahn, *Der Kampf um die Schule in Frankreich und Deutschland*, 6; and Steinhauser, *Neustes aus Frankreich*, 47.

[54] Gneist, *Der Rechtsstaat*, 166.

[55] M. Nordau, *Paris unter der dritten Republik. Neue Bilder aus dem wahren Milliardenlande*, 2nd edn. (Leipzig, 1881), 354–67; Schmidt, *Im Lande der Freiheit, Gleichheit und Brüderlichkeit*, 47–8.

[56] Fernau, *Die französische Demokratie*, 118.

[57] Kuhn, *Aus dem modernen Babylon*, 224.

Party conflict in the political state aggravated such lawlessness. In one of the principal histories of the Third Republic, *Die dritte französische Republik bis 1895*, Karl Vogel demonstrated its effects. In government, party politicians variously prevaricated, attempted to curry favour via amnesties, or sought through leniency to avoid controversy, showing in the process 'an often inexplicable forbearance with regard to crime', which led to acquittals by juries or pardons by the president: 'This can only cause an increasing confusion in moral beliefs, including the collapse of a sense of law and justice.'[58] Out of government, Vogel continued, politicians were much more extreme, railing against laws and governments alike, and blurring the distinction between liberty and licence:

Only legal freedom is to be understood under freedom in the life of the state. . . . To this understanding of it, no educated or thinking man, with the exception of those who harbour evil intentions, closes his mind. Since, however, there is never a lack of such intentions in the struggle of interests under any social circumstances, so there are many difficulties in all sections of the populace and even amongst the higher orders concerning a general compliance with the law and, accordingly, respect for authority. In no country is the line between freedom [*liberté*] and excess [*licence*] less clearly drawn.[59]

The scope for party interference in justice was great in France because the theoretical separation between judicial and executive functions had in practice been breached. It was true, as Joseph Haas's textbook confirmed, that judges were formally irremovable,[60] but Haas concurred with the journalist Karl Eugen Schmidt that their independence was diminished by ministerial control of promotion and appointment: 'I would, for my part, rather come into contact with a German, and much rather with an English, than with a French judge. . . . In the Third Republic the custom has become more and more common that judges decide according to the expressed and silent wishes of ministers, in all trials in which the government has an interest. The reason for this is obvious; the minister of justice cannot indeed dismiss judges, but promotion

[58] Vogel, *Die dritte französische Republik bis 1895*, 86–7.
[59] Ibid. 335–6; Andler, *Die Städteschulden in Frankreich und Preußen*, 41.
[60] Hintze, 'Der Beamtenstand' (1911), in *Soziologie und Geschichte*, 95; Roscher, *Politik*, 373.

depends on him.'[61] Moreover, public prosecutors, many of whom later became judges, had lost their irremovable status and consequently acted 'as a ministerial cipher', 'a blind instrument of ministers in political matters, a second and more respected prefect'.[62] As a result, Schmitz concluded, the judiciary avoided cases and judgements, which were likely to incur political criticism, for the sake of their careers. One alleged consequence was inertia throughout France's judicial system, with criminals of all kinds escaping punishment: 'Even in those criminal trials which have not the slightest thing to do with party-political considerations, one finds fewer and fewer judges who have the courage to come to strong judgements. Out of all the civilized countries [*Kulturländer*], life and property are least protected in the French republic. The odds of a murderer remaining unpunished are better than the prospects of success of most other independent professions.'[63] Since popular sensation produced criticism in the Assembly, even routine cases of the criminal justice system had, in effect, been subjected to political priorities.

Although he evinced how the French judiciary had previously been independent, Vogel went on to repeat the commonplace that a separate judicial competence no longer existed in France:

Unfortunately, French justice corresponds only very incompletely to Montesquieu's notion of the separation and independence of the three state powers. In this respect, it bears comparison neither with the body of judges on the other side of the Channel nor with the supreme court of the United States of North America. In the same way, France also stands far behind the German Empire, both with respect to the independence of judges and with regard to the cost of legal process.[64]

Of course, it was possible to argue that a strict division and complete independence of powers was unsustainable, since the executive would escape any form of control: the judiciary would have no right

[61] Schmidt, *Im Lande der Freiheit, Gleichheit und Brüderlichkeit*, 72. Haas, *Frankreich*, 100–1; Vogel, *Die dritte französische Republik bis 1895*, 344.

[62] Gneist, *Der Rechtsstaat*, 170; Hillebrand, *Frankreich und die Franzosen*, 111.

[63] Schmitz, *Das Land der Wirklichkeit*, 305.

[64] Vogel, *Die dritte französische Republik bis 1895*, 429. On the previous independence of the judiciary in France, see 343–4. On the fusion of functions, see also Schmitz, *Das Land der Wirklichkeit*, 303.

to judge its actions. Yet the different solutions to this conundrum adopted by France and Germany were indicative of their different attitudes to law.

The Third Republic proposed political control, it was held. The legislature determined the composition of the executive, which then interfered with the judiciary. As Haas observed, there was no question of such interference in the other direction, 'for the courts, according to the basic principle determining the division of powers, cannot give judgements on the activity of the administration'.[65] French judges were not competent to regulate and punish the executive. This, however, left the citizen exposed to government caprice: 'France's administration does not correspond to its political relations; for, despite the influence of the citizen in a state based on universal suffrage, the French citizen as such has no security at all vis-à-vis the administration.'[66] Under such conditions, the French police enjoyed a licence similar to that of its Russian counterpart, if Hermann Kuhn were to be believed, since it was subject only to the control of the minister of the interior. Because of this de facto legal irresponsibility, he went on, notorious crimes had gone unpunished.[67] Political control of France's system of justice appeared to have led to blatant cases of injustice.

The German solution to the same problem was the *Rechtsstaat*, or the regulation of state affairs by legal process. Whilst France's democratic history seemed to have encouraged a popularly elected legislature to interfere in executive and judicial affairs, Germany's experience pointed towards rational administration and predictable legality. As Otto Hintze remarked, the German bureaucracy was unusual because nearly all of its posts were filled by lawyers. It was they who had introduced the idea of a law-governed state from above: 'Everywhere in the old police state by the end of the eighteenth century, new ideas of a *Rechtsstaat* were emerging, and above all, officials strove to secure their position legally.'[68] Concerned for the security of their own posts, civil servants had brought the state under legal control. This joined with a much wider process of legal rationalization during the nineteenth century so that freedom and justice were associated in many Germans' minds with law rather than

[65] Haas, *Frankreich* 128.   [66] Ibid. 127.
[67] Kuhn, *Frankreich an der Zeitwende*, 16–17.
[68] Hintze, 'Der Beamtenstand' (1911), in *Soziologie und Geschichte*, 91.

with politics. By 1898 notions of legality were so deeply ingrained that the existence of private and public legal spheres was taken for granted. The main issue by that time, as has been seen, was how to prevent a state, which could claim to be acting in the national interest, from intervening unfairly in the private realm of individuals and corporations as it collected taxes, administered industries, and enforced conscription, social insurance payments, and attendance at school. Under such circumstances, the principle of legality seemed, to many Germans, to come into conflict with governments which were able, and too willing, to change and circumvent law. As the German state's functions increased, legality remained its main source of legitimacy, therefore. Naturally, this did not mean that all German political parties arrived at Gneist's antithesis between a legal state in Germany and a political state in France, nor that they subscribed to Treitschke's theory of legal and political freedom.[69] Nevertheless, they did use the rhetoric of the *Rechtsstaat* against the Third Republic and they did criticize French politicians' interventions in judicial matters. At no time was this so clear as during the years between 1898 and 1900, when a re-examined court martial of one adjutant, charged with passing on France's military secrets to the German embassy in Paris, brought the whole of the French legal system into question: if there was any doubt in Germany which solution—legal or political—best safeguarded law and justice, the Dreyfus affair banished it.

3. The Dreyfus Affair

'Die Affäre', as it was referred to in newspaper headlines, provoked diverse responses in Germany.[70] The Reich government and political parties received conflicting information from different sources in France, which sometimes led them to opposing interpretations and conclusions. The Centre Party organ, *Germania*, for example, was close

[69] Even Gneist himself was circumspect in this regard. His book was intended to warn Germans of the nefarious consequences of political intervention in justice.

[70] E.-O. Czempiel, *Das deutsche Dreyfus-Geheimnis. Eine Studie über den Einfluß des monarchischen Regierungssystems auf die Frankreichpolitik des Wilhelminischen Reiches* (Munich, 1966), details a series of different reactions to the Dreyfus Affair, determined in large part by attitudes towards the nation and national interest, on the one hand, and towards Germany's political system, on the other. Also, G. Krumeich, 'Die Resonanz der Dreyfus–Affäre im Deutschen Reich', in G. Hübinger and W. J. Mommsen (eds.), *Intellektuelle im Deutschen Kaiserreich* (Frankfurt a.M., 1993), 13–32.

to French clerics, who sympathized more or less openly with the army and the anti-Dreyfusards, whereas *Vorwärts*, the Socialist Party newspaper, published material by Dreyfusards like Jaurès. Unsurprisingly, such divergences were confirmed by discrepancies of political view. German conservatives, for instance, were not particularly well linked to their anti-German counterparts in France, but, nevertheless, their ideological disposition encouraged them to trust in the French military establishment during the early stages of the Dreyfus affair. In the same way, the instinctive reaction of left liberals was to heed the protests of Dreyfusard intellectuals. Recognition of these dissonances, however, should not drown out the concordant elements in German assessments of the case. Virtually all observers remarked throughout the affair that political priorities had overridden legal process, usually to the detriment of justice. The *Rechtsstaat*, whose rhetoric most German commentators adopted, appeared to be in danger in France. Furthermore, all political parties in Germany came to believe in the necessity of revision and in Dreyfus's innocence, often well before their French political equivalents. The result, sometimes explicit, was a distancing of the German parties from the Third Republic.

The stance of the Reich government, although informed by national interest, was similar to that of the parties. Of course, for the administration, the question of Dreyfus's guilt never really arose. From November 1897 onwards, most German leaders knew that Esterhazy had written the 'bordereau'—the main document which was said to have been passed on to Germany by Dreyfus—following a report by General Wilhelm von Hahnke, the chief of the military cabinet, to Hohenlohe, explaining the recall of Schwarzkoppen, Germany's military attaché in Paris.[71] Yet even uninformed officials such as Georg Herbert von Münster-Derneburg, the German ambassador to France, did not doubt that Dreyfus was innocent from the start: 'I never questioned the fact that the successful sentencing of Dreyfus was unjust,' he told the chancellor in October of the same year. Wilhelm II's annotation replied: 'Nor I.'[72] Government knowledge of Dreyfus's wrongful conviction reinforced the belief in the moral bankruptcy of French justice. Thus, Zola was likely to be condemned without a fair trial because the jury had been alarmed by the

[71] Czempiel, *Das deutsche Dreyfus-Geheimnis*, 32–4.

[72] Münster to Hohenlohe, 29 Oct. 1897, *Die Große Politik der Europäischen Kabinette 1871–1914*, xiii, no. 3591, 292–3. See also O. von der Lancken Wakenitz, *Meine dreissig Dienstjahre, 1888–1918* (Berlin, 1931), 38.

anti-Dreyfusard press—'The jurors are so terrorized...that an acquittal is hardly to be expected,'[73] whilst Dreyfus, it was held, had been convicted in the first place because French judges had been influenced politically: 'Trust in the unpartisan and independent character of judges had been maintained in France, despite all of its political upheavals, beyond expectation. Were that trust in the bench of judges to disappear, so this would be the surest sign of the moral decay of the country.'[74] Münster had already told Berlin in February 1898 that it was 'Sad and dangerous for this nation...that all trust in French justice, as well as in the leaders of the General Staff of the French army, must be lost.'[75] By July, after the initiating of proceedings against the French officers Picquart and Esterhazy, it was clear that the Third Republic was not only acting unjustly, but also illegally: 'The many house searches, which have been carried out during this affair, sometimes in the absence of those implicated, demonstrate how law and justice is being trampled on in the so-called free republic.'[76] It seemed that French, rights-based bombast had been repudiated by actual miscarriages of justice. When Münster wrote in January 1899 that a *League for the Defence of the Rights of Man* was to be founded in order to campaign for revision of Dreyfus's original trial, Wilhelm II retorted laconically: 'what's in a name?!'[77] The implication was that the language of rights espoused by the French political state had been proved empty.

Liberal newspapers, lacking the information available to government, started with certain assumptions about legal procedure and, in the light of new evidence, concluded not only that Dreyfus had been mistried, but also that he was innocent. The *National-Zeitung*, which was virtually the party organ of the National Liberals, was not unusual in its careful exposition of points of law, including those which worked to the disadvantage of the Dreyfusards. The Esterhazy trial in January 1898, it argued, had no bearing on the question of Dreyfus's guilt, even though it had cast doubt on Esterhazy's good character: 'We have in the course of the Dreyfus–Esterhazy affair voiced the opinion that the conviction of Esterhazy would not necessarily prove the innocence of Dreyfus. After the result of the trial,

---

[73] Münster, 22 Feb. 1898, AA R6592, A2324.
[74] Münster, 13 Apr. 1898, AA R6592, A4522.
[75] Münster, 22 Feb. 1898, AA R6592, A2324.
[76] Münster, 23 July 1898, AA R7125, A8617.
[77] Münster, 4 Jan. 1899, AA R6594, A258.

however, one must say that the acquittal of Esterhazy signifies just as little about the guilt of the prisoner on Devil's Island.'[78] Similarly, it was deemed right that Zola received a one-year prison sentence in July 1898, because his defence had failed to prove that the military court had acted 'under orders' in the Dreyfus case, as the author of 'J'accuse' had claimed.[79] In general, however, the *National-Zeitung* found, like most other liberal newspapers, that a strictly legal view of the Dreyfus affair tended to incriminate the military courts, the army, and the anti-Dreyfusards. Thus, Captain Lebrun-Renault's testimony that Dreyfus had confessed his guilt—one of the most important pieces of evidence in the original trial—was ruled inadmissable: 'Only an "authorised" confession by Dreyfus, which he had given in all clarity before the military court, could have been counted, . . . so that the testimony of Captain Lebrun-Renault, seen from the juridical point of view, appears thoroughly worthless.'[80] Still more damning was the admission in July of the war minister, Cavaignac, to the Assembly that he had secret information proving Dreyfus's guilt, which, impliedly, had not been disclosed to the defence: 'Since, according to the legislation of all civilized countries, such a process is improper, this one fact alone would already be enough to render the trial against Dreyfus invalid.'[81] The trial of Dreyfus in 1894 had manifestly contravened established legal procedure. In the interests of legality and the authority of the courts, revision was necessary.

By this time, however, it was also apparent to much of the liberal press that Dreyfus was innocent. The Zola trial had revealed illegality and deception in the army, despite the court's justified attempt to limit the defence to the pertinent facts of the alleged libel: 'It has become increasingly clear in the Parisian jury-trial proceedings against Zola that the French army administration, through its system of suppression and hushing up, is putting itself in the wrong in the eyes of all impartial observers, whilst the great majority of the nation seems to have lost its feeling for justice and legality.'[82] Confirmation of Dreyfus's innocence came on 31 August 1898, after another French officer, Henry, had committed suicide in gaol, having been arrested on suspicion of forging the only letter containing Dreyfus's name. The *National-Zeitung* heralded it as a triumph for justice and legality, although it was forced to add that most Frenchmen were

---

[78] *National-Zeitung*, 12 Jan. 1898.
[79] Ibid., 20 July 1898 and 3 Apr. 1898.   [80] Ibid., 24 Jan. 1898.
[81] Ibid., 8 July 1898.   [82] Ibid., 8 Feb. 1898.

slow to accept the consequences, in contrast to the rest of Europe: 'In the whole civilized world outside France, however, the alleged letter was recognized to be a gross forgery.'[83] Thereafter, there was a steady stream of evidence from independent sources exculpating Dreyfus. In September, for example, the same newspaper reported supposed disclosures by the Italian military attaché, Panizzardi, that Schwarzkoppen had written the 'petit bleu',[84] whilst in June of the following year the *Freisinnige Zeitung*, the principal mouthpiece of the left liberals, offered conclusive proof from twelve handwriting experts that Esterhazy had written the 'bordereau'.[85] Dreyfus, it was now evident to the liberal press, had been framed.

Given such beliefs, the series of political compromises countenanced by French institutions in 1899 appeared reprehensible. The first scandal, in January, was the transfer of revision proceedings from the the criminal chamber of the Cour de Cassation, which had conducted the initial inquiry into revision, to the united chambers of the same court, after Quesnay de Beaurepaire, the president of the civil chamber, had accused the criminal chamber of political bias. Both the *Freisinnige Zeitung* and the *National-Zeitung* reacted in similar fashion, calling Quesnay a soldier in a judge's toga and accusing him of a barely concealed political act.[86] Worse still, the government had connived in that act, undermining the republic's status as a *Rechtsstaat*:

> The French ministry has taken that fateful step, which stands in blatant opposition to the basis of every *Rechtsstaat* and which constitutes a strong attack on the independence of the judicial power. After the criminal chamber of the highest French court had been entrusted with the revision of the Dreyfus trial, it only needed the alleged 'revelations' of the president of the civil chamber, Quesnay de Beaurepaire, who had become famous through his lurid novels, in order to set up an investigation against members of the Cour de Cassation. This procedure is unheard-of in the annals of legal process.[87]

The second incident, in September, was the resentencing of Dreyfus by a military court in Rennes, sanctioned by the Cour de Cassation. The National Liberal press reacted wildly: 'The greatest

---

[83] *National-Zeitung*, 31 Aug. 1898.   [84] Ibid., 27 Sept. 1898.
[85] *Freisinnige Zeitung*, 1 June 1899.
[86] Ibid., 10 Jan. 1899; *National-Zeitung*, 12 Jan. 1899. The criminal chamber was reputedly Dreyfusard, *Cassation* in full session anti-Dreyfusard.
[87] *National-Zeitung*, 31 Jan. 1899.

crime which has been undertaken since the days of the inquisition and the burning of witches is therefore complete.'[88] The left-liberal party newspaper declared that the very possibility of reconviction was in itself 'troubling to the interests of mankind and compromising for the reputation of French jurisdiction'.[89] The formula of guilt with extenuating circumstances, allegedly suggested by a nationalist judge, merely underlined how far justice and due legal process had been corrupted by politics in France: '[Courts] should do nothing other than pronounce law, but instead they have twisted the law.'[90] In this respect, the pardoning of Dreyfus by President Loubet was an impoverished political solution rather than a reaffirmation of law, legality, and justice. The request of the war minister that Dreyfus be pardoned 'does all honour to the humanity of General Gallifet [*sic*], yet the question of law has thereby been passed over completely'.[91] Only in 1906, with the full acquittal of Dreyfus by the courts, was the judicial affair finally resolved: 'Satisfaction has finally been given to the pitiful victim of one of the most terrible miscarriages of justice.... It has taken long enough for fairness and honesty to triumph.'[92] Justice had prevailed in France, but the French system of justice had been compromised.

It was common in the liberal press to point to the isolation of France over the Dreyfus affair. The National Liberal *Hamburgischer Correspondent* noted that even Switzerland had been alienated by the legal improprieties of the French state, not to mention the Scandinavian countries.[93] The *Freisinnige Zeitung* expatiated on the same theme:

Events in Rennes have also given the reputation of France *abroad* a terrible jolt. Quite rightly, the 'Köln. Ztg.', in a leading article entitled 'A Cowardly Judgment', states that a dividing wall has been erected by the rest of the world, which indeed will not prevent diplomatic relations and restrict the exchange of goods, but which will be carried into the twentieth century by all of civilized mankind and will constitute a barrier, whose removal might require long and strenuous work.[94]

Responding to French criticism of accusations against Esterhazy in the German press, the *National-Zeitung* articulated what was implicit in many liberal articles: Germany could have no interest in publicizing

[88] Ibid., 10 Sept. 1899.   [89] *Freisinnige Zeitung*, 10 Sept. 1899.
[90] Ibid., 12 Sept. 1899.   [91] Ibid., 22 Sept. 1899.
[92] Ibid., 14 July 1906.   [93] *Hamburgischer Correspondent*, 10 Nov. 1898.
[94] *Freisinnige Zeitung*, 12 Sept. 1899.

Esterhazy's guilt other than that of justice and legality.[95] The Reich was thereby included in the circle of civilized states, which abhorred the injustices perpetrated by the French legal system. Moreover, these injustices were also linked to the Third Republic. The principal retrospective account of the affair in Theodor Barth's *Nation*, organ of the left-liberal *Freisinnige Vereinigung*, reminded readers that Dreyfus's innocence had been certain from relatively early on. The legal question had thereafter become a legal error, and eventually a legal rape, as more and more mistakes were made by the judiciary. The corruption of the army, judges, press, ministries, and parliament all betrayed the deep decay of French conditions under the republic.[96] Right-wing liberals drew the same conclusions. In any *Rechtsstaat* the failure of the prosecution to disclose evidence or the subsequent incrimination of leading witnesses, such as Henry and Paty du Clam, would lead automatically to a retrial, wrote the *National-Zeitung*. But not in France: 'In every law-governed state just one of these reasons would have been sufficient to justify taking up the case once more. In the French republic, however, whose public buildings carry the inscription: Liberté, Egalité, Fraternité, "Liberty, Equality, Fraternity", they use the alleged honour of the army as an excuse to twist the law.'[97] Politics, at least at the time of the Dreyfus affair, appeared to German liberals to have prevented justice.

The German socialist newspaper, *Vorwärts*, was, if possible, even more convinced than its liberal counterparts that Dreyfus had been a victim of French injustice.[98] As early as 11 January 1898, it protested that the prosecution in 1894 had succeeded on the evidence of the 'bordereau' alone, a document which was neither dated nor signed and which two out of five handwriting experts failed to attribute to Dreyfus. In the meantime, Esterhazy himself had conceded that the similarity between the script of the 'bordereau' and his own writing was 'shocking'.[99] Picquart, supported by his superior in the intelligence bureau, General Conse, began to suspect Esterhazy in 1895 and instituted an inquiry. Anti-Dreyfusards in the army reacted, silencing Conse and dispatching Picquart to Tunis, which prevented him from

[95] *National-Zeitung*, 11 July 1898.
[96] *Nation*, vol. 16, no. 6, Nov. 1898.
[97] *National-Zeitung*, 26 Sept. 1898.
[98] See also *Neue Zeit*, 16 Feb. 1898, no. 22, and 13 Sept. 1899, no. 52.
[99] *Vorwärts*, 11 Jan. 1898.

participating in Esterhazy's trial in January 1898, or so *Vorwärts* propounded, following Clemenceau's *Aurore*. With the principal witness excluded, the military court judge simply trusted Esterhazy's word of honour and acquitted him.[100] The entire proceedings suggested a cover-up, a fact which was later substantiated by Esterhazy's revelations to the *Daily Chronicle* that he had been protected by the General Staff.[101] Further revelations by *Le Figaro*, detailing the whole of the criminal chamber's report on the necessity of revision, provided still more proofs of Dreyfus's innocence and were relayed daily throughout April by *Vorwärts*, in the hope of destroying the anti-Dreyfusard case definitively.[102]

To the socialist newspaper's disappointment, however, the Dreyfus affair failed to come to a satisfactory conclusion, largely because of obstruction in the French judicial system. 'Civil, class justice',[103] as *Vorwärts* labelled it, had already besmirched itself during the Panama scandal, as the most powerful bourgeois parties had singled out scapegoats for trial, leaving the main culprits untroubled and half of the bribes unaccounted for. The jury had rightly acquitted these scapegoats and thereby indicted the whole system of 'party justice': 'The conclusion of the Panama trial.... is a pleasing indictment by the people's court [*Volksgericht*] of the system of justice, which has been so seriously demeaned by the Meline [*sic*] cabinet.'[104] Viviani's report for the Assembly committee on Panama went further, exposing a dishonest and self-interested judiciary as just one component of a greedy political system. The French socialist and parliamentarian appeared to have delivered a 'condemnation of the entire workings of the corrupt bourgeois republic... of the political power of high finance, the joint business deals between government men, parliamentarians, and founders of companies, the dirty work of the executive power and of the servile bench of judges trying to save the guilty.'[105]

German socialism's assessment of French justice continued during the Dreyfus affair, as civil and military courts worked out their respective jurisdictions and allegiances. For a short while in December 1898, after the Cour de Cassation had suspended the military trial of Picquart on the grounds of insufficient evidence, it

---

[100] Ibid., 14 Jan. 1898.   [101] Ibid., 7 Mar. 1899.
[102] Ibid., 5 Apr. 1899.   [103] Ibid., 14 Jan. 1898.
[104] Ibid., 6 Jan. 1898. See also, 5 Jan. 1898 for the reference to 'Parteijustiz'.
[105] Ibid., 3 Apr. 1898.

seemed to *Vorwärts*, in an article entitled 'Der Sieg der Zivilgewalt', that the civil power had triumphed in France over the military: 'we can now see the subordination of the military to the civil power in France as a complete and final fact... Germany, whose press for the most part raged self-righteously over France, now has just cause to examine itself and *to imitate France's example!*'[106] Yet, by January 1899, in a summary of French events of the previous year, the same newspaper declared that 'the decisive authorities' still preferred the counsels of the army to the dictates of civil justice: 'In such conditions, the "supremacy of the civil power" is nothing more than a phrase from a ministerial programme.'[107] The transfer of the decision over revision from the criminal chamber to the joint chambers of Cassation merely reinforced the notion that the bourgeois political state, in a law reminiscent of civil war, had removed the last remnants of an independent civil judiciary: 'Out of all the institutions of the French republic, the criminal chamber of the Cour de Cassation alone remained unscathed on legal ground.'[108] The other courts had already been discredited in the course of the affair. The verdict on Zola, for example, had dissipated the nimbus surrounding jury courts: 'These jurors, traders and industrialists,... [throw] civil and criminal law into the gutter in favour of the rule of the sword.... Once again, respect for the law is abandoned.'[109] Similarly, by acquitting Esterhazy in August 1898, the Chambre des Mises en Accusation had lost the little authority it had retained from the Panama scandal: 'Since then, the decisions of the court of indictments have lost any vestige of moral worth in the eyes of the legally conscious public.'[110] The French judiciary fell short of the standards and rhetoric of legality and justice demanded by *Vorwärts.*[111]

Forced to choose sides during the Dreyfus affair, the class-based political state had subordinated itself to the army: 'Power defeats law.... *Militarism is boss in France, the country of the rights of man*'.[112] There was no chance of republicans fundamentally reforming civil and military justice:

The liberal bourgeoisie is only prepared to countenance a few petty, tinkering reforms, which will alter nothing of the destructive nature of militarism. Apart from the class interests of the bourgeoisie in maintaining its most important

---

[106] *Vorwärts*, 10 Dec. 1898.   [107] Ibid., 4 Jan. 1899.   [108] Ibid., 31 Jan. 1899.
[109] Ibid., 25 Feb. 1898.   [110] Ibid., 16 Aug. 1898.
[111] Ibid., 1 Sept. 1898 and 15 Nov. 1899.   [112] Ibid., 25 Feb. 1898.

means of domination unchanged, the good, liberal bourgeoisie fears the possible resistance of the praetorian guards to fundamental anti-militarist reforms.[113]

Whether to avert a *coup d'état* or to pander to chauvinist voters, the Assembly passed emergency laws and circumvented established legal procedure—'It prefers to undermine the foundations of the *Rechtsstaat* in "legal" ways'[114]—whilst the president, in pardoning Dreyfus, avoided the question of law altogether.[115] Confronted by such bourgeois pusillanimity, illegality, and injustice, the socialist press in Germany tended at first to emphasize that only their French colleagues continued to support Dreyfus consistently: 'only Jaurès stands his ground, unshaken'.[116] But, as justice lost itself in politics, some German socialists, such as Wilhelm Liebknecht, began to denounce the whole affair as bourgeois and irrelevant: 'How does "the Affair" differ from hundreds of thousands of other "affairs" of social and political injustice and inhumanity?'[117] Such denunciations were prompted, at least in part, by an awareness that a legal case had been politicized, which in turn called for a reassertion of political forms of address. During the affair, wrote Liebknecht, 'one [has] almost become accustomed to viewing French party matters from the standpoint of the Dreyfus business, instead of the other way around.'[118] The salient politicization of justice, however, resurrected the priorities of party.

For the conservative press, too, party interference had brought the French legal system into disrepute. Initially, the conservative party newspaper, the *Neue Preußische Zeitung*, argued that the lawful judgement of a military court was being threatened by the political opportunism of the Dreyfusards: 'the man has rightly been sentenced'.[119] Only irresponsible factions challenged the integrity of the army. There was no possibility of a miscarriage of justice:

Now, every man here of calm judgement will say that a conscious judicial murder on the part of the military court is the last thing that a malicious mind could seize upon. These are the most elevated leaders of the French army who sat in the court. . . . It would be absolutely unheard of, if one were to accept that they consciously sacrificed an innocent man: only French party heat could come to such a conclusion.[120]

[113] Ibid., 15 Sept. 1899.   [114] Ibid., 14 Feb. 1899.   [115] Ibid., 15 Sept. 1899.
[116] Ibid., 1 Sept. 1898.   [117] Ibid., 27 July 1899.   [118] Ibid.
[119] *Neue Preußische Zeitung*, 22 Jan. 1898.   [120] Ibid., 26 Jan. 1898.

Consequently, it was difficult to question Dreyfus's guilt: 'Only a few people in Germany, to which we do not belong, doubt the fact of Dreyfus's guilt.'[121] Even in September 1898, after Henry's suicide, the same newspaper still maintained that the French army's code of honour vouched for Dreyfus's treason.[122] Zola's intention, in provoking a trial, was not to demonstrate the latter's innocence, but rather to sully the army's reputation by unfounded insinuation. By contrast, the court rightly adhered to just legal principles and disallowed references to the Dreyfus trial of 1894.[123] With the condemning of Zola in February 1898, the *Neue Preußische Zeitung* assumed that the affair had reached its end.[124]

Politics ensured that such expectations proved premature. Over time, it became clear that the French army's actions were politically motivated. This had been intimated by the severity of Dreyfus's punishment, with the authorities refusing his wife the privilege of accompanying him to Devil's Island,[125] and by the political manoeuvring of officers such as the Chief of Staff, General Boisdeffre, in the first Zola trial: 'It is precisely a republican general who is behaving like a French ministry, which resigns as soon as it is outvoted. In order to put pressure on the jurors during the first Zola trial, he threatened to hand in his resignation, thereby giving a group of citizens, who are not always marked out by their intelligence, a degree of direct influence over the army to which they are in no way entitled.'[126] Yet the decisive evidence for a politicized army was furnished by the arrest and suicide of Henry. Although the instinct of newspapers such as the *Staatsbürger Zeitung* was to reiterate their long-standing case against revision—that Dreyfus had been convicted in 1894 on other evidence, not the 'faux Henry'—the conservative press eventually associated and excoriated Henry, Esterhazy, and Paty du Clam.[127] As the *Neue Preußische Zeitung* wrote, Esterhazy was a base traitor, who had discredited the whole of the republican officer-corps: 'Those sort of scandalous events, which have taken place at the heart of the French General Staff, are up until now unique in the world.'[128] As a result, the need for revision was reluctantly acknowledged.[129] New facts had emerged, which German

[121] *Neue Preußische Zeitung*, 6 Apr. 1898.
[122] Ibid., 20 Sept. 1898.   [123] Ibid., 10 Feb. 1898.   [124] Ibid., 2 Mar. 1898.
[125] Ibid., 6 Apr. 1898.   [126] Ibid., 3 Sept. 1898.
[127] *Staatsbürger Zeitung*, 1 Sept. 1898.
[128] *Neue Preußische Zeitung*, 18 Nov. 1898, 1 and 29 Sept. 1898.
[129] Ibid., 19 Sept. 1898, 18 Nov. 1898 and 29 Apr. 1899.

conservatives deemed worthy of consideration, in the interests of justice, but which French public opinion ignored: 'Every calmly thinking person must concede that this revision, which in no respect prejudices yet another trial of Dreyfus, should be recognized as a moral necessity, after everything that has happened.'[130] Likewise, conservatives in Germany came to accept Dreyfus's innocence, whereas their counterparts in France did not.[131] It was as if the pervasive influence of politics under the republic had removed any neutral yardstick, such as law, by which things could be judged.[132] The political blinkers of French conservatives blinded them to political bias in the army.

For conservatives, of course, the military constituted the last citadel. The judiciary had long since ceded to the legislative power, whether during the Panama scandal, as the *Deutsche Zeitung* contended, or in the scandals of the 1880s.[133] The fusion of competencies within the state—'A more insane confusion of constitutional powers cannot even be imagined'[134]—and the force of public opinion within the political system, via the press, the chambers, and the street, had combined, in the opinion of the *Neue Preußische Zeitung*, to make justice political: 'One person wants to convoke the Assembly immediately, presumably to exacerbate still more the existing disorder.... Another—clearly mistaking M. Faure for the tsar—wishes the president of the republic to play the role of the judge, and so on *ad infinitum*.'[135] The Assembly, which was by definition partial and which legislated in all areas at will, was in no position to interpret law and dispense justice: 'Parliament, given its conspicuously political character, is truly not suited to solving a juridical question.'[136] Yet, the admission by the justice minister, Lebret, that Quesnay de Beaurepaire was a *quantité négligeable*, the repeated leaks in *Le Figaro* of the criminal chamber's findings on the revision question, and the compromise verdict of guilt with extenuating circumstances in Rennes all implied the predominance of politics.[137] 'For six months the state machine has worked to tear a purely juridical matter away from the

---

[130] Ibid., 20 Sept. 1898.

[131] Ibid., 5 Nov. 1898, depicted Dreyfus as an 'Opferlamm'. *Deutsche Tageszeitung*, 4 June 1899.

[132] Ibid., 20 Sept. 1898.   [133] *Deutsche Zeitung*, 7 Sept. 1898.

[134] *Neue Preußische Zeitung*, 1 Feb. 1899. See also, 5 Sept. 1898.

[135] Ibid., 5 Sept. 1898. On the influence and caprice of public opinion, see also, 5 Sept. 1898 and 2 Mar. 1899.

[136] Ibid., 27 Sept. 1898.

[137] Ibid., 10 Jan. 1899, 6 Apr. 1899, and 11 Sept. 1899.

political arena and to place it back on the correct course of official legal process,' reported the conservative party mouthpiece in February 1899.[138] But the state failed. The Dreyfus case remained political.

Both the pardoning of Dreyfus and the passing of a general amnesty for the affair were viewed by the *Neue Preußische Zeitung* as declarations of judicial bankruptcy in France and led to extended critiques of the political state. The pardon, which gave Dreyfus no satisfaction in law, was not only unworthy of a *Rechtsstaat*, it was postulated, but, in its caprice, it also contradicted the republic's slogan of liberty, equality, and fraternity.[139]

The administration of law is dilatory and, as soon as politics comes into play, partisan. The Dreyfus business not only brought the military courts, but also civil jurisdiction clearly into disrepute...so that the head of the republic and of the ministry, led simply by political points of view, finally had to intervene just to bring the endlessly drawn-out 'Affair' to a superficial conclusion. It is self-evident that this shameful fact has not exactly helped to retrieve lost trust in the justice and independence of French courts.[140]

The amnesty was, obviously, the pardon writ large, and was tantamount to confessing the inability of the judicial system to deal with any of the numerous infringements connected to the affair, not just the vexed issue of Dreyfus's guilt.[141] It evinced the striking disparity between republican symbolism, embodied in the 'Genius of Freedom' statue at the Palais de la Justice, and republican justice, with its scandals and amnesties:

But should one not smile at such symbols when one thinks that these liberators of foreign peoples cannot control themselves and that they had to extinguish the torch of freedom in order to kill off celebrated scandals, from the Wilson and Panama to the Dreyfus scandal? And is the whole question of an amnesty, which the chambers have already begun to deal with, not an admission of impotence, their inability to resolve pending questions by legal and judicial means?[142]

Germania, the Centre Party newspaper, followed a similar line to the conservative press. The army and the Méline Government were portrayed as the defenders of a French *Rechtsstaat* against the political hysteria of the Dreyfusards. The acquittal of Esterhazy was just, given that 'the Dreyfus clique's evidence against Esterhazy is in a

[138] *Neue Preußische Zeitung*, 2 Feb. 1899.
[139] Ibid., 20 Sept. 1899.   [140] Ibid., 28 Oct. 1900.
[141] Ibid., 6 June 1900.   [142] Ibid., 21 Nov. 1899.

very bad way',[143] and the decision during the Zola trial to prohibit references to the Dreyfus case was legally unchallengeable: 'an error of law is not present, and it is a question of a *res judicata*.'[144] Even after the Président du Conseil, Brisson, had initiated an inquiry into revision, in September 1898, *Germania* insisted that ministers were not convinced of Dreyfus's innocence.[145] Only those who orchestrated the 'shameless witch-hunts against the French government' doubted the prisoner's guilt, and more because of a sense of political advantage than a sense of justice: 'The real instigation of the Dreyfus clique's actions against the government is less the Dreyfus case as such than, much more, the desire to prevent, at any cost, the creation of a moderate government in France and, thus, to secure their own predominance.'[146] The entire affair, such as it was, had been artificially kindled by Zola and the Dreyfusards, before being fuelled by what Cavaignac called French 'party spirit'.[147] Now it was the duty of the government to quell it, before it ran out of control.[148]

As for the *Neue Preußische Zeitung*, the watershed for *Germania*, which separated it from its French counterparts, was Henry's suicide. In two front-page articles, the newspaper's correspondent in Paris signalled the change, with detailed criticism of the anti-Dreyfusards, which stood in contrast to previous encomium in the same columns.[149] France, he wrote, had hoped to end an unhappy period of conflict in September 1898: 'Formally, people sighed with relief after the suicide of Colonel Henry since a change for the better seemed possible.'[150] Yet such hopes were confounded, as anti-Dreyfusard politicians and press managed to manipulate public opinion:

However great the swing in [public opinion] was, which had occurred after Henry's forgery became public knowledge, it could not withstand the attacks of several widely read, cheap newspapers like Intransigeant, Libre Parole, Petit Journal.... It was also shaken by the numerous announcements of interpellations over the Dreyfus affair, in which revision was depicted for the most part as illegal and as a danger for the internal and external security of the country.[151]

The extremes of anti-Dreyfusard publicity, which included the possibility of bloodshed and civil war, subverted the morals of all

---

[143] *Germania*, 12 Jan. 1898. [144] Ibid., 9 Feb. 1898.
[145] Ibid., 6 Sept. 1898. This was, of course, after Henry's suicide.
[146] Ibid., 15 and 26 Jan. 1898.
[147] Ibid., 25 Feb. 1898, 10 Apr. 1898, and 19 Jan. 1898. [148] Ibid., 26 July 1898.
[149] Ibid., 26 Feb. 1898. [150] Ibid., 14 Sept. 1898. [151] Ibid.

sections of society, even those of good Catholics, in a frenzy of political hatred: 'Still more remarkable than this apparently groundless
volte-face in public opinion is the fact that amongst the opponents of
revision are highly respectable and conscientious people, who would
not for anything in the world allow themselves to be guilty of the
smallest infringement against that which, according to custom and
law, is considered to be right.'[152] Only the politicization of the
Dreyfus affair could explain the discomfort of these exemplary individuals: 'In fact, no explanation is to be found for this credulity of
the masses, on the one hand, and this molestation of truth and logic,
on the other, if Dreyfus alone was at stake...therefore, it is evident...to every impartial observer that the struggle for and against
Dreyfus has increasingly spilled over into *religious* and *political are-
nas*.'[153] The transformation of German Catholics' attitudes between
1898 and 1900 paralleled, albeit in specific form, the changing opinions of conservatives, liberals, and, to a lesser degree, socialists vis-à-
vis the Third Republic. At the beginning of the affair, *Germania* had
thought that politics threatened state justice. By its end, it was sure
that political conflict permeated all parts of French state and society
and that, as a result, the idea of justice had become chimerical.

The rhetoric of the *Rechtsstaat* was borrowed by all German political parties, as they reacted to the French political state, but it did not
alone determine their responses. Broadly, until the suicide of Henry
in August 1898, Catholics and conservatives used it in support of the
French army, anti-Dreyfusards and moderate republican governments, whilst liberals and socialists employed it in defence of
Dreyfus. This dichotomy of views can be seen as the translation of
political differences onto an international stage. Yet there was a point
at which cross-party, national conceptions of law, legality, and justice
began to divide equivalent German and French parties. Thus, the
SPD was more likely from the outset to criticize the Third Republic
as a bourgeois political state, with a class-based system of party justice, than Jaurès, Millerand, and the independent socialists; the
German liberals condemned the prevarication and opportunism of
their Radical and republican colleagues from early 1898 onwards;
and the Centre and conservative parties turned against French ultramontanes, nationalists and anti-Dreyfusards after Henry's death.
Naturally, anti-German feeling revealed during the affair encouraged

---

[152] *Germania*, 7 Aug. 1898 and 14 Aug. 1898.   [153] Ibid., 24 Nov. 1898.

national divisions, but it did not account for the timing of divergences between German and French political traditions. Nor did it explain why Catholics and conservatives had backed virulently xenophobic anti-Dreyfusards until August 1898. The solution to such conundrums was to be found in the different ideas of law and the state in Germany and France. The excesses of the Dreyfus case eventually alienated all German parties. They then subscribed to a critique of the French political state as a means of rationalizing that alienation. The historical and normative forms of legal redress common to the German *Rechtsstaat* were confronted most strikingly by the political forms of redress favoured by the Third Republic during the Dreyfus affair. Each party made the distinction between the two types of state at a different time and in its own way. But all came to distance themselves from the French political state and, by implication, came to acknowledge the German *Rechtsstaat*.

3

The Merger of Executive and Legislative Competencies

1. President, Senate, and Assembly

The *Rechtsstaat* was guaranteed, above all, by a formal separation of functions.[1] The legislature sanctioned laws, which were both initiated and administered by an autonomous executive and, in the case of disputes, interpreted and enforced by an independent judiciary.[2] The critical distinction, it was postulated, was that made between the enactment and administration of law, since a neutral and fair bureaucracy would adhere to legal principle of its own accord, without the strictures of the courts. Administrative law merely existed to limit and rectify the wrongful actions of a partial administration.[3] The reaction of most German commentators to the merger of executive and legislative competencies in France betrayed an underlying assumption of most German political thought: the two functions should be kept separate.[4]

---

[1] Admittedly, this separation was complex. Since the executive proposed laws, it participated in the *Gesetzgebung*, just as the Reichstag, in passing the budget, contributed to *Verwaltung*. Blurring of the critical line between enactment and administration of law was deliberately kept to a minimum, however. As Michael John has shown, in an unpublished paper on the German constitution of 1871, Laband denied that an absolute separation of powers existed in Germany, but then tried to re-establish an effective division of competencies through the doctrine of 'sanction', or compulsion to obey the law, which lay exclusively in the executive's power.

[2] E. M. Hucko (ed.), *The Democratic Tradition* (Oxford, 1987), 121–45. Art. 23 of the constitution gave the Reichstag a formal right to propose laws, but such proposals required the sanction of the Bundesrat before being enacted. Since the Reich government dominated the Bundesrat through Prussia, it was seen as the principal initiator of laws.

[3] Boldt, *Deutsche Verfassungsgeschichte*, ii. 42; M. Stolleis, 'Verwaltungsrechtswissenschaft und Verwaltungslehre 1866–1914', *Die Verwaltung*, 15 (1982), 52–72, 75–77.

[4] The German word 'Gliederung', used in preference by some authors to 'Trennung', expressed at once the integrity of different functions and the connections between them, analogous to the limbs of a body. See e.g. Gneist, *Rechtsstaat*, 166–7.

The only German treatise on the constitution of the Third Republic before the First World War was written by Siegfried Brie. It aimed to put the commonplace idea of a French political state into historical context, for the origins of the republic were marked by compromise and uncertainty. Notoriously, the constitutional laws of 1875 had not referred to the republican form, except in passing, in the Wallon amendment, which called the Chef de l'État the president of the republic. Nor did the laws contain a declaration of rights, explicit recognition of popular sovereignty, or confirmation of the division of powers,[5] which had the odd effect of distinguishing France, the progenitor of such declarations in the past, from other democracies and aligning it with constitutional monarchies:

> In any event it is a very remarkable fact that that state, which had earlier provided a model through its constitutional declarations for so many constitutions of other continental European states, now counted itself amongst those states with modern representative institutions but without a constitutional declaration of rights [i.e. constitutional monarchies]. Furthermore, France may be... the only state, in which modern representative democracy exists without a declaration of rights.[6]

Despite indicating such anomalies, however, Brie did not question the existence of a political state in France. The French Third Republic not only remained an emblem of rights-based popular sovereignty—an orthodox view, which Brie sought to revise, after all[7]—but it also retained many of the constitutional laws passed since 1789, albeit now deprived of their declaratory or constitutional character, belonging as they did to ordinary statute: 'If the validity of the principles of 1789 was not expressly acknowledged, there was and is little doubt that these must be regarded as fundamental for France's whole public legal order.'[8] Most important of all, Brie agreed with other authors that the separation of executive and legislative functions had been breached in France: 'The basic principle of a separation of powers has only been implemented... with very considerable modifications.'[9] Anxious to avoid a repetition of 1851 or 16 May 1877, the French Assembly had come to exercise the most significant powers within the state: 'The political predominance... of the chamber of

---

[5] Brie, *Die gegenwärtige Verfassung Frankreichs*, 17.
[6] Ibid. 16–17.   [7] Ibid. 3.   [8] Ibid. 19–20.
[9] Ibid. 21. Haas, *Frankreich*, 128; Schmitz, *Das Land der Wirklichkeit*, 303; Fernau, *Die französische Demokratie*, 12; Vogel, *Die dritte französische Republik*, 429.

deputies has been secured.'[10] In contrast to 1848, the president of the republic was denied the right of veto and initiation, as well as the legitimacy of popular election. Instead, he was nominated by the Assembly and Senate in joint session, which gave the former about two-thirds of the vote, given its numerical superiority.[11] Furthermore, although the president was formally irresponsible, except on the charge of high treason, his ministers were both legally impeachable and politically answerable. De facto, they were also chosen by the Assembly: '[this] is the parliamentary regime, as it exists in numerous constitutional monarchies according to the English model.... The president should not keep a single minister or ministry in office, if the chambers refuse to place their confidence in this minister or ministry.'[12] Unlike in the United States, where the separation of powers had enjoyed 'a barely modified implementation', the Assembly in France interfered in the affairs of the presidential executive and dominated the affairs of that executive's guardian, the Senate.[13]

The expositions of more popular academics, publicists, and journalists, together with those of government and the parties, coincided with Brie's analysis of the French constitution and political practice. The theoretical head of the executive, the president of the republic, was widely perceived to be a figurehead, a 'signature machine', as *Germania* put it, or an 'internal and external decoration', in Münster's phrase.[14] The office had been downgraded to such an extent, the ambassador went on, that the presidents of the republic, Senate, and Assembly were treated equally at the opening of the World Exhibition in 1900.[15] All presidents before that date had resigned because their powers had been so restricted, except Sadi Carnot, who had been assassinated.[16] Whereas, in the 1880s and 1890s, the presidency was still viewed with suspicion by many German observers,[17] by the 1900s no French president was depicted as an aspirant dictator. The passage of time appeared to have proved that the Chef de l'État was too constrained, both practically and constitutionally, to allow him to metamorphose, as Napoleon III had

---

[10] Brie, *Die gegenwärtige Verfassung Frankreichs*, 52.

[11] Ibid. 25.   [12] Ibid. 36.

[13] Ibid. 38. Jellinek, *Allgemeine Staatslehre*, 726–7.

[14] *Germania*, 11 Jan. 1906. Münster, 13 Apr. 1898, AA R6592, A4522. See also *Deutsche Tageszeitung*, 14 Jan. 1913.

[15] Münster, 18 Apr. 1900, AA R6596, A4912.

[16] Münster, 5 Jan. 1899, AA R6594, A259. Radolin, 21 Nov. 1903, AA R7062, A17412.

[17] Esp. in the aftermath of the 'seize mai' crisis. See below, Ch. 5, sect. 3.

done after 1848.[18] Virtually all German onlookers therefore treated Félix Faure and Raymond Poincaré, who were seen as potentially dictatorial in France, with relative equanimity and detachment.

Diplomats never doubted that Faure was merely playing the monarch, rather than aspiring to be one: 'The president... is clever enough to see that it is safer to play than to be the sovereign.'[19] It was precisely because the president had little real power, and little likelihood of achieving it, Münster continued, that such pomp came to seem pompous: 'Since Felix [*sic*] Faure can have no power in his own country, he believes that he is serving his country by playing the sovereign, notably with foreign sovereigns.... This has neither helped him nor his country, but it has, and this is dangerous in France, made him risible.'[20] Graf von Below-Saleske, the second secretary at the German embassy in Paris, recorded how Faure had scolded his host's grandson for addressing him without formal permission, whilst, for his part, Münster recalled a book about the royal hunt, given to him by the president, which began with Hugh Capet and Charlemagne, and ended 'with a celebration of the president'.[21] Such stories resounded throughout the German press. One cartoon in *Lustige Blätter*, entitled 'Les gens chics. Monsieur Félix Faure et Madame Gyp', portrayed the president in full ceremonial garb, leading the novelist by the arm to a ball. The sardonic caption, in the style of a gossip column, read: 'FELIX FAURE.... The whole Dreyfus affair appears to him, the great man, of course, infinitely small.'[22] It was evident to a German audience, the cartoon implied, that the president could never be a great man. In a front-page harangue to 'Infelix Faure', another liberal satirical journal, *Kladderadatsch*, juxtaposed the pretension of the president abroad with his powerlessness at home.[23] According to such accounts, Faure was just 'The vain parvenu', as *Vorwärts* said.[24] He had, concurred *Germania*, 'invited mockery of himself on repeated occasions through a pitiable concern for the maintenance of etiquette'.[25] Faure

[18] *Frankfurter Zeitung*, 18 Jan 1913. Kuhn, *Frankreich an der Zeitwende*, 3.

[19] Münster to Hohenlohe, 19 Oct. 1898, in K. A. v. Müller (ed.), *Fürsten Chlodwig zu Hohenlohe-Schillingsfürst. Denkwürdigkeiten der Reichskanzlerzeit* (Berlin, 1931), 395.

[20] Münster, 5 Jan. 1899, AA R7056, A259.

[21] Below, 15 Sept. 1898, AA R7019, A10623. Münster, 25 Nov. 1898, AA R7019, A13663.

[22] Cited in *Dreyfus-Bilderbuch*, 12.   [23] *Kladderadatsch*, 25 Sept. 1898, no. 39.

[24] *Vorwärts*, 16 Jan. 1913.   [25] *Germania*, 5 Jan. 1899.

appeared funny in the role of a great and powerful man because he possessed no greatness and little power.

Poincaré was different. Most newspapers recogized that the Lorrainer was intelligent and ruthless enough to exploit the powers of the presidency.[26] But few considered that the prerogatives of the office were sufficiently undefined to allow of dictatorship and many challenged the notion that Poincaré wanted to act dictatorially. Ironically, during a period of 'national renewal', most German commentators believed that the years from 1912 to 1914 vindicated a theory of presidential weakness. True, the constitution, as *Vorwärts* remarked, did not render Poincaré impotent: 'We see that powerlessness is not determined by the articles of the constitution, which are elastic enough.'[27] Moreover, conservative, Catholic, liberal, and socialist newspapers all believed that he would, unlike his predecessors, use the powers available to him,[28] especially the power of appointment, for the fragmented nature of French politics permitted him to play off the factions one against the other: 'In France there is no closed majority party, which has an acknowledged leader; therefore, the president is not presented with any politician, as happens in England, whom he has to make prime minister.'[29] Yet Poincaré, it was clear to most of the German press, worked within distinct parameters. Newspapers as different as the left-liberal *Frankfurter Zeitung* and the *Deutsche Tageszeitung*, organ of the radical conservative *Bund der Landwirte*, confirmed that the president of the republic had been forced 'to honour parliamentary logic': 'With one blow he has reduced to nothing all those hopes of him employing a miraculous cure against the excesses of the parliamentary regime.'[30] By April 1914, even the nationalist *Dresdner Nachrichten* was convinced that the 'president of the French republic [is] in truth merely a creature of parliament and a puppet of his ministry'. What was more, the same newspaper added that such prostration was inevitable: 'Even Herr Poincaré, who knows to give himself certain personal airs and graces, cannot change the course of things fundamentally but must,

[26] This was true across the political spectrum, from the *Neue Preußische Zeitung*, 22 Jan. 1913, on the right, to *Vorwärts*, 12 Jan. 1913, on the left. *Frankfurter Zeitung*, 18 Jan. 1913.
[27] *Vorwärts*, 12 Jan. 1913.
[28] *Neue Preußische Zeitung*, 22 Jan. 1913; *Frankfurter Zeitung*, 4 Jan. 1913; and *Germania*, 10 Jan. 1913.
[29] *Frankfurter Zeitung*, 4 Jan. 1913. See also K. E. Schmidt in the *Fränkischer Kurier*, 9 Dec. 1905.
[30] *Frankfurter Zeitung*, 12 Dec. 1913; *Deutsche Tageszeitung*, 31 Dec. 1913.

like his predecessors, pay tribute in all decisive questions to the ministerial and parliamentary urge to dominate.'[31] The perceived failure
of Poincaré was evidence of what had been surmised from the late
1890s onwards: the president's hands were tied.

It was almost routine in Germany to liken the theoretical powers of
the French president to those of a constitutional monarch.[32] Historically, they had, after all, been granted by Orléanists in 1875, who had
envisaged a legal reversion to monarchy. As the *Frankfurter Zeitung*
reminded its readers before the elections of 1906 and 1913, it had been
intended that the title 'president of the republic', which was to be
transferred every seven years, could simply be exchanged for that of
'king of the French', which was to be held in perpetuity.[33] Newspapers
across the political spectrum marvelled at the apparent extent of presidential authority in France: the president was, obviously, head of the
executive and could preside over ministerial meetings, appoint officials
and ministers, force a second reading of bills, and, with the concurrence
of the Senate, dissolve the Assembly; as the head of the French state
abroad, he could conclude treaties, perform representative duties, and
command the army and navy; and, as the head of the French state at
home, he was formally irresponsible, except on charges of treason, and
could pardon those condemned by due legal process.[34] However, the
same newspapers proceeded to demonstrate how constitutional small-
print and political practice in fact circumscribed the president's actions:
'There is no head of state who is so absolutely decorative as the president of the French republic. . . . The president has indeed, according to
the constitution, all those prerogatives which are conceded to heads of
state everywhere, but it is made certain that he does not come into a
position where he can exercise them independently.'[35]

In part, this presidential weakness was the result of republican
domination in France after 1877, which had allowed the head of
state's right to dissolve the Assembly, to speak before the chambers,
and to force bills to a second reading to fall into desuetude.[36]

---

[31] *Dresdner Nachrichten*, 10 Apr. 1914.   [32] *Frankfurter Zeitung*, 4 Jan. 1913.
[33] Ibid. Also ibid., 25 Nov. 1905.
[34] *Vorwärts*, 12 Jan. 1913; *Frankfurter Zeitung*, 4 and 18 Jan. 1913; *Berliner Börsenzeitung*,
30 Dec. 1905; *Kölnische Volkszeitung*, 21 Jan. 1906; *Dresdner Nachrichten*, 10 Apr. 1914; *Neue
Preußische Zeitung*, 22 Jan. 1913; and *Deutsche Tageszeitung*, 14 Jan. 1913.
[35] *Berliner Börsenzeitung*, 30 Dec. 1905. Radolin, AA R7065, A7039, observed that it
had been usual for ministers to neglect to brief the President of the Republic over policy.
Delcassé constituted an exception in informing Loubet before his colleagues.
[36] *Deutsche Tageszeitung*, 14 Jan. 1913.

Republican habit, noted Christian Scheier in *Der Tag*, had confounded royalist intention: 'During the last thirty years or so, after
the conservatives and monarchists who were obliged to found the
republic but then, powerless, had had to hand over the leadership of
government to republican parties, several of those [earlier] prerogatives have retreated into the background.'[37] But it was still necessary
to explain how republicans, who controlled the Assembly, had influenced the exercise of executive power. In other words, why had the
most important political powers of the president lapsed? The answer,
replied most of the German press, lay in the parliamentary logic of
the French political state. The president could only act with the
counter-signature of his ministers, who in turn required parliamentary support in order to legislate:

the...prerogatives of the president...are all subject, as in every parliamentarily
governed state, to the restriction that they can only be exercised through a
responsible ministry. All acts, statutes, and decrees of the president must be
counter-signed by a minister, who thereby accepts responsibility for them before
parliament and country. The president can select and appoint ministers, but
these ministers must have the trust of parliament, otherwise they cannot govern;
they must therefore be taken from the parliamentary majority.[38]

Whereas in the United States, the president of the republic retained
his veto and appointed and supported ministries, irrespective of
Congress's censure, the French president had to bow to parliamentary
pressure. According to the journalist Karl Eugen Schmidt, the
American president had powers roughly equivalent to those of the
German kaiser, and far superior to those of the French president and
the constitutional monarchs of England, Belgium, and Holland.[39]

The French and American presidents differed, ultimately, in the
amount of legitimacy they enjoyed. Both presidential executives
could in theory resist the will of parliament, as the president
alone appointed and dismissed governments. Yet, in France, when
MacMahon had indeed opposed the Assembly in 1877, the latter had
emerged victorious and, thereafter, dictated, through votes of no
confidence, which governments stood and which fell.[40] In the United
States, on the other hand, the president had suffered no such defeat

[37] *Tag*, 8 Jan. 1913.
[38] *Frankfurter Zeitung*, 4 Jan. 1913. See also ibid., 18 Jan. 1913, and *Münchener Neueste
Nachrichten*, 1 Mar. 1906.
[39] K. E. Schmidt in *Tag*, 9 Dec. 1905.   [40] Jellinek, *Allgemeine Staatslehre*, 735.

and claimed to be just as legitimate as Congress, since both had been elected by direct manhood suffrage. Whilst the French president was voted into office by the Assembly and Senate, and appeared to have been legitimized by them, the American president portrayed himself as the unmediated product of popular sovereignty. These were the two types of presidency identified by the constitutional lawyer Georg Jellinek. They were, he admitted, distinguished more by politics than by law: 'This distinction is more significant from a political than from a legal point of view, since the president who is elected by the people possesses much more authority vis-à-vis the chambers than does the one who is appointed by the chambers and is therefore dependent on them, even though they only function as a constituent organ of the people during the election [of the president].'[41] It was for this reason that the French presidential elections were conducted, in Schmidt's phrase, in felt-soled slippers, as if a corpse lay in the adjacent room, whereas the American ones were heralded by trumpets and cannon.[42] Because he did not have a direct, popular mandate, the French president had been eclipsed by the Assembly; and because he had been eclipsed, his election was largely ignored by the French populace. As *Germania* commented, the inauguration of a new head of state in France constituted a 'change of personnel', rather than an American-style 'change of system'.[43] As a result, French presidents and their ministers knew that they would be defeated, were they to provoke a confrontation with the Assembly.[44]

Of course, disputes between the head of the executive and the legislature were less likely in France because the former was elected by the latter. It was easier for republicans to influence the head of state in person and through party, than by means of formal powers and political confrontation. Since the election of the president was confined to the two chambers, the voters—deputies and senators—knew the candidates personally and vetted them politically: 'The National Assembly... includes... 895 representatives of the people, from which each belongs to a particular parliamentary group and from which each has an adequate knowledge of persons and policies. ... [It] is as good as ruled out that a president of the republic would be sought outside parliament.'[45] As long as the parties

[41] Ibid. 732–3.
[42] In *Tag*, 22 Dec. 1912. *Frankfurter Zeitung*, 1 Jan. 1913: *Berliner Blatt*, 5 Jan. 1906.
[43] *Germania*, 4 Jan. 1913.   [44] Ibid., 11 Jan. 1906.
[45] *Frankfurter Zeitung*, 1 Jan. 1913.

of the centre and the left retained a majority in the Assembly and Senate, they were able to choose suitably passive and solidly republican presidents, such as Emile Loubet and Armand Fallières. Both, it was agreed, had been ideal candidates, preferring to let their powers lapse than to disturb a putative constitutional harmony.[46] Loubet, German newspapers from across the political spectrum concurred, had been an unusually uncontroversial choice at a time of unprecedented political instability. A suspected, but not an active revisionist in the Dreyfus affair,[47] he had declared his election 'a new proof of France's trust in the republic' and had then proceeded to discharge his duties, which he insisted were limited in scope, with great forbearance, caution, and modesty; 'in a thoroughly comfortable and petty-bourgeois fashion', as the *Neue Preußische Zeitung* described it.[48] Although he had a weakness for aristocratic company, Loubet's successor, Fallières, was, if possible, even more emphatically a creature of the centre-left majority, it was claimed.[49] His winning feature, according to the *Vossische Zeitung*, was his colourlessness, which reassured republican parties of various hues that he would not obstruct their designs: 'He is a good enough republican to inspire trust in even the most advanced parties, and his colours are subdued enough . . . not to shock the moderates.'[50] It appeared in Germany that neither Loubet nor Fallières wanted to reassert the rights of the executive in France. From 1900 to 1913, therefore, questions about the exact nature of those rights simply did not arise.

German writers were well aware that this gagging of the president was intentional, and most believed that it was justified.[51] Given France's specifically continental conditions, including a large conservative-monarchical population, poor urban masses, and pronounced class conflict, French republicans had rightly heeded the warning of 1848, it was propounded. Even newspapers advocating greater presidential powers, such as the Catholic *Kölnische Volkszeitung*, recognized that the counter-example of the Second Republic was influential, if not compelling: 'In America a hundred

---

[46] *Germania*, 10 Jan. 1913.

[47] *Vorwärts*, 16 Jan. 1913; *Freisinnige Zeitung*, 20 Jan. 1906.

[48] *Freisinnige Zeitung*, 20 Jan. 1906; *Kölnische Volkszeitung*, 21 Jan. 1906; *Neue Preußische Zeitung*, 11 May 1900; *Germania*, 22 Feb. 1899.

[49] *Vossische Zeitung*, 25 Nov. 1905; *Germania*, 18 Jan. 1906; *Freisinnige Zeitung*, 18 Jan. 1906.

[50] *Vossische Zeitung*, 25 Nov. 1905.   [51] Ibid., 9 Jan. 1903.

years of experience has shown how good it is when the powers of the president are great and those of ministers not so great. Why do they not want to learn anything from these experiences in France? Because they still live in the fear that the president could, like Louis Napoleon Bonaparte, turn himself into an emperor.'[52] Georg Jellinek, professor of law at Heidelberg, made a similar point in the academic debate. After an American-inspired presidency had engendered the Second Empire, he contended, France had understandably imitated the English parliamentary system under the Third Republic.[53] His colleague in Berlin, Heinrich von Treitschke, went further, detaching American experiment from European experience. The centralization of French administration, he posited, did not permit a powerful, popularly elected head of state without a concomitant risk of dictatorship.[54] The United States, which was in effect thousands of small federal republics,[55] constituted an exception to the European pattern of increasing concentration in government. The *Berliner Tageblatt* rehearsed the same arguments for a wider audience:

In the American union of states, which is composed of so many single and different parts, a strong central power had to be created, and the election of the president, who incorporates this central power, became an important event, which deeply affected the interests of the people. In the French republic, which is a solid structure and suffers, if anything, from over-centralization, the constitution can limit the power of the head of state to the minimal possible, and the election, which only signifies a substitution as far as the people are concerned, remains the affair of narrowly defined political circles.[56]

The French political establishment, fearing the omnipotence of a demagogue-president in a centralized state, had come to dominate the executive.[57]

The supposed guarantor of separate constitutional spheres, the Senate, had succumbed to similar pressures. Initially, the upper house had attracted cross-party support in Germany as a necessary counterweight to the Assembly. It was, wrote *Vorwärts*, a dam

---

[52] *Kölnische Volkszeitung*, 14 Dec. 1913; *Dresdner Nachrichten*, 4 Jan. 1906; and *Frankfurter Zeitung*, 1 Jan. 1913.
[53] Jellinek, *Allgemeine Staatsrechtslehre*, 734.
[54] Treitschke, *Politik*, ii. 276–7.　　[55] Ibid. 299.
[56] *Berliner Tageblatt*, 12 Jan. 1906.　　[57] Treitschke, *Politik*, ii. 277.

against the turbulence of the lower house and of the population in general: 'As the protector of formal-republican institutions, the Senate has what one could call the virtues which correspond to its vices: its origin makes it altogether more resistant to currents which dominate the electoral masses, and to Caesarist currents which surface in France from time to time.'[58] But, like the presidency, the Senate had soon become captive to the demands of party. German socialists, conservatives, Catholics, and liberals converged in their descriptions of the ascendancy of the *bloc des gauches* in the upper chamber.[59] As a result, it was noted, Radicals had not only abandoned their previous opposition to the Senate, but they had also begun to look on seats there as tranquil and well-paid sinecures: 'Now the ministers and their followers will take great care not to characterize the "upper house" as superfluous or in need of reform; for they would be injuring themselves and be taking away a notorious welfare institution from their dear nephews.'[60] Instead of protecting the constitution and tempering the ambitious schemes of the lower chamber, the Senate had become a party device, which was used to veil government inaction. The factions passed radical bills in the Assembly only on the understanding that their colleagues in the Senate would reject them out of hand.[61] Party reputation was thereby salvaged, it was held, but at the cost of senatorial independence.[62]

The most significant touchstone for this change in German attitudes towards the French upper house was the fall of the third Briand ministry in March 1913. The details of the affair seemed straightforward. With the backing of Poincaré, the ex-socialist Président du Conseil had introduced an electoral reform bill, which had been accepted with a large majority by the Assembly but thrown out by the Senate. It was the only occasion between 1898 and 1914 on which a government had been forced to resign after a defeat in the upper chamber, despite having the support of both the lower chamber and the president. The incident served as a useful yardstick to gauge German opinion because two opposing interpretations appeared plausible. On the one hand, opponents of proportional

---

[58] *Vorwärts*, 7 Jan. 1903; *Germania*, 2 Mar. 1904.
[59] *Freisinnige Zeitung*, 21 Mar. 1913. For the other parties, see the following footnotes.
[60] *Germania*, 13 Jan. 1909; *Neue Preußische Zeitung*, 9 July 1912; *Vorwärts*, 9 Jan. 1912; *Germania*, 5 Jan. 1906; *Neue Preußische Zeitung*, 8 Jan. 1903; and *Vorwärts*, 9 Jan. 1912.
[61] *Vorwärts*, 6 Jan. 1898, 7 Jan. 1903, 16 Mar. 1909, and 14 July 1912.
[62] Vogel, *Die dritte französische Republik*, 340.

representation argued that the Senate was safeguarding the constitution against hasty and ill-considered reform. On the other hand, proponents claimed that the Radicals, who were favoured by the existing system of constituency voting, were abusing their last power base in order to secure party interests. Regardless of their political affiliation, German newspapers took the second view. The Senate, explained the *Freisinnige Zeitung*, had avoided conflict with the Assembly before 1913, not because the constitution had stood unchallenged, but because the Radicals and their allies had been preponderant in both houses: 'Chamber and Senate have always, despite all sorts of differences, got on well or at least tolerably with each other, as long as the majority in both bodies was homogeneous....More pronounced opposition between Chamber and Senate was first established after the predominance of the Radicals in the Chamber started to disintegrate.'[63] As soon as that party unity across the chambers had disappeared, the Radical domination of the Senate was exposed for what it was; the unmitigated self-interest of a political faction. Both *Vorwärts* and the *Neue Preußische Zeitung* blamed the politicking of the Radical upper chamber for the most serious constitutional crisis since 1877: 'it was above all things a *favourable opportunity to throw Briand out*....It is well-known that these Radicals have never liked Poincaré.'[64] The constitutional function of the Senate, which had been designed to counteract the worst effects of factional extremism in the Assembly, was seen in Germany to have been subverted by party interests.

Political parties had formed in the Assembly and had then used the powers of the lower chamber in order to infiltrate the executive. A predominant chamber brought party interference in its wake, it was assumed. In his major work, *Regierung und Volkswille*, the historian Hans Delbrück attempted to demonstrate how a powerful lower house was to be prevented from becoming preponderant. The Reichstag, in spite of its defects, was his model. It had, he argued, different origins to those of English, French, and American parliaments. Whereas the latter had forced their way into government, sometimes replacing the previous regime in the process, the former had been created by existing authorities: 'In all other states, where

[63] *Freisinnige Zeitung*, 21 Mar. 1913.
[64] *Neue Preußische Zeitung*, 20 Mar. 1913. The idea that the ministerial crisis was the most serious since 'seize mai' was relayed unquestioningly from the French press by *Vorwärts*, 20 Mar. 1913.

similar representative institutions of the people exist, in particular in England, France, and America, they achieved power by forcing aside or completely toppling the existing government. In Germany, the representative institution emerged because the government called it into being and placed it beside itself.'[65] Because it had been assigned a special role by the German government, from above, the Reichstag had a different rationale and different powers from the Assemblée des Députés or the House of Commons, which had struggled for their authority haphazardly, until, eventually, they dictated the composition and actions of the administration. Whilst the exigencies of conflict in England and France had obscured the separation of legislative and executive competencies, the lower house in Germany had been designed to fit into a scheme of government, which was founded on the distinction between *Gesetzgebung* and *Regierung*: 'It is correct that those other parliaments have much greater power than our Reichstag. Those parliaments themselves determine the government; the ministry is composed from the leaders of the majority.... There can be no talk of this in Germany. The German Reichstag, in accordance with its completely different origin, exercises only influence over the government.'[66] In order to preserve distinct legislative and executive functions, which were seen in Germany to guarantee government neutrality and the exclusion of party from administration, the Reichstag had been planned as a mechanism assuring a popular veto on all legislation: 'Here, the gap between, for example, Germany and France appears to be infinite. Here there is a professional government with popular assembly as a sort of organ of control [*Kontrollstation*], there an elected popular government.'[67] Lacking the practical means to appoint governments, the German lower house, unlike its English and French equivalents, rejected laws, but it did not dictate them.

The French Assembly effectively nominated the government, German authors maintained, not only by electing the president, but also by obstructing and voting down ministries which affronted the majority coalition. With deputies having the right to interpellate ministers at any time and to give votes of no confidence at will, obstruction and dismissal were virtually built into the political system, it was held.[68] As a result, wrote Karl Vogel, the Assembly had

---

[65] Delbrück, *Regierung und Volkswille*, 59.   [66] Ibid. 59–60.   [67] Ibid. 66.
[68] Fernau, *Die französische Demokratie*, 19. On the right of interpellation, see *Frankfurter Zeitung*, 20 July 1909; *Vossische Zeitung*, 22 May 1914.

come to govern France, in contrast to the United States, where Congress remained comparatively weak:

> How very differently it [the Assembly] behaves in France, where the congress of both chambers, not the people itself, elects the president of the republic, and the cabinet, which is nominated by the president but which is taken from the lap and accords with the suggestions of the chamber of deputies, must as such be responsible for everything and must be dependent on the mood of the Assembly, keeping in step with it, in order to keep itself in office.... On the other hand, this practice gives to the French chamber of deputies, really and apparently, a predominance, which overshadows the head of state, limits the powers of the ministers, and lames the executive, by laying bare the constant interventions of the deputies.[69]

Although the president of the republic sometimes exploited the lack of unity in the chamber to appoint one Président du Conseil instead of another, his choice was circumscribed. In a strict sense, there was no majority party, able to impose its own candidate, but there was a loose coalition of republican groups, which had begun as the *concentration républicaine*—the 'domination of the republican pact or ring', in Hermann Kuhn's formulation[70]—before becoming the Radical-dominated *bloc des gauches* at the turn of the century. Even academic authors of textbooks such as Richard Mahrenholtz referred to this coalition as a single party: 'In general, ministers are taken from the majority party, *although the constitution does not require this.*'[71] In most German accounts, such a republican core was not, of course, characterized by consensus over policy, but rather by a common identification of outsiders, or non-republicans. Thus, it was possible to explain the apparent contradiction between the fragmentation of French politics and the political hegemony of French republican parties.[72] Unable to settle on an agreed political programme, the factions nevertheless united in the exercise of political power.

The notion that each republican party provided a few members of each government was so well established that the technical term 'les ministrables' had been coined to describe them, reported the *Neue Preußische Zeitung* in 1898.[73] The phrase resurfaced regularly in

---

[69] Vogel, *Die dritte französische Republik*, 342–3.
[70] Kuhn, *Frankreich an der Zeitwende*, 15.
[71] Mahrenholtz, *Frankreich*, 160.
[72] Münster, 25 Nov. 1898, AA R7019, A13663.
[73] *Neue Preußische Zeitung*, 29 June 1898.

German articles thereafter, not least because it appeared to encapsulate the oligarchical nature of French political life.[74] The implication was that specific republican parties dictated who was to be included in a ministry, and who was not. This domination of politics by the Assembly and, more particularly, by the 'ministrables' of each republican faction was assumed by most correspondents in their dispatches about ministerial crises and new governments. The *Neue Preußische Zeitung*, for example, observed that even the Caillaux government, which had proclaimed itself a strong and independent antidote to the weak and ineffectual Monis administration, drew its members entirely from party coteries: 'Completely new names will under no circumstances emerge; one remained within the circle of party ministrables.'[75] *Vorwärts* agreed, adding that those party leaders who had eschewed the last government were to be bribed, by offers of posts, into supporting the new one.[76] Unsurprisingly, the parties and politicians deemed to be 'républicain' and 'ministrable' changed over time,[77] but, at any given moment, it appeared necessary for ministries to command 'une majorité républicaine'.[78] For most of the period between 1898 and 1914 this meant a majority based on a Radical and Radical-Socialist kernel: 'In a chamber in which Radicals have the majority, a French prime minister cannot govern with a majority whose composition depends unavoidably on monarchists and clericals.'[79] From 1908 onwards, German newspapers conjectured that the Radical core of republican majorities was starting to splinter.[80] Nevertheless, nearly all remained certain that there were republican groups which presidents and governments could not ignore, and republican bounds beyond which they could not go. The *Vossische Zeitung*, *B.Z. am Mittag*, *Neue Preußische Zeitung*, and *Vorwärts* all expected the immediate failure of the Ribot ministry in June 1914, despite its concessions to the Radicals, because the Président du Conseil was suspected of reactionary leanings, which placed him beyond the republican pale.[81] After the government had indeed fallen on its first day in office, the *Berliner*

---

[74] Fernau, *Die französische Demokratie*, 31–2.
[75] Ibid., 28 June 1911.   [76] *Vorwärts*, 29 July 1911.
[77] Ibid., 20 Jan. 1905.   [78] *Neue Preußische Zeitung*, 9 Mar. 1912.
[79] Ibid., 26 Feb. 1911; *Münchner Allgemeine Zeitung*, 11 Mar. 1911; *Neue Preußische Zeitung*, 18 Sept. 1906.
[80] *Vorwärts*, 27 July 1909; *Freisinnige Zeitung*, 30 June 1911 and 20 Mar. 1913.
[81] *Vossische Zeitung*, 8 and 13 June 1914; *B.Z. am Mittag*, 13 June 1914; *Neue Preußische Zeitung*, 8 and 13 June 1914; *Vorwärts*, 13 June 1914.

Tageblatt explained why: President Poincaré had tried to impose a ministry on an unwilling majority in the Assembly—a step which had proved to be 'extremely questionable'.[82] The French 'Deputiertenherrschaft', as the diplomat Herbert von Hindenburg called it, remained intact.[83]

Max Nordau's extended essay on Robert de Jouvenel's book, *La République des camarades*, which appeared in the *Vossische Zeitung* in June 1914, summarized many of the assumptions made by Germans about French political parties, the Assembly and the separation of functions.[84] Nordau was one of the most prolific writers in Wilhelmine Germany and one of the acknowledged German-speaking experts on France. In books such as *Paris unter der dritten Republik*, first published in the 1880s, but reissued in the 1890s, he had demonstrated his sympathy for the Third Republic.[85] By 1914, however, he concluded, with Jouvenel, that the republican experiment in France had foundered. His premiss was that the French republic, in asserting that it was a democracy, required that the populace surveyed, controlled, and directed all government dealings, which in turn necessitated a strict division of competencies. Unfortunately, in France, the proximity and mutual interests of deputies, ministers, and bureaucrats, who were not adequately or formally separated, had led to a species of camaraderie, which blurred distinctions between functions and thereby subverted democracy:

The French republic is theoretically a democracy. The essential core of such consists of the people watching over and directing all government actions.... In order for [popular] surveillance to be possible, powers must be separated. Previously, there were three of them: legislative, executive and judicial. Now a fourth has been added: the press. Basically and in outline, they are still separate. But they are good neighbours....Thus, the powers are not yet fused, but already closely connected.[86]

A strict separation of legislative and executive competencies had not been preserved, continued Nordau, because ministers and deputies

---

[82] *Berliner Tageblatt*, 13 June 1914.

[83] H. v. Hindenburg, *Am Rande zweier Jahrhunderte* (Berlin, 1938), 105. Hindenburg was the grandson of the German ambassador to France, Münster. *Neue Preußische Zeitung*, 12 Apr. 1906.

[84] *Vossische Zeitung*, 6 June 1914. Jouvenel's book was also reviewed in other newspapers, such as the *Deutsche volkswirtschaftliche Korrespondenz*, 13 June 1914.

[85] Nordau, *Paris unter der dritten Republik*, 8–27, 64–74.

[86] *Vossische Zeitung*, 6 June 1914.

came from the same pool of 'camarades' and remained interdependent, meeting in the morning as friends and political partners, before confronting each other in the afternoon as government and legislature. Under such circumstances, the monitoring and control function of the parliament was undermined at the same time as its coercive and punitive sanction, the interpellation of ministers, started to be abused by self-interested factions and individuals: 'They continue to interpellate, but behind every interpellation is a secret coalition or very open ambition.'[87] This inability of parliament to monitor, control, and punish, together with the concomitant shortcomings of the French judiciary and bureaucracy, accounted for the failure of the Third Republic: 'the sterility of party struggles, the difficulty of reform, the fossilization of administration, the peculiarity of certain judgments in large trials, the ability of certain politicians to have their say despite being held, generally, in low esteem: camaraderie suffices to explain all this.'[88] Closely tied factions and individuals had come to dominate the French Assembly, and the Assembly had come to dominate the French republic.

Underpinning the preponderance of the lower chamber, postulated most German commentators, was the idea of popular sovereignty. As has already been seen, this was the reason most commonly given for the subordinate position of the president. It was also the explanation favoured by authors such as Haas and Vogel for the precedence of Assembly over Senate.[89] German opinions on the question of sovereignty in general were divided. But they tended to converge over the issue of French sovereignty. It was, as Treitschke pointed out, the French who had first used the term 'sovereignty' scientifically, to mean ultimate and indivisible authority: 'they maintained the unity of the state with intelligence and will-power, and a Frenchman found the appropriate scientific word for it.'[90] This notion of undivided sovereignty matched Treitschke's own theory: there had to be an ultimate repository of power within the state; either king, populace, or God.[91] Jellinek admitted the force of such argument, but suggested that, although sovereignty was indivisible, competence was not: 'A division of competencies is possible, but not

[87] *Vossische Zeitung*, 6 June 1914.   [88] Ibid.
[89] Vogel, *Die dritte französische Republik*, 340; Haas, *Frankreich*, 104.
[90] Treitschke, *Politik*, i. 36.
[91] Ibid. 7; Treitschke's three types of state were thus monarchy, republic, and theocracy.

the splitting of power.'[92] The United States managed to separate such competencies to an extent but it, like France, tended to grant most power to the lower chamber.[93] According to Jellinek, the Assembly had been singled out as the principal secondary organ of state, partly because it possessed superior constitutional powers, and partly because it stood closest to the will of the people, which constituted the primary organ of state in democratic legal theory:

Especially instructive in this respect is the stance of the French Constituent Assembly, which proclaimed the principle of the separation of powers in its declaration of the rights of man [but which]..., more importantly, created an organ in the legislative, in which all powers were united. Abstractly [too], however, the theory of popular sovereignty, which formed the basis of democratic ideas, only allowed the separation of powers to be a subordinate principle.[94]

It was thus no coincidence that parliament had been the predominant element in all French constitutions since 1789, for 'All these constitutions rest, like France's first one, on the principle of popular sovereignty'.[95] Since only the Assembly was elected by direct, manhood suffrage, it could portray itself as the sole representative of the sovereign nation. Both Roscher and Gneist agreed with Jellinek that the notion of popular sovereignty had promoted a transfer of power to the lower chamber and a fusion of executive and legislative functions.[96] It remains to be seen to what extent Germans believed that the Assembly actually expressed the will of the people, or *Volkswille*. But, first, it is necessary to examine the perceived consequences of the merger of *Gesetzgebung* and *Regierung*.

2. Party and Faction

To German observers, party had permeated all areas of government in France. Such practice ran directly counter to the political ideology of the *Kaiserreich*, which insisted that a neutral administration of experts should stand above the competing factional interests of a popular legislature.[97] The former, using its expertise, was to draft and initiate bills, whilst the latter, representing the diverse interests of the nation, was to block measures which were unacceptable to majority opinion. The German system, wrote its apologists, ensured rationality and national

---

[92] Jellinek, *Allgemeine Staatslehre*, 501.
[93] Ibid. 499, 556.   [94] Ibid. 499, 556, 735.   [95] Ibid. 523–5.
[96] Roscher, *Politik*, 321; Gneist, *Der Rechtsstaat*, 166–8.
[97] Bülow, *Denkwürdigkeiten*, iii. 325.

efficiency, because ministers were trained bureaucrats, materially and mentally detached from political, social, and economic interest groups; it offered continuity, since administrations were not dependent on the Reichstag; and it promised fair government, both because ministerial officials were tied functionally to the national interest and because each bill was passed on its own merits by a different coalition of parties. To defenders of the *Kaiserreich*, party government appeared to portend instability, conflict, deadlock, and disaffection.

Although it is certainly true that the German parties themselves were less alarmed by the prospect of party government and more critical of so-called neutral government in the *Kaiserreich* than were ministers, they nevertheless remained sceptical of the party-based political system in France. There, as in Germany, political fragmentation seemed to offset the potential gains of parliamentarism, for each party worried that it alone was too weak to assume office. Lust for power constantly struggled against fear of power, forcing parties to choose whether they preferred bureaucrats or opponents as their political masters. Britain, with its stable, two-party parliamentary regime, constituted an alternative model, yet even left liberals such as Friedrich Naumann conceded that such conditions did not obtain in Germany.[98] Few disputed Otto Hintze's claim that 'our people in its entirety actually has no unified, political form'.[99] Germany, it appeared, lacked the national, regional, confessional, and economic unity necessary for a parliamentary system.[100] Not only were its parties too numerous and inimical to admit of lasting coalitions, they were also too radical to agree on an acceptable form of government. As Hans Delbrück observed, in a parliamentary regime such extreme diversity threatened constant alternation between monarchy and republic, as monarchical and republican parties acceded to office one after the other:

It is not possible to let parties alternate, when they are so far apart from each other that one is monarchist and the other republican. If there was again a majority of believers in monarchy, who again established monarchy, and then after a number of years there was a republican majority, which re-established a republic, and so on, with one change after another, the state would collapse. . . . If this were

---

[98] Düding, *Der Nationalsoziale Verein*, 81.

[99] Hintze, 'Das monarchische Prinzip und die konstitutionelle Verfassung', in *Staat und Verfassung*, 372.

[100] Ibid. 377–8; Delbrück, *Regierung und Volkswille*, 130; Treitschke, 'Die Freiheit', in *Historische und politische Aufsätze*, 15.

translated to Germany, what would become of Germany, if we alternated between a clerical and a social-democratic government?[101]

It was easier to predict what would happen in Germany by assessing what had occurred in France. Most commentators acknowledged that political disunity and radicalism were common to both countries. Authors of textbooks such as Richard Mahrenholtz tried to distinguish composite political strands—in this case, royalist-clerical, republican-anticlerical, and socialist-anarchist—but were then obliged to admit that the actual number of factions was much greater, and the probability of long-term cooperation between them correspondingly smaller: 'within these three [groupings] there are further factions of different sizes, which sometimes feud with each other and sometimes unite, either for election purposes or to topple ministers and presidents.'[102] By 1914, Delbrück could still identify nine parties in France and ten in Germany.[103] What was more, similar types of political fragmentation were witnessed in the two states. Individualism, anticlericalism, monarchism, and socialism were cited as the main causes of French factionalism, but all seemed to be equally applicable in Germany.[104] Perhaps most significant of all, some French factions, like their German counterparts, were known to have disavowed the parliamentary republic altogether, thereby precluding a two-party system, warned Delbrück, even if factionalism could be eradicated: 'In any case, the two-party system, as it predominates in England and America, is ruled out in France because a large part of the people do not want a republic at all: in their hearts, they do not recognize it in the slightest degree.'[105] Given such circumstances, the decision to allow party into government proper appeared reckless.

The German government and press, with the exception of socialist newspapers, which shall be treated separately, were united in their criticism of political disorder in France. Articles were littered with words such as 'Parteizerwürfnisse', 'Zerrissenheit', 'Uneinigkeit', 'Wirrnisse', 'Staatskomödie', and 'politische Spaltung', which revealed latent doubts about the viability of the French regime even

---

[101] Hintze, 'Das monarchische Prinzip', in *Staat und Verfassung*, 127–8.
[102] Mahrenholtz, *Frankreich*, 318.
[103] Delbrück, *Regierung und Volkswille*, 129–30.
[104] Kuhn, *Aus dem modernen Babylon*, 37; Vogel, *Die dritte französische Republik*, 378–9.
[105] Delbrück, *Regierung und Volkswille*, 129. M. Exner, *Die französische Armee in Krieg und Frieden*, 2nd edn. (Berlin, 1894), 2.

from publications which, ostensibly, continued to support the Third Republic. A good pictorial example of the same ambivalence was the cartoon, 'The New French Parliament', which appeared in the socialist satirical journal, *Der wahre Jacob*, in June 1902.[106] It depicted chaos in the French Assembly, with the many factions brawling and fencing with each other, ignoring President Loubet's admonition in the caption that 'Unity makes for strength'. Despite the fact that the *bloc des gauches* was the most stable coalition between 1898 and 1914, the largest circulation socialist publication forgot its backing of the French administration in its struggle with the Church and showed to its readers the unmitigated disunity of French politics. The symbol of French government, Loubet, was left powerless, calling in vain for order.

As was to be expected, the conservative press was most zealous in its caricaturing of this 'absolutely modern French comedy', as Münster labelled it.[107] After the nationalist deputy, Syveton, and the justice minister, Vallé, had come to blows in the lower chamber, for instance, the *Reichsbote* eagerly implicated the entire French parliamentary regime: 'It really seems as if modern parliamentarism wanted to prove that it can no longer live life sufficiently to the full within parliamentary confines, that it cannot go on living without insults and acts of violence.'[108] Yet the liberal press also characterized French politics in similar terms—'interpellations, accusations, fistfights, in short, everything which the parliamentary season has to offer', in the words of the *Hannoverscher Courier*[109]—so that more favourable, pro-French editorials were sometimes obscured by allusions to disarray and faction in daily reportage.

It was implicit in newspaper and diplomatic coverage of French events that faction was endemic in the Third Republic. Politics in France was explained to a considerable extent by political fragmentation. The fall of the Méline ministry and the failure of Brisson's *concentration républicaine* in June 1898 were, according to Münster, attributable to the same lack of coherence in France's party structure noted by the *Neue Preußische Zeitung*: 'The parties in the chamber are...disunited, as has been demonstrated by the recent attempt to form a homogeneous ministry.'[110] The *National-Zeitung* predicted

[106] *Der wahre Jacob*, 17 June 1902, no. 415.
[107] Münster, 15 Aug. 1899, AA R6595, A9720.   [108] *Reichsbote*, 9 Dec. 1902.
[109] *Hannoverscher Courier*, 13 July 1904; *Berliner Tageblatt*, 17 June 1902.
[110] Münster, 30 June 1898, AA R7125, A7717. *Neue Preußische Zeitung*, 1 June 1898.

that Brisson's government of reconciliation and unity would collapse in the same ignominy as it had done in 1885, 'because reconciliation and unity between ultra radicals and moderate republicans was impossible, and will also prove to be so in the present and in the future.'[111] It was thus no surprise that Waldeck-Rousseau's ministry of talents was greeted with incredulity exactly one year later: a government 'faute de mieux', sneered the conservative press; 'the "cabinet of improbabilities"', as their left-liberal rivals phrased it.[112] Münster was convinced that what *Germania* called 'such colourful society' had only succeeded temporarily by exploiting the imminence of the World Exhibition and by alternating between the votes of the centre and those of the left: 'In a chamber like the present chamber of deputies, in which a proper majority does not exist and where majorities are merely created ad hoc each time, no cabinet can consider its future assured.'[113] *Germania* agreed: 'Given the complicated relationships between parties in France, a majority can easily change into a minority.'[114]

In the period after the Dreyfus affair, as the *bloc* established itself under Combes, German newspapers vacillated between opposing views of French politics. At times, it appeared from their reports that the affair had created two parties, Radical or socialist Dreyfusards and clerical, nationalist, or royalist anti-Dreyfusards, which had replaced the previous party structure in all but name. Thus, the right-wing *Hamburger Nachrichten*, which was inclined politically to overstate party confusion under the Third Republic, declared in 1902: 'in reality there are now... only two great parties in the country, which are mutually exclusive.... The Dreyfus affair did not create such oppositions, but merely laid them bare; it was not the cause of the split, but its consequence; thus, the split cannot simply be removed from the face of the earth.'[115] At other times, however, it seemed that the Dreyfus affair had simply exacerbated political fragmentation, by adding the battle between Dreyfusards and anti-Dreyfusards to the accumulated conflicts of French party history.[116] This suspicion was confirmed by the belief of virtually all

[111] *National-Zeitung*, 28 June 1898.
[112] *Neue Preußische Zeitung*, 3 Nov. 1900; *Freisinnige Zeitung*, 28 June 1899.
[113] *Germania*, 27 June 1899. Münster, 21 Jan. 1900, AA R6596 A971. Münster, 25 May 1900, AA R7127, A6526.
[114] *Germania*, 29 Nov. 1901.
[115] *Hamburger Nachrichten*, 5 Mar. 1902.   [116] *Germania*, 16 Oct. 1903.

German correspondents that the Radicals had begun to disintegrate under Clemenceau, Briand, Monis, and Caillaux, who were in office from 1906 to 1912. During those years, commented the *Hannoverscher Courier*, genuine liberalism had become mere 'Sektentum', or faction.[117]

Under Poincaré, notwithstanding French boasts of ralliement, the process of political disintegration appeared to many German newspapers to have been proved decisively. 'The Great Ministry', as Poincaré's first ministry was heralded in January 1912, was after all an admission, even to the liberal *Berliner Tageblatt*, that faction dominated French politics: 'Obviously, it was the intention of President Fallières to set up a *bloc* of renowned men, which would guarantee parliamentary work a large degree of stability, against the confusion of the chamber of deputies. The last ministries, such as those of Monis and Caillaux, were created out of the agitation of party struggle.'[118] Although Poincaré's own ministry survived, despite many voices, identified by the German ambassador in Paris, prophesying its downfall,[119] his sobering experiences as president with the Barthou administration, which he appointed to pass the three-year law, evinced that 'Party Chaos in France' still determined the form of national politics.[120] Barthou fell after eight-and-a-half months, before he had secured funding for increases in the length of military service. The *Freisinnige Zeitung* observed 'that it might be extremely difficult, with the fragmented state of relations between parties, to find a successor to Barthou.'[121] In the aftermath of the ministerial crisis, in January 1914, its left-liberal partner, the *Frankfurter Zeitung*, counted eleven political groupings in France.[122] The problem of factionalism had clearly not been resolved under the Third Republic. Indeed, because it had become a problem of government, with the fusion of executive and legislative functions, faction had almost become a symbol of the Third Republic in much of the German press.

The socialist press appeared to be different. According to party doctrine, the bourgeois centre was expected to disintegrate, as precapitalist political groupings were forced by economic imperatives to

---

[117] *Hannoverscher Courier*, 5 May 1909; *Augsburger Abendzeitung*, 2 Dec. 1909.
[118] *Berliner Tageblatt*, 15 Jan. 1912.
[119] Schoen, 19 Apr. 1912, AA R7135, A7065.
[120] The phrase was the title of a major article in *Vossische Zeitung*, 11 Mar. 1914.
[121] *Freisinnige Zeitung*, 5 Dec. 1913.   [122] *Frankfurter Zeitung*, 31 Jan. 1914.

choose sides. It was postulated that industrial society necessarily divided between the owners of the means of production and the suppliers of labour. Although industrialization in France had been slow and concentrated in the northern departments,[123] *Vorwärts* predicted the polarization of French politics throughout the 1900s: 'With the heightening of class oppositions, the political party struggle in France must also increasingly become a *class struggle*, which no longer tolerates a democratic middle party between the socialist party and the capitalist parties.'[124] Rouvier, Clemenceau, Briand, and Poincaré were all greeted as harbingers of a new age of capital and labour.[125] Disintegration and faction were thus portrayed, not as an enduring French problem, but as a prelude to polarization.

There were, however, two senses in which factionalism was associated in socialist thinking with the Third Republic. First, *Vorwärts* confessed repeatedly that French parties had refused to merge and organize themselves in the prescribed way. Thus, socialist reporting of French affairs took on a regular form, prematurely extending congratulations to their French colleagues and then retracting them, as it became evident that old political practices and institutions remained intact.[126] During elections and conferences, the bourgeois political groupings were mercilessly exposed and criticized for their inadequate party organization.[127] The 'disintegration of the bourgeois parties'[128] in France constituted one of the recurring themes of *Vorwärts*'s articles, even at the height of the *bloc des gauches*: 'Large, homogeneous parties... are as little in evidence in France as elsewhere, or even less so.... In order to be able to govern, several parties must unite to form a cartel.... The political dividing line, which is visible to all, does not therefore run along deep and enduring class borders, but along... the furrows which divide the individual factions of the propertied classes from each other.'[129] Even if a trend towards organized, mass parties could be discerned in France, socialist correspondents were bound to admit that notable politics, or *Honoratiorenpolitik*, continued to prevail for the moment: 'This

---

[123] *Vorwärts*, 15 Oct. 1904.   [124] Ibid., 10 May 1898.

[125] Ibid., 10 Nov. 1905, on Rouvier; 26 May 1906 on Clemenceau; 3 Nov. 1910 on Briand; 2 Oct. 1913 on Poincaré.

[126] Ibid., 9 Dec. 1913 and 13 June 1914.

[127] On the elections, ibid., 10 May 1898, 9 May 1900, 27 July 1909, 11 May 1910; for the joint Radical and Radical-Socialist congresses, ibid., 15 Oct. 1904, 23 Oct. 1906.

[128] *Vorwärts*, 9 May 1900.   [129] Ibid., 6 Jan. 1903; ibid., 5 Jan. 1905.

market of cliques and nepotism, or this cliquish organization, which is more or less supported by parties, is rooted, of course, in the essence of bourgeois parties of all countries. But in France it is more sharply defined than in all other European countries with universal suffrage, and it continues to be so, despite the unmistakable beginnings of organization during the last few years.'[130] France was perhaps moving towards modern forms of political organization, but, if so, its progress was slower than had been anticipated.

Second, to *Vorwärts*, modern parties and polarized politics were themselves only a brief staging-post between bourgeois republic and socialist *Zukunftsstaat*. Their historical appearance signalled that a society was on the verge of a new, universal and socialist era. Per se, they were no more a part of that era than they were a part of the old, class-based, bourgeois epoch. In other words, organization and polarization were not features of either stage of history—bourgeois or socialist—rather they were both cause and effect of a transition from one stage to another. The result was that faction and political disintegration were tied all the more closely in socialists' minds to the republican system of government. The republic was a bourgeois political form, it was reasoned, and bourgeois politics were characterized by the factional infighting of propertied interest groups and routine subjugation of labour. It was only as the proletariat began to organize itself, in preparation for the *Zukunftsstaat*, that diffuse bourgeois groups were obliged to unite their forces: 'if the Radicals have broken with the system of favouritism for the first time, then it is because they have begun, at the most sensitive point, to feel the pressure and competition of the socialists.'[131] The impulse for the bourgeois republic to change therefore came from outside, from the socialist parties, who were in fact the vanguard of a new society. Hence, it was tempting for socialists to deduce that the real republic was a republic of competing commercial interests and disintegrating historical combinations. At the level of word association, republic undoubtedly equalled faction.

The distinction made between party and faction varied from author to author. The commonest terms in German—'Partei', 'Fraktion', and 'Klüngel'—suggested a blurring of boundaries between the two ideas, with 'Fraktion', for example, connoting both faction and parliamentary party. To academics such as Delbrück,

---

[130] *Vorwärts*, 15 Oct. 1904.   [131] Ibid.

parties represented particular interests, which often contradicted the national interest represented by the state: 'each party is an organization, filled with a particular spirit, governed by general principles, which are not necessarily subordinate to the idea of the state.'[132] Since the emphasis was on the particularity of party interests and the universality of the state interest, the two concepts—party and faction—were frequently equated.[133] To politicians, however, who rarely distinguished their own party interest from the national interest, it was important to keep 'Partei' and 'Klüngel' separate. Whereas the former usually signified an organized group, preferably with a mass membership and necessarily with a canon of political principles and policies, the latter tended to imply a loose or tactical alliance of private interests, often without an ideology or a following. The deputies of parties, it was claimed, represented their electorate's ideas and interests: the deputies of factions pursued their own ideas and interests.

Regardless of the words used, most German commentators assumed at some time that French parties were little more than self-interested factions and virtually all agreed, albeit on different occasions, that the policies of French parties in government contravened France's national interest. Somehow, it was necessary, as Vogel said, to create a sense of national well-being above the desire for immediate personal satisfaction:

For the exemplary development, that is, for the internal prosperity and lasting existence of every well-ordered, ideally unchallengeable state...one thing...is absolutely necessary: what Montesquieu...somewhat emphatically called civic virtue (vertu), and what we, for our new, European conditions, consider to be well-enough described by the word public spirit [*Gemeinsinn*], namely an inculcated and acknowledged sense of the country's well-being, of civic duties and of strict legality.[134]

Yet, however this sense of duty to the nation was best to be nurtured, it was clear that the French system was ruled by other passions and interests: 'Yet, just how little of this [sense of public spirit] is to be found in the dominant majority of the French chambers, there can be no doubt. For a long time, their internal agitation, like the election struggle which produces it, have been more of an

[132] Delbrück, *Regierung und Volkswille*, 179.
[133] Ibid. 129–30, talked of 'Fraktionen' and 'Dieselbe Vielheit der Parteien' in the same paragraph.
[134] Vogel, *Die dritte französische Republik*, 346.

argument about party, local, and private interests than about the general interests of the country.'[135] Factional, parochial, and personal interest all came before national interest in French government, Vogel inferred.

Such opinions were commonplace in both government and press. French politics, it seemed, from a reading of the newspapers, had been reduced to an unprincipled struggle of politicians and their dependents for power and state income: 'The French government and the majority in the chamber know the saying that the well-being of the collectivity is the highest law only in theory: in practice, they keep unshakeably to that basic principle, which is evident to every egotist, that one has to look after one's own interests first. Their endeavour to keep themselves in the saddle for as long as possible is unmistakable and comes before all other considerations.'[136] Elections, in particular, demonstrated the poverty of political principle in France. The *Welt am Montag*, a mass-circulation weekly newspaper, which stood close to the left-liberal *Demokratische Vereinigung*, examined the French parties before the Assembly elections in 1910 only to find that the 'great questions of principle have been almost entirely excluded from the election contest'.[137] Whilst in England the elections turned on fundamental issues such as free trade and land reform, in France they were marked by personal insult and ambition: 'Here, one reads little more than phrases and personal insults in the so-called explanations of candidates' programmes.... Each has just one aim: *Ote-toi que je m'y mette!* Away with the other one, so that he himself can come to the trough!'[138] Münster had observed the same in 1899, after most candidates had sworn allegiance to parties, whose manifestos they did not believe in, simply to be elected. 'The whole of political life is, in this country, lies, deception and egotism', wrote the ambassador.[139]

When such deception and egotism were translated into government, the results were often damaging for France, it was contended. German newspapers from all political traditions attributed many of the significant junctures of French politics to personal and factional motives. Of course, there were variations. Whereas liberal criticisms

---

[135] Vogel, *Die dritte französische Republik*, 346. Also Kuhn, *Frankreich an der Zeitwende*, 103.
[136] *Germania*, 17 Nov. 1907; *Deutsche Tageszeitung*, 16 June 1902; *Rheinisch-Westfälische Zeitung*, 10 Aug. 1899.   [137] *Welt am Montag*, 25 Apr. 1910.
[138] Ibid. *Weser Zeitung*, 12 May 1914; *Frankfurter Zeitung*, 4 June 1902.
[139] Münster, 4 Dec. 1899, AA R7127, A14332.

of self-interest increased markedly after 1905, socialist, conservative, and Catholic condemnations were spread more or less evenly across the period.[140] *Germania*, for example, explained the fall of the Méline ministry, the resignation of Waldeck-Rousseau, the longevity of the Clemenceau administration, the success and demise of Briand, the dismissal of Millerand and the departure of Doumergue all in terms of personal and factional infighting.[141] As was to be expected, national interest was frequently lost amidst the welter of other competing interests, which were described by one writer as 'the unrelenting, most ruthless and selfish party struggle that can be imagined'.[142] Since the state actually consisted of such competing interests rather than balancing them, it could no longer coordinate consistent policies: 'Everywhere the lack of a fixed centre point, or of a basis, can be felt: individuals rock and sway, as does the whole.'[143] Even foreign policy, which was conducted consensually until the turn of the century, had been subordinated to faction,[144] as appeared to have been evinced by the collapse of the Sarrien and Caillaux ministries in March 1906 and January 1912, at the height of the Moroccan crises.

Because the priority of factions was power and office, new ministries were common and new policies rare, since incumbent administrations, constantly under attack from the opposition, found inactivity the best means of defence. Whereas unstable party government would have occasioned rapid and violent swings in policy, as one set of political priniciples replaced another, France suffered, in the German ambassador's estimation, the unstable government of factions, 'whose existence and programmes, subject more to personal than to

[140] *National-Zeitung*, 14 Jan. 1905; *Hamburgischer Correspondent*, 28 Oct. 1908, on Clemenceau; *Freisinnige Zeitung*, 12 Jan. 1912, on Caillaux; *Vossische Zeitung*, 12 Nov. 1910 and 19 Mar. 1913, on Briand. For the conservatives, see *Neue Preußische Zeitung*, 1 July 1898, on Brisson; ibid., 15 June 1899, on Dupuy; ibid., 18 Apr. 1900, on Waldeck-Rousseau; ibid., 20 Oct. 1906 and *Reichsbote*, 2 June 1907, on Clemenceau; *Münchner Allgemeine Zeitung*, 5 Nov. 1910 and 11 Mar. 1911, on Briand; *Neue Preußische Zeitung*, 28 June 1911, on Caillaux; ibid., 15 Jan. 1912 and 9 Mar. 1912, on Poincaré. For the socialists, see *Vorwärts*, 26 June 1898, on the Radicals and the mooted Sarrien Government; ibid., 29 June 1898, on Brisson; ibid., 6 May 1899, on Dupuy; ibid., 3 Dec. 1901, Waldeck-Rousseau; ibid., 10 Mar. 1906, on Rouvier; ibid., 11 Nov. 1906, on Clemenceau; ibid., 15 Apr. 1910 and 14 Jan. 1913, on Briand; ibid., 29 July 1911, on Caillaux; ibid., 14 June 1914, on Viviani.

[141] *Germania*, 25 June 1898, 22 May 1902, 11 Jan 1907, 1 Mar. 1911, 13 Jan. 1913, and 2 June 1914, respectively.

[142] Anon., *Das heutige Frankreich* (Hamm, 1903), 21. See also Münster, 25 May 1900, AA R7127, A6526; *Reichsbote*, 2 June 1907.   [143] Anon., *Das heutige Frankreich*, 21.

[144] *Neue Preußische Zeitung*, 8 Sept. 1900.

substantial influences, are still continually in flux'.[145] Thus, when factions acceded to office, they not only lacked their own distinctive political programme, they also lacked any incentive to act.[146] The trick in politics under the Third Republic, asserted Vogel, was to avoid responsibility in order to maintain power: 'People are courageous enough only to utter half the truth, and they never dare to stand against the tide. Almost everywhere, those at the helm and at the summit of the present republic think only in their own period of office of accepting the least possible responsibility.'[147] However, because most deputies in the Assembly behaved equally irresponsibly, Vogel continued, ministers were habitually abandoned by their erstwhile supporters, 'as it seemed advisable, from personal motives, to one set or the other. The result of this is the complete disintegration of parliamentarism.'[148] The immediate consequence, though, was ministerial instability.

It would be difficult to overstate the frequency of references in the German literature to the ephemerality of French ministries. France under the Third Republic had had so many administrations, it was said, that the populace no longer knew nor cared whether there was anyone in charge at all: ' "Do we have a ministry?" people have been asking each other jokingly in the street and at social gatherings for ten, or actually twelve, days now. No one takes the repeated failure of coalitions tragically, for it is just a question of candidates who have grabbed a portfolio in vain.'[149] It was standard form in the press and in diplomatic dispatches to record the number of each new ministry and the duration of each departed one, as if it were an ongoing joke at France's expense and, paradoxically, a repeated warning for Germany's edification. It will suffice here to examine German responses to just one such ministerial crisis, provoked by the resignation of Doumergue in June 1914. The headline of the *Deutsche Tageszeitung*, 'The 55th Ministerial Crisis of the Third Republic', was echoed by the German ambassador to France, Wilhelm von Schoen, who noted that the Ribot ministry was not only the fifty-fifth in the forty-four year history of the Third Republic, but also the fourth administration of the short presidency of Raymond

---

[145] Schoen, 16 Apr. 1911, AA R6608, A6308. Münster, 17 Sept. 1898, AA R7019, A10796; *Neue Preußische Zeitung*, 10 Oct. 1913.

[146] *Frankfurter Zeitung*, cited in *Germania*, 25 June 1898.

[147] Vogel, *Die dritte französische Republik*, 89.   [148] Ibid. 89.

[149] *National-Zeitung*, 28 June 1898.

Poincaré.[150] In an article in *Der Tag*, entitled 'French Crises', Franz Wugk attempted to put the crisis into context. The austere figures calculated by the in-house mathematicians of the Palais Bourbon did not do justice to the inconstancy of government in France, he claimed, which in fact had been a feature of French politics since 1789, and had merely reached its nadir after 1870: 'Actually, France has not emerged from crisis since 1789, and the Third Republic is one, single enduring crisis. Long-lived ministries are rare exceptions.'[151] In a similar vein, publications as diverse as the nationalist *Rheinisch-Westfälische Zeitung*, the conservative-Protestant *Reichsbote*, and the liberal *Vossische Zeitung* all discussed the congenital instability of government under the republican regime.[152]

The most obvious cause of ministerial instability was the dependence of government on the Assembly. Lawyers such as Siegfried Brie and Georg Jellinek recognized that a high turnover of administrations was the obverse side of the fusion of executive and legislative functions. By avoiding a stricter division of competencies, the French republic had avoided the risk of stalemate between president and parliament, but at the expense of ministerial continuity. Once again, the United States served as a corroborative counter-example, having secured stable government by separating its functions:

The French system is better suited to guard against conflicts between these organs or at least to bring them to a rapid end but, on the other hand, it easily impairs the stability and energy of the government. The dependence of ministries on parliamentary majorities must in any event be seen as highly questionable so long as those parties which oppose the present constitutional structures out of principle are inclined and in a position to use every opportunity to bring down the incumbent ministry.[153]

Newspapers like *Germania* made the same point for a lay audience, equating 'monarchy' with a separation of executive and legislative competencies and 'republic' with their merger: 'In monarchies, ministers resign when they incur the displeasure of their ruler or when they have entered a cul-de-sac, which they do not know how to get in or out of. In republics, every small stone on the path can cause

---

[150] *Deutsche Tageszeitung*, 3 June 1914.   [151] *Tag*, 7 June 1914.
[152] *Rheinisch-Westfälische Zeitung*, 3 June 1914; *Reichsbote*, 27 June 1914; *Vossische Zeitung*, 4 June 1914.
[153] Brie, *Die gegenwärtige Verfassung Frankreichs*, 40–1. Jellinek, *Allgemeine Staatslehre*, 728.

their fall from office.'[154] The assumption underlying such assertions was that the Assembly would want to bring down the government at every opportunity. In other words, it was assumed that there was no majority party or lasting coalition of parties, but rather a number of greedy factions, anxious to gain power: 'Such an [ordered and secure] majority is only conceivable where organized, strong, and principled parties are in existence.... We seek a majority in the French parliament in vain, so we look for a dominant party instead; we find neither one nor the other and, consequently, no stable government.'[155] Moreover, the presence in the lower chamber of at least some non-republican groups, who voted against the government almost indiscriminately, lent the opposition 'false' weight, to be used against all administrations.[156] At worst, warned the *National-Zeitung*, this could lead to a meeting of the extremities and permanent political instability: 'For it is again only a question of time until these extreme left-wing party groups find themselves, given a suitable occasion, in the same camp as the extremes of the right, and ministerial crises without end will from then on become a standing institution again.'[157] To many German commentators, French governments were dependent on a chamber which was composed of opportunist factions in the centre and anti-republican parties in the wings. Whichever element was stressed most—opportunism or anti-republicanism—the outcome was the same: instability.

If the transience of ministries was one immediate consequence of faction in government, at least to German correspondents, the inefficacy of administrations was another. The individual responses of officials and parties will be examined in Chapter 5, but it is necessary here to show how lack of reform was linked in German accounts to the subordination of the legislature to the executive, and to the concomitant entry of unstable, self-interested factions into government. Liberals, who were the last to become disenchanted with the parliamentary republic, in the mid-1900s, still wavered between absolute condemnation of the Radicals' cynicism and avarice, on the one hand, and belief in their good intentions, on the other.[158] Yet even newspapers like the *Vossische* and the *Frankfurter Zeitung*, which maintained

---

[154] *Germania*, 13 Jan. 1913.
[155] Steinhauser, *Neuestes aus Frankreich*, 10.
[156] Delbrück, *Regierung und Volkswille*, 129.
[157] *National-Zeitung*, 16 Jan. 1905.   [158] See below, Ch. 5, sect. 5.

that the core of a reformist Radical Party remained intact, were obliged to admit that that core was surrounded by such a tangle of factions that reform had inevitably been thwarted:

> The legislative session which is now coming to an end has been a completely fruitless one. . . . The deeper reason for this fruitlessness lies in the fact that there is no majority in parliament which is large and coherent enough to implement its will to reform. There are, indeed, majorities, but only coincidental ones; they are subject to change and are more suited to obstructing good causes than realizing them.[159]

The right-wing press in Germany was less guarded in its criticism than its liberal counterpart. It took the agreed weaknesses of government-by-faction in France—instability, greed, obstruction, irresponsibility—and related them gleefully to government inefficacy. In an article headed 'Ein Schwatzrekord', the *Berliner Neueste Nachrichten*, for example, examined obstructionism in the Assembly: 'Let us take a parliamentary country "par excellence", for example France, and see how they go about their "work" there.'[160] When parliament desired, the newspaper continued, it could pass the budget in three weeks, as in 1907, but usually it chose to block government, as in 1913, when budgetary proposals were still not settled after nine months and 663 speeches, delivered by 598 different speakers.[161] The *Dresdner Nachrichten*, for its part, seized upon greed as an explanation for the stilling of France's reforming zeal: 'Wherever you look, *reforms* are *needed urgently*. But the deputies care far too much about their parliamentary seat that they can do anything for the country. This, however, is less their fault than that of the *parliamentary system*, which is dominant in France.'[162] What all such reports had in common was a willingness to harness perceived individual shortcomings of French government to a general critique of the parliamentary system. As shall be seen later, this proclivity was shared, sometimes with qualifications, by liberal, Catholic, and socialist newspapers, as well as by official correspondence.[163]

By their own criteria, French governments had failed, concluded the *Tägliche Rundschau*. They continued, of course, to advert to the great

---

[159] *Frankfurter Zeitung*, 4 Nov. 1913; *Vossische Zeitung*, 6 Apr. 1914.
[160] *Berliner Neueste Nachrichten*, 6 Apr. 1913. See also Osten, *Die Fachvereine und die sociale Bewegung in Frankreich*, 95–6; Kuhn, *Aus dem modernen Babylon*, 39.
[161] *Berliner Neueste Nachrichten*.
[162] *Dresdner Nachrichten*, 23 Apr. 1910.   [163] See below, Ch. 6.

future tasks of French policy making, but had neglected to enact even
the minimal pledges of Gambetta's Belleville programme of 1869.
Politics in the Third Republic had become the idle sport of self-
interested men—'Fünfzehntausend-Franken-Männer', as deputies
were called, after their salaries had been raised from 9,000 to 15,000
francs in 1906—and political reforms languished behind displays of
rhetoric:

As impartial spectators of French parliamentary sport, we ask ourselves how our
fifteen-thousand-franc-men would deal in six weeks with the military question,
with the defence of irreligious elementary schools, with the socialist legislation,
with nationalization projects, with proportional representation and, above
all, with fiscal and tax reform—for these trivialities are still outstanding from the
old republican agenda.[164]

It appeared that faction in government had hindered necessary changes
in laws regulating polity, society, and economy in France. But that was
not all. It also allowed faction into the bureaucracy, which, of course,
implemented existing laws: not only did the French political state fail to
pass just law, it was said, it also failed to administer law justly.

3. Bureaucracy and Bureaucratization

In Germany, France was paraded as the archetype of centralization.[165] Even for an ardent defender of state sovereignty such as
Treitschke, the extent to which power had been centralized in
the neighbouring state was 'off-putting'.[166] Yet most academics
acknowledged that the concentration of power in some form or other
was the *conditio sine qua non* for the rise of European great powers in
the eighteenth and nineteenth centuries. Germans, wrote Treitschke,
were particularly sensitive to the need for state power, having suffered under barely protected princely states before 1871. The anti-
state proclivities of British and French liberals simply betrayed
complacent ignorance: 'How wonderful that we Germans, with our history of fragmented states, must warn a Frenchman and an Englishman
to think more highly of the state! Mill and Laboulaye both live in a
strong, respected state; they take this rich blessing as self-evident and

---

[164] *Tägliche Rundschau*, 30 May 1914.
[165] *Germania*, 9 Feb. 1899; Mahrenholtz, *Frankreich*, 162; Schmitz, *Das Land der Wirklichkeit*, 119.
[166] Treitschke, *Politik*, i. 43.

see in the state only a frightening power, which threatens people's freedom. We Germans have had our perception of the state's worth sharpened by a painful absence.'[167] France, which was regarded as the greatest continental power for most of the eighteenth and nineteenth centuries, appeared to prove the connection between an extensive, centralized bureaucracy and a powerful state. Because of its association in the minds of German observers with the successful foreign policies of absolutist and Napoleonic regimes, French bureaucracy still elicited some praise during the Bismarckian and Wilhelmine eras.

Following the thesis of Alexis de Tocqueville, it was widely believed that a 'modern' French bureaucracy had been conceived by the absolutist rulers of the *ancien régime*, who used salaried *intendants*—the forerunners of *préfets*, it was claimed—to circumvent an unwieldy system of venal offices.[168] Otto Hintze, author of one of the main analyses of bureaucratization, was manifestly Tocquevillian in his approach, for example, emphasizing that there was no necessary link between centralization, bureaucracy, and democracy, since paid, removable and interfering bureaucrats were already in place before the democratic reforms of the French revolution:

The government helped itself out by introducing a new category of official beside these venal and heritable offices, which in contrast to the old posts was based only on a revocable contract and was kept in the strictest dependency, and in whose hands real political power and responsibility was now concentrated: these were the provincial intendants, the precursors of today's French prefects.... These intendants now became the real political organs of the French government during the ancien regime.[169]

The motive for such administrative innovation amidst the rococo extravagance of eighteenth-century France seemed, in the first instance, to be efficiency—'The modern state is a "business"', in Weber's phrase—and, in the second instance, power, for this above all was seen in Wilhelmine historiography to characterize French absolutism.[170] Absolute monarchy in France found the approval of authors of textbooks and polemics alike because it was perceived to have concentrated and rationalized power in order to build the

---

[167] Treitschke, 'Die Freiheit' (1861), in *Historische und politische Aufsätze*, iii. 15.
[168] Tocqueville, *L'Ancien Régime et la Révolution* (Paris, 1967). The work first appeared in France and, translated, in Germany in 1856.
[169] Hintze, 'Ber Beamtenstand' (1911), in *Soziologie und Geschichte*, 88–9.
[170] Ibid. 121; Weber, *Wirtschaft und Gesellschaft*, 825.

nation-state.[171] To Haas, Schmitz and others, restricted freedoms
and centralized bureaucracy were necessary components of the
Nationalstaat, even if, from a twentieth-century perspective, France
appeared to have gone too far: 'Absolute monarchy thus remained the
French form of government until 1789. Traces of any limitation of the
monarchical will are to be found nowhere; no hint of political freedom,
nor guarantees of the rights, freedom and property of the inhabitants.... This form of government allowed France to achieve national
unification earlier than Germany or Italy. On the other hand, it
favoured the establishment of that *over-exaggerated centralization*,
which is characteristic of the French state.'[172] To Hintze, both
Germany and France had needed some form of absolutism and some
degree of centralization in order to achieve great-power status.[173]

This link between centralization and power appeared to be confirmed by the Napoleonic pedigree of the French bureaucratic
machine. It was a truism in Germany that Bonaparte's restructuring
of administration and concentrating of authority had helped him to
conquer most of Europe.[174] Even critics of twentieth-century French
bureaucracy, such as Hermann Fernau, acknowledged that it had
been effective as it had been introduced, at the start of the nineteenth
century: 'At the time of Napoleon, this strict centralization and love
of stamped paper was an impressive achievement, which indeed
served as a model for most other states.'[175] It was hard to deny that
Napoleonic forms of administration had then remained in place for
the next 110 years.[176] Until the 1890s, at least, it had been common in
Germany, not only to praise the efficiency of the French bureaucracy,
which was one institution that Heinrich von Sybel thought worthy of
imitation,[177] but also to contend that bureaucrats actually ran the
French state and determined policy, since ministerial portfolios were
passed on so quickly that incumbents had neither the time nor the
knowledge to overrule their departments: 'only ministers [are
replaced] not ministries. The immediate subordinate of the minister
knows and practises all the secrets of state service.... He and the
staff of lower officials remain when ministers come and go. By this

[171] Vogel, *Die dritte französische Republik*, 31.
[172] Haas, *Frankreich*, 65–7. Schmitz, *Das Land der Wirklichkeit*, 103.
[173] Hintze, 'Der Beamtenstand' (1911), in *Soziologie und Geschichte*, 89.
[174] Haas, *Frankreich*, 127.   [175] Fernau, *Französische Demokratie*, 39.
[176] Vogel, *Die dritte französische Republik*, 2; Haas, *Frankreich*, 120.
[177] Sybel, *Was wir von Frankreich lernen können*, 12.

means alone is the continuation of business possible.'[178] It seemed
that a professional, Napoleonic bureaucracy constituted the unseen
backbone of the Third Republic. According to Weber, this fact
accounted for the constancy of government in France, despite frequent changes of regime.[179]

If French administration continued to profit from the legend of a
powerful and efficient Napoleonic regime, it was also connected by
Germans to the French revolution and democracy.[180] This apparent
contradiction between the bureaucracy as part of an absolutist-
authoritarian tradition, on the one hand, and of a democratic tradition, on the other, was mitigated by a German propensity to link
French absolutism, Caesarism, and republicanism to equality.
Absolute monarchs, dictators, and republican ministries, it was
claimed, all worked against the inequality of inherited administration
by notables.[181] In this respect, mass democracy in France was simply
the last of a series of regimes which had sought to replace feudal,
patrimonial, and plutocratic privileges in government with a professional bureaucracy.[182] It differed from those other regimes, however,
in seeking to achieve equality for its own sake, that is, to redistribute
power more equally. Democracy and bureaucracy therefore enjoyed a
special relationship, Max Weber argued: 'Within the state administration itself, the growth of bureaucratization in France, North
America and now England is evidently a parallel process of democracy.'[183] The problem for democracies, though, was that functionaries, by virtue of their specialist knowledge and their security of
tenure, threatened to escape popular control: 'Hence, wherever possible, political democracy strives to shorten the term of office by
election and recall and by not binding the candidate to a special
expertness. Thereby democracy inevitably comes into conflict with
the bureaucratic tendencies which, by its fight against notable rule,
democracy has produced.'[184] This restriction of the power of the
bureaucracy by means of political interference did not, however,

[178] J. Reber, *Ein Blick auf Frankreichs Schulwesen. Eine pädagogische Skizze*
(Aschaffenburg, 1897), 5; Haas, *Frankreich*, 132. *National-Zeitung*, 28 June 1898.

[179] M.Weber, in Eisenstadt (ed.), *Max Weber*, 77.

[180] Haas, *Frankreich*, 120. Weber, in Eisenstadt (ed.), *Max Weber*, 73: 'In France, the
Revolution and still more Bonapartism have made the bureaucracy all-powerful.'

[181] Weber, in Eisenstadt (ed.), *Max Weber*, 73.

[182] Ibid. 71.

[183] Weber, *Wirtschaft und Gesellschaft*, 568.

[184] Ibid. Eisenstadt (ed.), *Max Weber*, 72.

increase the populace's influence on administration, which was the real sense of democratization, but merely served, in Weber's opinion, to substitute autocratic party leaders for unanswerable civil servants.[185] Democracy, he continued, had set in train a process of bureaucratization and subsequent bureaucratic politicization which merely levelled the governed without empowering them.[186]

It was accepted by all German political parties that the Third Republic had adopted France's centralized bureaucracy without contradicting its own principles. To socialists such as Friedrich Engels 'the oppressive power of the hitherto centralized government' was welcomed by all regimes as an instrument of class domination: 'In reality, the state is nothing more than a machine for one class to oppress another, and indeed no less so in a democratic republic than in a monarchy.'[187] To liberal and conservative newspapers such as the *Hannoverscher Courier*, *Post*, and *Deutsche Tageszeitung*, democratic centralization arose out of the logic of a political system rather than the domination of a social class. It was expected that democratic, parliamentary governments, unchecked by a strict division of competencies, would appropriate powers and destroy intermediate bodies, which stood between citizen and state: 'Republicanism follows exactly the same line as absolutism in the polarization [*sic*] of power towards a supreme authority.... Mistrustful, fearing that somewhere and somehow an independent power might establish itself, undermining state power, central government wishes to order and oversee everything which happens in the state by itself; no independence for local organs.'[188] To many German writers, this elimination of rival centres of power appeared, perhaps unsurprisingly, to be an expression of the tyranny of the majority over the minority, for which Jacobinism had become the watchword in Germany.[189] As Max Weber observed, a centralized state bureaucracy acted on behalf of the whole nation: its actions were superior to mass or community actions, because it represented the wishes of more people: 'under otherwise equal conditions, well-planned, ordered and directed "societal action" is superior to any

---

[185] Eisenstadt (ed.), *Max Weber*, 72–3.   [186] Ibid.

[187] F. Engels, *Einleitung* to K. Marx, *Der Bürgerkrieg in Frankreich*, 3rd edn. (Berlin, 1891), 12–13.

[188] *Deutsche Tageszeitung*, 24 Apr. 1910; *Hannoverscher Courier*, 24 Sept. 1907; *Post*, 10 Nov. 1898.

[189] Osten, *Die Fachvereine und die sociale Bewegung in Frankreich*, 5–8; P. Rühlmann, *Der staatsbürgerliche Unterricht in Frankreich* (Leipzig, 1912), 1.

resistance put up by "mass" or "communal action".'[190] Bureaucratic centralization seemed to suit parliamentary democracy.

A centralized bureaucracy was, of course, perceived to be particularly susceptible to political interference in a parliamentary state such as France. For Hintze, differences between the bureaucratic structures of the *Kaiserreich* and the Third Republic were rooted in constitutional soil: 'Naturally, general political and constitutional factors play a role in the creation of a law for the civil service. Our German bureaucratic estate [*Beamtenstand*] rests to a considerable degree on the monarchical-constitutional form of government which we have, in contrast to the parliamentary means of government in other countries.'[191] First, the French republics, in abolishing the monarchy, had broken with the past and renounced historical in favour of political legitimacy. This had exorcised any hint 'of the old spirit of princely service', which characterized the allegedly dutiful German bureaucracy, and replaced it with revocable commissions, which encouraged short-term self-interest.[192]

Second, the tiered, unitary structure of the French state granted, as Vogel noted, extensive formal powers to French ministers of the interior: 'Thus, the ministry of the interior constitutes one of the main pillars of the domestic government and administration of France, from which the net of state power envelops the whole country.'[193] The fulcrum of the system was the prefect, who was directly responsible to the interior minister and who oversaw local councils, conscription, tax collection, departmental expenditure, the appointment and dismissal of teachers, the running of prisons, and the building of roads and bridges.[194] Whereas in the *Kaiserreich* ministers were bureaucrats themselves and were further limited by the separate jurisdictions of the federal states, for example over education, it seemed to German authors that French politicians were able to use the French state to intervene politically in all areas.

Third, the practice of purging the administration with the accession of each new ministry to office was seen by Hintze and others to be a specifically parliamentary principle: 'The parliamentary

[190] Weber, *Wirtschaft und Gesellschaft*, 570.
[191] Hintze, 'Der Beamtenstand' (1911), in *Soziologie und Geschichte*, 95.
[192] Ibid. [193] Vogel, *Die dritte französische Republik*, 381.
[194] Haas, *Frankreich*, 136–7, 157; F. Brüggemann and F. Groppler, *Volk- und Fortbildungs-Schulwesen Frankreichs im Jahre 1900* (Berlin, 1901), 9–13; Rühlmann, *Der staatsbürgerliche Unterricht in Frankreich*, 9.

principle of replacing civil servants in accordance with the fortunes of party governments is of course also practised in France, here on a much greater scale even than in England.'[195] The 'Präfektenschub' and 'Unterpräfektenschub', which accompanied changes of government, were a regular source of comment in diplomatic and newspaper correspondence.[196] What was more, dismissals from so-called political posts in the upper echelons of the system created uncertainty lower down, it was said, because of prefects' formidable influence over a wide range of appointments and promotion, from postmen to police commissioners.[197] The result, continued Hintze, was that civil servants tended, at least in public, to toe a political line rather than giving balanced advice: 'A functionary must be very skilful in his political manoeuvring in order to escape the effects of the feared épuration, which removes all political opponents of the new political system.'[198]

Fourth, bureaucrats in France were, it was held, protected neither by law nor by ordinance, which allowed politicians to threaten and cajole them. Haas's list of French failings in this regard had reached a wide German audience by the mid-1900s, at the latest, as newspapers reported on Clemenceau's attempt to appease teachers and postal workers with the promise of a full 'Beamtengesetz', such as had existed in Prussia in all but name since 1851:[199] there was under the Third Republic no law over the appointment and payment of bureaucrats; no formal qualifications were required for many posts, including prefectures; appeals against unfair dismissal were referred to a political tribunal; and pension rights applied only after 30 years of service.[200] Because politicians in power benefited from a lack of regulation and security in civil service ranks, the system had not been reformed, despite functionaries' plaints. It followed, wrote Vogel, that the French political state would want to maintain a political bureaucracy:

Arbitrariness in the replacement and appointment of new civil servants takes place very often since fixed norms for the taking on and promotion of employees

[195] Hintze, 'Der Beamtenstand' (1911), in *Soziologie und Geschichte*, 97.
[196] *Neue Preußische Zeitung*, 22 July 1898; *Germania*, 24 June 1902, 19 July 1904, and 13 July 1906. See e.g. Münster, 30 June 1898, AA R7125, A7717 and 23 July 1898, AA R6592, A8617, on the Brisson government, and Radolin, 31 Oct. 1906, AA R7283, A18399, on Clemenceau.
[197] Vogel, *Die dritte französische Republik*, 349–50; Kuhn, *Frankreich an der Zeitwende*, 4–5.
[198] Hintze, 'Der Beamtenstand' (1911), in *Soziologie und Geschichte*, 97.
[199] Ibid. 92.   [200] Haas, *Frankreich*, 131–2, 137.

only exist for very few branches of the civil administration. . . . These serious shortcomings are the result of strict centralization itself and of the absolutist stamp of the entire administrative machine, which was set up very elaborately by the first Napoleon and which continues to operate with very few changes to its structure. Nevertheless, such shortcomings have become more and more noticeable with the rapid alternation of parties and people at the head of the state. Moreover, there has never been a lack . . . of loud complaints about this. As soon as a party gets into power, however, it shrinks from doing anything which could diminish the fullness of its power and it allows itself again and again to be gratified by . . . the unlimited nature of that power, all the more so since there is never a lack of pressure from those who desire or need posts.[201]

The most obvious consequence of such political control of the bureaucracy was political appointment and nepotism. Concepts like 'Vetternwirtschaft', 'Günstlingswesen', 'Gönnerschaft', 'Freibeuterei', and 'l'assiette au beurre' became leitmotifs in German accounts of French administration. This was particularly true of liberal reports of 1907–1910, which contained numerous references to corruption and favouritism, and of conservative articles of 1898–1900, 1905–6, and 1909–12.[202] The Third Republic had, as the *Münchner Allgemeine Zeitung* commented, neglected the separation of politics and administration—'the separation of politics and administration [is] something incomprehensible [in France]'—with the result that the parties came to look upon the bureaucracy as a type of 'Placierungsbureau' for relatives, friends, clients, and voters.[203] To Vogel, as to many other German commentators, the parties which constituted the majority in the Assembly looked upon politics, not in terms of national interest, but as a struggle for power and spoils: 'the acquisition of power and control over the budget, namely ministerial portfolios and miscellaneous offices and posts, rich salaries, sinecures, preferments of all kinds'.[204] All classes had self-interestedly come to see the state as a source of income rather than the instrument of the

---

[201] Vogel, *Die dritte französische Republik*, 348–9.
[202] For the liberal press, for instance, see *Frankfurter Zeitung*, 4 June 1902, 15 May 1907; *Hamburgischer Correspondent*, 17 Mar. 1907; *Hannoverscher Courier*, 24 Sept. 1907; *Vossische Zeitung*, 19 Mar. 1908, 19 Mar. 1909; *Berliner Tageblatt*, 25 July 1909; *Welt am Montag*, 25 Apr. 1910. For conservative newspapers, see, e.g. *Neue Preußische Zeitung*, 9 June 1898, 7 July 1898, 19 Jan. 1899; *Dresdner Nachrichten*, 23 Aug. 1899; *Neue Preußische Zeitung*, 18 May 1900, 14 Dec. 1900, 28 July 1905; *Hamburger Nachrichten*, 28 Jan. 1906; *Reichsbote*, 26 Sept. 1909; *Münchner Allgemeine Zeitung*, 15 Jan. 1910; *Reichsbote*, 8 Nov. 1910; *Allgemeine Zeitung*, 11 Mar. 1911; *Deutsche Nachrichten*, 13 July 1912.
[203] *Münchner Allgemeine Zeitung*, 15 Jan. 1910.
[204] Vogel, *Die dritte französische Republik*, 346.

general good.[205] At first, place-finding had been restricted, as Kuhn
admitted, to the higher administrative levels—the *Vossische Zeitung*
noted that by 1908 each minister had up to twelve private secretaries[206]—but 'since these no longer sufficed, all lower-level posts
were filled by politicians, or according to political considerations.'[207]
Instead of the handful of patrons of a court, 900 senators and deputies
clamoured to distribute the largesse of the state in order to serve their
own interests and secure their own political positions.[208]

Inevitably, German correspondents asserted, the French
bureaucracy increased in size. This, then, was a third type of
bureaucratization, associated with parliamentary systems of government. If the first bureaucracies had been created by a war-pressed
need for efficiency and succeeding bureaucratization had been perpetuated by a democratic struggle against notable privilege, the new
parliamentary-political state expanded of its own accord, like a
private company serving the interests of its own employees and
shareholders, at the expense of the national interest. Naturally, the
other impulses towards bureaucratization remained: Otto Hintze
and Max Weber were merely the most celebrated of many prophets
of an ineluctable expansion of the state.[209] Yet, from different quarters, Germans acknowledged that the French state had expanded
anomalously. The figures in textbooks were clear enough: 'The
number of civil servants has increased greatly since 1870, indeed it
has doubled in many branches, so that there are about 350,000 functionaries with 454–455 million francs salary.'[210] But the interpretations of the political press were much more telling. It was no
surprise that its estimations of the size and of the cost of the French
bureaucracy exceeded those of the textbooks.

As was to be expected, Catholic and conservative newspapers portrayed French bureaucratization as the product of unbridled nepotism amongst republican factions. *Germania*, for instance, pointed
out that there were fewer pressures in France towards bureaucratic
expansion, since its population had barely altered since 1846.

[205] Vogel, *Die dritte französische Republik*, 306.
[206] *Vossische Zeitung*, 19 Mar. 1908.
[207] Kuhn, *Frankreich an der Zeitwende*, 4–5.
[208] Vogel, *Die dritte französische Republik*, 347.
[209] Hintze, 'Der Beamtenstand' (1911), in *Soziologie und Geschichte*, 68–70, on the
increases in the size of the German bureaucracy, and 121, on the inevitability of bureaucratization even in the United States and Britain, where conditions were different.
[210] Mahrenholtz, *Frankreich*, 311–12.

Nevertheless, its bureaucracy had increased threefold:

Government and parliament compete with one another to create as many new civil service posts as possible and thereby to provide and care for their creatures. At present, France has 608,511 state and 262,078 communal functionaries.... Whoever gains power and a reputation in France wants to dispose, as 'Patronus', of as numerous a 'Clientela' as possible...and this goal is best achieved when clients are placed at the state trough, where possible in the most sought-after feeding places. That is what one calls serving the republic![211]

The *Neue Preußische Zeitung* agreed. Between 1896 and 1901, the number of French state employees had risen by 82,000 to 625,000, at a total cost of 1,000 million francs.[212] Most of this was spent on the small but numerous salaries of lower civil servants,[213] whose superfluous posts had been created by political protectors: 'This French civil service, which cannot be compared to the German one, has become a real menace for the life of the French people. People push their way to the state trough in order to earn an assured, albeit scarcely adequate income. The government accommodates this tendency and unrelentingly creates new legions of officials.'[214]

Less expectedly, perhaps, liberal newspapers such as the *Hannoverscher Courier* coincided with the *Neue Preußische Zeitung* in contending that bureaucratization had taken off under the Third Republic.[215] In a three-column, front-page article, entitled 'Der Bureaukratismus in Frankreich', the newspaper reassured its readers that German difficulties concerning bureaucratization paled in comparison with those experienced by France: 'Repeatedly, bitter complaints were made in the Prussian Landtag about bureaucratism, which has come to predominate in our country, but however bad it might be in the land of pure reason: beyond the Vosges there is a much bigger and richer harvest of official pen-pushers.'[216] In 1873 there had been only 285,000 French civil servants, costing 340 million francs; by 1890, there were already 416,000, costing 627 millions. Whereas state administration amounted to 15.7 francs per head in Prussia, in France it stood at 24.07. Such expansion, the *Courier* continued, was driven more by push than pull. Frenchmen had become accustomed to the comfortable security of positions within

[211] *Germania*, 27 Mar. 1908.
[212] *Neue Preußische Zeitung*, 12 Sept. 1906.
[213] Ibid., 17 May 1899.   [214] Ibid., 12 Sept. 1906.
[215] *Hannoverscher Courier*, 24 Sept. 1907; *Neue Preußische Zeitung*, 28 July 1905; *Vossische Zeitung*, 11 May 1909.
[216] Ibid.

the state and expected posts to be found for them there: 'Why should one send one's only son to the hard school of independent struggle, into the world, when one can shelter him in a civil service career by the proved and rarely, if ever, failing means of nepotism.'[217] Because the French political state proved unable to resist the demand for an ever-greater number of new posts, the bureaucracy went on increasing in size, to the point where it threatened to bankrupt the state itself.

French administrative practice ran counter not only to German bureaucratic procedure, but also to the political ideology of the *Kaiserreich*. According to apologists such as Delbrück, the German system of constitutional government turned on the integrity of the bureaucracy, which constituted 'die politische Intelligenz' required to initiate and carry out policy.[218] 'Politics' simply consisted of finding majorities for bills in the Reichstag: it did not impinge on the formulation and implementation of laws, which came within the purview of a government of bureaucrats. It was essential that the bureaucracy remained impartial, for, in suggesting and executing laws, it was, in effect, the real power within the political system: 'the civil service [constitutes] a neutral point [*Indifferenzpunkt*] in our state.'[219] Bureaucratic impartiality had been achieved in Germany, Delbrück concurred with Hintze, by insisting on technical specialization, with administration dominated by lawyers, technicians, and engineers, on social equilibrium, with middle-class functionaries outnumbering their noble counterparts, and on functional neutrality, with a salaried, pensionable bureaucracy standing apart from conflicts between capital and labour: 'the state is certainly not an economic enterprise...its purpose is not economic profit, it does not wish to produce goods, but law, peace, security, and power...the central idea within the civil service is duty, not economic and social self-interest.'[220] The German bureaucracy was, in short, a class in itself, or *Stand*, tied by function to the interests of the nation. Imbued with values such as loyalty, welfare, and legality, it was lauded by Hintze as the best administration in the world:

On the whole, German civil service law is the best in the whole of Europe, i.e. in all the world. Germany is the classic bureaucratic country in the European world, like China in Asia and Egypt in the ancient world. These comparisons

---

[217] *Hannoverscher Courier*, 24 Sept. 1907; *Neue Preußische Zeitung*, 28 July 1905; *Vossische Zeitung*, 11 May 1909.

[218] Delbrück, *Regierung und Volkswille*, 187.   [219] Ibid. 181.

[220] Hintze, 'Der Beamtenstand' (1911), in *Soziologie und Geschichte*, 75–6, 99–113; Delbrück, *Regierung und Volkswille*, 183.

show that it is only a question of a conditional lead here. Nevertheless, this lead in Germany at least rests on the idea of the *Rechtsstaat* and with feelings of loyalty and welfare, with which the civil service is strongly imbued—factors, in short, of which we do not need to be ashamed.[221]

By contrast, the French bureaucracy had, in Hintze's and in Delbrück's opinion, surrendered its integrity to the logic of the political state. The unofficial policy of nepotism and intervention practised by French ministers, who were of course politicians and not bureaucrats, had undermined the technical competence, political independence, and moral disinterestedness of French administration: 'it is of importance whether or not a country has a specialized, reliable, and independent civil service, and genuine reformers in France wish to achieve this. The Panamists, however, and everything connected to them, wish to carry on enjoying the sweet fruits of the present system forever, since it offers to those who are incumbent a comparatively secure, long-term post.'[222] It was significant that both Hintze and Delbrück continued to label French political and bureaucratic practice 'Panamist', 20 years after the first disclosures of governmental corruption during the Panama affair.[223] Not all Germans went so far. Nevertheless, there was cross-party agreement that the Third Republic had created conditions conducive to bureaucratic disaffection: its civil service was characterized by low-pay, insecurity, and political vetting: 'Yet more damaging, though, are the consequences which this insecurity of official positions... creates for public service itself and for the spirit of the bureaucratic estate. There can be little talk here of full commitment to one's post.'[224] The emergence and disobedience of teachers', rail, and postal workers' unions in the mid-1900s horrified most German observers, at the same time as underlining the nefarious consequences of political interference in administration. More important still, such interference was seen to preclude a whole range of policies, including nationalization, social insurance, and income tax, because the public did not trust in the fairness, impartiality, and competence of French bureaucrats. As Bülow remarked, few things occasioned more resentment than

---

[221] Hintze, 'Der Beamtenstand' (1911), in *Soziologie und Geschichte*, 95.

[222] Delbrück, *Regierung und Volkswille*, 25.

[223] Hintze, 'Der Beamtenstand' (1911), in *Soziologie und Geschichte*, 97.

[224] Ibid.; Münster, 7 June 1898, AA R7170, A6843, the German consul in Le Hâvre, 19 Oct. 1910, AA R6607, A17617, and Schön, 15 Apr. 1911, AA R6608, A6309. Vogel, *Die dritte französische Republik*, 350.

injustices perpetrated by seemingly omnipotent state functionaries. Compared to France, few compatriots denied the chancellor's assertion that Germany had escaped lightly.[225] The fusion of executive and legislative functions at the top of the French political system had eventually impaired the administration of policy at the bottom.

[225] Bülow, *Deutsche Politik*, 213. Hillebrand, *Frankreich und die Franzosen*, 124–5.

4

Universal Suffrage and the Spectre of Dictatorship

1. Equality, Individualism, and Control

The connection between nation-building and popular participation predisposed Germans of virtually all political persuasions towards some sort of elected, representative chamber. European experience during and after the revolutionary wars seemed to have demonstrated that the new nation-states of the nineteenth century required popular support, ultimately because such regimes appeared to be more stable in peacetime and stronger in times of war than their undemocratic predecessors. The best way to tie the populace to the nation's fate was to give it a role in government, it was held.[1] The post-medieval state should be 'a real popular power..., acting within fixed forms and bound to the will of the majority of citizens', wrote Treitschke.[2] Oskar Schmitz, whose leanings were similarly to the right, expanded Treitschke's point: the French Revolution, above all, had broken the fissile feudal bonds of the Middle Ages and bound the 'Kräfte der Gesellschaft', or social resources, to the nation-state; absolutism, which had been necessary to unify German and French territories under Richelieu, Mazarin, Friedrich Wilhelm I, and Friedrich II, had now been superseded by stronger *Nationalstaaten*, which had cultivated national consciousness by allowing the populace to administer its own affairs.[3] Likewise, for the left, of course, popular involvement in government was recognized to be both desirable and necessary. Once again, the French Revolution was depicted as the most important juncture. To Hermann Fernau,

---

[1] Delbrück, *Regierung und Volkswille*, 45–6.
[2] Treitschke, 'Die Freiheit' (1861), in *Historische und politische Aufsätze*, iii. 7; Delbrück, *Regierung und Volkswille*, 147.
[3] Schmitz, *Das Land der Wirklichkeit*, 103.

for instance, it had allowed the expression of popular consciousness for the first time: 'Democracy, which achieved dominance with the revolution of 1789, was thus less of a counterfeit of popular tradition by power-hungry demagogues than the correction of earlier misrepresentation of popular conscience by the monarchy and aristocracy.'[4] To the pacifist Alfred Fried, changes in technology and communication had combined in the 'political' era after 1789 to make the 'democratic ethos... the leading ethos in Europe': 'Under "democracy" we should understand... the development of the masses into a political factor, which has come into being since the French revolution, and especially since the middle of the previous century.... The masses have... become thinking critics,... who, even if they do not yet possess the means of direct influence in all states, are nevertheless strong enough to impose their will by indirect means.... Hitherto, the mass was the buffer and the anvil of all the historical actions of the elite.'[5] Championed in Europe during the French Revolution and, indeed, under subsequent French regimes, popular participation, it appeared, had become, at the very least, an important element of government and, often, political regimes' principal source of legitimacy.

It proved easier for German commentators to agree on the significance of popular participation in government, however, than on the best means to achieve it. Democracy in large, modern states such as France and Germany could not, as Weber acknowledged, mean the governance of all citizens by all citizens.[6] Even referendums in small states such as Switzerland had proved inadequate: not only were they impracticable for day-to-day policy, but they also failed, given voter indifference, to gain the sanction of the majority for any policy whatever.[7] The task of officials, politicians, and political scientists, therefore, was to determine which system most effectively met the wishes of the populace on most issues:

In this context, it is, of course, necessary to observe that the name 'democratization' can be misleading: the demos in the sense of an unconnected mass never 'administers' by itself in larger associations, but is itself administered and only changes the

---

[4] Fernau, *Französische Demokratie*, 5.

[5] A. Fried, *Deutschland und Frankreich. Ein Wort über die Notwendigkeit und Möglichkeit einer deutsch-französischen Verständigung* (Berlin, 1905), 32–3, 36–7; K. Holl, *Pazifismus in Deutschland* (Frankfurt a.M., 1988), 43–5.

[6] Eisenstadt (ed.), *Max Weber on Charisma and Institution Building*, 72. Vogel, *Die dritte französische Republik*, 339–40.

[7] Delbrück, *Regierung und Volkswille*, 31.

means of selecting the dominant leaders of the administration and the amount of influence which it, or more accurately: other circles of people from its own core, is in a position to exert, through the influence of so-called 'public opinion', on the content and direction of the activity of the administration. 'Democratization' in the sense intended here does not necessarily mean an increase in the active participation of the ruled in ruling within the relevant social structure.[8]

In large polities, popular sovereignty could only signify popular representation, for the mechanisms, which bound popular plenipotentiaries, or deputies, to the populace itself, were imperfect. One general election every four or five years seemed, at best, a questionable guarantee of political accountability and good conduct on the part of ministers and deputies.[9]

The impossibility of direct democracy was taken by the Reich's apologists as a further argument for the strict separation of executive and legislative functions. The minimum requirement of any popular government, they argued, was the people's right of control and veto, so that the populace could censure those in power and block measures unpalatable to majority taste.[10] Because popular, direct means of controlling ministers were imperfect, however, it appeared that indirect means were necessary; that is, the representative chamber should criticize and regulate government on behalf of the people. Yet, apologists continued, that chamber could only perform its critical function if it were formally separate from the executive. To Delbrück the advantages of this division of competencies were clear. On the one hand, the head of state, his ministers and administration were recognized to be fallible and their actions, accordingly, could be checked by the lower house.[11] On the other hand, the populace was tied more closely to its representatives, most obviously because power did not divide them—deputies, having no chance of office themselves, acted as unambivalent popular critics of government— but also because each measure had to find genuine majority support from a different coalition of parties, since bureaucrats-as-ministers were much less likely to demand and avail themselves of party discipline than were politicians-as-ministers. With deputies frequently siding with their party colleagues in office, often against the wishes of their electorate, popular government appeared to be threatened in

---

[8] Weber, *Wirtschaft und Gesellschaft*, 568.
[9] Jellinek, *Allgemeine Staatsrechtslehre*, 581–3; Delbrück, *Regierung und Volkswille*, 86.
[10] Delbrück, *Regierung und Volkswille*, 66.   [11] Ibid. 187.

parliamentary regimes, continued Delbrück. By contrast, in constitutional regimes such as the German Empire, there was little incentive for popular representatives to ignore their constituents in favour
of the government, for the spoils of office were closed to them:

> The motions which are introduced by the popular assembly, the controls which
> the people exercise, the necessity of justifying oneself before the representative
> body, to negotiate with it, to debate sometimes with this part, sometimes with
> that, to come to compromises, to draw the people together on a point, this
> makes up the particularity of our strength.... The decisive thing for the effec-
> tiveness and successes of a state constitution is that the historically created
> resources of the people... work together as comprehensively as possible for the
> purposes of the state.[12]

It is arguable that the separation of executive and legislative competencies was seen in Wilhelmine Germany to be more germane to the
functioning of a political system than the form of suffrage adopted
by that system. The meanings of terms such as 'Volksgewalt',
'Volksregierung', 'Demokratie', and 'Demokratisierung' merged with
each other in common usage. Since direct democracy, or democracy
narrowly defined, was seen to be unattainable, the word
'Demokratie' was often used to denote popular government in its
broad sense, and 'Demokratisierung' to imply a movement towards
popular influence in any part of government or administration.
Although the idea of universal suffrage was sometimes attached to
'Demokratie' and, less commonly, to 'Volksgewalt', it did not constitute a necessary component of either concept.[13] Given that direct
rule by the populace was perceived to be unrealizable, the significance of the suffrage question correspondingly diminished: even if
all men voted, their votes per se, it was contended, did not determine government action; other mechanisms were needed to convert
popular preferences into popular policies. As a result, German disagreements over the desirability of universal suffrage and the political reliability of the populace did not lead to dichotomous depictions
of the French polity. No German party declared the Third Republic
doomed to failure, or assured of success, by its suffrage alone.

The diversity of German reactions to the French electorate
was marked. Unsurprisingly, much of the right opposed the idea of
universal suffrage altogether. It was argued that part of the populace
in France, as elsewhere, was uneducated and ill-informed.

---

[12] Delbrück, *Regierung und Volkswille*.   [13] Ibid. 15.

Consequently, it appeared reckless to give all men the vote.[14] Individuals and groups were to be included in the political nation as they proved themselves politically mature: 'The necessity of a general popular assembly is widely acknowledged, but it would only be realizable in the form of a reasonable, well-structured electoral law, in addition to which a suitable plan would take account of the degree of personal responsibility of each individual, as well as higher national and local interests of state.'[15] The main charge against direct, universal suffrage in France, where it stood virtually unchallenged,[16] in contrast to Germany, where restricted federal and municipal franchises continued to limit its effect, was that it rested on an unstable and impressionable electorate. The conservative organ the *Neue Preußische Zeitung* was not unusual in its criticism. It compared French public opinion to a unit of storm troopers, sweeping all before it in victory, but turning in panic in defeat: 'The public at large' was 'deaf to all reasonable arguments', moving constantly 'from one extreme to the other', so that foreigners were left with the impression that they were in a madhouse.[17] Preoccupied by scandals at home, the electorate seemed blind to France's national interest abroad.[18] Divided and misled by the passions and biases of party, French voters rejected out of hand any measured and sensible policy, whoever proposed it.[19]

At important junctures, such as the Dreyfus affair, similar views were aired in liberal newspapers like the *National-Zeitung*: 'Something new and unexpected happens, which draws the gaze and attention of the French, above all Parisians, in another direction. This happy-go-lucky people is satisfied as long as a new horizon is opened to its fantasy for a while.'[20] Yet, for the most part, the German liberal press trusted in the French public and welcomed democratization under the Third Republic. Even ministers such as Clemenceau, who were criticized for their opportunism and obstructionism, were at the same time praised for their democratic zeal: 'The democratization of France has advanced a long way under

---

[14] G. Schmoller, *Skizze einer Finanzgeschichte von Frankreich, Österreich, England und Preußen* (Leipzig, 1909), 19; Kuhn, *Aus dem modernen Babylon*, 43.
[15] Vogel, *Die dritte französische Republik*, 478.
[16] Fernau, *Die französische Demokratie*, 7.
[17] *Neue Preußische Zeitung*, 5 Sept. 1898, 20 Sept. 1898, and 24 Aug. 1899.
[18] Ibid., 6 Sept. 1898 and 14 Feb. 1906.
[19] Ibid., 26 July 1902 and 12 Apr. 1906.
[20] *National-Zeitung*, 19 Feb. 1899. See also ibid., 8 Feb. and 31 Aug. 1898.

Clemenceau.'[21] Both the *Berliner Tageblatt* and the *Frankfurter Zeitung* traced this process of democratization in France back to the turn of the century and beyond, to the late 1870s.[22] The premiss of such accounts was that the populace would act responsibly, if it were balanced by other parts of the political organism or machine— significantly, the choice of metaphor varied. This assumption drew, in turn, on a recurrent and cross-party notion that the French people, when they escaped the machinations of the Parisian press, were essentially peaceable and conciliatory, if only because business prospered most under such conditions: 'The real people, namely the rural population, are quiet, wish to earn and save money, but know very well that this is only possible in peacetime. . . . The restless ones are the press, parliamentarians, and politicians, who topple ministers and would like to replace them in office', wrote Georg Herbert von Münster-Derneburg, the German ambassador in Paris.[23] At certain times and subject to important qualifications, then, diplomats, conservatives, liberals, and socialists agreed that the French populace could act reasonably, provided that it was not led astray.[24] Under the Third Republic, however, caveat appeared to have become fact: when it was combined with the fusion of executive and legislative functions and the myth of the political state, the populace did not, despite universal suffrage and a predominant lower chamber, seem to constitute an adequate, rational check on government action.

One reason was the absence of an independent, self-governing, and politically educated populace in France, it was proposed. The French political state was supposedly, at least in the opinion of many German commentators, a contractual association of rational individuals. The details and ramifications of this political thesis were outlined by Adolf Tecklenburg, who wrote the principal work in German on French electoral law. According to the tenets of the Enlightenment, which were enacted during the French Revolution,

---

[21] *Freisinnige Zeitung*, 22 July 1909. See also *Berliner Börsenzeitung*, 16 Mar. 1906, and *Berliner Tageblatt*, 11 Jan. 1907.

[22] *Berliner Tageblatt*, 23 June 1906, and *Frankfurter Zeitung*, 6 Nov. 1906.

[23] Münster, 17 Oct. 1898, AA R6593, A11973; Münster, 30 Oct. 1898, AA R6593, A12458; *Münchner Allgemeine Zeitung*, 16 Mar. 1899; *Deutsche Zeitung*, 15 Aug. 1899; *Post*, 24 Aug. 1899. They also had a long history, however—see e.g. Chlodwig zu Hohenlohe-Schillingsfürst, *Denkwürdigkeiten der Reichskanzlerzeit* (Stuttgart, 1931), ii. 268—and continued to appear after the Dreyfus affair; Lancken, 23 July 1909, AA R7039, A12360.

[24] Fernau, *Die französische Demokratie*, 12.

he argued, similar individuals had contracted to form a state in order to regulate their transactions in society. The will of the state corresponded to the sum of individual wills:

> Enlightened philosophy had transferred the yardstick for judging all things to individual people. Thus, the final decision was said to rest on the individual and his opinion. Humanity was atomized. In addition, the entire organization of the state was regarded as the product of the will of individuals. They, indeed, had founded the state in the social contract; in its being, the will of the state was no more than the will of the sum of all individuals.[25]

Such premisses allowed the classic English theory and the 'dominant school in France, too', whereby sovereignty was located in the nation, which was understood as an integrated personality, but only because it would act, through the state, in accordance with the wills of the individuals of which it was composed.[26] Since, theoretically, the state represented the wishes of each rational, individual will on each issue, intermediary bodies between state and citizen were deprived of any justification other than that of unfairly benefiting one group of citizens at the expense of others, which was what revolutionaries claimed had happened during the *ancien régime*: 'The social groupings of the *ancien régime* tied together in a whole the individuals who belonged to them, in the entirety of their relationships. The individualism of the revolution opposed this organization of members of the state and destroyed it by law.'[27] Tecklenburg concurred with the French sociologist Charles Benoist that such abolition and restriction of intermediate corporations had produced a century of anarchy in France, a fact which had eventually been acknowledged by movements as different as the Catholic revival and academic sociology, but which had been more or less ignored, legislatively, by the Third Republic.[28]

---

[25] A. Tecklenburg, *Die Entwicklung des Wahlrechts in Frankreich seit 1789* (Tübingen, 1911), 159; Steinhauser, *Neuestes aus Frankreich*, 46–7; Spahn, *Der Kampf um die Schule in Frankreich und Deutschland*, 5. The theory of the French contractual state was also rehearsed by non-Catholic academics and publicists: *Neue Preußische Zeitung*, 10 July 1907, the economist Andler, *Die Städteschulden in Frankreich und Preußen*, 41, and the publicist Schmitz, *Das Land der Wirklichkeit*, 101–2.

[26] Tecklenburg, *Die Entwicklung des Wahlrechts*, 240–1.

[27] Ibid. 233; Osten, *Die Fachvereine und die sociale Bewegung in Frankreich*, 5; W. Kulemann, *Die Berufsvereine*, 2nd revised edn. (Berlin, 1913), iv. 180; Kuhn, *Frankreich an der Zeitwende*, 87.

[28] Tecklenburg, *Die Entwicklung des Wahlrechts*, 161–70, 261.

Corporations, associations, and intermediary forms of government, separate from the state, were judged by nearly all German
writers to enhance rather than undermine the strength of the
nation-state. Even an apostle of a sovereign central power, such as
Treitschke, criticized French liberals for failing to recognize the
benefits of 'Germanic', self-governing provinces and communes.[29]
Instead, the Third Republic continued to centralize administration,
so that improvements in social conditions, for instance, only seemed
possible through the state.[30] As a result, the populace lost the habit
of self-reliance and became dependent on the bureaucracy, which
was the real meaning of the word *Etatisme* according to one author:
'Everything... is expected from the state, especially material welfare; the state is made responsible for everything, especially all losses
and damage. The Frenchman has coined the word "Étatisme" for
this form of suspension of personal and private initiative.'[31]
Whereas German civil servants worked with regional and local governments and helped to bind them together, French functionaries
stood apart from provincial circles and administered *départements*
from above rather than from within: 'The state is served by an army
of uprooted people, who are never local, can be transferred any-
where and are not tied to their work by any inner involvement.'[32] To
close observers of the French provinces like the academics Karl
Hillebrand and Max Andler, it was not surprising, therefore, that
honorary posts such as that of mayor were regularly left unfilled and
that local politics under the Third Republic, in contrast to those of
Wilhelmine Germany, had withered and died: 'the new flowering of
Germany's cities is not only founded on the new, uninterrupted
influx of the masses; and the lack of a freshly pulsing communal life
in the neighbouring country is not only caused by the absence of
such an influx. Another great and secret source of strength of
German city life is the legal freedom "to set the boundaries of one's
sphere of activity oneself".'[33] Even Paris, noted Hermann Kuhn,
had been affected by political indifference, itself born of a feeling of

---

[29] Treitschke, 'Die Freiheit' (1861), in *Historische und politische Aufsätze*, iii. 5.
[30] Vogel, *Die dritte französische Republik*, 585. Schoen, 16 Apr. 1911, AA R6608, A6308.
[31] Rühlmann, *Der staatsbürgerliche Unterricht in Frankreich*, 1–2.
[32] Schmitz, *Das Land der Wirklichkeit*, 119; Hillebrand, *Frankreich und die Franzosen*, 115–16.
[33] Andler, *Die Städteschulden in Frankreich und Preußen*, 19. Hillebrand, *Frankreich und die Franzosen*, 121.

political impotence. The capital's bourgeoisie, 'even down to the smallest craftsmen and shopkeepers', had abandoned politics to *la bohême*: 'Students, workers, and sundry people without families'.[34] Deprived of associational life and political responsibility, French citizens, it seemed, had forgotten how to influence the parliamentary state by means of concerted criticism. It was difficult to imagine such a disparate and irresponsible populace constituting an adequate check on government.

The obverse side of individualism and social atomization was equality. As has been seen, revolutionaries had attacked corporations, it was said, because the latter had promised advantages to members and, logically, disadvantages to non-members. It appeared to be in the nature of the French political state, as it emerged during the French Revolution, to seek to integrate all citizens by offering them equal opportunities and equal chances of redress, through the state. Naturally, such aspirations were not limited to France, as Karl Eugen Schmidt observed: 'In other countries, one demands the same, of course, and it would be a nice state, according to modern ideas, which wrote the opposite into its constitution. But in other countries, one holds it to be self-evident... and one does not see the necessity of painting it on all public buildings.'[35] Yet the French political state differed in kind from other states, which pledged, as far as possible, to treat their citizens equally, because it looked to equality as its main source of legitimacy, it was argued: unlike states which also appealed to history and historically based laws, the French republics saw and portrayed themselves solely as a willing association of equal, rational individuals; their political structures not only guaranteed a hearing for the wishes of all citizens, they were themselves, professedly, the very expression of those wishes, so that they could be changed at will by the citizenry, in contrast to the structures of historical states.[36] The political state, having repudiated history as a form of self-justification, had to enlist the support of the populace directly. It did so by empowering, or claiming to empower, citizens equally.

Equality, as Vogel noted, was perceived to underpin democracy: 'It is still true that no democracy can exist without equality.'[37] It was

[34] Kuhn, *Aus dem modernen Babylon*, 38.
[35] Schmidt, *Im Lande der Freiheit, Gleichheit und Brüderlichkeit*, 71.
[36] Gneist, *Der Rechtsstaat*, 166. See above, Ch. 2, sect. 2.
[37] Vogel, *Die dritte französische Republik*, 337; Treitschke, *Politik*, i. 62.

also linked, sometimes via democracy, to France, so that the two terms—equality and France—were compounded and opposed to the 'German' principles of freedom and self-government: 'Germans strive above all for freedom, French above all for equality. The German has a strong sense of the particularity of his person, town, and province; he does not wish to be disturbed by the state in such matters.... The Frenchman knows nothing of municipal and provincial patriotism, and has no respect at all for personal individuality', wrote Heinrich von Sybel in the 1870s.[38] Such supposed truisms were perpetuated in the works of academics like Treitschke and Roscher in the 1890s and of journalists such as Oskar Schmitz in the 1900s: 'The difference between a popular assembly which is based on the old order of estates and one which is posited on the human rights of the individual is that only the order of estates produces freedom, albeit without equality, whereas the French system produces equality without freedom.'[39] The true meaning of equality for French democracy was betrayed, in the opinion of many German onlookers, by the latter's preoccupation with electoral figures.[40] As the constitutional lawyer, Siegfried Brie, remarked, the number of voters per deputy in France was regular and the electoral colleges of the Senate, although not absolutely uniform, had been adjusted in line with varying communal populations in 1884.[41] At its most extreme, such numerical preoccupation led to private companies providing information on each *député* and on the *Assemblée*, which included calculations of the real number of electors consenting, through their deputy, to each vote in the chamber. Only then could the 'puissance morale' of each ballot be measured, sneered newspapers like the *Leipziger Neueste Nachrichten*.[42]

In theory, French equality merely implied equality before the law: 'Obviously, the inventors of the motto [liberty, equality, fraternity] only thought of equality before the law.'[43] Yet, in practice, it appeared to be founded on social envy: 'The other magic word, on

[38] Sybel, *Was wir von Frankreich lernen können*, 12. Also from the 1870s, Hillebrand, *Frankreich und die Franzosen*, 23.

[39] Schmitz, *Das Land der Wirklichkeit*, 104; Treitschke, *Politik*, ii. 251–5; Roscher, *Politik*, 395.

[40] Fernau, *Die französische Demokratie*, 25.

[41] Brie, *Die gegenwärtige Verfassung Frankreichs*, 42, 49–50.

[42] *Leipziger Neueste Nachrichten*, 13 Apr. 1906; *Hamburger Nachrichten*, 18 Apr. 1906.

[43] Schmidt, *Im Lande der Freiheit, Gleichheit und Brüderlichkeit*, 69. Also Vogel, *Die dritte französische Republik*, 337.

which most Frenchmen dote more than on freedom, is equality. Yet one must be clear about this. What actually attracts them to it is the claim of each individual against the dispensations and privileges of others.'[44] It was no coincidence, wrote Max Nordau, that woman-kind—'an enemy of social equality'—also deplored French democracy, nor that the sartorial symbol of social equality—black tails—had originated in France during the Revolution: 'Black tails were famously adopted during the first revolution as a kind of uniform of the third estate, as an expression of equality. They soon achieved general domination and have maintained the same until now, a full century later.'[45] According to Treitschke, French democracy was simply the political manifestation of such social equality: Lamartine's declaration of 1848 that no Frenchman, after the advent of universal suffrage, could accuse his neighbour of dominating him, smacked of envy rather than of freedom.[46] Envy was dangerous as a political motive, continued Treitschke, because it lowered the level of political discourse—a point which even the left-liberal *Frankfurter Zeitung* endorsed[47]—and sought to achieve the chimerical goal of complete equality, which eventually culminated in tyranny:

When we observe the febrile paroxysms, which have shaken the nation at the other side of the Rhine—still great despite everything—for seventy years, we find, ashamedly, that the French, despite all their enthusiasm for freedom, have only ever known equality, and never freedom. Yet equality is a concept without content: it can just as well mean the equal servitude of all as the equal freedom of all. And it certainly means the former when it is sought by a people as the single, highest political good.[48]

When equality and social atomization were combined with a democratic French parliamentary state, one likely outcome, postulated many German commentators, was the tyranny of the majority over the minority.[49] Rousseau had invented the specious theory,

[44] Vogel, *Die dritte französische Republik*, 337.
[45] Nordau, *Paris unter der dritten Republik*, 164; Kuhn, *Aus dem modernen Babylon*, 144; Vogel, *Die dritte französische Republik*, 337; Hillebrand, *Frankreich und die Franzosen*, 139.
[46] Treitschke, 'Die Freiheit' (1861), *Historische und politische Aufsätze*, iii. 10.
[47] *Frankfurter Zeitung*, 4 June 1902.
[48] Treitschke, 'Die Freiheit' (1861), *Historische und politische Aufsätze*, iii. 10; id., *Politik*, ii. 14–15.
[49] In an extreme form, this tyranny of the majority in France was equated with the rule of the mob, or ochlocracy, which were terms used more often by the right-wing press—for instance, *Neue Preußische Zeitung*, 9 May 1906, *Deutsche Tageszeitung*, 1 Jan. 1910—but which also found their way into the works of liberal academics such as Max Weber, in Eisenstadt (ed.), *Max Weber*, 220.

wrote Treitschke, that equal individuals would only have to obey themselves, whereas, in fact, they obeyed the majority: 'Rather, he [the individual] obeys the majority, and what prevents this majority from behaving even more tyrannically than an unscrupulous monarch?'[50] Where the myth of equality prevailed, populations could call on no other authority than that of number.[51] Thus, in a society such as the United States the pressure of public, or majority, opinion was just as restrictive as formal state coercion, since it dictated the bounds of common decency: 'Not only can the power of the state be tyrannical; the disorganized majority of society can also, through the slow and unnoticed, but irresistible, force of its opinion, subject the feelings of citizens to a hateful pressure.'[52] Political, parliamentary states such as the Third Republic ruled in the name of the majority, unhindered by historical notions of law and unopposed by corporations, it was claimed. Against such absolute authority, as Schmitz termed it, minorities felt powerless, deprived of local forms of self-government and historical, legal guarantees of their liberties.[53] This was the essence of Treitschke's reply to Rousseau: 'in democracies, the majority is held to be the whole'.[54] The only hope for democratic minorities was that they would, one day, become part of the majority themselves.[55] But, even if they did join the majority, how could they defend themselves against a government, which professed to act on behalf of most of the populace? Isolated individuals had no means of knowing how many of their fellow citizens were similarly discontented. If complaints to the deputy were ignored, as often appeared to be the case, for deputies seemed to prefer to listen to ministers rather than to electors, to whom should the aggrieved citizen turn? Roscher's question was rhetorical. His answer borrowed directly from Tocqueville: an appeal to public opinion appeared pointless, because the citizen felt himself to be in the minority; the popular chamber claimed to act in the name of that public; and the bureaucracy and judiciary were, in turn, controlled by the chamber.[56] All channels of redress appeared to have been blocked. The impotent individual was confronted by the omnipotent parliamentary state.

[50] Treitschke, 'Die Freiheit' (1861), in *Historische und politische Aufsätze*, iii. 9.
[51] H. Delbrück, *Regierung und Volkswille*, 131.   [52] Ibid. 14.
[53] Schmitz, *Das Land der Wirklichkeit*, 105; Sybel, *Was wir von Frankreich lernen können*, 12.
[54] Treitschke, *Politik*, ii. 253, paraphrasing Herodotus.   [55] Ibid. 255.
[56] Roscher, *Politik*, 379, cited Tocqueville.

The two most significant points of contact between government and citizen—elections and the press—had, it seemed, been subverted under the Third Republic. All German political parties were critical of the biases and excesses of French newspapers, denigrating them as 'a libel press', 'bawlers', and 'demagogic rags'.[57] Given that titles such as *Petit Journal* had a circulation of more than one million by the early 1890s and were read, according to Hermann Kuhn, by as many as one-third of the population,[58] no one in Germany doubted the assertion of *Germania* that the press in France was extremely powerful: 'If that famous saying, which fashions the press into the *seventh great power*, is justified in any country, then it is in *France*. Nowhere does the press enjoy such a reputation and nowhere does it have so great an influence on the people as in France.'[59] Disagreements did occur in Germany, however, over the issue of impartiality in the French press.

On the one hand, it appeared to some German commentators that newspapers such as *Matin* and *Petit Journal* were so large that they could be neither coerced nor courted by government.[60] On the contrary, the owner of the former, Bunau-Varilla, boasted to the German ambassador in Paris, for instance, that he could topple ministries at will.[61] The Dreyfus affair, in particular, seemed to demonstrate that the French press was a political power in its own right—in Münster's words, 'The mischief of the press gets more and more irritating and no one feels himself strong enough to restrict it'[62]—yet such claims were common both before and after the affair as well: 'The government or the governing party does not always make decisions in France about the most important affairs of the country; it is only too often swept along by public opinion and *this is manufactured by the press*.'[63]

On the other hand, it appeared that French newspapers were unusually venal and manipulable. As Hans von Flotow, a counsellor

[57] *Germania*, 5 Jan. 1899; *Freisinnige Zeitung*, 31 Jan. 1899; *Vorwärts*, 8 Sept. 1912; *Neue Preußische Zeitung*, 5 Oct. 1898.

[58] Kuhn, *Aus dem modernen Babylon*, 181–2, undoubtedly exaggerated the readership of the *Petit Journal*—a third of all Frenchmen—but attested to the perceived popularity of the French press. See also *Germania*, 3 Sept. 1901 and 8 July 1908.

[59] *Germania*, 9 Feb. 1899.   [60] Kuhn, *Aus dem modernen Babylon*, 182.

[61] Radolin, 5 Nov. 1905, AA R7065, A19700.

[62] Münster, 12 Apr. 1899, AA R6594, A4374; Münster, 30 Oct. 1898, AA R6593, A12458; 21 Feb. 1899, AA R7057, A2098; Below, 6 July 1899, AA R7126, A8225. *Germania*, 7 Sept. 1898.

[63] H. Semmig, *Czar, Empereur und Republik, oder Frankreich vor dem Richterstuhl des gesunden Menschenverstandes* (Leipzig, 1894), 18; Schmoller, *Skizze einer Finanzgeschichte*, 19.

at the German embassy, recorded, the structure of the press under
the Third Republic encouraged a blurring of boundaries between
journalism, politics, and finance.[64] Not only were the major publications concentrated in Paris, and therefore not subject to the independent criticism of the provinces, as in Germany, they were also, with
few exceptions, too small and financially insecure to withstand the
bribes of government and commerce: 'As far as the press here is concerned, its corruptibility in general can hardly be doubted. Only a few
papers, like the "Petit Parisien" and "Matin", generate such profits,
because of their extremely large circulation, that their owners and
editors are in a position to renounce illicit sources of income.'[65] Since
it was common knowledge in diplomatic circles that French newspapers could be bought, even for the purposes of German foreign
policy, it did not surprise the *Auswärtiges Amt* that journals were
manipulated as a matter of course by politicians such as Clemenceau
and financiers like Cornelius Herz, who also acted as editors and
owners.[66] Schmidt, Vogel, and others made the same points in public.[67]

Whichever view of the French press was preferred—unstable,
extreme, but independent, or corrupt and malleable—the fact
remained that newspapers did not safeguard a flow of reliable information between citizen and state, which was necessary, if the populace were to criticize and check government effectively. At best,
citizens, it seemed, would remain in a mute state of ignorance. At
worst, they would become a noisy, uninformed and unpredictable
element in an unbalanced political system:

'L'opinion est comme la reine du monde, mais la force en est le tyran,' according
to Pascal. Now, however, nowhere is it more difficult to gain a healthy expression of public opinion, if one understands by this clear, scrupulous responses to
current questions of state, than in democratic France, under the pressure of a
completely unintegrated, equal, universal suffrage, which is dominated by numbers and the masses, who are not in a position to form an opinion about the most
significant things lying beyond their horizons and who, beyond their drives, are
forced to follow blindly, yet who nevertheless usually tip the scales.[68]

[64] Flotow, 28 Nov. 1905, AA R6601, A21458.

[65] Ibid. *Neue Preußische Zeitung*, 14 Feb. 1906.

[66] Flotow, 28 Nov. 1905, AA R6601, A21458; O. von der Lancken Wakenitz, *Meine
dreissig Dienstjahre, 1888–1918* (Berlin, 1931), 77.

[67] Schmidt, *Im Lande der Freiheit, Gleichheit und Brüderlichkeit*, 68; Vogel, *Die dritte
französische Republik*, 84; S. Feldmann, *Paris gestern und heute. Kulturporträts* (Berlin,
1909), 196; *Germania*, 9 Feb. 1899; *Berliner Volkszeitung*, 27 Oct. 1906; *Frankfurter
Zeitung*, 31 Mar. 1914.

[68] Vogel, *Die dritte französische Republik*, 477.

The precise political role of public opinion in the Third Republic depended, of course, less on the issue of press representativeness and accountability than on the separate question of political representativeness and political accountability. In other words, even if French politicians equated press and public opinion, how far did political mechanisms dispose them to listen to the public at all? To most German observers, the mechanism on which the popular component of the political system turned was the parliamentary election.

It was widely believed in Wilhelmine Germany, especially amongst Catholics, conservatives, and socialists, that elections during the Third Republic were fixed, irrespective of which party was in power.[69] Thus, the conservative *Neue Preußische Zeitung* accused Méline of 'influencing elections' in 1898, despite supporting him in the Dreyfus affair, and the socialist organ *Vorwärts* admitted that the Waldeck-Rousseau ministry, which included Millerand, ' "fixed" the elections' in 1902.[70] It was, continued the former, understandable that French deputies defended the integrity of 'their' system against foreign criticism, but the same politicians were known to acknowledge in private that the republic's electoral procedure was flawed. Nevertheless, having acceded to office, French parties consistently refused to reform voting practice:

in spite of all kinds of vanity in their dealings with foreigners, they see domestic conditions, when they are amongst themselves, through very sharp lenses and destroy the reputation of democratic institutions so relentlessly that impartial foreign critics can hardly keep up with them. One should not allow oneself to be deceived by this astounding honesty of the gentlemen parliamentarians, however...when the same gentlemen take over the rudder themselves, they do not do a jot better.[71]

---

[69] Chlodwig zu Hohenlohe-Schillingsfürst, *Denkwürdigkeiten der Reichskanzlerzeit*, iii. 151. *Germania*, 29 Apr. 1902, 16 May 1908, 10 Jan. 1913, 22 Jan. 1913, 14 Mar. 1914. For conservatives, *Neue Preußische Zeitung*, 1 June 1898, 20 Sept. 1905, 18 May 1906; *Deutsche Tageszeitung*, 29 Apr. 1902, 25 Apr. 1910; *Dresdner Nachrichten*, 16 Mar. 1906; *Leipziger Neueste Nachrichten*, 1 Nov. 1907; *Münchner Allgemeine Zeitung*, 15 Jan. 1910, 11 Mar. 1911. For socialists, *Vorwärts*, 13 May 1902, 7 May 1912. *Reichsbote*, 27 June 1914, rightly declared that even left liberals and socialists in Germany admitted that France was a country characterized by election-fixing. Hintze, 'Das monarchische Prinzip und die konstitutionelle Verfassung', *Staat und Verfassung*, 380.

[70] *Neue Preußische Zeitung*, 1 June 1898; *Vorwärts*, 13 May 1902.

[71] *Neue Preußische Zeitung*, 28 Jan. 1906. *Germania*, 18 May 1910; *Vorwärts*, 3 Dec. 1901, 4 Jan. 1902; and *Neue Preußische Zeitung*, 2 June 1914.

There were, if Hermann Kuhn were to be believed, twelve accepted ways of fixing an election in France.[72] Some relied on technical devices and tricks, employed during polling day, others necessitated threat and enticement over a longer term. Most methods required the involvement of the state. The first type—electoral ruses—had been developed from the 1870s onwards and had, by the 1890s, been 'perfected to an unexpected degree.'[73] Many of them turned on the political leanings of the mayor, who both controlled the voting list and chose the election committee. Although *maires* were appointed by the town council, which was itself elected by the commune, they could be removed by the Ministry of the Interior, acting through prefects. As long as the mayor sided with the government, a whole series of malpractices were possible, Kuhn continued, from the keeper of the voting-urn filling in uncollected slips or damaging those slips handed to him by the voters, by smearing oil on his finger, to the mayor himself supplementing the voting list with the names of dead and absent constituents, whose votes he then used.[74] With the connivance of the mayor and the prefect, who could annul the election of opposition candidates on the slightest pretext, voters were intimidated 'not only [by] life-threatening crowds, but also by riots' and votes were bought, for between one and ten francs each.[75] Extreme cases of corruption, such as de Greffuhle's attempt to buy Dieppe's seat for 100,000 francs in 1898, were possible, implied *Germania*, only because electoral bribery and favours were endemic throughout France:

The organizers were inexhaustible in their invention of new 'tricks'. Naturally, all that glinted was not gold. Much or almost all was deception and trumpery which was only designed to show one off in a flattering light to the voters at home.... *Cheese for soldiers, pardons for poachers, deserters, and the politically condemned..., free tickets on the trains* for outlying *voters on the day of the election*...etc., etc. These are a few of the dishes of the parliamentary kitchen of the Palais Bourbon.[76]

Other tricks were more spectacular. Governments, it was said, did not balk at creating and uncovering spurious conspiracies just before elections, in an attempt to muster a defensive vote for the status quo,[77]

[72] Kuhn, *Frankreich an der Zeitwende*, 160–93. Mahrenholtz, *Frankreich*, 313–14.
[73] Kuhn, *Frankreich an der Zeitwende*, 26.   [74] *Germania*, 8 May 1909.
[75] Kuhn, *Frankreich an der Zeitwende*, 161. Mahrenholtz, *Frankreich*, 313–14.
[76] *Germania*, 5 Apr. 1902 and 20 Mar. 1898.
[77] *Deutsche Tageszeitung*, 2 May 1906; *Neue Preußische Zeitung*, 22 May 1906.

nor at moving entire battalions into safe constituencies, to increase the electorate above 100,000 and thereby gain another seat.[78] Deceptions large and small were bracketed together by German newspapers under the heading 'Wahltriebwerk' and were attributed to the parliamentary regime. As the *Kölnische Zeitung* reminded its readers in 1910, reform of electoral procedure had been on republican programmes in France since the Second Empire, yet even simple improvements, such as polling booths and mixed election committees, had proved elusive.[79] Parties in office were unlikely to use power to their own disadvantage.

Behind the immediate contrivances of the election period was, most German journals agreed, an enduring political structure, which was weighted in favour of incumbent parties. The state itself, partly because of expansion under the Third Republic, was perceived to be electorally significant in its own right, with state employees comprising one-tenth of the electorate, one-fifth of actual voters, and one-third of *bloc* voters, according to figures produced by *Germania*.[80] More important still, the bureaucracy was depicted as chiding and threatening the rest of the electorate into supporting government candidates. 'From the prefect down to the concierge', it seemed, in the words of the *Neue Preußische Zeitung*, that 'civil servants [are] a natural tool for the influencing of elections, which is carried on in such great style in France'.[81] Confronted by prefects, mayors, tax collectors, teachers, and other petty bureaucrats, villagers frequently appeared to forfeit their vote for the sake of a quiet life: 'When one is exposed to all the official torture on the part of mayors, tax collectors, schoolmasters, gamekeepers etc., one votes for the party of government just for the sake of a peaceful life.'[82]

Moreover, if the state was used by parties in power to chastise and punish recalcitrant voters, it was also manipulated in order to reward supporters, it was claimed.[83] This was most pronounced in the case of tactically useful supporters such as innkeepers, whose premises were hired out for political meetings and whose alcohol was given out as a form of electoral bribe: 'It has been said that it is impossible

---

[78] Kuhn, *Frankreich an der Zeitwende*, 191.

[79] *Kölnische Zeitung*, 5 Feb. 1910; *Freisinnige Zeitung*, 12 May 1914.

[80] *Germania*, 27 Mar. 1908; ibid., 5 Apr. 1906; *Vossische Zeitung*, 11 May 1909.

[81] *Neue Preußische Zeitung*, 17 May 1899; *Germania*, 10 Mar. 1906; *Münchner Allgemeine Zeitung*, 15 Jan. 1910; *Vorwärts*, 6 May 1906.

[82] *Germania*, 18 May 1904. *Vorwärts*, 10 Nov. 1905. Hillebrand, *Frankreich und die Franzosen*, 115.

[83] *Germania*, 12 Apr. 1910; *Neue Preußische Zeitung*, 29 Apr. 1902.

in France to govern against the wishes of the landlord, since the party of the "petit verre" is the only one in the republic which has a powerful organization.'[84] As a result of tax concessions, the number of bars increased by 25 per cent to 660,000 during the first twenty years of the Third Republic, which in turn appeared to promote alcoholism, disorder, and criminality: on average, four litres of pure alcohol was consumed by each Frenchman every year.[85] According to the liberal *National-Zeitung*, the notorious connection between alcohol and voting in France constituted a classic example of the malfunctioning of democracy.[86] Such favouritism extended not only to strategically important groups, however, but to whole constituencies. Indeed, it seemed to many German onlookers, including liberal newspapers like the *Hamburgischer Correspondent*, that the political system was built on favouritism at the local level, for villages and towns knew that state funds were available almost exclusively to government supporters: 'For the custom had already become entrenched under the Second Empire that the deputy was the fixer, the mediator of all favours of state for his voters. Of course, only the acceptable, pro-government deputy gained the full measure of such favours.'[87] Roads, railway lines, schools, hospitals, civil service posts, and exemptions from military service all seemed to depend on the political colours of the deputy.[88] It was for this reason that up to 60 deputies per election were 'mal élus', or elected under the wrong party label.[89] The only way for critics of government to enter the Assembly, it appeared, was to disguise their intentions. Elections, which were designed, in much German political thought, to guarantee the critical function of the lower chamber, had become an occasion on which communes displayed their political support for government:

The opposition holds out for a few years, because its supporters believe in a reverse of fortune on the Seine.... But once the prospect of seeing another

---

[84] *Neue Preußische Zeitung*, 8 Dec. 1910.

[85] Ibid. Kuhn, *Frankreich an der Zeitwende*, 161–2.

[86] *National-Zeitung*, 23 Nov. 1909.

[87] Anon., *Das heutige Frankreich* (Hamm, 1903), 9. *Hamburgischer Correspondent*, 17 Mar. 1907; *Germania*, 13 May 1906. Delbrück, *Regierung und Volkswille*, 24; Kuhn, *Aus dem modernen Babylon*, 54; id., *Frankreich an der Zeitwende*, 182.

[88] *Reichsbote*, 5 May 1908; *Germania*, 4 Jan. 1913.

[89] *Frankfurter Zeitung*, 12 Oct. 1913, 14 Apr. 1914; *Vossische Zeitung*, 10 Dec. 1913. For conservatives, *Neue Preußische Zeitung*, 2 May 1902. For socialists, *Vorwärts*, 27 May 1898, 5 Jan. 1909.

party come to the helm disappears, then one is obliged, whether one wants to or not, to support whichever colour is trumps in the Palais Bourbon. This is true of the individual who wants to get on in business or a career, just as it is for communes, which rely on the backing of the state and which, without the sun of governmental favour, could starve.[90]

Granted that the fusion of executive and legislative competencies gave those party politicians who were in office the power of the purse, elections, it was held, could not be expected to secure a popular check on government action.[91]

2. Competence and Corruption

The absence of an independent, self-governing, and politically educated French populace and the failure of popular control over the Assembly necessarily affected the composition and conduct of the lower chamber, it was contended. First, there was the double-edged issue of talent and aptitude. The former—political talent—appeared, to some German authors, to have been levelled by an ill-informed and ill-educated electorate, which preferred like-minded or demagogic representatives. This effect had been remarked in Germany by authors of major works on political suffrage such as the old-school liberal Wilhelm Roscher and the conservative historian Georg von Below.[92] In France, the same effect was likely to be amplified by the merger of executive and legislative competencies, since incompetent or bombastic deputies could become ministers. Oskar Schmitz, drawing on Emile Faguet's book, *Le Culte de l'incompétence et l'horreur de la responsabilité*, gave one of the most critical expositions of such democratic levelling and its consequences for French government:

He proves that pure popular rule not only leads to the rule of incompetents, but that logically it must lead to this. Where this, as in England, is not yet the case, it is because still more powerful aristocratic forces are present within the democratic polity. In France, the people votes, according to the law of the majority, *those* into parliament who force themselves on them, i.e. who pay for their

---

[90] *Neue Preußische Zeitung*, 22 Aug. 1906.
[91] *Germania*, 26 Mar. 1913.
[92] G. v. Below, *Das parlamentarische Wahlrecht in Deutschland* (Berlin, 1909), 34; Roscher, *Politik*, 319.

drinks and are most like them or seem most like them, namely the ignorant or market criers, in any case incompetents.[93]

Diplomats such as Münster and Radolin, lamenting the inexperience and the 'constantly sinking level of parliamentarians who are sent here by universal suffrage', authors like Schmitz and Kuhn, lambasting 'the mediocrity of the chambers' and the desperateness and ignorance of ministers, and newspapers such as the liberal *Vossische Zeitung*, criticizing the parochialism of French ministries, which were composed 'for the most part of the great men of provincial taprooms', all made a similar point: the people's choice was not always the best choice.[94]

This, in turn, raised the question of aptitude, for, even if it were conceded that the prospect of office lured France's most ambitious and talented young men into politics, it was also commonplace for German sources to assert that such talents and ambitions had been misled and abused under the Third Republic.[95] To Radolin, it was preposterous that proven skills, experience, and specialist training had been eclipsed as qualifications for high office by avarice and ambition: 'Every ambitious and half-outstanding man believes himself to be predestined to assume leadership of the government.'[96] The consequences appeared clear enough: the wrong men acceded to the wrong positions. 'How many newspaper literati, administrators, advocates, doctors with or without a practice, engineers, even artists and poets do not joyfully indulge in the dream, which has already become real for so many colleagues, of winning a seat on the benches of deputies, senators, and ministers.'[97] Only in a parliamentary regime did it seem likely that a professor of chemistry would be made foreign minister, an engineer minister for the colonies,

[93] Schmitz, *Das Land der Wirklichkeit*, 302–3. Another acknowledged specialist on France, Käthe Schirmacher, whose advice found a government hearing, also agreed with Faguet in *Der Tag*, which was cited by the *Kölnische Volkszeitung*, 29 May 1910.

[94] Münster, 27 May 1898, AA R7170, A6454; Münster, 25 Nov. 1898, AA R7019, A13663; Below, 10 Nov. 1898, AA R7019, A13005; Radolin, 21 Nov. 1903, AA R7129, A17415, and 25 Apr. 1905, AA R7065, A7039. Kuhn, *Frankreich an der Zeitwende*, 14; Schmitz, *Das Land der Wirklichkeit*, 105; Vogel, *Die dritte französische Republik*, 376. *Vossische Zeitung*, 16 Jan. 1912; *Schlesische Zeitung*, 11 June 1902.

[95] Delbrück, *Regierung und Volkswille*, 66–7; Schmoller, *Skizze einer Finanzgeschichte von Frankreich, Österreich, England und Preußen*, 63.

[96] Radolin, 14 Apr. 1902, AA R7171, A5907; Radolin, 10 June 1902, AA R7128, A9080.

[97] Vogel, *Die dritte französische Republik*, 338, 349, 702.

an apothecary finance minister, and a doctor navy minister.[98] Such men gained their posts by virtue of eloquence rather than competence, implied newspapers like the *Vossische Zeitung*, which attributed the overrepresentation of southerners in the chambers to the fact that they were good speakers and excellent liars.[99] It was no coincidence, suggested Münster, in a list of deputies' professions, which he termed, sardonically, 'an extremely interesting natural history', that there were 104 lawyers, 22 notaries, 22 ex-magistrates, 52 doctors, and 40 journalists in the Assembly.[100] The popular and articulate professions appeared to have displaced government technicians and specialists, often at the expense of administrative efficiency.

Second, there was the temptation for deputies and ministers to enrich themselves, since popular censure through the press and during elections was rare and ineffective. In the eyes of many Germans, the most notorious example of such enrichment was the increase in deputies' salaries from 9,000 to 15,000 francs in 1906, which was sanctioned by a large majority in both chambers. Whilst the measure soothed politicians' tempers, according to Radolin, just as petroleum calmed turbulent waters, it inflamed public opinion.[101] The *Vossische Zeitung* compared popular contempt and anger to that of December 1851:

Now deputies are not called 'the twenty-five francs', but 'the fifteen-thousand', 'Les Quinze-Mille' or, corresponding to the custom of abreviations, 'Les Q.M.', and if they ever call on the people to make an effort, or for a well-meaning gesture, then the echo of their call is not just met with the mocking laughter of 2 December 1851, but with a cry of anger, an eruption of insults.... What has the chamber of May 1906 achieved in the three years of its existence? The people, which loves simple lines and succinct summaries, says: 'They have raised their salary from 9,000 to 15,000 francs, and that is all.' And this judgement is not incorrect.[102]

---

[98] J. Reber, *Ein Blick auf Frankreichs Schulwesen. Eine pädagogische Skizze* (Aschaffenburg, 1897), 5. Münster, 9 Nov. 1898, AA R6593, A13005. *Germania*, 25 June 1898; *Neue Preußische Zeitung*, 13 Nov. 1905. Sternfeld, *Französische Geschichte*, 187; Vogel, *Die dritte französische Republik*, 379.

[99] *Vossische Zeitung*, 11 Apr. 1911. *Neue Preußische Zeitung*, 8 Mar. 1910. S. Feldmann, *Paris gestern und heute*, 224, on Gambetta and, 185–8, on Paul Deschanel, who was named 'Ripolin' after a well-known varnish.

[100] Münster, 31 May 1898, AA R7170, A6586.

[101] Radolin, 6 Jan. 1908, AA R7174, A341. *Germania*, 19 Apr. 1914; *Neue Preußische Zeitung*, 24 Nov. 1906; *Vorwärts*, 25 Nov. 1906.

[102] *Vossische Zeitung*, 7 Apr. 1909.

In a similar vein, Delbrück recalled an anecdote, which had circulated widely in the press, about a deputy who, having become embroiled in an argument on an omnibus, declared that he was a member of the legislature, in an attempt to assert his authority: 'But instead of making a good impression in this way, the public turned on him immediately: "Un quinze mille! Un quinze mille! A la porte! A la porte!" and threw him out.'[103] The politicians, it was said, made laws to suit themselves, regardless of taxpayers' wishes.[104] It was no wonder, continued the *Neue Preußische Zeitung*, that a record number of candidates stood for election to the Assembly in 1910. Avignon alone had 52.[105]

Most German correspondents depicted the *quinze mille* affair merely as the legal façade of bribery and corruption on a grand scale under the Third Republic.[106] Such descriptions appeared in major liberal newspapers like the *Hamburgischer Correspondent, Münchner Neueste Nachrichten, Vossische Zeitung, Berliner Tageblatt,* and *Welt am Montag,* as well as in conservative publications.[107] Indeed, one of the most detailed indictments came from Hermann Fernau, a left-wing admirer of the republic. Although he praised France's democratic political culture, Fernau was convinced that the French parliamentary regime was corrupt. The Bank of France, with its eighteen 'regents' and its enormous budget, which was larger than that of the state, allegedly led a closed financial elite of 2,000 people, 'who had rightly been called the "kings of the republic" '.[108] This elite was able to dictate French policy by suborning deputies, secure in the knowledge that most dealings would be neither exposed nor punished: 'In order to achieve ascendancy in a parliamentarily governed democracy like France, capital must necessarily gain control of the parliaments. Thus, for the deputy, the chamber in France today has become, in nine out of ten cases, a place to do business, under the

---

[103] Delbrück, *Regierung und Volkswille,* 22.

[104] Kuhn, *Aus dem modernen Babylon,* 44, calculated that the Assembly and Senate cost France 12,145,088 francs p.a., whereas parliament cost Britain 1,298,100 francs p.a., and the Reichstag cost Germany only 479,000 francs p.a.

[105] *Neue Preußische Zeitung,* 25 Apr. 1910. *Germania,* 11 Jan. 1907, 1 Mar. 1911, 5 May 1914; *Vorwärts,* 6 Jan. 1898.

[106] Kuhn, *Frankreich an der Zeitwende,* 103; Mahrenholtz, *Frankreich,* 163.

[107] *Hamburgischer Correspondent,* 11 May 1899, 17 Mar. 1907; *Münchner Neueste Nachrichten,* 26 July 1907; *Vossische Zeitung,* 2 July 1908; *Berliner Tageblatt,* 25 July 1909; *Welt am Montag,* 25 Apr. 1910.

[108] Fernau, *Die französische Demokratie,* 25–7.

agreeable cover of general welfare.'[109] Deputies were, in Fernau's opinion, particularly corruptible not only because they were insufficiently checked by the populace, via elections and the press, but also because they were subject to considerable financial pressures. Election costs themselves averaged 50,000 francs per deputy and election committees had to be repaid with posts, decorations, and banquets, which required additional spending, sometimes in the form of bribes and sweeteners. Under such circumstances, it was easier for deputies to justify morally reprehensible actions: 'should the poor representatives of the people live off their meagre 15,000-franc salary alone? . . . No, for the banks, great industrialists, and entrepreneurs of all kinds are there.'[110] In return for arranging contracts, premiums, subsidies, concessions, and reduced tariffs, the politician received positions in companies, honorary directorships, shares, fees, and allowances, by means of which he could supplement his income, but at the cost of his political independence: 'Thus, of course, he becomes more or less the dependent tool of financial people.'[111] Deputies, senators, and ministers appeared to be selling their powers, which they held in trust for the nation, to the highest bidder.

For conservative academics and publicists, there seemed to be a direct connection between parliamentary democracy and corruption.[112] Whereas in England, wrote Vogel, the continuing political influence of the aristocracy protected politics to an extent from the bribery and plotting of financiers, in France there was no longer any counterweight to money: 'Things are different in Paris. Here, in the daily traffic of business and private life, there is no steady counterweight to the powerful magnet, which is in the hands of the financial world—that is, in the broader sense of great capitalists, stock-exchange and commercial barons, railway companies, and industrial firms.'[113] Whatever liberals and socialists thought of Vogel's comparison with England and the desirability of aristocracy, they felt obliged to agree that the impediments to political corruption in France had proved inadequate.[114] It was generally acknowledged

---

[109] Ibid. 29.   [110] Ibid. 29–30. Anon., *Das heutige Frankreich*, 20–1.

[111] Fernau, *Die französische Demokratie*, 30. Mahrenholtz, *Frankreich*, 314; Kuhn, *Aus dem modernen Babylon*, 18. *Tägliche Rundschau*, 24 June 1911.

[112] Treitschke, *Politik*, ii. 136, 251, 281–92; Delbrück, *Regierung und Volkswille*, 46, 49; Schmitz, *Das Land der Wirklichkeit*, 104; Vogel, *Die dritte französische Republik*, 363.

[113] Vogel, *Die dritte französische Republik*, 84.

[114] The conservative press, of course, concurred. *Dresdner Nachrichten*, 5 Apr. 1914; *Neue Preußische Zeitung*, 7 Mar. 1900.

that the Third Republic had been tarnished, if not endangered, by a series of scandals. In an article entitled 'Die französischen Skandale', which appeared in March 1914, the left-liberal *Freisinnige Zeitung* marvelled, not without disquiet, at the regularity of French crises: 'Before the whole world, "Marianne" now washes her dirty linen. The republic has already experienced many scandals, many dirty affairs of corruption.'[115] To the socialist organ *Vorwärts* such regularity was easily explained within a Marxian schema: French *affaires* were indicative of the gradual, but inevitable breakdown of the republic, betraying 'the law of development of the bourgeois republic, the constant procession of scandals and crises'.[116] To liberal newspapers like the *Münchner Neueste Nachrichten* the causes were more complex. In the hope of unseating ministries, the French opposition, it was argued, exhumed case after case of government corruption, which were then usually obstructed and stifled by the ruling parties in the two chambers. Votes in parliament, the courts, the press, and counter-allegations were all effective means of limiting damage during scandals. It was never doubted, however, that corruption existed in the first place:

When faced with revelations of French 'scandals', great scepticism is to be advised. Especially if political personalities are involved. Not that there are no scandals. Heavens above! But we have too often experienced that such revelations are announced with great pomp and then that...it all comes to nothing....This can happen in a parliamentary vote. The courts have the possibility of letting an enquiry drag on....There are also ways and means in France to impose a meaningful silence on the press. And often enough, the threat of counter-revelations suffices to create quiet.[117]

French journals, reported the left-liberal *Welt am Montag*, were full of '"Affairs", of which there are always some in France.'[118] Scandals were so common, continued another liberal newspaper, the *Hamburgischer Correspondent*, that Parisians, in blacker moments of sarcasm, affected to be proud of them: 'For the Parisian, there is no greater pleasure than a scandal. They are proud of having the greatest and most scandalous scandals, just as they are proud of their sweet, little girls....For filth is one of the achievements of culture, too, and France finds great worth in being the oldest and principal

[115] *Freisinnige Zeitung*, 22 Mar. 1914; ibid., 30 Mar. 1906.
[116] *Vorwärts*, 8 Mar. 1900.   [117] *Münchner Neueste Nachrichten*, 26 July 1907.
[118] *Welt am Montag*, 25 Apr. 1910.

cultural power of the world.'[119] German newspapers not only followed major scandals avidly—Panama, Dreyfus, Humbert, Edgar Combes, Duez, Rochette, Caillaux, the last of which was covered extensively throughout the second half of July 1914, despite the Sarajevo crisis and the outbreak of the First World War[120]—but also devoted columns to less well-known affairs such as Vallé, Chaumié, and Ceres and Marix.[121] In many respects, the great scandals of the 1890s set the tone for the 1900s. After Panama and Dreyfus, Germans of all parties came to expect affairs in France, which would shake the political foundations of the Third Republic or, at least, would be seen to do so. As has already been noted, the word 'Panamist' was still used as a technical term for parliamentary corruption almost a generation after the actual bribery had been uncovered.[122] Both *Germania* and the *Freisinnige Zeitung* heralded the Duez affair as 'Das neue Panama' in 1910.[123] The failure of a republican government to end Guérin's occupation of a house in central Paris, which hit small businesses in the *quartier*, was compared by the *Neue Preußische Zeitung* to the failure of republican ministries to stop fraudsters deceiving small investors during the Panama share flotations.[124] In much the same way, loans to Russia in 1906 were assumed by *Vorwärts* to have generated more than 100 million francs of bribes, simply because a similar percentage of illegal earnings had been made from the Panama canal project.[125] Even the Dreyfus case was labelled a military Panama affair—'It is a new, a military Panama affair, which casts its shadow before it'[126]—before it, too, became a point of reference for Germans, by which the affairs of the next one and a half decades were measured and interpreted.

It is probable that the scandals associated with Panama and Dreyfus helped to focus the doubts of German liberals vis-à-vis the French parliamentary state. The persistence of such doubts explains the ambivalence of liberals and socialists during the crises of the *bloc*

---

[119] *Hamburgischer Correspondent*, 15 Mar. 1910.
[120] The *Vossische Zeitung*, for example, carried major reports of two columns or more on 18 and 20–29 July. There were three such reports on 23 July, two, including one of some eight columns, on 24 July, and two on 29 July.
[121] *Neue Preußische Zeitung*, 10 June 1902; *Münchner Neueste Nachrichten*, 26 July 1907; *Berliner Tageblatt*, 17 May 1909.
[122] Delbrück, *Regierung und Volkswille*, 22. Delbrück was writing in 1914.
[123] *Germania*, 17 Mar. 1910, *Freisinnige Zeitung*, 15 Mar. 1910.
[124] *Neue Preußische Zeitung*, 18 Aug. 1899.   [125] *Vorwärts*, 24 Apr. 1906.
[126] Ibid., 14 Jan. 1898. Ibid., 15–16 and 19 Jan. 1899.

era, in spite of their committed support for Waldeck-Rousseau and
Combes in the struggle against the Catholic church. Thus, although
newspapers like *Vorwärts* and the *Freisinnige Zeitung* strenuously
denied the pertinence of analogies between Panama and the
Humbert affair, which involved the fraudulent borrowing of 50 million francs on the strength of Senator Humbert's name and connections, the former did admit that the scandal had exposed the
rottenness of the republic's judiciary.[127] Whilst much of the liberal
press remained tight-lipped, expressing neither support nor criticism, liberal satirical journals were unable to suppress their mirth.
In a cartoon entitled 'Monte Carlo', *Simplicissimus* envisaged Mme
Humbert walking confidently at the head of a pageant of admirers:
' "You know that our prince has offered Therese Humbert a home
here?" "Of course, that's the best thing that he could do; thus, he
renders the competition harmless",' ran the caption.[128] The implication was that the Humberts had become celebrities by bringing the
republic into disrepute. *Kladderadatsch* went further, suggesting that
other spectacular frauds perpetrated against the political and economic establishment were, in the words of the article's headline,
'Nach französischem Muster'.[129] France under the Third Republic
appeared to exemplify fraudulence. The Edgar Combes affair, in
which the son of the Président du Conseil was accused of demand-
ing one million francs in return for the state authorization of
Carthusian monasteries, did little to restore the republic's image.
Granted, liberal newspapers like the *Berliner Tageblatt*, *Freisinnige
Zeitung* and *Hannoverscher Courier* defended the integrity of Emile
Combes and charged the Assembly commission with nationalist
incitement,[130] yet most were circumspect on the question of Edgar
Combes's innocence. A socialist publication like *Vorwärts* went so far
as to lament, with the commission, that Combes Sr. had abused his
office and had tried to intervene in the workings of justice.[131]
Moreover, *Kladderadatsch* was, once again, unforgiving: 'The
bribery affair has still not been explained, and that is enough for

---

[127] *Vorwärts*, 17 May 1902, *Freisinnige Zeitung*, 13 May 1902; *Der Westfale*, 4 May 1902.
[128] *Simplicissimus*, vol. 8, no. 25.
[129] *Kladderadatsch*, 18 Dec. 1904, no. 51.
[130] *Berliner Tageblatt*, 11 June 1904; 13 July 1904, *Hannoverscher Courier*, 13 July 1904;
Freisinnige Zeitung, 8 July 1904.
[131] *Vorwärts*, 3 July 1904.

those with influence and weight to claim that the business has been dealt with.'[132] Uncertain of the facts, the instinctive reaction of republican governments was to obfuscate and ignore the truth, it was conjectured. This was the gravamen of the Catholic and conservative response to both cases.[133]

German liberals were less ambiguous in their reactions to major scandals in the decade before the First World War, as they became disenchanted with French Radicalism. The *National-Zeitung* gave the uncompromising details of the first such affair, which involved a liquidator of church property called Duez. It seemed to evince the catastrophic power of connections in the Third Republic: 'The reputation of patronage of influential circles has, through the acquisition of this personality, suffered a heavy blow.'[134] Duez, continued the National Liberal newspaper, had been an assistant in a department store, until he had made the acquaintance of Humbert, through whom he eventually became a legal administrator, although he knew nothing of law or accountancy. According to the *Hamburgischer Correspondent*, 250 million francs of sequestered church property had been misappropriated by the handful of liquidators and lawyers who had been appointed by republican ministers, after the separation of church and state in 1905.[135] No appeal against state liquidators had ever been successful, despite the capricious circumstances of their appointment, concluded the *Vossische Zeitung*.[136] German liberals, socialists, Catholics, and conservatives all concurred that the name of the republic had been tarred by Duez.[137] The same was true of Rochette, his friends and his enemies. The immediate premonition of the *Freisinnige Zeitung* as the affair first came to light was that 'the outbreak of a great political scandal is unavoidable'.[138] Socialist newspapers such as *Vorwärts* and publications close to the National

---

[132] *Kladderadatsch*, 3 July 1904, no. 27.
[133] On the Humbert affair, see *Deutsche Tageszeitung*, 30 May 1902 and 14–23 Aug. 1903, when lengthy reports appeared daily; *Berliner Neueste Nachrichten*, 30 May 1902; *Neue Preußische Zeitung*, 13 May 1902 and 6 Jan. 1903; *Germania*, 26 Aug. 1903. On the Edgar Combes affair, see *Neue Preußische Zeitung*, 9 July 1904; *Germania*, 22 June 1904 and 5 July 1904.
[134] *National-Zeitung*, 10 Mar. 1910.
[135] *Hamburgischer Correspondent*, 15 Mar. 1910.
[136] *Vossische Zeitung*, 19 Mar. 1910.
[137] *Deutsche Tageszeitung*, 9 Mar. 1910; *Neue Preußische Zeitung*, 13 July 1910 and 23 June 1911.
[138] *Freisinnige Zeitung*, 12 July 1910.

Liberal Party, like the *Kölnische Zeitung*, confirmed the fears of the left-liberal press:

With the regularity, with which summer replaces winter, scandals have, for a considerable number of years, been following one after the other in the republic. And recently they even seem to want to eclipse each other. For the liquidation scandal has not yet been dealt with and the embezzlement of many millions of francs of sequestered monastical property has not yet been fully cleared up and atoned for, and already the Rochette case is drawing a whole world of people, of private individuals and high-ranking officials of the republic before the forum of public accusations of the same kind: the prohibited, deceitful pursuit of Mammon.[139]

If *Vorwärts* were to be believed, Rochette was a well-connected but fraudulent financier, who was arrested at the instigation of powerful business rivals, including Clemenceau's brothers, in 1910.[140] His arrest caused a panic on the stock exchange, which led to significant losses for 50,000 shareholders, but to large gains for the few speculators, who had been forewarned of the financier's imprisonment. Once Rochette was in gaol, however, ministers like Caillaux, Monis, and Briand, it was alleged, intervened to delay and, ultimately, quash his trial, since they were worried about revelations of political corruption, which a court case might unearth.[141] The affair appeared, to *Vorwärts* and others, to discredit France's entire political system, not merely this or that political party: 'Above all—the whole mystery of the state collapses. Like justice, politics too—not that of one or the other party, of this or that statesman—but bourgeois politics as a whole is recognizable in its true state.'[142] Although they remained divided by detail, German left and right agreed that affairs such as Duez and Rochette had damaged the standing of the Third Republic.

German interpretations of French scandals implied a degree of alienation between populace and politicians in France. Corruption was perceived to be both cause and effect of this alienation, for it was seen to result, in part, from the disjunction between the people and their political leaders, which was permitted by the failure of popular checks on government, and then, when it actually occurred, it seemed to reinforce popular contempt for government. The same

---

[139] *Kölnische Zeitung*, 13 July 1910. *Vorwärts*, 12 July 1910.
[140] *Vorwärts*, 12 July 1910.   [141] Ibid., 27 Mar. 1914.
[142] Ibid. *Vossische Zeitung*, 14 Mar. 1914. For conservative criticism of Rochette, see *Neue Preußische Zeitung*, 21–22, 24–25, 28 Mar., 2 Apr. 1914; *Deutsche Tageszeitung*, 1 Apr. 1914; *Fränkischer Volksfreund*, 26 Mar. 1914. For Catholic censure, see *Germania*, 28 Mar. and 2 Apr. 1914. Schoen, 21 Mar. 1914, AA R7135, A5772.

could be said of technical incompetence, for it seemed to many Germans that there was nothing to promote administrative aptitude in the French political system. The populace was left with the feeling, it was postulated, not only that it could not control government, but also that government was not working for it. When such interpretations were added to other common German myths of France— opposition between Paris and the provinces, notions of 'les deux Frances', the revolutionary tradition, residual monarchism, and Bonapartism[143]—it seemed, under certain circumstances, that a change of regime was possible. To different German parties at different moments, 'La République en danger' appeared to be more than a hollow republican slogan.

3. Caesarism and the Danger of Collapse

There were two overlapping hypotheses in Germany, which tried to explain the apparent fragility of the Third Republic. One propounded that significant parts of the French population and political system had remained monarchist in all but name after 1870, so that reversion to monarchy or to dictatorship was easier to envisage. The other posited that democracy contained within itself the promise of its own demise, because it tended to produce either anarchy or oligarchy, the instability of which promoted a dictatorial restoration of order. Although the two theories had varying elements—it was common, for instance, for prophets of democratic degeneration to assume that reversion to monarchy was unlikely—they coincided in important respects. Both presupposed a strong state, enforced order and authority, and both assumed the rejection of a republican synthesis of liberty, equality, and national unity.

The notion of a resistant, right-wing anti-republicanism in France found most adherents in the 1890s, although it resurfaced in the 1900s and 1910s. In part, it was the consequence of the German historiography of the Third Republic, which stressed the conservative origins of the republican regime. Hermann Kuhn, for example, disputed all election results after those of 1871, which had yielded a right-wing majority, because they had been subverted by republican bribes and administrative coercion: 'Now, the only time in this

---

[143] See both Catholic newspapers such as *Kölnische Volkszeitung*, 31 Mar. 1907, and liberal publications like *Vossische Zeitung*, 14 July 1906, and *Kölnische Zeitung*, 8 June 1914.

century, according to the trustworthy testimony of Thiers, that the real opinion of the people was expressed through universal suffrage, in 1871, a strong, monarchical, conservative majority was elected. It was only as this [majority] placed all powers in the hands of Thiers, from too great a trust in his hypocritical protestations, that the republicans first rose to the top. What the high pressure of the authorities does not achieve during elections, money takes care of.'[144] Yet even the results after 1871 evinced continued support for the right: in 1876, continued Kuhn, there were still 3,202,333 monarchists against 4,028,153 republicans; and, in 1889, 3,378,352 against 4,012,353.[145] What was more, in 1885, after the introduction of proportional representation, 176 conservatives had been elected in the first round, and only 127 republicans: 'The election [was] a sign that republican domination was not so secure that royalists had to give up all hope of coming to power again,' wrote Haas.[146] The other textbook authors agreed in outline, if not in detail. Richard Sternfeld, one of the principal German historians of France, for example, contested the strength of the royalists, but then went on to demonstrate the power of the ultramontanes, who led the right-wing opposition to the republic and who influenced Méline in the 1890s.[147] In a similar fashion, Richard Mahrenholtz, who had written another of the standard works on France, did not allow the undoubted popularity of republicanism in the late 1870s to obscure the success of the anti-republican right in the late 1880s: 'The republic was never more threatened than during the time of Boulanger.'[148] Anti-republicanism, whether monarchist, ultramontane, or Bonapartist, whether private or public, appeared to have entrenched itself in French politics. Even in 1914, when, it seemed to Delbrück, monarchists were destined to perpetual opposition— 'the monarchists have become a mere opposition party in France'— they were still judged to be significant enough to combine with other malcontents to block republican policies and depose republican governments: 'There is still a quite important monarchical minority in France... what is the consequence of this? That they are in a position to topple each government as soon as it does not have a very great percentage of republicans behind it.'[149]

---

[144] Kuhn, *Frankreich an der Zeitwende*, 99.   [145] Ibid., 25–6.
[146] Haas, *Frankreich*, 118.   [147] Sternfeld, *Französische Geschichte*, 178–83.
[148] Mahrenholtz, *Frankreich*, 142–4.
[149] Delbrück, *Regierung und Volkswille*, 128–9.

It was common, especially in the 1890s, for conservative and Catholic newspapers in Germany to contrast popular discontent under the republic with contentment under the monarchy. *Germania*'s anxiety that the Third Republic was at greatest risk from its own people, particularly its social elite, which was not ready for the sobriety of democracy, found echoes in nationalist newspapers like the *Rheinisch-Westfälische Zeitung*: 'especially now, a return to monarchy cannot be ruled out, if the right man comes forward. One must not forget that the Third Republic is actually a re-Christened monarchy, and that the French people, with the exception of the republican rulers of the day, has remained monarchical at heart and longs for a firm hand.'[150] Such fears could not be banished completely even from a left-liberal article on the 'Rückgang des monarchischen Sinnes im Auslande', which appeared in the *Freisinnige Zeitung* in 1910. German observers, it seemed, were never able to rule out the restoration of monarchy or, more often, dictatorship completely. Of course, the newspaper went on, monarchist and clerical enemies of the republic had almost disappeared, but the 'danger of a dictatorship, the establishment of a military empire cannot for France either, of course, be ruled out for ever. The feelings of the people could, under certain conditions, allow it again.'[151] Perhaps, 120 years after the abolition of the legitimate Bourbon monarchy, the French populace was still not prepared for democracy.[152] It was unrealistic to expect the German people, with its purportedly uninterrupted history of monarchy and empire, to adjust to democracy more quickly, or more successfully, it was implied.

Karl Eugen Schmidt, a correspondent of one of Germany's few independent newspapers, *Der Tag*, and a self-confessed man of the people, wrote one of the principal analyses of residual monarchism and the main critique of republican rhetoric, in a book entitled *Im Lande der Freiheit, Gleichheit und Brüderlichkeit*, in which he confronted republican intentions with political, social, and economic reality in France. The republic was simply alien to French soil, he contended, unlike in Hamburg and Bremen, where it had grown up gradually, 'like a tree in the forest'.[153] In the 1870s, the monarchists

[150] *Rheinisch-Westfälische Zeitung*, 10 Aug. 1899. *Germania*, 17 Jan. 1899.
[151] *Freisinnige Zeitung*, 13 Oct. 1910.
[152] It was frequent to depict the French monarchies of the 19th cent. as compromised experiments rather than legitimate monarchies.
[153] Schmidt, *Im Lande der Freiheit, Gleichheit und Brüderlichkeit*, 4–5.

had enjoyed a large majority and the republicans 'did not make up three baker's dozens between them'.[154] But they had been unable to agree on a pretender, so that the continuance of the republican form seemed to France's cautious peasantry and petite bourgeoisie to portend greater stability than a reversion to monarchy.[155] Such prudent republicanism was not to be equated with social egalitarianism, however: 'it is the people itself which does not want to know anything of *égalité*. The German people has been called a subservient people, and there is some truth in this view. But it is hardly better in France.'[156] Throughout France, it remained the ambition of villagers to serve in the local *château*, whereas in western Germany these vestiges of servitude had disappeared: 'In short, everywhere in French villages it is like it is in the German Empire only eastwards of the Elbe. A proud, democratic estate of farmers, as can be found in the villages of the Rhine and in the whole of West Germany, does not exist in France.'[157] Similarly, in towns, the nobility remained France's social elite, which explained why commoners continued to buy and counterfeit titles: 'this respect for nobility is universal amongst the French people to the extent that nobles not only have social advantages, but are also helped by their title in their careers.'[158] It was one of the legends of the French Revolution, perpetuated by foreigners' reliance on the reports of aristocratic émigrés, Schmidt declared, that the French nobility had been virtually wiped out. In fact, the Prussian aristocracy had lost ten times as many members as its French counterpart between 1789 and 1815. Furthermore, Napoleon had created another 9 princes, 32 dukes, and 1,090 barons, and the restored Bourbons another 17 dukes and 215 barons, many of whom still received state pensions, including the King of Sweden and Berthier, Prince de Wagram, who received 234,151 francs per annum, or four times as much as a French minister.[159]

The Third Republic had inherited the social hierarchy of the Bourbon monarchy, suggested Schmidt, and it was only in such terms that its legitimacy was understandable. France's conservative populace had come to accept the republic because, in many respects, it was an ersatz monarchy: 'And so the French republic was born,

[154] Schmidt, *Im Lande der Freiheit, Gleichheit und Brüderlichkeit*, 5.
[155] Ibid. 7–8.   [156] Ibid. 76.   [157] Ibid. 77.
[158] Ibid. 77–9. *Neue Preußische Zeitung*, 4 Oct. 1898. J. E. Schermann, *Von Paris zurück* (Ravensburg, 1901), 124.
[159] Schmidt, *Im Lande der Freiheit, Gleichheit und Brüderlichkeit*, 81–5.

not because the French were unhappy with monarchy, but because they could not agree about the monarch; not because the people absolutely demanded a change, but on the contrary because it realized that the republic was and is nothing other than a disguised monarchy. All the institutions of state remained exactly what they were before, except that the labels were altered.'[160] Schmidt was, by the mid-1900s, unusual in labelling French institutions like the police, judiciary, and bureaucracy unreservedly monarchical.[161] In the 1890s, however, it was more common to describe the French republic as the embodiment of imperial and monarchical assumptions and practices. German fears, which were often either elicited or exacerbated by French foreign policy, centred on the Président de la République, as Mahrenholtz, writing in 1897, explained:

Although France has now been a republic for 26 years, there is too much missing for the monarchical tradition of so many centuries to have lost its influence over the spirit of the French people. Now as then, the *centralization* of all public affairs, emanating from Paris, persists, and the head of this, in the popular consciousness, appears to be the president, not the parliament. In addition, the powers at the disposal of the former, since so many civil servants and also the commanders of the armed forces depend on him, since he gives out much-coveted decorations, and since he is the visible external representative of the unity of the state, are in themselves substantial enough.[162]

If political constraints were ignored—and this proviso was what divided Hermann Kuhn, Richard Mahrenholtz, and other authors of the 1890s from most journalists and writers of the 1900s[163]—it seemed that the French head of state possessed the power of the purse, since loans were generally rubber-stamped by the Assembly, the power to declare war, with campaigns in Tunis, Tonkin, Dahomey, and Siam proving that the consent of the Assembly was not required, in spite of constitutional law, and the power to appoint ministers, functionaries, judges, and officers: 'That the president appoints all civil servants or lets them be placed by his high officials, he has in common with all rulers. But he is bound by fewer restrictions and regulations in this than any prince in Europe.'[164] When such powers were added to the vainglory of presidential protocol and

---

[160] Schmidt, *Im Lande der Freiheit, Gleichheit und Brüderlichkeit*, 8.
[161] Also anon., *Deutschland und Frankreich. Politisch und militärisch verglichen* (Stuttgart, 1912), 14–15.
[162] Mahrenholtz, *Frankreich*, 162. [163] Kuhn, *Frankreich an der Zeitwende*, 4.
[164] Ibid.

the republic's adoption of monarchical and imperial institutions, it appeared to Kuhn, in 1895, that French history betrayed a proclivity towards centralization, independent of political change: 'For centuries, the political development of France has not deviated by a hair's breadth from its original direction, which aims at the constant accumulation of power for the government and especially the head of state.'[165] The only difference between the Third Republic and the *ancien régime* was that government was hindered by corporations in the latter, and aided by technology and administrative innovation in the former.[166] Despite their varying points of view, both Kuhn and Schmidt agreed that popular subservience and the demand for strong government in France were the corollary of such institutional habit:

> The French people are as good as drilled only to be governed by a real, powerful master, a dictator. France came about through the monarchy, and became a great, prestigious, and illustrious empire. Thus, all Frenchmen, however loudly they proclaim themselves to be republicans or swear themselves to be socialists and anarchists, have remained monarchists in their basic views and habits. True, they do not themselves see or believe it: the more they fill their mouths with the republic, the less they are actuated by it in their dealings.[167]

Although some German authors assumed that real democracy had been obstructed in France by the persistence of monarchical and Bonapartist institutions, many commentators, particularly after the turn of the century, expected some sort of institutional coincidence between democracy, absolute monarchy, and dictatorship. As has already been seen, centralization, bureaucratization, and the tyranny of the majority were frequently linked to parliamentary democracy by German writers. It was, therefore, no surprise to publicists like Karl Vogel, who wrote in the 1890s, that a republic preserved much of its monarchical and imperial inheritance: 'France, the single large republic, just as earlier it had been the oldest monarchy in Europe, has not for a long time changed so much in its innermost being, despite all the revolutions which it has undergone, as it might appear from a distance. Also, however much the rising pole of democracy has come closer in recent times to the opposite pole of tsarist autocracy and however much this takes one's breath away, this fact is justified by the old proverb "les extrêmes se touchent".'[168] Both democratic and

---

[165] Kuhn, *Frankreich an der Zeitwende*, 9.   [166] Ibid. 9–10.
[167] Kuhn, *Frankreich an der Zeitwende*, 13. Schmidt, *Im Lande der Freiheit, Gleichheit und Brüderlichkeit*, 24–5, 38–44, 49–50.
[168] Vogel, *Die dritte französische Republik*, 32–3.

despotic states had grown, declared Max Weber, by accumulating the powers of independent notables. Either regime could produce an efficient, centralized bureaucratic machine, which, once it existed, stood at the disposal of anyone who knew how to use it: 'The objective indispensability of the apparatus, once it has come into existence, together with its own unique "impersonality", means that it—in contradistinction to feudal orders, which rest on personal piety—can easily be made to work for anyone who has discovered how to take control of it.'[169] The transition from democracy to dictatorship, or vice versa, did not imply a complete restructuring of the state.[170]

It appeared to many German commentators that dictatorship might succeed democracy in France because French democrats were inclined to push equality to political extremes. The attempt to translate the idea of equality directly into political practice had been based on the assumption that politically equal individuals could govern themselves. Yet, to German observers, this argument ignored the difficulties of representation in large democracies and of coordinating a myriad of popular interests and preferences, for it was widely agreed that individuals were neither culturally nor economically identical. Was it likely that dissimilar individuals would manage to agree on consistent policies? And, even if like interests and preferences could be discerned and united, how were self-interested, power-hungry factions to be prevented from neglecting popular wishes? By overlooking such problems, the Third Republic courted anarchy, it was held, as unstable factions immersed themselves in scandals and political infighting and failed to pass necessary laws: ' "Both tendencies, which Rousseau nurtured, which revolution developed further..., namely the anarchist tendency and the tendency to despotism, can be found again and again in our history for the last 90 years..." But one could also put forward these words as a motto for the last 30 years of French history', wrote the conservative historian Theodor Schiemann, citing Taine.[171] Similarly, to the liberal historical economist Wilhelm Roscher, extreme democracy was tantamount to anarchy: since democrats were not prepared to limit and regulate their freedoms, each individual had no choice but to fight every other in order to impose his own absolute liberty. It was at this point that the military power, which constituted the first

---

[169] Weber, *Wirtschaft und Gesellschaft*, 570; Vogel, *Die dritte französische Republik*, 358–9; Haas, *Frankreich*, 127.

[170] Weber, *Wirtschaft und Gesellschaft*, 571.   [171] *Neue Preußische Zeitung*, 10 July 1907.

characteristic of a social group to emerge and the last to disappear, took control of government, imposed order and ended the inaction of anarchy.[172] Because extreme democracies had usually espoused the rhetoric of equality and concentrated power by destroying intermediary corporations, argued Roscher, military dictators, who claimed to be the first above equals and who centralized authority in the people's interest, appeared to be the natural heirs of democracy: 'Equality, which according to v. Treitschke "is a concept without content"', underpinned both types of regime: 'it can just as well mean the equal servitude of all as the equal freedom of all.'[173] In France, democracies such as the First and Second Republics, which had destroyed rival centres of power and then proved themselves unworkable, had cleared the way for dictators like the Bonapartes: 'It was very helpful to Napoleon, . . . that the revolution had destroyed all particularities, privileges, corporations etc., that it had effected the most extreme centralization, but at the same time had brought trade, industry, art, science etc. into desperate straits.'[174]

If French egalitarianism promoted anarchy, it also encouraged oligarchy, continued Roscher. As has been seen, many German authors believed that the faith of French republicans in the complementarity of liberty and equality was naive. In the absence of state regulation, the removal of corporate restrictions—or enforced freedom—in trade and industry seemed to create disparities of wealth and social polarization rather than the harmonious cooperation of equal individuals: '*Freedom of trade*, this democracy in the sphere of industry, which higher culture almost regularly brings in its wake, indeed increases the volume and as a rule also the quality of industrial production, but also makes the distribution of products more unequal.'[175] This was particularly visible in areas of Paris such as St Antoine and Du Temple, where an increase in industry and economic freedom had been accompanied by the growth of a large, dissatisfied, and potentially revolutionary proletariat.[176] Similarly, the equal division of inheritances—or enforced equality—demanded by egalitarian legal codes eventually produced a capitalized land market, in which sons sold their plots of land, which were too small to farm, to speculators and large-scale cultivators.[177] Egalitarianism

---

[172] Roscher, *Politik*, 588–9; Kuhn, *Aus dem modernen Babylon*, 30–1.
[173] Roscher, *Politik*, 592.   [174] Ibid. 590.   [175] Ibid. 479.   [176] Ibid. 480.
[177] Ibid. 475.

thus connived, despite itself, with plutocracy: 'Two great political parties...regularly work together towards the dissolution of the medieval ties of familial property, namely the democratic and the plutocratic party.'[178]

The Third Republic appeared, to Roscher, to resemble a plutocracy.[179] Partly because democracies found it difficult to impose taxes, which were likely to be unpopular, the French regime had saddled itself with large debts, many of which were secured by politically influential financiers.[180] As oligarchs corrupted and manipulated the centralized state at the same time as mouthing the phrases of democracy—'Since it [plutocracy] is a daughter of degenerate democracy,...so it cannot deviate too brusquely in form from the principle of equality'[181]—they exacerbated the tension between democratic aspiration and plutocratic practice and thereby fostered the growth of socialism. In Roscher's opinion, plutocratic democracy created the conditions necessary for communism: 'A). A crude opposition of rich and poor...B). A high degree of division of labour...C). High expectations and demands on the part of the lower classes as a consequence of the democratic movement...D). A strong shaking, indeed confusion of the public sense of legality through revolutions...E). General decline of religiosity and morality of the people.'[182] In turn, the threat of socialism and communism provoked a reaction in favour of dictatorship: 'Hitherto, the outcome of almost all really significant communist threats has been either Caesarism or at least absolute monarchy.'[183] Faced with the possible collectivization of goods, Roscher went on, the propertied classes backed any power likely to block communism, whilst communists themselves were indifferent to the various forms of bourgeois state, whether democratic or dictatorial.[184] Roscher's schema, which, in its last stages, passed from democracy, via plutocratic-proletarian regimes, to Caesarism, was clearly influenced by eighteenth- and nineteenth-century France, although its references ranged from ancient Athens to modern America. In 1892, as *Politik* was published, it still seemed to Roscher that dictatorship was one possible, perhaps even probable, consequence of democracy. When figures as representative as Thiers and Comte showed obvious leanings towards Caesarism, it appeared that the French Third Republic

[178] Ibid.   [179] Ibid. 497.   [180] Ibid. 493–4.
[181] Ibid. 496.   [182] Ibid. 535–6.   [183] Ibid. 563.   [184] Ibid.

would, at the very least, be menaced by the spectre of dictatorship: 'Were the old legitimate monarchy to be re-established in present-day France, it would be extremely well-advised to retain many of the peculiarities of Caesarism.'[185] French history suggested that democracy and dictatorship were connected.

The two German theories of French dictatorship—residual monarchism and democratic degeneration—recurred sporadically throughout the Wilhelmine period. Even in 1905, during the Rouvier ministry, a liberal newspaper like the *Münchner Neueste Nachrichten* could be found speculating about *coups d'état*.[186] Likewise, in 1909, during the dispute over proportional representation, one of the staunchest German defenders of the Third Republic, the *Frankfurter Zeitung*, suggested that the *scrutin de liste*, although it was necessary, nevertheless eased the transition towards dictatorship in France.[187] Predictably, the frequency of such references increased at times of crisis, most notably 1898–1900 and 1908–1910. The first of the two periods, which centred on the Dreyfus affair, will suffice here to demonstrate the breadth and uniformity of German prophesies of Caesarism in France.

The German embassy in Paris, although it knew that Méline himself did not fear a coup, was a case in point.[188] The ambassador, Münster, was convinced at various junctures that the corruption of French public life and the atrophy of French institutions presaged dictatorship. His predictions expanded on Roscher's theory of plutocracy by conjecturing that Bonapartists were not only ready to profit from an ailing, venal regime, but also that they were prepared to replace it by means of bribery: 'A coup cannot even be attempted in this corrupted country without extremely significant pecuniary resources.'[189] It was rumoured that just one of Victor Napoleon's backers possessed a fortune of 800 million francs, which was to be used to buy support in the army and the administration: 'With such means a *part of the army* and civil servants will allow themselves to act favourably.'[190] Perhaps more important still, Münster added, the monied interest, especially the Jewish part of it, had decided that dictatorship would constitute a more effective dam against socialism and anti-Semitism: 'I have also heard that the great Israelite

[185] Roscher, *Politik*, 714.   [186] *Münchner Neueste Nachrichten*, 16 Dec. 1905.
[187] *Frankfurter Zeitung*, 4 Feb. 1909.
[188] Münster, 27 Feb. 1899, AA R7170, A2413.
[189] Münster, 10 Jan. 1899, AA R6594, A394.   [190] Ibid.

financiers are supporting the Bonapartists and will give them significant sacrifices of money. The Dreyfus case and hatred of the Jews
has become dangerous for them and the struggle of socialists against
capital is rightly making them anxious. They hope that a new empire
will protect them better than the republic.'[191] In January 1899, the
ambassador anticipated a coup after the fall of the Dupuy ministry,
during the subsequent period of pro- and anti-socialist stalemate, or
after an unsuccessful colonial war with Britain.[192] Although such
analyses were founded on a critique of democratic corruption and
inefficacy, they also included the premiss that monarchist values in
the army were both desirable and inevitable, since command and
obedience could only rest on hierarchy, assigned duties, and granted
freedoms, not on equality, negotiated responsibilities, and freedoms of
right. Such values were apolitical in the sense that the army would
work with the republic, so long as republicans did not intervene in
military affairs. But, continued Münster, if republicans insisted on
politicizing the army, then officers would react in favour of dictatorship: 'A great danger lies in the army, whose discipline, first eaten
away by Boulanger, has very much suffered during the Dreyfus
affair.'[193] Even the second secretary, who had previously tempered
Münster's apocalyptic dispatches, agreed with his ambassador by June
1899 that a reversion to Caesarism was conceivable.[194] All that had
been lacking in recent months was a charismatic and ruthless leader:

If a political upheaval in France remains improbable for the foreseeable future,
since the necessary prerequisite for it is lacking, namely a suitable personality, it
is still unmistakable that discontentment, not so much with the republic itself,
as with the present form of it, *increasingly grips more and more circles*. The most
menacing symptom is, according to the unanimous judgement of the most
diverse, experienced observers, that the *malaise in the army, i.e. amongst officers,
is steadily increasing*.[195]

One month later the *Berliner Lokal-Anzeiger*, a conservative newspaper with government connections, rehearsed the same arguments
for the 500,000 German households in which it was read: only the
absence of a suitable general or pretender had allowed the survival of
the Third Republic.[196] This belief of German conservatives in the

[191] Ibid. Münster, 10 July 1900, AA R7189, A9173.
[192] Münster, 10 July 1900, AA R7189, A9173.   [193] Ibid.
[194] Below, 16 Jan. 1899, AA R6594, A638, and 4 Feb. 1899, AA R6594, A1464.
[195] Below, 16 June 1899, AA R6594, A7334.
[196] *Berliner Lokal-Anzeiger*, 28 July 1899.

ineluctability of a *coup d'état* in France was not part of a wider faith in the French right, however. The *Neue Preußische Zeitung*, which remained ardently monarchist, was convinced by 1898, 'that the restoration of the throne is becoming increasingly improbable, and that the monarchical parties, if things continue, must finally disappear.'[197] The Orleanists were portrayed as powerless and ineffectual conspirators, whilst Paul Déroulède, the leader of the nationalists, was variously ridiculed as a 'trouble-maker', an 'operetta hero' and Don Quixote.[198] Rather, German conservatives' premonitions of dictatorship were prompted, directly, by the Third Republic itself or, at least, by a conservative conception of the French republic. As the *Leipziger Neueste Nachrichten* expatiated, during the siege of the Parisian headquarters of the anti-Semites in the rue Chabrol, figures such as Guérin, Déroulède, and Buffet constituted no threat in themselves to the republic, yet they were nevertheless representative of a much more widely felt dissatisfaction with republican government: 'Herr Guérin and his kind belong precisely to those masses, the number of which is not at all to be underestimated, who are moved by a deep hatred of the republic of Mammon, of a state form, which secured the robbery perpetrated by those terrible Panama fellows and allows corruption to flood far into the circles of representatives of the people, justice, officer corps, ruling elites.'[199] In the words of the *Dresdner Nachrichten*, France was now reaping the rewards of the frivolous games with state authority, which it had played during the preceding thirty years: 'the political horse-trading, nepotism in the civil service, the unconcealed, money-bag regime with its shameless corruption, all this is now taking revenge on its initiators and supporters.'[200]

Given that France was perceived to be in a state of dissolution, with its populace angered by republican corruption and its army alienated by political interference, it was understandable that German conservatives took the menace of dictatorship seriously.[201] Initially, almost all right-wing groups in France were seen to endanger the

[197] *Neue Preußische Zeitung*, 25 July 1898. Also ibid., 20 Jan. 1898 and 4 Mar. 1898.
[198] Ibid., 8 Dec. 1898, 1 Mar., 19 Sept., 27 Oct. 1899; ibid, 27 Sept. 1898, 25 Feb. and 13 July 1899. Ibid., 3 June 1899.
[199] *Leipziger Neueste Nachrichten*, 15 Aug. 1899.
[200] *Dresdner Nachrichten*, 23 Aug. 1899.
[201] *Neue Preußische Zeitung*, 1 and 2 Feb., 27 June, 7 July, 13 Sept. 1899 and 2 Mar., 20 Sept., 1 Nov. 1898. *Reichsbote*, 4 Aug. 1899.

republic's existence. In 1898, for example, the Ligue des Patriotes was depicted as a resurrected Boulangist movement, with the same potential for disruption and change as its predecessor.[202] Similarly, on occasions, the Bonapartists were paraded as France's next rulers, with the *Neue Preußische Zeitung* confident, that 'Napoleon is the only name which still has a good reputation today in France'.[203] As late as November 1899, the same newspaper cited six monarchist, nationalist, or Bonapartist plots against the republic in that year to prove that the idea of a *coup d'état* was achieving an ever-wider political currency.[204] Yet the principal threat of dictatorship was seen to come from the army. The *Deutsche Tageszeitung* routinely predicted the advent of a French military regime, in spite of confirming the weakness of French forces: 'Today, we could even contemplate a military dictatorship in France, which will happen in the short or long run anyway, without a concern for a disturbance of the peace, since a military dictator, too, would not dare suddenly to start a war with Germany.'[205] Officers like Zurlinden, Marchand, Gallieni, and Mercier were presented one after the other as potential dictators, but none of them had possessed the courage, in the opinion of German conservatives, to do more than posture.[206] Partly as a response to republican intervention, some French generals had been drawn into politics: the result was frequent, politically motivated declarations against the republic, rather than a nationally motivated *coup d'état*. This was the true meaning of critical conservative allusions to Spanish conditions in the French army: 'France has a surplus of such sickly, somewhat Spanish generals, and that alone is alarming.'[207] The point was not that dictatorship was indefensible, but, on the contrary, that French generals were too cowardly, partial, or self-interested to establish a genuine, national military regime, which would serve the nation by ending anarchy: 'There is no lack of symptoms for severe illness of the capitalist republic. . . . It cannot be doubted that an energetic hand could topple the whole republican house of cards. But, unfortunately, nothing of such a consiously powerful, well-guided hand has yet been felt.'[208] Yet, at least during the crises of 1898–1900,

---

[202] *Neue Preußische Zeitung*, 29 Sept. 1898.   [203] Ibid., 5 Oct. 1898.
[204] Ibid., 8 Nov. 1899.   [205] *Deutsche Tageszeitung*, 15 Aug. 1899.
[206] Ibid., 26 Sept. 1898, 27 May 1899 and 16 Aug. 1899 on Zurlinden, Marchand, Gallieni, and Mercier, respectively.
[207] Ibid., 15 Mar. 1899. Ibid., 26 Sept. 1898 and 18 Jan. 1898.
[208] Ibid., 7 June 1899.

few German conservatives doubted that a sure and forceful hand would pick up the reins of power in France. Even though it denied that revolution and *coup d'état* were imminent in September 1899, as the liberal *Berliner Tageblatt* had prophesied, the *Neue Preußische Zeitung* did agree that political collapse was almost inescapable. Moreover, when it occurred, the republic would be unable to restore order: 'Once the cards have been dealt out, it is almost impossible to get them back in, and the first of these things has already happened in France.'[209] To German conservatives, the Third Republic appeared doomed to failure. Dictatorship looked likely.

German socialists were of the same opinion. Like conservatives, they proposed that Caesarist regimes usually replaced corrupt republics. Unlike conservatives, they portrayed Caesarism as an extension of that republican corruption rather than as an antidote to it. Whilst conservatives thought that surviving monarchical traditions within and without the French state would merge with modern, dictatorial reactions to the republic, socialists believed that bourgeois republicans would willingly join forces with monarchists, Bonapartists, and nationalists against the proletariat. It was for this reason that *Vorwärts* envisaged the creation of a 'military republic' and wrote of the 'dictatorship' of the Radical war minister, Cavaignac: it seemed that the military republic was simply a step on the way to dictatorship.[210] German socialists were able to fuse the two concepts—republic and dictatorship—since they viewed both as oppressive oligarchies in terms similar to those of Roscher's theory of plutocracy: 'In both cases [Dreyfus and Panama] the ruling clique did its best, for the purpose of the crude [*grob-materiell*] salvage of the pillars of order [*Ordnungsstützen*]—here the principal Panama men [*Panamisten*], there the military oligarchy [*militärische Oligarchie*]—to destroy justice completely.'[211] Under the republic, as under dictatorial regimes, corruption and oppression appeared to be partners; hence the association of base materialism (*grob-materiell*) and pillars of order (*Ordnungsstützen*), fraudulent politicians (*Hauptpanamisten*) and officers (*militärische Oligarchie*), oligarchy (*Oligarchie*) and army (*militärisch*). During the transition to dictatorship, only the external configuration of political institutions would change, not the underlying configuration of class interests.

---

[209] *Deutsche Tageszeitung*, 13 Sept. 1899.
[210] *Vorwärts*, 1 Sept. 1898 and 10 July 1899.
[211] Ibid., 6 Jan. 1898.

The socialist press frequently assumed that bourgeois republicans had been tainted by militarism. In part, this was seen as a response to defeat in 1870: 'The enemies of the republic must hide themselves behind national or nationalist masks in order to lend an air of popularity to their plans.'[212] But it was also linked to class domination and the maintenance of a praetorian guard by the bourgeoisie. Fear of a democratic militia had persuaded republicans to adopt German methods of military organization:

After the smashing of France in the war of 1870/71, the creation of a great army was a requisite of national renaissance. Since, at that time, the spirit of democracy was not yet strong enough to effect a general arming of the people and the establishment of a militia, similar to that of Switzerland, an organization of the army on the model of the victorious German army was seized upon, and with this organization militarism entered the French republic, too, somewhat milder, but in essence just as dangerous for civic freedom as over here. In 1877, the new French army came within an ace of being used in a *coup d'état* against the republic. Since then, the danger, which is attached to militarism, faded into the background for a long time.[213]

In this intervening period, when militarism seemed to constitute less of a threat to France's political system, republicans had supported the army unthinkingly, observed *Vorwärts*. During the Dreyfus affair, however, the French military had reasserted itself and republicans, fearing that the republic was too weak to resist, had given way: 'Earlier, it [the Assembly] obeyed the General Staff more out of foolish chauvinism and—before elections—from fear of chauvinist voters. Now, it obeys ever more visibly and cynically out of a naked *fear of a military coup d'état*.'[214] Since, to socialists, the change from republic to dictatorship did not imply a significant shift—indeed, the French bourgeoisie had already shown that it could live comfortably under either regime[215]—it was easy for them to imagine the disappearance of the Third Republic. *Vorwärts* carried articles predicting a French *coup d'état* in February, September, and October 1898 and January, February, March, August, and September 1899.[216] German liberals were more circumspect than socialists about the connection between a corrupt republic and dictatorship. On the whole, they identified residual monarchism in France as the enemy of

---

[212] *Vorwärts*, 21 Sept. 1899.   [213] Ibid., 27 Oct. 1898.
[214] Ibid., 14 Feb. 1899.   [215] Ibid., 21 Sept. 1899. See also ibid., 25 Feb. 1898.
[216] Ibid., 25 Feb., 1 Sept., 27 Oct. 1898, 4 and 15 Jan., 7 and 16 Feb., 2 Mar., 13, 18 and 21 Aug. 1899.

the republican state, whereas German socialists believed in the collusion of republicans, monarchists, Bonapartists, and nationalists under the auspices of that same state. Although both German liberals and conservatives assumed the opposition of republicans and Caesarists, the sympathies of the former lay with the republic and those of the latter with dictatorship. What united liberals, conservatives, and socialists in Germany was the fact that they all anticipated the collapse of the republican regime and the coming of dictatorship in France. During French crises, liberals were often unambivalent in distinguishing republican friends and anti-republican foes, but they were equally certain that the republic really was in danger, despite the weakness of its enemies. As a result, most of the plots of right-wing parties, however amateur, were adjudged *coups d'état* rather than publicity stunts, which is how they were often treated by the German right. The *Freisinnige Zeitung*, for instance, referred to the Déroulède débâcle of February 1899 as 'Staatsstreichpläne in Frankreich' and warned its readers against complacency: 'According to various reports, the attempt was by no means so harmless.'[217] The moderate *National-Zeitung*, although it was calmer in its reporting, nevertheless thought that the affair had exposed latent anti-republicanism at the very core of the French state: 'Actually, there existed and still exist today numerous officials of all categories and grades, who would play a very ambiguous role in a plot from a reactionary or revolutionary direction, and on whom the government could not rely, because of their affiliation with the troublemakers, even though they do not have the slightest intention of going against their duty.'[218] Likewise, the government's uncovering of a conspiracy in August 1899, which occasioned the searching of royalists' and nationalists' houses, was generally taken seriously by liberal newspapers. The *Frankfurter Zeitung*, *Freisinnige Zeitung*, and *National-Zeitung* all reacted in similar fashion: 'Now, it would be ill-advised to take the entire conspiracy lightly and mock the vigilance of the government. . . . The Rocheforts and Drumonts are merely waiting cleverly in the wings until the time comes openly to lead the movement, and the case of General Négrier has revealed that there is no lack of elements in the army who would be ready one day to march against the republic.'[219]

---

[217] *Freisinnige Zeitung*, 1 Mar. 1899 and 28 Feb. 1899.
[218] *National-Zeitung*, 28 Feb. 1899.
[219] *Frankfurter Zeitung*, 15 Aug. 1899. *Freisinnige Zeitung*, 13. Aug. 1899; *National-Zeitung*, 15 Aug. 1899.

Such party plotting was accorded great weight by German liberals because it seemed to implicate parts of the French state, particularly the army. Left-liberal and National Liberal newspapers talked of 'the spread of a dangerous, anti-republican spirit' and 'of an ultramontane-led, military dictatorship' without further explanation, since it was obvious to them after the Dreyfus affair that military circles in France harboured dictatorial ambitions.[220] With hindsight, it was this threat of dictatorship, combined with the threat of revolution from the left, which appeared to have characterized the first thirty years of the Third Republic: 'The great and, as it now seems after thirty years' experience, insuperable difficulties of the republic are being created for it, not by external opponents, but by domestic parties. It is constantly threatened by conspiracy and *coup d'état*, on one side, social-democratic revolution on the other.'[221] If the ultimate test of a political regime was its own survival, then the French Third Republic, German observers of all political parties were convinced at some time or other, was about to fail.

4. Republic *faute de mieux*

French crises revealed that German declarations of support for the Third Republic were founded more on hope than on conviction. Few Germans trusted resolutely in the strength of the republican form of government in France. Indeed, some conservatives remained sceptical about its survival until 1914.[222] Yet, between crises, many Wilhelmine correspondents came to believe that the republic would probably endure. Haas, Schmitz, Vogel, and others all employed the standard form of words: 'The republic is more solid today than ever.'[223] Unsurprisingly, liberal newspapers joined the chorus: 'the republic itself rests on an almost thirty-year-old habit of rule. All powers, constitutional as well as usurpatory, which have replaced each other since 1789, have not had nearly as long an unchallenged period of domination.'[224] Such testimonies, however,

---

[220] *Freisinnige Zeitung*, 26 Sept. 1900, and *National-Zeitung*, 10 Sept. 1899.

[221] *National-Zeitung*, 6 Nov. 1904.

[222] *Posener Tageblatt*, 9 Jan. 1900; *Post*, 9 June 1902; *Neue Preußische Zeitung*, 12 May 1904; *Reichsbote*, 7 Nov. 1908 and 12 July 1911; *Agrarpolitische Wochenschrift*, 1 Mar. 1913 and 1 Nov. 1913.

[223] Schmitz, *Das Land der Wirklichkeit*, 264. Haas, *Frankreich*, 119; Vogel, *Die dritte französische Republik*, 478.

[224] *National-Zeitung*, 19 Feb. 1899. See also, *Frankfurter Zeitung*, 29 Apr. 1908.

were always carefully qualified. The Third Republic had, after all, narrowly escaped revolution and *coups d'état* during its short existence: its survival was a talking-point precisely because it appeared so precarious, even to liberal publications like the *National-Zeitung*: 'each time, republican institutions have shown themselves to be stronger than all threats, and alleged and real plots.'[225]

The reasons commonly given by German authors for the endurance of the republican regime in France were almost all negative. True, some writers referred to a republican or democratic faith—'France is republican because, by an overwhelming majority, it earnestly and decidedly wants the republic'[226]—but most pointed to conservatism, fear, apathy, and the weakness of the French right as causes of the republic's longevity: 'No one will claim that... the country, with respect to its parliamentary life and its government, has brilliant experiences to boast of. What speaks for the probability of the continued existence of the... Third Republic... is the remarkable weakness and lack of direction with which its adversaries, the pretenders and leaders of the monarchists and Bonapartism, have opposed it until now.'[227] Frenchmen had come to accept the republic, conservative writers such as Vogel agreed with liberal newspapers like the *Berliner Tageblatt*, not because they believed in the republican system, but because they could not think of a better alternative. Both their dissatisfaction and their acceptance were motivated by political disillusion and apathetic, cynical envy:

> The broad masses in France have no political ideals whatever today—no political system which they would like to put in the place of the present system.... The present government does not have a great anti-republican party to fight, but it sees itself confronting a mood of annoyance, jealous curses, and irritated listlessness, for whose growth the sins of the ruling groups just as much as the undermining mole's work of their opponents are to be blamed.[228]

Time had worked in the Third Republic's favour, it was argued, so that a change of regime appeared to threaten disruption, violence, and impoverishment. Even in 1899 the *National-Zeitung*, in its sober moments, recognized this principle of inertia: 'The mass of the people

[225] *National-Zeitung*, 19 Feb. 1899. See also *Freisinnige Zeitung*, 30 June 1902, and *Berliner Börsenzeitung*, 25 Sept. 1901.

[226] Steinhauser, *Neuestes aus Frankreich*, 8. Fernau, *Französische Demokratie*, 126.

[227] Vogel, *Die dritte französische Republik*, 4. Schmoller, *Skizze einer Finanzgeschichte von Frankreich, Österreich, England und Preußen*, 18.

[228] *Berliner Tageblatt*, 10 Jan. 1900. Vogel, *Die dritte französische Republik*, 96-7.

will always, as long as conditions do not become unbearable, prefer what exists to all other prospects, however brilliant, which could only be realized by an insurrection.'[229] Republicans, it seemed, had been able to use popular fear of instability and revolution in order to ostracize the French right, which was effectively excluded from the political nation. The nationalists, who had gained control of Paris in the municipal elections of 1900, lost so many votes in the Assembly elections of 1902 by ignoring popular anxiety about anti-republicanism that they never recovered their political position: 'They overlooked the fact that a very great proportion of voters, who are otherwise not particularly partial to the present governors, fear nothing more than a revolution, a change of regime [*Staatsform*].'[230] As long as the republicans commanded an overall majority in the chambers, then republican governments could treat the right-wing parties, which were deemed anti-republican, as if they did not exist: 'Although they almost matched the left in strength—310 against 340—the right was excluded systematically from the leadership of the chamber...as well as from all important committees, especially the budget committee. Yes, the rule was established, and used many times, of treating conservative votes as if they did not exist.'[231] This was the reason that moderate and right-wing republicans like Sadi Carnot and Raymond Poincaré paid such attention to 'la majorité républicaine' and consistently snubbed monarchists and nationalists.[232] It was also the other reason, in addition to election-fixing, for the significant number of French deputies, who canvassed under the wrong party label.[233]

To German commentators, it was one of the paradoxes of the French Third Republic that it had used its own weakness to deflect criticism and isolate opposition. Republicans, it appeared, had been able to rely on the slogan 'La République en danger' to rally forces precisely because most Frenchmen genuinely believed that the republic was near to collapse and wished to avoid the disruption which that collapse would cause. In other words, the fragility of the

---

[229] *National-Zeitung*, 19 Feb. 1899. Steinhauser, *Neuestes aus Frankreich*, 7.

[230] Anon., *Das heutige Frankreich*, 18.

[231] Ibid. 7. Kuhn, *Aus dem modernen Babylon*, 227. *Neue Preußische Zeitung*, 23 May 1906.

[232] Kuhn, *Aus dem modernen Babylon*, 12–13, noted that, on his tours of France, Sadi Carnot tried to avoid stopping in conservative areas at all, but, if it proved unavoidable, he insisted on excoriating the conservative reception party.

[233] Fernau, *Die französische Demokratie*, 22; Steinhauser, *Neuestes aus Frankreich*, 8.

republican regime seemed to be its greatest strength. It was not to be confused with progress or success. This was the conclusion of Richard Sternfeld's history of France:

The domestic political life of France shows no progress. The republic has been consolidated not through love and the republican virtue of the French, but through the fear that they might be faced with still worse conditions and new unrest under a different form of government. Now as before, the capital dominates the provinces; more than ever, the nation is split into broad conservative strata, who support the Catholic church and obey the clergy, and into a free-thinking minority, who voice the democratic theories of the great revolution and wish to bring up children without religion. The hunt for office, the search to obtain a post and to use it for profit are fed by changing ministries and by the clientele of civil servants and deputies; behind closed doors, financiers and stock-brokers exercise great and damaging influence over politicians and press. It is rare for someone to expose the failings of the nation, without flattery or party-interest, and to urge that they be counteracted.[234]

The proud hopes of the French political state, which had been based on democracy, had, in the opinion of many Germans, been confounded by overambition. A priori assumptions about liberty and equality underpinned the republic, rather than inherited practices and adapted institutions. As a result, it had been expected that governments, which had been popularly elected, would be answerable to and informed by the populace. This trust in a popular check on government had, ultimately, led to the merger of executive and legislative functions, in the name of popular sovereignty, it was claimed. It seemed to many German onlookers, however, that less consideration had been given in France to practical, historically proven difficulties such as societal atomization, conflicts of economic interest or cultural preference, political fragmentation, abuse of the press, corruption, and demagogy. Each of these difficulties had come to beset the Third Republic, they went on, to the point where the very survival of the French regime appeared open to doubt. The implication of such German arguments was not that universal suffrage and democracy, however defined, inevitably produced anarchy, oligarchy, or dictatorship, but rather that they could have such effects, if means were not found to avert them. The French Third Republic did not seem to have found such means.

[234] Sternfeld, *Französische Geschichte*, 188–9.

5

German Rejection of the French Parliamentary Republic

German statesmen, diplomats, politicians, journalists, and writers all subscribed, with some qualifications, to certain core elements of a political myth of France in the Wilhelmine period. Often to their own surprise, they found their sensibilities affronted by French political practice under the Third Republic. Through criticism, they came to define the weaknesses of the parliamentary republic in France and, frequently despite themselves, the strengths of the constitutional monarchy in Germany. This criticism, definition, and identification occurred in diverse fields and on different levels and produced dichotomies such as those between the German *Rechtsstaat* and the French political state, between German notions of freedom and French conceptions of equality, and between a German separation of functions and French parliamentarism. As has been seen above, these dichotomies were linked to concrete observations about the Third Republic, as well as being connected to each other in a broader political typology. It is the purpose of the next chapter to examine the external form and the internal parts, the extent, the limits, and the contradictions of this typology. First, however, it is necessary to chart the varying courses of political parties and of government in rejecting the Third Republic as a political paradigm which was worthy of imitation. For, although most German groups criticized the French regime in similar ways throughout the Wilhelmine period, such criticism coexisted, sometimes uneasily, with other judgements of French politics. Nevertheless, over time, criticism appeared to eclipse panegyric. By 1907, it was possible to discern a cross-party German rejection of the French republic.

1. Diplomats and Statesmen

Diplomats and statesmen, it was widely believed in Germany, had a unique understanding of foreign affairs.[1] According to a British envoy

[1] P. G. Lauren, *Diplomats and Bureaucrats* (Stanford, Calif., 1976), 57.

in 1906, the first question posed by an average German, confronted
by newspaper reports on events abroad, was whether coverage was
official or not. Only government-inspired articles were seen to be
trustworthy.[2] The Foreign Office, it was believed, was privy to con-
fidential information, from spies and politicians in camera, on secret
treaties and clouded affairs. Moreover, diplomats were supposedly
tied by profession to the national interest, above the preferences of
party, whilst at the same time being free of national prejudices, which
distorted perception and alienated foreigners:

For we diplomats are not sent abroad to live there as we please, but to win friends
for ourselves and therefore for our fatherland. If national opposition and a caste-
like ethos put obstacles in our way, it is necessary for us to try our luck with those
who are less prejudiced—and all the more so, as we also have the important and
gratifying task of getting to know a country and its people and to form as comprehensive a judgement as possible about their doings and dealings in politics and
economy, art and science.[3]

In theory, the importance of the diplomat's task—to secure
Germany's national interest—combined with specialist training in
order to ensure that he understood foreign institutions as they really
were, before going on to answer dependent questions concerning
foreign policy.

In practice, however, diplomats knew that biases and misunder-
standings were inevitable. This was especially true in parliamentary
democracies, where foreign affairs appeared to have passed into the
public domain, with its numerous and conflicting parties, presses, and
lobbies. Ambassadors and their secretaries constantly had to determine which group their interlocutors belonged to, before assessing
how those groups influenced policy making. Further, they had to
interpret foreign manners correctly, but resist being seduced by them.
In a letter to Maximilian Harden, which was published in *Die
Zukunft*, Graf Harry Keßler, a writer and diplomat, who had
spent much of his life in Paris, demonstrated how the two dangers—
misinterpretation and assimilation—could merge:

The German, who is used to rather poor or, let us say, all too straightforward
manners, and who comes to Paris for the first time in his mid-twenties or thirties
as a diplomat or journalist, takes the agreeable outward forms of the French, who
are always as careful and tactful as possible, to be friendliness and heart-felt

[2] P. G. Lauren, *Diplomats and Bureaucrats*, 55.
[3] K. v. Pückler, *Aus meinem Diplomatenleben* (Schweidnitz, 1934), 27–8.

emotion; with his eyes accustomed to cruder lines and colours, he does not see the nuances. He then falls, after a set amount of time, into one of two traps: either he declares all French people to be false and hates them forthwith, or he believes them all to be Germanophiles and pays back all their gambling chips with gold.[4]

Friedrich von Holstein, the most powerful counsellor in the Foreign Office, divided Germans into 'l'Allemagne prussienne', of which he himself was a representative, and 'l'Allemagne française', which had been won over by French manners and culture.[5] Radolin, who was the German ambassador in Paris from 1901 to 1910, was branded by his former sponsor as one of the latter. His dispatches, it was said, were weighted in favour of the French regime, with which the ambassador wished Germany to come to an agreement: 'At the moment, you are completely preoccupied by the idea of effecting a rapprochement between ourselves and France. Because of this fata morgana, you are neglecting your real task: observation and reporting of events in the entire political sphere.'[6] Radolin, continued Holstein, gave a partial view of France in his diplomatic correspondence. Such accusations were common in the Foreign Office, however, and seemed to turn on specific policy differences rather than on biased reporting. Holstein himself was charged by Alexander von Hohenlohe, the son of the chancellor, with mistaking the Third Republic of the 1870s, when he had been attached to the German embassy in Paris, for that of the 1900s: 'His whole policy, as far as France was concerned, rested on totally false foundations. He still lived as if confronted by the France of the seventies, during which he had been in Paris. He would not be deflected from this and allowed his policy to be based on entirely false ideas.'[7] Radolin extended the charge, inculpating the whole of the *Auswärtiges Amt*, which, he wrote, formulated German policy towards France on foundations of ignorance and misconception.[8] Both sides, it appeared, had translated particular disagreements over strategy— Radolin favoured rapprochement, Holstein brinkmanship—into

---

[4] H. Rogge (ed.), *Holstein und Harden* (Munich, 1959), 144.

[5] Ibid. 24.

[6] Holstein to Radolin, 6 Nov. 1901, in M. H. Fisher and N. Rich (eds.), *Die Geheimen Papiere Friedrich von Holsteins* (4 vols.; Göttingen, 1956), iv. 242; F. Thimme, 'Aus dem Nachlaß des Fürsten Radolin', *Berliner Monatshefte*, 15 (1937), 748, for another warning from Holstein on 14 June 1902; H. Raulff, *Zwischen Machtpolitik und Imperialismus* (Düsseldorf, 1976), 29.

[7] A. v. Hohenlohe, *Aus meinem Leben* (Frankfurt a.M., 1925), 317.

[8] L. Cecil, *The German Diplomatic Service, 1871–1914* (Princeton, 1976), 248.

general allegations about the misreading of French events, practices, and institutions, when, in fact, they differed little in their assessment of the republican regime in France. Accusation and counter-accusation contained in themselves no guarantee of truth, however distant and occluded. Although Radolin's reports were labelled pro-French by Holstein, they were alleged, by Bülow, Rosen, and Kühlmann, to be transcripts of Holstein's own memoranda.[9] Even Münster, who was depicted by some as an exemplary German ambassador to France, had been dubbed a French puppet by others.[10]

Pro-French sympathies were not the only grounds for allegations of diplomatic bias, however. It seemed to some observers, including insiders such as Wilhelm von Schoen, that the social exclusivity of German envoys, the majority of whom were noble, was inappropriate and might promote political partiality.[11] Münster, for example, was renowned for his aristocratic hauteur, whilst Radolin, his successor, was related by marriage to the Talleyrands, Rohans, and Castellanes.[12] When such connections and predispositions were added to a residual suspicion of republicans, which affected figures as different as Holstein and Ludwig II of Bavaria, who refused to meet MacMahon on his visit to Paris in 1876 because the latter was president of a republic, then it appeared probable that German ambassadors would be influenced unduly by French monarchists, nationalists, and Bonapartists.[13] Yet diplomats themselves went to considerable lengths to demonstrate the breadth of their range of contacts and acquaintances. Radolin claimed on several occasions that he had striven to ensure, that there was 'a simultaneous circulation of government circles and of the Faubourg [St Germain, a byword for French aristocracy] in the imperial embassy, on which I have placed great weight, so that the German embassy does not fall behind the other embassies where, likewise, representatives of all sides circulate'.[14] The list of republicans— Galliffet, Delcassé, Millerand, Pelletan, Loubet, Combes, Viviani,

[9] B. v. Bülow, *Denkwürdigkeiten* (Berlin, 1930), i. 496–7; R. v. Kühlmann, *Erinnerungen* (Heidelberg, 1948), 240; Thimme, 'Aus dem Nachlaß des Fürsten Radolin', 742.

[10] Bülow, *Denkwürdigkeiten*, i. 495; H. Rogge (ed.), *Holstein und Hohenlohe* (Stuttgart, 1957), 360; E. Oncken, *Panthersprung nach Agadir* (Düsseldorf, 1981), 151.

[11] Lauren, *Diplomats and Bureaucrats*, 66.

[12] Cecil, *The German Diplomatic Service*, 64; Thimme, 'Aus dem Nachlaß des Fürsten Radolin', 738, 743.

[13] Hohenlohe, *Aus meinem Leben*; N. Rich, *Friedrich von Holstein* (2 vols.; Cambridge, 1965), i. 63.

[14] Radolin, 4 Feb. 1904, AA R6827, A1917.

Caillaux, Briand, and Pichon—with whom Münster, Radolin, and Schoen had private audiences, appeared to substantiate the claim.[15] Indeed, the Germany embassy, it was said, was one of the few places in France where legitimists could meet their republican counterparts.[16] In an essay entitled 'Pariser Stimmung', which was published in *Die Zukunft* in 1907, Harden imagined Edward VII confiding in Clemenceau: 'I'm pleased that you have him [Radolin] here and that he and the princess are happy in Paris. Are loved, so I hear, not only in the Faubourg, but also by red republicans and are very proud that *citizen* Millerand sits at their table next to a Castellane. Each has his own particular ambition.'[17] German diplomats in France, it seemed clear, were not unreceptive to republican advances.

By the turn of the century, German aristocrats appeared to have come to terms with the French republic. As wealth began to impinge on title, Paris continued to set the tone for 'society' and, therefore, for diplomacy, despite the fact that it was republican: for Bülow, at least, the 'cosmopolitan-French airs of society' still constituted a requirement for diplomatic service.[18] Russian dukes, American heiresses, British peers, German princes, and French republicans all rubbed shoulders in a world of international luxury, in Philipp Eulenburg's phrase, regardless of reproaches at home: 'The times of the Holy Alliance were over. . . . Even after the republican form of government had established itself in France, not only externally but also internally, European princes and dukes led pilgrimages to Paris, as they had for decades sought out the Paris of the Bourbons, the Orléans, and the Bonapartes. The English heir to the throne and Russian grand dukes, by their good and more often bad example, showed all the others the way.'[19] This atmosphere of social promiscuity in republican

---

[15] Münster, 25 May 1900, AA R7127, A6526; Radolin, 3 Mar. 1901, AA R7058, A3395; Radolin, 4 June 1901, AA R7127, AA8433; Radolin, 10 June 1902, AA R7128, AA9080; Radolin, 4 Nov. 1903, AA R7062, A16341; Radolin, 11 Nov. 1904, AA R7129, A17839; Radolin, 30 Oct. 1906, AA R7131, A18395; Radolin, 14 Feb. 1907, AA R6680, A2692; Lancken, 21 Oct. 1910, AA R7040, A17738; Schoen, 29 Oct. 1910, AA R7069, A18122.

[16] Thimme, 'Aus dem Nachlaß des Fürsten Radolin', 743; Hohenlohe, *Aus meinem Leben*, 77.

[17] Rogge (ed.), *Holstein und Harden*, 123. The article appeared on 8 Feb. 1907 and does not seem to have been inspired by Holstein, who wrote a letter to Harden the day after criticizing the references to Radolin.

[18] J. C. G. Röhl (ed.), *Philipp Eulenburgs politische Korrespondenz* (Boppard, 1976), i. 616.

[19] Bülow, *Denkwürdigkeiten*, iv. 479. B. v. Hutten-Czapski, *Sechzig Jahre Politik und Gesellschaft* (Berlin, 1936), i. 91; P. zu Eulenburg-Hertenfeld, *Erlebnisse an deutschen und fremden Höfen* (Leipzig, 1934), 150.

France affected much of the German diplomatic establishment, which had served there, including Holstein, Hohenlohe, Eulenburg, Kiderlen-Wächter, Schoen, Metternich, and Pourtalès, and many others, such as Eckardstein, who sojourned there.[20] Bülow, for instance, who was second secretary in Paris during the late 1870s and early 1880s, mixed with republicans as diverse as Gambetta, Galliffet, Waldeck-Rousseau, Scheurer-Kestner, and the Cambon brothers in the salons of Roger du Nord and Georges Pallain, the director of the Banque de France.[21] Relations seemed to be so cordial at one point that the Président du Conseil, Freycinet, considered, if Bülow were to be believed, marrying his daughter to the German ambassador's son.[22] The aristocratic German diplomatic corps appeared to harbour few social scruples vis-à-vis republican France.

Envoys did harbour other prejudices, however. These tended to merge in what might be described as a functional adaptation of a conservative myth of the French parliamentary republic. It was the function of the Foreign Office, of course, to assess how France was likely to act and how Germany should counter her actions. This, in turn, involved a calculation of France's strength: how much of a threat did France pose to the security of the Reich? It was here that conservative conceptions of republican government came into play: in general, German answers in the Wilhelmine period followed Bismarck's maxim that the republic weakened France most.[23] By the 1880s, it had become a truism within the *Auswärtiges Amt* that the French republican regime had been kept alive by German interventions alone. According to diplomats such as Herbert von Bismarck and Chlodwig zu Hohenlohe-Schillingsfürst, this had been accepted in France by republicans—'The republicans know very well that they were mainly kept afloat by us'[24]—and monarchists alike: 'From the remarks above, it is clear how much the monarchist party...is convinced that the republic survives only through the good wishes and offices of Germany.'[25] What was more, the legend of a French republic protected

---

[20] H. v. Eckardstein, *Lebenserinnerungen und politische Denkwürdigkeiten* (3 vols.; Leipzig, 1919).

[21] Bülow, *Denkwürdigkeiten*, iv. 466–73.   [22] Ibid. 484.

[23] Cecil, *The German Diplomatic Service*, 198.

[24] W. Bußmann (ed.), *Staatsekretär Herbert von Bismarck. Aus seiner politischen Privatkorrespondenz* (Göttingen, 1964), 168.

[25] F. Curtius (ed.), *Chlodwig, Fürst zu Hohenlohe-Schillingsfürst. Denkwürdigkeiten* (2 vols.; Stuttgart, 1906), ii. 350.

by Germany for its own purposes persisted until 1914 and beyond. Alexander von Hohenlohe, who had become a republican under Weimar, still maintained that the French political system had only survived during its first two decades because of Bismarck.[26] Likewise, Bernhard von Bülow, despite emphasizing 'the life-force and elasticity' of France, which had been proven during the First World War, nevertheless recorded that the Third Republic corresponded to the German chancellor's wishes, since it was less likely to go to war, for fear of dictatorship: 'This corresponded with the wishes of Prince Bismarck and the goals of his policy. He was convinced that a democratic and republican France would be more peaceful than a monarchical one.'[27] In a letter to Eulenburg in March 1893, he spelled out his position: 'Parliamentary anarchy' in France was to Germany's advantage, he wrote:

We do best if we give the impression that we are indifferent to domestic events in France, and yet keep a sharp eye on these and secretly favour those elements which are most damaging to France's position of power, namely the doctrinaire Opportunists and headless Radicals.... When the pestilential boils on the French body slowly and gradually seep into the juices and blood, when chronic infirmity results and the weakened and dishonoured republic goes on vegetating, we can congratulate ourselves.[28]

Wilhelm II made the same point, more bluntly, in 1904: 'As for France, we both know that the radical or anti-Christian party, which for the moment appears to be the strongest one, inclines towards England, the Crimean tradition, but is opposed to war, because a victorious general would mean certain destruction to this republic of miserable civilians.'[29] Unlike German political parties, the Reich government not only mouthed the commonplace that republics were weaker than other political systems; it actually acted by that commonplace.

The German administration's suspicions about the Third Republic were confirmed by the perceived disintegration of the French state. They focused above all on politicization, mutiny, and anti-militarism in the army and on strikes within the civilian state. The significance

---

[26] Hohenlohe, *Aus meinem Leben*, 394.
[27] Bülow, *Denkwürdigkeiten*, iv. 478.
[28] Bülow to Eulenburg, 13 Mar. 1893, cited in P. Winzen, *Bülows Weltmachtkonzept* (Boppard, 1977), 47; Rogge (ed.), *Holstein und Hohenlohe*, 176.
[29] William II to Nicholas II, 30 Oct. 1904, cited in B. v. Bülow, *Deutschland und die Mächte* (Dresden, 1929), 150.

of the former was underlined by Bülow, who wrote a detailed memo-randum on the decline of the French military for Bethmann Hollweg, just before resigning in 1909. It was the only essay written by a German chancellor on French domestic affairs between 1898 and 1914.[30] At its core was the premiss, shared by many of Bülow's col-leagues, that a republic was, ultimately, incompatible with an efficient army: 'The army, in particular, despite commendable individual efforts, lacks both seriousness and momentum. Political and social conditions, as they have developed in France, are decisive in this respect. For a republic, it is in any case very difficult to keep the army at the height of its powers, for an overall chief, which soldiers naturally need, is lacking.'[31] As far as officers were concerned, continued the chancellor, republican governments could never replace an overall commander of the army, because their interventions were political, capricious, and incompetent. Promotion was dictated by political reli-ability and favouritism rather than by courage, honour, experience, and capability. As a consequence, the *état-major* divided along polit-ical lines, which necessarily impaired chains of command: 'Under these conditions, politics can barely be separated from military dis-cussion and endeavours. Supporters and opponents of the government are split. In this way, trust in superiors, subordinates, and colleagues suffers. . . . In no monarchy is the system of protection and patronage so well-developed as in the French republic.'[32] For conscripts, the politicization of the French military was, if anything, even more unsettling, for it ended the special status of the army as an apolitical, national institution. As soon as political parties began to interfere routinely in military affairs, service appeared to become a matter of political preference. Moreover, it also allowed political parties, whose ideologies ran counter to obedience-based military values, to denounce the army with impunity:

Will the good and warlike attributes of the French soldier remain in existence over the long term? All the more so as revolutionary propaganda seeks, through refutation, to shake these qualities and to make the estate [*Stand*] of soldiers contemptible? This process of undermining begins in the schools. For the anti-militarists famously have most supporters precisely amongst elementary-school teachers. And the struggle of civil servants against the state as boss... gives an indication in which direction men are led in later life. The army

---

[30] Or, at least, the only such essay in the 'Frankreich' files of the *Auswärtiges Amt*.
[31] Bülow, 15 May 1909, AA R6605, A8510.   [32] Ibid.

cannot remain fully foreign to such fermentation, which moves such broad sections of the people.[33]

To Bülow, the French army had been drawn into the internecine conflicts of the political state and, as a result, had been weakened.[34] German envoys, counsellors, and attachés came to similar conclusions.[35]

In his memorandum, Bülow adverted to the second focus for German worries about the French state: the unionization of civil servants, which culminated in the postal workers' strike of March 1909 and the rail strike of October 1910. As with the army, German diplomats reacted strongly to the incursion of socialism into the state: 'The mutinous character of this time's strike movement of post and telegraph functionaries shows how much socialist-revolutionary feelings and, as it were, purposeful, systematic unruliness against higher authorities have now spread to state employees too.'[36] To French socialists, it was contended, the state was merely another capitalist employer run by corrupt and 'Manchesterite' political parties. It appeared natural, therefore, for the 800,000 'prolétaires de l'Administration', in Jaurès's phrase, to resort to strikes and sabotage to improve their working conditions: 'Understandably, unconcerned about the interests of the public service and of the country itself, they regard the state as a tough employer, which must be fought with the same weapons, with strike threats, even with sabotage—destruction of tools and machines—and deliberately poor work, just like any other "boss".'[37] As Oskar von der Lancken-Wakenitz, one of the secretaries of the German embassy in Paris, retorted to Briand's question about the probable response of the Reich government to a rail strike, such events still seemed inconceivable in Germany, with its tradition of neutral administration: 'I replied that our railway employees felt themselves to be civil servants and had not, to my knowledge, thought about a struggle against state and society.'[38] French governments had

[33] Ibid.

[34] H. Rogge (ed.), *Friedrich von Holstein. Lebensbekenntnisse in Briefen an eine Frau* (Berlin, 1932), 286; J. Penzler (ed.), *Fürst Bülows Reden* (3 vols.; Berlin, 1907), iii. 411.

[35] Eulenburg, 18 Jan. 1898, AA R6740, A679; Münster, 10 Oct. 1898, AA R6593, A11682; the navy attaché, Siegel, 26 Nov. 1902, AA R6783, A17553 and 7 Dec. 1903, AA R6783, A18922; the military attaché, Hugo, 12 Aug. 1905, AA R6747, A14624; Radolin, 20 Oct. 1908, AA R6786, A17423; Winterfeldt, 27 May 1910, AA R6751, A9196, 30 Aug. 1911, AA R6753, A13921, and 11 May 1912, AA R7041, A8607.

[36] Radolin, 16 Mar. 1909, AA R6605, A4831.

[37] Ibid. Lancken, 29 July 1909, AA R7174, A12703.

[38] Lancken, 21 Oct. 1910, AA R7040, A17738.

been forced by the logic of parliamentarism to tolerate socialism and unions within the state, for they had often required socialist votes in the chamber in order to stay in office. Radolin had observed that 'the authorization to state employees to form unions' had been government policy as early as March 1906, to which Wilhelm II's response, in the margin, had been '!!!'[39] He also noted, along with Lancken, that the ministers confronted by the unions—Clemenceau and Briand—had themselves previously encouraged unionization and strikes from the opposition benches.[40] Under such circumstances, it appeared unlikely that ministries would legislate either to improve the poor conditions of state employees, who were underpaid and unprotected against nepotism, or to make strikes within the state illegal. The French parliamentary regime, which was eager to profit from *l'assiette au beurre*, yet which was fearful of antagonizing socialists and union members, found itself deprived of both carrot and stick.[41] To German diplomats, the consequence seemed to be the near-collapse of administration in France.[42] For 48 hours during the postal strike, the French Foreign Office had been completely cut off from its embassies and consulates. If a war had started, the government in France would not have known about it. Wilhelm II's annotation was laconic but expressive: 'Republic!'[43]

There is evidence that chancellors, envoys, secretaries, and counsellors all associated the parliamentary and republican system of government with the decline of France.[44] For statesmen such as Hohenlohe, French republicanism was only infectious for neighbouring monarchies when it was in opposition: as soon as republics had been declared, they had served as a warning rather than as an example to German onlookers.[45] Likewise, for Bülow, Paris, although enchanting,

---

[39] Radolin, 13 Mar. 1906, AA R7131, A5268.

[40] Radolin, 16 May 1907, AA R7174, A8053; Lancken, 16 Oct. 1910, AA R6607, A17414.

[41] Khevenhüller, 14 Dec. 1907, AA R6604, A1054; Lancken, 16 Oct. 1910, AA R6607, A17414.

[42] Radolin, 24 May 1909, AA R6607, A17617.

[43] Radolin, 24 Mar. 1909, AA R6605, A5414.

[44] F. Fischer, 'Das Bild Frankreichs in Deutschland in den Jahren vor dem ersten Weltkrieg', *Revue d'Allemagne*, 4 (1972), 507–8, and Raulff, *Zwischen Machtpolitik und Imperialismus*, 17, 31–9. One exception to such Foreign Office critics appeared to be Bethmann Hollweg's personal secretary and adviser on foreign affairs, Kurt Riezler [pseud. J. J. Ruedorffer], *Grundzüge der Weltpolitik in der Gegenwart* (Berlin, 1913), 82–3.

[45] Curtius (ed.), *Chlodwig zu Hohenlohe-Schillingsfürst*, ii. 330, citing Duclerc; 'Die französische Republik sei für die benachbarten Monarchien nur dann ansteckend, wenn sie nicht existiere. Die Monarchie könne sich in Frankreich nie lange halten, und ihrer Zusammenbruch bringe weithin fühlbare Erschütterungen mit sich. Ich habe Duclerc meine ganze Zustimmung zu seiner Auffassung ausgesprochen.'

was nevertheless an 'Afterzivilisation', with radicalism and parliamentarism existing as both symptom and cause of its decay.[46] In the French capital itself, German representatives concurred with their chancellor. Whereas in Germany 'we can talk of a turn for the better', reported Münster, in France it was regrettable that 'everything was going downhill'.[47] Eight years later, and in very different circumstances, Radolin rehearsed the same argument 'that France was going backwards, militarily, politically and socially'.[48] Four years after that, Schoen returned to Paris as ambassador, having worked in the embassy as a secretary in the 1890s. His summary of the changes, which had occurred in France between 1895 and 1911, constituted the most extensive indictment of French republicanism to be found in Foreign Office archives.

Granted, the Third Republic had established itself, conceded the ambassador: 'Twenty years ago, the republican form of state was still, even if elections returned strong republican majorities, by no means a phenomenon which was defended adequately against every attack.... Today, these tremors in France's body of state, which were provoked by monarchist agitation, can be seen as having been overcome. The republic emerged from those crises victorious.'[49] But that was all. Schoen's analysis started from the premiss that the republic's constant course towards the left carried chaos, corruption, and deadlock in its wake. Even radical ministers such as Clemenceau and Briand had felt compelled to oppose the excesses of anti-clericalism, anti-militarism, and revolutionary syndicalism, which republican demagogy had fostered in France:

The gaping abyss, which the republic has carefully to avoid, if it wants to retain its present form, is on the left, not on the right. In the same measure that the republic has become the master of its monarchist opponent, it has got onto the steep and slippery slope of Radicalism, drunk with victory, and has slid down this so quickly that the efforts of every clear-sighted and duty-bound government should be aimed at stopping this damaging trend.[50]

Schoen went on to explain how French decline under the Third Republic had created a fear of war and had thereby curbed revanchism.

[46] Bülow to Eulenburg, 10 July 1889, Röhl (ed.), *Philipp Eulenburgs politische Korrespondenz*, i, on 'die Pariser Afterzivilisation'. Rogge (ed.), *Friedrich von Holstein*, 289.
[47] Münster, 5 Jan. 1899, AA R7056, A259.
[48] Rogge (ed.), *Friedrich von Holstein*, 285.
[49] Schoen, 5 Jan. 1911, AA R6608, A319.   [50] Ibid.

During the last two decades, Frenchmen had come to realize that Germany's army was not merely more numerous, potentially, than its own, but also more reliable: 'In addition, there is for France, as an unfavourable and serious factor, the contamination of broad strata of the population with anti-militarism, which contains serious dangers for mobilization, deployment, and discipline.'[51] Moreover, Germany's military superiority was reinforced by the performance of its industry, the expansion of its trade, the strength of its banks, improvement in its living standards, the depth of its education, the precision of its science, the loyalty of its bureaucracy, the excellence of its public institutions, and the exemplary nature of its welfare system. By contrast, France seemed to have stood still or gone backwards, sometimes because of weakness of character—lack of entrepreneurial spirit, self-interest, superficiality—more often because of politics: 'Industry is hindered by the tendency of workers, encouraged by the democratic system, towards extreme demands and strikes.'[52] Parliamentary republicanism appeared to Schoen to have vitiated many of France's advantages:

To all this can be added the unavoidable ramifications of this type of state and of republican practices for public life. Carelessness, short-sightedness, and incapacity, hidden by petty bureaucracy in state and communal administrations, slackness in public works and transport. Everywhere an attitude of let-it-go and let-it-happen, everywhere a perceptible lack of order and subordination. As spiritual nourishment for the people, a press of a low moral level. In the life of business, a developed system of mutual cheating....In the social round, a noticeable displacement of exemplary, old forms by republican and petty-bourgeois values. Even Paris, the dazzling world city, the metropolis of intellect, beauty, delights, and elegance, has lost much of its previous lustre. With regard to its external development and internal administration, to its transport system, to the friendliness of carefully prepared street scenes, it has been overtaken by Berlin by far.[53]

The ambassador's advice was to continue Bismarck's *politique du pire*, supporting the republican regime unostentatiously so 'that French decadence progresses all the more rapidly'.[54] In 1911, as in 1871, the Foreign Office remained convinced that the Third Republic was best for Germany because it was worst for France.

---

[51] Schoen, 5 Jan. 1911, AA R6608, A319. [52] Ibid.
[53] Ibid. William II's annotation concerning the reference to Berlin was an exulted 'so!'
[54] Ibid.

2. Conservatives

Like the correspondence of the Foreign Office, German conservatives' articles on France were concerned above all about army and
state, although more because the French *Armée* and *État* safeguarded
internal order than because they posed a threat to the Reich. Whereas
diplomats' prejudices against the republic were constantly tested by
their need to assess France's strength as objectively as possible, conservatives tended to see everything through an anti-republican and
anti-parliamentary filter. In other words, there was less tension
between ideology and strategy. The Dreyfus affair constituted a
significant watershed for the conservative press in Germany because
it proved conclusively that two of the principal institutions of the
French state—the judiciary and the military—had acted unjustly and
dishonestly. Since, to conservatives, partiality, injustice, and dishon-
esty were attributes of parliamentary republics rather than of armies
or judiciaries per se, French institutions were said to have been implicated in republican corruption. The practices and values of politics
appeared finally to have infected the state.

As has already been shown, the army was discredited in the eyes of
German conservatives during the Dreyfus affair. As details of the case
first came before the public, the *Neue Preußische Zeitung* was convinced that unscrupulous republicans were attacking the military,
which remained the only untainted state institution, for their own
short-term political advantage: ' "the whole world has gone mad", in
the words of Saint-Gest, and is eagerly trying to add serious injury to
the only vital force which the republic still has at its disposal, the
army and navy.'[55] The charge of fabrication levelled against the
republic seemed all the more credible to German conservatives
because they were able to identify a whole series of *bêtes noires* in the
affair. An ill-informed populace, a demagogic press, a self-interested
parliament, revolutionary socialism, and venal Jewry all appeared regularly in the columns of conservative newspapers, goading, bribing,
and coercing each other to extremes. The French public, which was
capable of supporting the generals one day and Jaurès the next, stood
at the centre of the system: 'The entire French nation has showed
once again that it is ready at any moment to go overboard when it
comes across a sensation.'[56] It was worked upon by polemical politicians

---

[55] *Neue Preußische Zeitung*, 8 Feb. 1898.   [56] Ibid., 2 Mar. 1898 and 5 Sept. 1898.

and irresponsible newspapers: 'the worst thing, which can be predicted with certainty, is that the final decision that France makes will
not be reached by the best and most prudent heads in the country...,
but by the 50 market criers, who think up the headlines in the Parisian
press.'[57] Worst of all, parliamentary politics and corruption exposed
the populace to the machinations of Jews, who sought to save one of
their own, and of socialists, who wanted to remove the army as the last
obstacle to revolution: 'I know, unfortunately, that Vaillant...only
seeks to remove that which most stands in the way of the realization
of his revolution plans, namely the army.'[58] With hindsight, both
the *Neue Preußische Zeitung* and the *Deutsche Tageszeitung* claimed
that the Dreyfus case had been artificially aggravated by Jewish newspapers and money.[59]

During the affair, however, in spite of occasional invectives against
the 'Goldene Internationale', conservatives came to recognize that
the army had acted illegally. It was at this point, after Henry's suicide,
that part of the military was denigrated as republican, and thereby
materialist, self-seeking, and immoral:

> The Dreyfus case has nothing at all to do with the anti-Semitic question, but with
> the degeneration of the republican officer corps, and it only has a cultural-historical
> and political significance for this reason. It demonstrates that materialism and
> selfishness, the absence of *sens moral* and feelings of duty, that these cancers, to
> which the republic might succumb, have also not spared the army, or at least its
> leaders. It is not anti-Semitism which is to blame for the lack of conscience of an
> Esterhazy, Paty du Clam, Henry, Zurlinden, or Boisdeffre.[60]

Henry, it was now certain, had been 'a very limited mind' and
Esterhazy, who had just published 'Die Dessous der Dreyfus-Sache',
'a notorious traitor and rogue'.[61] Both cast a long shadow over
the republican army, which had protected them, went on the *Neue
Preußische Zeitung*: 'what a light the thing throws on the *republican
officer corps*, which for so long tolerated an Esterhazy within its
ranks!'[62] Moreover, every day, it appeared, another corrupt republican
officer was added to the list, so that, by September 1898, the same

[57] *Neue Preußische Zeitung*, 5 Oct. 1898. Ibid., 22 July and 27 Sept. 1898 and 7 Nov. 1899.
[58] *Münchner Allgemeine Zeitung*, 31 Aug. 1898.
[59] *Deutsche Tageszeitung*, 21 July 1906. *Neue Preußische Zeitung*, 10 Jan. 1900.
[60] *Neue Preußische Zeitung*, 25 Nov. 1898.
[61] Ibid., 3 Sept. 1898 and 22 Nov. 1898.   [62] Ibid., 29 Sept. 1898.

newspaper was already referring to 'The Dreyfus-Esterhazy-Piquart-Dupaty-Henry-Boisdeffre-and-Pellieux question, which gets longer by another name each day'.[63] The conservative press harboured few doubts that the French army had been all but destroyed by the Third Republic—'What depths the republic has brought the French army to!'[64]—not least because it had dared to inculpate Wilhelm II, who was alleged to have written to Dreyfus on his own account.[65] By the end of 1898, German conservatives had extended their definition of republican to include incriminated officers, war ministers, and a phalanx of unnamed 'overambitious men in the General Staff', as well as moderate and left-wing politicians, newspaper editors, and Jews: 'The named officers, together with the five war ministers and other overambitious men in the General Staff, who have let themselves get involved in this dirty business, are children of their time, the real sons of the republic, which is going to ruin because of its materialism.'[66] After the Dreyfus affair, army and judiciary in France were unable to redeem themselves to the satisfaction of German conservatives. In the articles of the right, they remained part of the besmirched republican regime.

To German observers, it seemed unlikely that political conflict would be banished from the French state, since France's monarchists, Bonapartists, nationalists, and right-wing republicans were too weak to challenge the ascendancy of Radicals and socialists. German conservatives' feelings towards their French counterparts had always been mixed because of the pronouncedly anti-German stance of the right in France, including Catholics, who wished to intervene in the German *Kulturkampf* in the 1870s, Boulangists, who were demonized by Bismarck in the 1880s, and anti-Dreyfusards, who railed against German spies in the 1890s. Virtually all German reports between 1903 and 1914 were critical of demagogic, extremist right-wing parties and none predicted success at the polls for them. Before that date, conservative newspapers had been divided between those such as the *Hamburger Nachrichten*, which had discounted the nationalist victory in the Parisian municipal elections of 1900 as anomalous, and those like the *Deutsche Zeitung*, which depicted the result as the start of a shift towards the right.[67] The *Neue Preußische Zeitung* had warned in

[63] Ibid., 3 Sept. 1898.   [64] Ibid., 12 Nov. 1898.
[65] Ibid., 10 Sept. 1898.   [66] Ibid., 25 Nov. 1898.
[67] *Hamburger Nachrichten*, 9 May 1900, and *Deutsche Zeitung*, 9 May 1900.

1901 that it would be 'a disastrous mistake' to write off the nationalists and was surprised when they lost votes in the Assembly elections
of 1902.[68] Thereafter, it appeared to the conservative press that the
French right had failed. In 1904, after the nationalists had lost control
of Paris, it was envisaged that the right-wing parties would disappear
altogether.[69] 'For a long time now, the unity of the nationalists has
been inconceivable,' recorded the conservative party mouthpiece two
years later: 'Nationalism in the form in which it was dominant during
the Dreyfus era finally no longer has any prospects of success.'[70]
Similarly, the resurgence of monarchism after 1905, under the Camelots
du Roy and Action Française, was treated as puerility rather than as
politics by German royalists: 'These attacks by the Camelots du Roy
are more risible than dangerous, but do the young men not realize that
they are simply damaging the cause which they hold to be a good
one?'[71] From 1899 onwards, when Baron Christiani attacked
President Loubet at the Auteuil races, French monarchism had been
portrayed in the German conservative press as decadent and mean-
ingless extremism, conducted by the false aristocrats of the republic:
'For a long while, not even a tenth of the so-called French nobility has
been authorized to bear a coat of arms. The other nine-tenths are a
product of the republic; it alone is responsible for this dizziness.'[72]
Real aristocrats, it was implied, would not have lapsed into such corruption and demagogy: they would not, in other words, have adopted
the supposed habits of republican politics.

Confronted by the political chicanery of the Third Republic, the
respectable part of the French populace was forced, according to conservative observers in Germany, not to turn to right-wing parties,
which were as culpable as those of the left, but to eschew politics
altogether. This had already begun to happen during the Dreyfus
affair: 'the nice people have long ago withdrawn altogether from anything which has even the most distant relation to politics, and leave the
direction of public affairs to conscienceless, pushy types and ambitious
or greedy fixers, who want to get rich at the public's expense and to
dispose of the *faveurs* of the state, and that is what is sad for France.'[73]

[68] *Neue Preußische Zeitung*, 25 Jan. 1901 and 2 May 1902.
[69] Ibid., 12 May 1904; *Hamburger Nachrichten*, 8 May 1904.
[70] *Neue Preußische Zeitung*, 16 Feb. 1906 and 9 May 1906.
[71] Ibid., 19 Feb. 1909. See also 21 Nov. 1910.
[72] Ibid., 18 July 1899. Ibid., 7 June 1899.
[73] Ibid., 22 Nov. 1898.

German conservatives' belief in a disaffected populace, completely withdrawn from the usual workings of politics, persisted until the First World War. As has been seen, it explained their conviction that a French *coup d'état* was probable in the long run, even in the absence of suitable political leaders.[74] It also informed their reaction to the French *Kulturkampf*, in which, it was assumed, the silent majority would finally be provoked into challenging France's republican political regime: 'The Combes ministry has achieved what few French governments have succeeded in doing: it has mobilized not only Paris but the whole of France against the ruling clique, and that is to say a great deal, when one takes account of the total political indifference of the French provincial.'[75] The fact that moderate newspapers such as the *Hamburger Nachrichten* agreed with traditional publications like the *Neue Preußische Zeitung* that a broad section of Frenchmen had countenanced active opposition to *bloc* government between 1902 and 1905, made it easier for conservative readers in Germany to accept that the French populace was close to civil disobedience in 1906, as the administration compiled inventories of church goods.[76] France, it was held, had become so disillusioned with the republic that it was prepared to take its orders from Rome instead: 'Combism has not reinforced the republic, but undermined it. On the extreme left, former government parties rebel against the authority of the state and follow the orders of the revolutionary syndicate dictators; on the right, the entire people, which has remained true to the church, awaits from Rome the decision over its future.'[77]

It became clear, after the elections of May 1906 failed to produce a swing away from the anti-clerical republican parties, that German conservatives' presentiments of a Catholic backlash in France had been mistaken: 'The "black menace" is not manifest any more. The elections have certainly shown that the church is not loved and that its sufferings are matters of indifference to the majority of the people.'[78] The notion of a silent, discontented majority in France reappeared, however, most notably between 1912 and 1914, under the ministry and presidency of Raymond Poincaré. For a brief period, conservative newspapers in Germany anticipated that popular discontentment

[74] See above, Ch. 4, sect. 3.
[75] *Deutsche Tageszeitung*, 22 July 1902.
[76] *Hamburger Nachrichten*, 6 Mar. 1904; *Neue Preußische Zeitung*, 5 Feb. 1906.
[77] *Neue Preußische Zeitung*, 19 Apr. 1906.
[78] Ibid., 22 May 1906.

would be translated into support for right-wing republicans, some of whom had pledged to reform the political regime from within. Such predictions betrayed a long-standing, if qualified, sympathy on the part of German conservatives for French *progressistes*:

At a time when radical-socialist and nationalist demagogy overshadows the whole of political life, it is gratifying still to find a strong, parliamentary party, which honours good, old, French *bon sens....* From the practical Realpolitiker of the opportunist era have come the clever theoreticians of today, whose plans are all the more comprehensive, as they have no prospect in the foreseeable future of being carried out. Nevertheless, a progressive government still lies closer to the realm of possibility than a nationalist-conservative one.[79]

Six years later, in 1912, it seemed to newspapers such as the *Agrarpolitische Wochenschrift* that the chances of a moderate republican government had improved, as the populace gradually turned to reactionary parties, and away from Radicalism.[80] Whereas, during the 1870s, Paris had called for a progressive democracy and the provinces had opposed it, by 1900, the capital had already begun to react against republican 'progress', despite provincial support for it.[81] Eventually, the restoration of monarchy itself might be possible, suggested the *Deutscher Kurier*, but only in the distant future.[82] In the meantime, the strengthening of the presidency under Poincaré and electoral reform under a moderate republican ministry seemed nearer to achievement. But even such readjusted hopes were quickly dashed. By March 1912, for example, less than two months after the formation of the Poincaré ministry, it was already evident to newspapers like the *Neue Preußische Zeitung* that the Président du Conseil remained beholden to the Radicals under the terms of the *majorité républicaine*: 'One did not believe that one had heard correctly...we are going back to *see-saw politics*.'[83] By December of the following year, German conservatives had given up the idea of constitutional reform under the Third Republic completely: 'With one blow he [Poincaré] brought all hopes of a wonder-cure against the excesses of the parliamentary regime to nought. Other presidents before him did exactly the same.'[84] Proportional

[79] *Neue Preußische Zeitung*, 12 Apr. and 9 May 1906.
[80] *Agrarpolitische Wochenschrift*, 1 Nov. 1913.
[81] Ibid., 1 Mar. 1913.
[82] *Deutscher Kurier*, 7 Apr. 1914.
[83] *Neue Preußische Zeitung*, 9 Mar. 1912.
[84] *Deutsche Tageszeitung*, 31 Dec. 1913.

representation had, in any case, always been depicted as an uncertain palliative rather than as a panacea.[85] By 1914, it appeared that all attempts to harness popular disaffection had failed. As far as the conservative press in Germany was concerned, the French populace stayed the same; indifferent to republican politics, dissatisfied with republican policies.[86]

For German conservatives, of course, the most worrying feature of the Third Republic was its relationship with socialism. The elections of 1898, when socialists gained 9 per cent of the seats in the Assembly, had finally established the idea of a left-wing threat from within the republican regime itself, and had disproved the thesis that there had been a freak result in 1893, when the same groups had increased their share from 2 per cent to 8 per cent: 'The socialists are arming themselves for a lightning attack and the propertied classes have eventually understood that the complete basis of their life and existence is threatened.'[87] Since Radicals felt obliged to withhold their support for Méline, who had accepted monarchist backing, they were forced to cooperate at the polls with socialists, who were intent on storming the lower chamber, according to the alarmist report of the *Neue Preußische Zeitung*.[88] The consummation of socialist electoral success and, allegedly, their reward for electoral cooperation came one year later, when Millerand was appointed minister of trade in the Waldeck-Rousseau ministry. As the first socialist to participate in the government of a major European state, Millerand immediately became the bugbear of German conservatives and a symbol of the inefficacy and imbalance of the French republic, for the latter had, in the words of one correspondent, chopped off its own head in order to cure toothache:[89] 'The worst compromise, most laden with consequences, is that which this [republican regime] has made with the self-confessed revolutionary socialist party. Like the bear-keeper of the tale to the devil, it has signed itself over to socialism and will later be forced to pay back extortionate rates of interest.'[90] Once they had entered the *bloc*, however informally, socialists exploited their position ruthlessly, backing trade unions and dictating policy.[91] Moderate ministers like General Galliffet, who supposedly had resigned

---

[85] *Dresdner Nachrichten*, 13 July 1912; *Kieler Neueste Nachrichten*, 16 July 1912.
[86] *Deutscher Kurier*, 7 Apr. 1914; *Dresdner Nachrichten*, 29 Apr. 1914; *Deutsche Tageszeitung*, 13 May 1914; *Reichsbote*, 27 June 1914.
[87] *Neue Preußische Zeitung*, 4 Jan. 1898.   [88] Ibid., 1 Jan. 1898.
[89] Ibid., 11 July 1899.   [90] Ibid., 18 Apr. 1900.   [91] Ibid., 3 Nov. 1900.

because of Millerand, never felt comfortable in the administration of
Waldeck-Rousseau, which, it was contended, constituted a change in
kind from preceding ministries: 'Governments follow one another—
extremely quickly under the republic!—but they are not all the same:
and the Waldeck-Rousseau ministry is least like its predecessors.
What makes this ministry interesting for us, detached observers, is
the fact that this is the first time that socialism has been entrusted
with the reins of government.'[92] Despite apparent differences
between ministries, it seemed to German conservatives that the Third
Republic remained captive to socialism after 1899.

The actions of French governments, particularly with regard to the
church, the army, and striking workers, appeared to betray the influence of socialists within the republican regime.[93] According to the
Tägliche Rundschau, Waldeck-Rousseau had had the choice in 1900 of
excluding socialism or ceding to it. Famously, he had chosen the latter course: 'One is waiting for the final decision from Herr Waldeck-
Rousseau whether socialism is to be excluded from government or
whether, as appears might be the case, it will create the basis of the
future form of government.'[94] Fourteen years later, it seemed to the
conservative historian Theodor Schiemann that the proclivity of
French politics had stayed the same: if the Doumergue ministry fell,
it would be replaced by Jaurès rather than by Briand.[95] In the interim,
the socialist leader had been greeted as the real leader of the Combes
government, as one of the main advocates of the separation of church
and state under the Rouvier administration, as a ghost in the past of
Clemenceau and Briand, as one of the men behind Monis's cabinet,
and as one of the vanquishers of Poincaré.[96] Such influence appeared
plausible to German conservatives because the electoral tide moved
throughout the period in favour of French socialists. After the final
results in 1898, when socialists had increased their share of seats in
the Assembly from 52 to 57, or 9 per cent, the *Neue Preußische Zeitung*
already noted an unambiguous shift to the far left: 'On the extreme
left, which includes the Radicals, the Radical-Socialists, and the most

[92] *Neue Preußische Zeitung*, 26 Apr. 1902 and 30 May 1900.
[93] *Schlesische Zeitung*, 1 Apr. 1901; *Neue Preußische Zeitung*, 25 June 1903; *Deutsche
Tageszeitung*, 9 Aug. 1904. On the army, *Berliner Neueste Nachrichten*, 14 Sept. 1904; *Neue
Preußische Zeitung*, 1 Nov. 1904, 2 Nov. 1904. On strikes, *Deutsche Zeitung*, 22 May 1907;
Deutsche Nachrichten, 14 Oct. 1910.
[94] *Tägliche Rundschau*, 27 Oct. 1900.   [95] *Neue Preußische Zeitung*, 13 May 1914.
[96] *Deutsche Tageszeitung*, 21 Nov. 1902; *Neue Preußische Zeitung*, 11 Apr. 1905, 14 Mar.
1906, 3 Mar. 1911, and 13 May 1914.

progressive, completely revolutionary socialists, a shift to the left is clearly visible.'[97] After the elections of 1902, the same newspaper was convinced that 'the socialization of France [will] be completed more and more quickly',[98] just as it was sure four years later that the ascendancy of the Radical-Socialists within the Radical block, which coincided with the recent growth of the far left, presaged cooperation with revolutionary socialism: 'The social-revolutionary movement has made more rapid advances in France during the last years than in Germany.'[99] Between 1893 and 1906, the article continued, the number of voters for French socialist parties had risen by more than 100 per cent, from 0.5 to 1.15 million, whereas the number of German socialist voters had increased by just over 50 per cent, from 1.9 to 3.1 million, despite the fact that the working-class in Germany was larger and expanding more quickly than in France.[100] In 1910, the united socialists gained another 20 seats and, in 1914, the combined socialist parties achieved 100 seats in total, or 16.6 per cent.[101] To the *Dresdner Nachrichten* full collaboration between Radicals and socialists was now inevitable, and on the latter's terms.[102] This looked all the more credible to German newspapers because party boundaries in France were blurred by self-interest, deception, and faction, which, in turn, had enabled informal cooperation between socialist and Radical parties during the previous one-and-a-half decades. Although Radical-Socialists were sometimes recognized to be bourgeois, believing in the sanctity of property, they were accused all the same of borrowing socialist rhetoric to acquire votes at the polls and to acquire support in the Assembly for their coalition governments.[103] As a result, argued the *Hamburger Nachrichten*, the French public had become inured to the idea of socialists in power.[104]

To German conservatives, such popular desensitization to the dangers of socialism in France did not correspond to an actual diminution of the socialist menace. Occasionally, ex-socialists like Millerand were still depicted as revolutionary, in spite of their participation in government.[105] More often, however, they were perceived to be the

---

[97] *Neue Preußische Zeitung*, 1 June 1898.   [98] Ibid., 14 May 1902.
[99] Ibid., 30 May 1906.   [100] Ibid.
[101] Ibid., 10 May 1910 and 13 June 1914.   [102] *Dresdner Nachrichten*, 3 June 1914.
[103] *Hamburger Nachrichten*, 22 June 1901; *Neue Preußische Zeitung*, 14 June 1907; *Dresdner Neueste Nachrichten*, 23 Apr. 1910.
[104] *Hamburger Nachrichten*, 27 July 1909.
[105] *Neue Preußische Zeitung*, 26 Apr. 1902.

opponents of radicals such as Jules Guesde and of union activists in the Confédération Générale du Travail (CGT): 'Famously, here in France, the two main groups of Guesdists, who stick to unadulterated Marxist theory and do not want to know about a compromise with the bourgeoisie, and the more opportunist-minded supporters of a Jaurès, Gérauld Richard, Millerand etc. more or less stand in direct opposition to each other.'[106] The effect, though, was the same, argued the conservative press in Germany. By their radical rhetoric and their participation in government, Millerand, Briand, Viviani, and other independent socialists encouraged and legitimized revolutionary socialists and syndicalists without integrating them into the republican regime. From the start, the *Neue Preußische Zeitung* had rejected out of hand the claims of some French politicians that socialists could be tamed: 'They believe that the election of Millerand to trade minister has changed the socialist party into a political one and the revolutionary party into a parliamentary one.... Over the long term, however, the socialists will not keep the peace and deny their entire past and their revolutionary principles because of Millerand making eyes at the bourgeois parties.'[107] By 1904, the radical-dominated St Etienne congress had pledged to control ministerial socialists, and Guesde, whose predictions included an eleven-minute working-day and a socialist revolution in 1910, appeared to have the upper hand over Jaurès.[108] What was more, these changes within the socialist parties were accompanied by the perceived radicalization of the CGT and by a series of strikes and demonstrations, which affected most regions of France, from the miners' strike in Montceau-les-Mines and the dockworkers' strike in Marseilles, both in 1901, to the strike of the Parisian electricians' in 1907, from the wine-growers' revolt in Languedoc of the same year and the Champagne growers' demonstrations in 1911 to the national strikes of postal workers and railwaymen in 1909 and 1910.[109]

Experience seemed to have proved to conservative newspapers in Germany that the number of militant socialists in France would always exceed the number of ministerial apostates:

The Radical-Socialists have always been of the opinion that this revolutionary phrase-mongering is not meant so badly, and they are right as far as Jaurès and

[106] *Neue Preußische Zeitung*, 22 Aug. 1900.   [107] Ibid., 29 Mar. 1900.
[108] Respectively, *Post*, 18 Feb. 1904; *Neue Preußische Zeitung*, 22 May 1906; *Deutsche Tageszeitung*, 15 June 1906.
[109] *Deutsche Tageszeitung*, 3 Dec. 1910 and 31 Dec. 1910; *Reichsbote*, 21 Dec. 1910; *Neue Preußische Zeitung*, 17 May 1911.

company are concerned. What will this educated gentleman, who in any case is suspect, have to say in the next four years? There will be people in the new parliament for whom revolution is *not* just a way of speaking, and if these people should become listless in the nerve-racking air of the Palais Bourbon, the Levys and the Bronchoux are standing out in the street with bomb-making confédérates [*Confédérierten*] in order to remind the 'intellectuals' that the 'people' expect actions from them.[110]

Extremism appeared to be in the logic of parliamentary socialism, for ministers such as Millerand and Briand were prevented by their own rhetoric and history from treating strikers and revolutionaries with necessary force and impartiality. Instead, Pelletan had encouraged the unionization of state arsenal workers, Briand had entrusted teachers' welfare to *amicales*, which were de facto unions, Clemenceau had attempted to bargain with unrecognized *syndicats* during the miners' strike in Lens, and governments of all colours had, according to the *Reichsbote*, subsidized the CGT.[111] Unsurprisingly, socialists, syndicalists, and workers all understood such actions as signs of weakness or support, so that they could act with impunity: 'Everyone knows the government and the deputies well enough to know that the mildest imaginable treatment of the strikers is assured.'[112] The Third Republic, contended German conservatives, had neither improved workers' conditions nor suppressed workers' revolts. The most obvious consequences of such failings were the paralysis of the state and the collapse of social order. In other words, republican political practice was held up as the actual enactment of a conservative's nightmare. The string of causes, by which France, allegedly, had been reduced to anarchy, was relatively simple: socialism had been stimulated above all by the inefficacy and demagogy of faction-ridden republican administrations; those ministries had then felt compelled to cooperate with socialist parties against right-wing, anti-republican parties, which had begun to imitate their own parliamentary tactics, and against self-interested republican factions, whose principal aim was to regain power; since executive and legislative functions had been merged in France, socialists became ministers and began to undermine the authority of government from within; and when revolutionaries and syndicalists outside parliament took such appointments as a licence for illegality, socialist-backed ministries proved unable to control them.

---

[110] *Neue Preußische Zeitung*, 22 May 1906.
[111] Ibid., 16 Nov. 1905, 11 Apr. 1906; *Reichsbote*, 26 Apr. 1906.
[112] *Neue Preußische Zeitung*, 25 Mar. 1909.

For German conservatives, 'the licentiousness of the socialist terror' in 1910 was the product of forty years of French republicanism.[113]

3. The Centre Party

The response of the German Catholic press to the Third Republic was conditioned ultimately by the latter's attitude to the French Catholic Church. Conservative newspapers in Berlin such as *Germania* and liberal publications in the Rhineland like the *Kölnische Volkszeitung* agreed that French Catholics should cooperate with moderate republicans, as Leo XIII had urged in the 1890s through his policy of *ralliement*, which seemed, to Wilhelmine Catholics, to envisage a 'German' model of political Catholicism, working within the accepted moral and legal confines of the nation-state. During the 1900s, with the proscription of Catholic orders, closure of Catholic schools, and separation of church and state, *ralliement* had, clearly, failed in France. Many articles which appeared in the German Catholic press attempted, implicitly or explicitly, to explain why French Catholics had not managed to collaborate successfully with the Third Republic, given that their German counterparts had achieved a modus vivendi with the *Kaiserreich*.

The turning-point in German reporting of French politics was the resignation of the Méline ministry in June 1898. Although it was neither clerical nor conservative—'The Radicals see ghosts; in fact, Méline is by no means a great friend of the conservatives'[114]—the moderate republican administration of Méline seemed to German Catholics to offer the possibility of reconciliation between clericals and anti-clericals, between reaction and revolution.[115] When the Assembly backed the ministry against imputations of anti-clericalism, *Germania* was unambiguous in its praise: 'This is a thoroughly pleasing fact, which shows that healthy, political common sense is currently ascendant in the French chamber.'[116] Equally, at the start of the Dreyfus affair, its criticism of Dreyfusards—'The Dreyfus clique's shameless witch-hunt against the French government'[117]—was usually linked to a defence of the Méline administration, as if Dreyfus's guilt were proven beyond all doubt by the protestations of the

[113] *Neue Preußische Zeitung*, 2 Nov. 1910.
[114] *Germania*, 15 Mar. 1898. Ibid., 23 Jan. 1898.
[115] Ibid., 14 Apr. 1898 and 23 Aug. 1898.
[116] Ibid., 23 Jan. 1898.   [117] Ibid., 15 Jan. 1898.

government: 'The real motor behind the Dreyfus clique's action against the government is less the Dreyfus case as such, but rather, to a far greater extent, the quest to obstruct at all costs the establishment of a moderate government in France and to secure supremacy for itself.'[118] Likewise, in the elections of 1898, it was anticipated that Méline would win and that rapprochement between Catholics and republicans would be vindicated: 'Better prospects have now emerged for a more enduring era of political calm in France, which was inaugurated by the Meline [*sic*] cabinet.'[119] When, eventually, it became evident that the moderate republican ministry had lost, and therefore felt obliged to resign, *Germania* continued to believe that *ralliement* would survive in a different form under the sham-Radical administration of Brisson: 'the Brisson cabinet constitutes a new edition, with a Radical cover, of the Meline [*sic*] cabinet.'[120] Soon, however, it was apparent that neither Brisson nor Dupuy intended to pursue Méline's policies. Rather, they marked the transition to the undisguised, unsuccessful Radicalism of Waldeck-Rousseau's and Combes's ministries: 'The new prime minister Dupuy will not succeed in pulling the wagon out of the morass into which Brisson, the freemason, had driven it. He could have done if he had followed in Méline's footsteps.'[121] France's only hope of peace and prosperity, it seemed to German Catholics, was to choose Méline's *via media*. Instead, it had opted for Radicalism and, consequently, had experienced sixteen years of political and social conflict, anti-clericalism, and economic decline.

The Catholic press in Germany was perplexed by the enduring nature of French Radicalism. One reason that it was tolerated by the populace, it appeared, was the irresponsibility of the French right, which could be portrayed by Radicals as a menace to the existence of the Third Republic: 'The conservatives in France only want to pursue politics under a monarch, and otherwise not at all.... Not completely without cause, they are seen by republicans as most dangerous revolutionaries. Despite the rejection on the part of the masses of old-world phrases about a new "restoration", a reinstitution of kingship, they do not stop peddling their outdated ideas throughout the land.'[122] At times, French royalists, Bonapartists and nationalists were depicted merely as buffoons: Déroulède's attempted *coup d'état* was

---

[118] Ibid., 26 Jan. 1898. See also ibid., 9 Feb. 1898.
[119] Ibid., 17 May 1898. Also, ibid., 12 Jan. 1898.
[120] Ibid., 5 July 1898. Ibid., 25 May 1898.   [121] Ibid., 29 Dec. 1898.
[122] Ibid., 10 Mar. 1908.

seen as 'childlike' and 'naive'; Guérin's occupation of 'Fort Chabrol' 'is gradually starting to take on the character of a burlesque'; and Baron Christiani's attack on Loubet at Auteuil was condemned as a 'chaotic sham directed at the existing institutions of state by a frivolous clan'.[123] At other times, however, right-wing conspirators were taken at their word. After the suicide of Henry in September 1898, observed *Germania*, anti-Dreyfusards refused to accept the legality of revision and attempted to push the French populace towards civil war:

Just as the pro-Dreyfus press exerted itself violently..., so the anti-Dreyfusard press, at the decisive moment, now stubbornly opposes revision of the Dreyfus case, which it would like to prevent even at the price of civil war.... Whoever judges the present situation from an impartial point of view, whoever is familiar with the mood of the Parisian population, must admit that the Dreyfus business is more threatening than ever in its present phase; it would not surprise us if this blindness and passion does not eventually lead to acts of violence and even the spilling of blood by the misled, incited people.[124]

Similar articles on the excesses of the nationalist press and probability of open revolt could be found in the columns of the same newspaper in 1899.[125] To *Germania*, at least, there seemed to be some truth in the case for republican defence against the far right, even if the danger of anti-republicanism had, subsequently, been exaggerated.[126]

As a result, German Catholic publications distinguished carefully between Catholicism, which was preponderantly republican, and right-wing political parties, which sought to restore either monarchy or dictatorship.[127] Dreyfusard accusations that the army was dominated by anti-republican, Catholic generals were refuted angrily: in fact, only one out of six officers implicated in the Dreyfus affair had been educated by Jesuits; furthermore, one had been Protestant: 'The fairy tale about the alliance of the army with the *clergy* for the purpose of insurrection appears still to frighten those with anxious constitutions.'[128] Even the charge that most officers were monarchist, after thirty-six years of constant change, was 'laughable'.[129] Whereas the army, like the church, remained one of France's most reliable

[123] *Germania.*, 26 June 1901, 15 Aug. 1899, and 7 June 1899, respectively. See also ibid., 22 Sept. 1899.

[124] Ibid., 7 Sept. 1898. On the extremism of the right-wing press, see 14 Sept. 1898.

[125] Ibid., 16 Mar. 1899. Ibid., 5 Jan., 22 Feb., and 22 Aug. 1899.

[126] Ibid., 13 Aug. 1908.   [127] Ibid., 8 Apr. 1906.

[128] Ibid., 16 Nov. 1898. Ibid., 5 Jan. 1904. Ibid., 24 Jan. 1898.

[129] Ibid., 28 Oct. 1906.

institutions, despite occasional lapses, right-wing political parties were self-interested and dilettante. Officers and clerics were not to be confused with royalists and nationalists: 'What a Parisian vicar-general recently said to a reporter is still true. Where are the Catholics, then, the latter asked, with regard to church fees. "Oh, them", replied the cleric, "they're off driving automobiles." '[130]

Monarchists, Bonapartists, and nationalists had betrayed the church on three counts. First, they had claimed disingenuously to represent Catholic opinion, although many of their leaders, such as Charles Maurras, were not believers.[131] They were prepared to avail themselves of the prestige and following of the church, yet they failed to defend clerics against the state, in 1901, over the law of association, and in 1905, over the revocation of the concordat.[132] Second, right-wing parties were disunited, allowing republicans to tar the church with the same brush: 'All *conservatives* are *Catholic*, but the label conservative conceals a complete mosaic of fractions and factions... that come to parliamentary elections in a fragmented state and are thus beaten by the enemies of the church.'[133] Third, the far right was generally anti-republican and conspiratorial, which allowed left-wing governments to ostracize them:

First, such fragmentation so dominates party relations that a united front of all conservatives under the Catholic flag cannot by any means be counted on.... Since the inception of the Third Republic, all French conservatives have fought the republican state constitution as if it were treasonous. That was their first mistake and the Figaro... rightly wrote: 'If the right had ever expressly placed itself on constitutional ground, to champion conservative tenets in this way, it could have played a decisive role.' It preferred to split up into special interest-groups.... Since all these parties found their supporters in the Catholic nobility, they awoke a steadily growing mistrust on the part of republicans. Since, on the other hand, the republican parties preferred to tend towards the left, in fighting the monarchists they fought above all the church, and the *Kulturkampf* in this fashion took on the air of a justified defence of the existing state constitution.[134]

According to *Germania*, Leo XIII had recognized that only republican parties accorded with the prudent, peaceable instincts of the French populace, whereas right-wing parties had lost any sense of popular feeling: 'It has been known for a long time that the conservatives

---

[130] Ibid., 1 May 1908 and 10 May 1906.   [131] Ibid., 27 Feb. 1909.
[132] Ibid., 16 Oct. 1903.   [133] Ibid.
[134] Ibid., 7 Apr. 1906. Ibid., 27 Feb. 1909.

in France endeavour quite desperately to avoid even the loosest contact with the people and go on trying further to distance themselves from them.'[135] Consequently, Catholic *ralliés*, who wished to collaborate with republicans, were ridiculed by the rest of the French right—'They were treated as complete imbeciles'[136]—rather than being welcomed by them: 'It was immediately apparent how little in common real Catholicism had with the efforts of the conservatives.'[137] Since the struggle against the Third Republic had become central to monarchism and Bonapartism by the 1900s, representatives of the two political strands were prepared to exploit the *Kulturkampf* and endanger the church in order to undermine the republican regime: 'It is obviously regrettable that individual royalists and Bonapartists misuse the tension between government and the church to make declarations against the republican form of state and constitution.'[138] For their part, Catholics reacted against such exploitation and short-sightedness by abandoning the French right altogether, continued *Germania*: 'Can one really blame [them]... if they prefer to stand with the parliamentary left rather than the right?'[139] It was well-known that Catholic bishops, clerics, and politicians all backed the republican form of government.[140]

The enemies of the church alone equated Catholicism and anti-republicanism after the turn of the century, resurrecting anti-clericalism because it united the disparate factions of the left rather than because clerics threatened the existence of the Third Republic: 'Combes and his distant helpers know just as well as we do that the majority of French Catholics today are supporters of the republic, and their aim is not the defence of the republic, but simply the struggle against any form of positive, religious life.'[141] Radicals and socialists had, it appeared to German Catholics, managed to blur the distinction between opposition to the particular form of the Third Republic and outright rejection of republican government. The *ralliés* had been isolated by the French left, it was claimed, not because they had rejected the republic but because they wished to improve it: 'Since they... too cannot approve of a republic as the Radical-Socialists understand it, they are simply labelled enemies of the republic by the *bloc* people, just like the monarchists.'[142] Republicans had exposed the weaknesses of the French parliamentary state in the pursuit of their own political

---

[135] *Germania*, 10 Mar. 1908.   [136] Ibid., 7 Apr. 1906.   [137] Ibid.
[138] Ibid., 19 Feb. 1909. Ibid., 16 Oct. 1903.   [139] Ibid., 10 Mar. 1908.
[140] Ibid., 16 Oct. 1903; ibid., 10 Jan. 1913.
[141] Ibid., 29 Aug. 1903. Ibid., 10 May 1906.   [142] Ibid., 7 Apr. 1906.

advantage, which, it seemed, was best served by demonizing the Catholic Church.[143] Corruption and political interference were perceived to be so widespread and destructive in France that the Third Republic had been reduced to little more than a parody of the republican form. Only the republican right, which aimed to increase the powers of the president and decrease those of the Assembly, could salvage the French political system without replacing it *in toto*:

> It is more probable, after the collapse of the fourth estate, that the forces of order will end the present parody or caricature of a republic and set up a real republic, which is honourable and national and respects all freedoms, above all religious freedom. Such a disinfection of the republic has been tried twice already, once by Boulangism, once by nationalism. Both attempts failed because the necessary unity and cohesion, spirit of sacrifice and self-abnegation was lacking.[144]

If the Catholic press in Germany were to be believed, the French political state had failed to safeguard the rights of fellow-believers. It seemed that left-wing politicians had been able to manipulate the bureaucracy in order to discriminate against Catholics in France: 'Their [bureaucrats'] whole attention is given over to the "menace of the clergy".'[145] Whereas prefects allowed departmental councils' expressions of support for government anti-clericalism, even though such *conseils* were forbidden by law to intervene in national politics, they would not hesitate to prosecute those councils which censured ministerial policies.[146] It was impossible, therefore, to assess provincial reaction to national policies. When the commission into religious orders did actually consult municipal councils in 1903, 1,075 were found to be in favour of orders and only 458 against.[147] Similarly, Radical election-fixing, locally and nationally, obscured real, anti-government sentiment amongst the French populace.[148] In 1904, for instance, nine out of fifteen cities with a population exceeding 100,000, where large electorates worked against electoral corruption, had voted against ministerial candidates.[149] Even in December 1905, the *Kölnische Volkszeitung* was convinced that the majority of the French population was opposed to the separation of church and state, and that, consequently, the Assembly was acting undemocratically in assenting to it.[150]

[143] Ibid., 26 Sept. 1908. [144] Ibid., 13 Aug. 1908.
[145] Ibid., 30 July 1908. [146] Ibid., 29 Aug. 1903. [147] Ibid., 15 Mar. 1903.
[148] Ibid., 29 Apr. 1902, 18 May 1904, 10 Mar. 1906 and 27 Feb. 1909.
[149] Ibid., 18 May 1904.
[150] *Kölnische Volkszeitung*, 9 Dec. 1905. See also, ibid., 8 Apr. 1906. *Germania*, 29 Aug. 1903.

Radicals and socialists appeared to have used the fusion of executive and legislative functions in France in order to deny to Catholics
due legal process in their fight against the abolition of religious con-
gregations, the closure of Catholic schools, the compilation of church
inventories, and the separation of church and state. After 1899,
French ministers were referred to as 'Jacobins' and 'dictators', enact-
ing 'exceptional laws' and pursuing a 'policy of persecution' against
the Catholic Church.[151] Those judges who dared to oppose the
government were, it was said, either silenced or removed: 'Such
men, who steadfastly defend law and justice, are naturally a thorn in
the flesh of the French government, because they are not "republican" enough. For it is, of course, an undoubted sign of republican
spirit when one excels oneself in the *Kulturkampf.* It has already
been reported how Briand is trying to gag the judges completely;
namely, he has acquired by means of decree a monopoly over their
appointment and promotion.'[152] As a rule, wrote *Germania*, judiciaries constituted a reliable source of information, but the politicized
French judiciary was an exception: 'That would be correct if in
France, as in other civilized countries, the judicial authorities
acted independently and were not under the thumb of the Justice
Ministry.'[153] Clemenceau's dictum that 'En politique il n'y a pas
de justice' appeared to have been borne out by the practices of
the French political state under Radical tutelage: in 1902, for example, Combes's ministry had decreed that 2,500 schools had to be
closed within a week, despite a flagrant contravention of the legal
sanctity of property, for laymen, not monks, were often the owners
of such schools.[154] As the Catholic Church struggled unsuccessfully with the French state, it became obvious to German Catholics
that 'the Radical-socialist-freemason clique' was using its twin
powers—as executor and legislator—to create, misinterpret, and sub-
vert law in its own interest: 'The way in which existing law is messed
around with in France is altogether unworthy of a cultural state
[*Kulturstaat*].'[155] For Catholic newspapers, the rhetoric of the French
republic had been turned on its head: 'Things are getting more and
more insane in the country of human rights and, with the exception

---

[151] *Germania*, 17 Mar. 1906 and 1 May 1908, 23 Oct. 1906, 17 Feb. 1906, 29 Dec. 1905.
[152] Ibid., 27 Mar. 1908.
[153] Ibid., 1 May 1906.
[154] Ibid., 15 Mar. 1903 and 22 July 1902, respectively.
[155] Ibid., 22 July 1902 and 13 Jan. 1909.

of Russia, there is no European country in which freedom, equality, and fraternity are more arbitrarily measured.'[156]

In 1899, *Germania* left the question of republican responsibility for France's woes unanswered.[157] By 1911, the same publication had reached a verdict, and had found against the Third Republic:

France is sliding unstoppably down the slippery slope, onto which the damaging policy of its statesmen has pushed it in recent years. There is a kernel of truth in the claim of Frenchmen themselves that the proud republic is governed by a handful of career politicians, who unscrupulously arrange everything in their own interest and force their will on each cabinet. For this reason, there can be no talk in this parliamentarily governed country *par excellence* of a government which stands above parties. Rather, the government directs its attention fully towards its current clients and changes its opinion daily, if it must. Just as it followed the promptings of the freemasons and atheists alone, whose influence dominated France's domestic policy in the sphere of church and school, in the struggle against religion, so it is dependent in foreign policy for the most part on a few great capitalists and banks, whereas in economic and social questions it is fully under the thumb of the most extreme elements of the people.[158]

The same catalogue of failings—stagnation, inefficacy, profligacy, nepotism, individualism, factionalism—was to be found in the *Kölnische Volkszeitung*, the *Bayerische Kurier*, and the *Schlesische Volkszeitung*: it was evident to all that parliamentary republicans had not found a suitable remedy.[159] Although Catholic newspapers supported the movement for proportional representation in France, they did not see it as a cure for all the ills of the Third Republic: 'However many advantages electoral reform can boast, it does not seem suited to France's thoroughly sick parliamentary body.'[160] At least one correspondent anticipated that electoral reform would work against Catholics and weaken the republic, by giving a fillip to socialists.[161] Frenchmen under the parliamentary republican regime, concluded the *Kölnische Volkszeitung*, were like dogs, which, having lost their way, simply stood and barked at the moon.[162] The only solution was to restructure the entire system, not by replacing the republic, but by removing excessive parliamentarism, which had destroyed it. Käthe

---

[156] Ibid., 6 Jan. 1909. [157] Ibid., 5 Jan. 1899.
[158] Ibid., 16 May 1911. Also, ibid., 4 July 1912.
[159] *Kölnische Volkszeitung*, 6 Nov. 1909; *Bayerischer Kurier*, 31 July 1907; and *Schlesische Volkszeitung*, 16 Dec. 1913.
[160] *Germania*, 4 July 1912. *Kölnische Volkszeitung*, 7 Jan. 1910.
[161] *Kölnische Volkszeitung*, 12 Mar. 1913. [162] Ibid., 25 July 1908.

Schirmacher's review of Emile Faguet's book, *Le Culte de l'incompétence*, made the point more precisely: 'Faguet's acute observations
touch great, open wounds and demonstrate conclusively that France
has *not* managed to solve the problem of *democratic* government. This
by no means concerns democracy as such, for we shall see below that
the United States has happily managed to avoid the evils censured by
Faguet.... In America, above all things, the separation of the legislative, executive, and system of courts is strictly enforced.'[163] There
were, of course, other explanations for the failure of the Third
Republic, including irreligion, moral lassitude, and political fatigue,
but the gravamen of the Catholic case against the French political
state was that it had merged its executive and legislative functions.[164]
This failing alone had translated the anti-clerical demagogy of French
Radicals, socialists, and republicans into anti-clerical policy.

4. The SPD

Unlike German Catholics and liberals, socialists could call on a comprehensive ideology, which defined, explained, and evaluated the
republican form of government. Since, as Richard Calwer noted in
the *Sozialistische Monatshefte*, France and Germany enjoyed roughly
compatible social and economic conditions, despite the notorious tar-
diness of French industrialization, the Third Republic and its predecessors were observed carefully by the SPD as precursors of German
development.[165] The histories of both nations had been characterized
after 1850 by decadence, which, in the words of a front-page article in
Vorwärts, had plagued 'Das alte Europa':

In no field did decadence manifest itself so crassly and tangibly as in that of politics.... The era of decadence is not new—it began shortly before the middle of
this century... with the birth of the *März revolution*.... The *June Days* completed the division of the political and economic world into two inimical camps.
And the propertied class... from that time on, no longer had a positive, creative
policy, but only a negative, destructive one. It only thinks about the *retention* of
power, about the *preservation* of *class interests*, about the *exploitation* of *political
power* for two reasons: to defend its own economic position and keep its opponents

---

[163] *Kölnische Volkszeitung*, 29 May 1910.

[164] *Germania*, 6 Jan. 1909 and 4 July 1912.

[165] R. Calwer, 'Deutsch-Französische Annäherung', *Sozialistische Monatshefte*, 1908,
665. There were, of course, references to the slowness of French industrialization—for
instance, *Vorwärts*, 16 May 1906, but, in general, it was not treated as different in kind from
Germany.

down. The governments of the European continent have not known any other policy since the middle of this century. Notably in France and Germany, this stands out clearly.[166]

Given such perceived political decadence in both countries, German socialists began to question whether a republic was preferable to a monarchy in all cases.

Marx's answer was unambiguous, at least according to Karl Kautsky, the principal ideologue of the German socialist party. In an article entitled 'Republik und Sozialdemokratie in Frankreich', which was published in seven parts in *Neue Zeit* in 1904, Kautsky applied Marx's theory of class conflict to the Third Republic, which he acknowledged as typifying republican government *tout court*.[167] The republic—that is, parliamentarism—was the only type of regime, he continued, which would produce the dictatorship of the proletariat and, thereby, a socialist *Zukunftsstaat*. It alone allowed the domination of the bourgeoisie as well as the organization of the proletariat, since it was founded on the rhetoric of free association and expression. As the owners of the means of production managed to exploit and impoverish workers, the latter reacted by forming socialist parties and trade unions, which in turn planned the replacement of the republic altogether:

If, owing to its class position, it [the proletariat] can only come to power in a republic, and if this is the only possible form for the 'dictatorship of the prole-tariat', the bourgeoisie can exercise domination in the state under any political form.... Yet it can rule most directly in a parliamentary republic or in a parlia-mentary monarchy, whose head is a mere decoration. The parliamentary form of government corresponds most to its class interests.... Thus, the same republic, which constitutes the ground for the emancipation of the proletariat, at the same time becomes the ground for the class domination of the bourgeoisie, a contra-diction which is no more peculiar, for example, than the contradictory role played in capitalist society by the machine, which is at once the indispensable prerequisite of the freeing of the proletariat and the means of degrading and enslaving it.[168]

Despite Kautsky's certainty that the bourgeois republic constituted a necessary stage between feudal monarchy and socialist society, other members of the SPD were demonstrably confused. The *Neue Zeit* article was itself, of course, a response to such confusion. As Kautsky

---

[166] *Vorwärts*, 19 May 1898.
[167] K. Kautsky, 'Republik und Sozialdemokratie in Frankreich', *Neue Zeit*, 1904, 263–4.
[168] Ibid. 262.

admitted, the bourgeois press, Jaurès, and even *Vorwärts* had declared
that Jules Guesde and August Bebel were indifferent to the relative
merits of republic and monarchy: 'On the basis of a series of statements, which came out in Amsterdam, Guesde and Bebel were
credited with indifference towards the republic, even a certain preference for monarchy.'[169] The issue had arisen when Millerand, a socialist, had entered the Waldeck-Rousseau ministry in 1899. The Second
International, meeting at Paris in 1900, had rejected Guesde's claim
that non-participation in bourgeois governments was a matter of
principle in favour of Kautsky's resolution that it was a purely tactical question, which had to be decided ad hoc.[170] If socialist support
were needed in order to prevent regression from a bourgeois republic
to a feudal monarchy, then it should be given. Although republics
were not preferable to monarchies in principle, because both
oppressed the working classes, tactically, it was in the interest of the
proletariat to maintain the former, since the transition to a socialist
society could only occur from a republican starting-point.
Nevertheless, Kautsky was of the opinion that the predicament of the
Third Republic in 1900 did not necessitate Millerand's participation
in government.[171] He made the same point more forcefully when the
International reconvened at Amsterdam in 1904: 'A socialist cannot
afford to tolerate any revolting promiscuities, cannot acknowledge any
unacceptable declarations of solidarity, cannot countenance the possibility of intrigues, which only cause confusion in the consciousness
and in the ranks of the proletariat.'[172] Yet Millerand and Jaurès, who
continued to back Combes's ministry, should still not be expelled
from socialist ranks, continued Kautsky, because they had not contravened first principles, but had merely erred tactically.[173]

Kautsky's line of argument failed to convince either the right or the
left of the SPD. On the one hand, it proved difficult for socialists to
back republican regimes on the grounds that they produced the greatest impoverishment of the proletariat, and hence political polarization
and revolution: 'Precisely in the fact that under these conditions class
oppositions bang into one another more directly and brusquely than

[169] K. Kautsky, 'Republik und Sozialdemokratie in Frankreich', *Neue Zeit*, 1904, 260.

[170] E. David, 'Der internationale Congress und die "Einigung" der französischen
Socialisten', *Socialistische Monatshefte*, 1900, 706–8.

[171] Ibid.

[172] K. Kautsky, cited in J. Droz, *Einfluß der deutschen Sozialdemokratie auf den französischen Sozialismus* (Opladen, 1973), 12–13.

[173] Ibid. 13.

they would in a monarchy of a similar level of economic development, we Marxists see the advantage of the republic.'[174] Even a centrist and orthodox Marxist such as Bebel demonstrated such ambiguities at Amsterdam in 1904, when Jaurès accused the SPD of cooperating complacently with a sham parliament—since the Reichstag had no executive powers—instead of introducing a parliamentary system of government, as in France. Bebel retorted that the French republic, no less than the German Reich, was a class-dominated society, 'which it is not worth allowing oneself to be beaten up for', and which suppressed strikes brutally at the same time as failing to enact social insurance and improve working conditions. By comparison, bureaucratic government in Germany had served workers well in some respects, implied the leader of the SPD.[175] Similarly, Wilhelm Liebknecht opposed the involvement of French socialists in the Dreyfus affair and the participation of Millerand in the ministry of Waldeck-Rousseau, which he labelled the most reactionary administration since MacMahon. In a long article in *Vorwärts*, he applauded Guesde's policy of non-cooperation with the Third Republic: 'Thus, it is not at all remarkable that the most trusted of our party comrades in France—Guesde, Lafargue, Vaillant, Deville and others *oppose* the demand to make the Dreyfus case a party affair.'[176] For left-wingers such as Rosa Luxemburg, collaboration in any form with an allegedly exploitative republican regime was, likewise, out of the question.[177]

On the other hand, Kautsky's case for increasing bourgeois exploitation of labour under the French republic was rejected by German revisionists in the SPD. The Millerand case, wrote Eduard David in the *Sozialistische Monatshefte*, had been taken as a pretext by Guesdists to attack moderate French socialists such as Jaurès, for, as Kautsky had conceded, there was no principle at stake: 'The Millerand case was not the cause, but only the external, *welcome*

---

[174] Kautsky, 'Republik und Sozialdemokratie in Frankreich', 263.

[175] A. Bebel, cited in Droz, *Einfluß der deutschen Sozialdemokratie auf den französischen Sozialismus*, 13.

[176] *Vorwärts*, 27 Sept. 1899. David, 'Der internationale Congress und die "Einigung" der französischen Sozialisten', 706.

[177] R. Luxemburg, cited in Droz, *Einfluß der deutschen Sozialdemokratie auf den französischen Sozialismus*, 12. Also R. Abraham, *Rosa Luxemburg* (Oxford, 1989), 62–5; Luxemburg wrote articles on the socialist crisis in France for the *Neue Zeit* between 1900 and 1902, in which she castigated Jaurès and Millerand and denied that the Third Republic was in any real danger.

pretext for opponents to wield anew the battle-axe of fratricidal war.'[178] Whereas Bebel and Kautsky considered Millerand's participation in a bourgeois government tactically unjustified, revisionists saw it as the start of a gradual transition towards socialist society. In an essay on the Parisian meeting of the Second International, for instance, Eduard Bernstein challenged Marxist premisses. Why could socialists not take power step by step, even in centralized political systems such as France? Why should the entry of a socialist minister into a bourgeois cabinet not be seen as the normal starting-point of a socialist assumption of power?[179] David was equally ebullient:

I am of the opinion, in stark opposition to Kautsky, that the conquest of the power of government can and will only happen in a piecemeal fashion in parliamentarily governed states....In France and elsewhere, the socialists do not yet have the power of government because the overwhelming majority of the people is not inclined to give it to them. The change in the opinion of the majority of the people will not be sudden. Only step by step, from election to election, will our comrades succeed in multiplying their parliamentary mandates.... The Millerand case will be repeated; it will become a 'normal' occurrence in France and, in all probability, elsewhere. Then, one will no longer justify the entry of socialists into a mixed ministry by saying that it is, exceptionally, *necessary*, but by acknowledging that it is, normally, *useful*; useful for the progress of positive work transforming existing conditions in the direction of democratization and socialization.[180]

There was no evidence, declared Bernstein, that the real interests of workers had been damaged by Millerand's participation in government. On the contrary, it had become the norm in the most advanced, parliamentary states for socialists to enter bourgeois ministries and empower workers from within the existing political system: 'In short, precisely in the most advanced countries, we see happening in fact that which the resolution [of Kautsky, in Paris] described as the "abnormal" start of the conquest of political power. Reality is in the unfortunate position of being "abnormal".'[181] In 1900, at least, German revisionists believed that the parliamentary regime of the Third Republic, with its proclivity towards the left, presaged the future of more backward states like the *Kaiserreich*.

---

[178] David, 'Der internationale Congress und die "Einigung" der französischen Sozialisten', 1900, 706.
[179] E. Bernstein, 'Paris und Mainz', *Sozialistische Monatshefte*, 1900, 715.
[180] David, 'Der internationale Congress und die "Einigung" der französischen Sozialisten', 708–9.
[181] Bernstein, 'Paris und Mainz', 716–17.

In the next fourteen years, such expectations were confounded. Even revisionists became disillusioned with the French republic. Readers of the *Sozialistische Monatshefte* were presented with a series of dispiriting reports from French correspondents such as Gabriel Deville, who claimed that social and economic reforms were routinely blocked by the Senate, and Jules Louis Breton, who thought that the republic had been caught in a web of material self-interest: 'Without doubt, we are experiencing a period of political decline in France. Our public morality seems to get worse from day to day. To succeed at any price, even by the most unscrupulous means, appears to have become the rule for the behaviour of most candidates, whichever political party they belong to.'[182] By 1913, Albert Thomas could write of 'Die Krise in der innern Politik Frankreichs', 'that at the same time opened up a crisis for the system of government.'[183] For his part, Bernstein had changed his tone and his French political allies by 1910: 'I do not feel the need to act as the advocate of Briand and his ministerial colleagues, Millerand and Viviani. Rather the opposite.... The entry of socialists into a government, as long as the social order is still essentially capitalist, is something which, in *all* circumstances, brings great difficulties in its wake.'[184] True, Bernstein had not given up the idea of socialist participation in bourgeois governments altogether, but he had been forced to recognize the difficulties encountered by Millerand, Briand, and Viviani. It appeared that there were times in the life of bourgeois ministries when ministers would be forced to choose between their own socialist principles and the directives of the government. In a political system which encouraged political conflict and faction, such tensions seemed ineluctable. For the moment at least, continued Bernstein, the Third Republic was not likely to furnish ministries suitable for socialist participation.[185]

Whilst German revisionists, in general, shifted from enthusiasm to doubt in their depictions of French republicanism, Marxists moved from guarded, tactical approval to outright rejection. The columns of *Vorwärts* marked the change. Initially, the regular correspondent of

---

[182] J. L. Breton, 'Die französischen Wahlen 1910', *Sozialistische Monatshefte*, 1910, 676. G. Deville, 'Betrachtungen über die Kammerwahlen und die Sozialisten in Frankreich', *Sozialistische Monatshefte*, 1906, 570.

[183] A. Thomas, 'Die Krise in der innern Politik Frankreichs', *Sozialistische Monatshefte*, 1913, 960–5.

[184] E. Bernstein, 'Strömungen und Gegenströmungen beim Generalstreik der französischen Eisenbahner', *Sozialistische Monatshefte*, 1910, 1482.

[185] Ibid.

the newspaper agreed with occasional contributors such as Kautsky and Bebel that French socialists should cooperate with Dreyfusards in order to prop up the bourgeois republic against reactionaries in the period before the proletariat was ready to assume power:[186]

Soldiers, priests, the privileged strata of large-scale capital and the declining elements of society have formed a pact, which is directed against those strata of the bourgeoisie who are not only not privileged, unlike the enormous capitalists and agrarians, but also not in the grip of atrophy, unlike small craftsmen. But the only battle-ready part of the anti-reactionary strata is the proletariat; the duty of the pre-struggle, with all its burdens, falls to it, even though it is not in a position immediately to gain great practical benefits.... All this means, though, when applied to the Dreyfus case, that French Social Democracy had the task of *putting itself at the head of the movement for revision.*[187]

To Bebel, this cooperation with Dreyfusards was so evidently necessary that Guesde's opposition and the consequent split in the ranks of French socialists was incomprehensible: if the Dreyfus case had occurred in Germany instead of France, all German Social Democrats, including Liebknecht, would have joined the movement for revision.[188] To fight for Dreyfus was, in effect, to defend the Third Republic, and *Vorwärts* did not doubt, in 1899, that the republican regime in France was worth preserving: 'France can be counted amongst those few countries where civic democracy is still of a remarkable and admirable greatness.'[189] The ministry of Waldeck-Rousseau, which was formed in order to resolve the Dreyfus affair, was welcomed accordingly by the socialist press, despite the inclusion as war minister of General Galliffet, who had suppressed the Commune.[190]

As has already been seen, this socialist support for the republic did not imply participation in bourgeois ministries. Both Kautsky and Bebel believed that French socialism had been weakened, and the French government barely strengthened, by the appointment of Millerand to the Ministry of Trade in 1899.[191] Ordinarily, however, *Vorwärts* was more circumspect. Millerand's entry into government had only split French socialists because of the presence of General Galliffet, a veteran of the suppression of the Commune in 1871, not

---

[186] See K. Koszyk, 'Sozialdemokratie und Antisemitismus zur Zeit der Dreyfus-Affäre', in L. Heid and A. Paucker (eds.), *Juden und deutsche Arbeiterbewegung bis 1933* (Tübingen, 1992), 73.

[187] K. Kautsky in *Vorwärts*, 1 Aug. 1899.

[188] A. Bebel in ibid., 17 Sept. 1899.   [189] Ibid., 23 July 1899.

[190] Ibid., 29 June 1899.   [191] Ibid., 1 Aug. 1899 and 17 Sept. 1899.

because of a clash of principles between independent socialists, who voted for the Waldeck-Rousseau ministry, and Guesdistes, Alemanistes, and Blanquistes, who voted against: 'One should remember the depth of hatred which the heinous crimes of the "slaughterer of the Commune" Galliffet have produced in the breast of every French worker.'[192] The division within French socialist ranks was perceived to rest merely on tactical disagreement.[193] Ideologically, they were still seen to be similar: 'at bottom, i.e. as far as acts and not words are concerned, it is simply a question of different *shadings*, which is underpinned by a narrower or broader conception of class conflict or an evaluation of reform work.'[194] Whereas Guesdists were criticized for their divisive dogmatism, Jaurès was lauded for his attempts at conciliation.[195] What was more, Millerand was praised in a series of articles, which appeared between 1899 and 1901, for his social and economic reforms.[196] His bill to introduce a state-run system of arbitration, for example, had long been an aim of German Social Democrats, reported *Vorwärts*. It was, therefore, disappointing that most left-wing French socialists had rejected the project on the grounds that non-socialist workers and the state would be allowed to distort the economic struggle between capital and labour: 'Such a discussion and consequent decision about an important bill seems rather odd to German Social Democrats. . . . The grounds for rejection by the French majority are for German Social Democrats quite surprising.'[197] The conciliatory gestures and sensible legislation of Millerand and Jaurès had been obstructed, it seemed, by Guesde, Vaillant, and Allemane.

Between 1901 and 1902, however, *Vorwärts* altered its stance, as disunity within the French federation of workers' parties persisted and Millerand's reformism failed to meet socialist expectations. By the end of May 1901, it could no longer be denied 'that Millerand's ministerial position and all that is connected with it is gnawing away more and more perniciously at the body of the party' and that the solution 'can only be found through the removal of the ministerial question'.[198] By January of the following year, the minister of trade was already being described as a counterfeit socialist, 'who, as is well-known, is energetically opposed by the majority of socialists'.[199]

---

[192] Ibid., 15 July 1899.   [193] Ibid., 23 July 1899.   [194] Ibid., 4 Sept. 1900.
[195] Ibid.
[196] Ibid., 29 Dec. 1899, 23 Jan., 1 Apr., 21 Sept., 11 Oct. 1900, and 22 Feb. 1901.
[197] Ibid., 8 May 1901.   [198] Ibid., 26 May 1901.   [199] Ibid., 22 Jan. 1902.

He continued to use the term 'socialist', like the *radicaux socialistes*, as a flag of convenience rather than as a sign of conviction: 'It is obvious that the counterfeiting of socialism for electoral purposes has now spread, in an ugly way, more widely than ever, even than in 1893, when socialism had attracted the attention of the voting masses as a new party... as in the forties of the previous century, the word socialism has totally lost its real meaning for the great masses.'[200] The ministry of Waldeck-Rousseau, which had been greeted as a coalition for the defence of the republic, was decried as a mere stopgap government by October 1901 and Millerand, who, it had been said, wished to turn defence into reform, was disparaged as a political failure: 'For it [the government] has disappointed all classes and strata of the population, who had expected serious reforms from it.... The best elements of the proletariat regard the Waldeck-Rousseau government with just as much antipathy or mistrust as the bourgeoisie.'[201] Even Jaurès and his supporters were seen to have been tarred by the same ministerialist brush, after 'their group in the chamber had acted like a mere appendage of bourgeois democracy'.[202] By the summer of 1902, *Vorwärts* had not only rejected the idea of socialist participation in bourgeois ministries, it had also begun to criticize any other form of cooperation with the Third Republic.

The rest of the pre-war period confirmed the change of 1901–1902. As was to be expected, a socialist such as Briand, who joined and led republican governments, was reviled at various times by the mouthpiece of the SPD as 'a dishonourable scoundrel', 'slave of plutocracy', 'ruthless politician', and 'the bourgeoisie's man,'[203] whilst Viviani was denigrated as an untouchable, despite having resigned over the Briand ministry's conduct during the rail strike of 1910.[204] More significantly, however, Jaurès was condemned for simply supporting Combes's ministry and independent socialists were discounted en bloc as 'a pendant of bourgeois Radicalism'.[205] Such aspersions were motivated, above all, by *Vorwärts*'s fears concerning party unity.[206] SPD leaders, who believed that the strength of their

---

[200] *Vorwärts*, 26 Apr. 1902.   [201] Ibid., 22 Oct. 1901.

[202] Ibid., 26 Apr. 1902.

[203] Ibid., 24 Apr. 1906, 16 May 1907, 13 and 29 Oct. 1910.

[204] Ibid., 29 Oct. 1910 and 27 July 1909.

[205] Ibid., 17 May 1906. For criticism of Jaurès, see 31 May and 24 Aug. 1904, and 23 Feb. 1906.

[206] See, for instance, ibid., 15 Oct. 1904, which urged the socialist groups in France to unite in opposition to Radicalism, which had begun to develop its party apparatus.

own party lay in its organization, were shocked by the fragmentary nature and vituperative infighting of French socialism, which had been displayed to the world at the Paris and Amsterdam meetings of the Second International in 1900 and 1904. When, finally, a single socialist party was established in 1905, allegedly at the behest of the International, the mainstream socialist press in Germany had already decided that ministerialism and parliamentarism were responsible for previous disorder and division in France:

The work of unification in 1905 is the necessary result of prolonged, many-sided secession crises.... The practical overcoming of ministerialism expressed itself in the continued strengthening of the *left* wing of the PSF itself, which eventually won a majority on the national committee of this party. This event was the most important factor in the unification and is the most secure guarantee for its longevity.[207]

Now that internal conflict and parliamentarism had been banished from French socialism, the taming of France's radical, anti-parliamentary unions also seemed possible: 'Hopefully, the unification of the party will serve to tie the French union organizations spiritually to the party. Because of the division and fragmentation of the party, on the one hand, and parliamentarism, which was taken too far, on the other, many union circles were alienated from the party altogether.'[208] Their public protestations notwithstanding, German socialists continued to treat the SFIO as a precious and fragile object. Any challenge, it appeared, would destroy the whole structure. Since the most obvious challenge was the resurrection of turn-of-the-century parliamentary tactics, those French socialists who advocated them were ostracized in the German socialist press. By 1905, at the latest, the possibility of participation and reform in the Third Republic had been discounted by much of the SPD.

Ministerialism, parliamentarism, and reformism in France were never considered by most German socialists to be more than interim strategies, of course. Eventually, it was anticipated, the polarization of French politics into proletarian socialism, on the one hand, and bourgeois, republican reaction, on the other, would remove the question of involvement and support. Republicans and Radicals would become the political representatives of the bourgeoisie alone, leaving workers no alternative to revolutionary socialism. Class opposition would turn

---

[207] Ibid., 3 May 1905.   [208] Ibid., 29 Apr. 1905. Also, ibid., 25 Aug. 1906.

party conflict into open class conflict, it was predicted: 'This intensi-
fication of party struggle is expressed, apart from in the election
results, in the fact that capitalist parties in France have, for the first
time, *united* against the socialists and, backed by the government, have
behaved in the most ruthless way—such as one, until now, has not
been accustomed to in France.'[209] Before and after each Assembly
election, *Vorwärts* was convinced that a bifurcation of French politics
was in train. In 1898, it appeared until the eleventh hour that the
Radicals would side with nationalists in a reactionary, anti-socialist
bloc.[210] The failure of this polarization to occur immediately was
attributed to the confusion wrought by the Dreyfus affair.[211] By 1902,
however, a left-wing republican coalition had been formed in response
to the right-wing majority, which had predominated under Méline.[212]
Although bourgeois parties were still little more than factions,[213] some
of which were linked to French socialism, the trend seemed clear
enough and looked set to be tested after 1906, when the Radicals
gained an absolute majority at the polls: now the myth of Radical
social and economic reform would be exploded and the propertied,
capitalist basis of the party would be exposed:[214] 'The money for the
clash between capital and labour is now free. Radicalism must choose
between one of the two conflicting parties. Perhaps class oppositions,
which are developing with increasing speed, will destroy the unified
association of Radicalism.'[215] The same predictions were made in
1910 and 1914.[216]

Vorwärts's accounts of French politics tended to concentrate on
Radicalism, which was seen as the bulwark of the bourgeois republic.
How strong were the Radicals and what role did they play in government? How likely were they to countenance social and economic
reform and, consequently, extend the republican phase of French history? These were the leading questions which socialist journalists in
Germany asked themselves. Although their reports were shaped by
the belief that Radicalism would disappear eventually, as politics
divided between capital and labour, their assessment of the timing
of that disappearance and the strength of the *Parti radical* fluctuated. During the ministries of Waldeck-Rousseau and Combes, it

---

[209] *Vorwärts*, 10 May 1898.
[210] Ibid., 5 June 1898.   [211] Ibid., 4 Jan. 1899.   [212] Ibid., 13 May 1902.
[213] Ibid., 6 Jan. 1903.   [214] Ibid., 14 June 1906.   [215] Ibid., 26 May 1906.
[216] Ibid., 11 May 1910 and 26 Apr. 1914.

had become evident that the prophesies of the Méline era, which had anticipated '*new party groupings* or the beginnings of lasting party shifts', had been premature:[217] the Radicals had showed themselves powerful enough to defend the republic against its enemies.[218] This, as one report in April 1914 put it, had been the last heroic period of French Radicalism.[219] Thereafter, during the ministries of Rouvier, Clemenceau, and Briand, it had merged with the forces of capital and reneged on its promises of reform. Losing seats in the elections of 1910 and 1914, Radicals were perceived by *Vorwärts* to have given their last breath in preventing Poincaré's imposing a government in December 1913, rather than having revitalized their party.[220]

This perceived bankruptcy of French Radicalism was significant because it was seen by German socialists to affect the nature and durability of the Third Republic. Granted, those same socialists had already rejected the idea of cooperation with the republican regime, since it seemed to endanger the unity of the French workers' parties. But the debasement of the Radical republic into an unequivocally capitalist republic was a useful justification for that pragmatic rejection. Here, after all, was the proof that parliamentary democracy was nearing its end in France, to be replaced by the direct, economic democracy of socialist society:

Petty-bourgeois short-sightedness, which does not recognize deeper relations and sticks to the visible appearances of the surface of things, is quick to see the *cause* of democracy's lack of results in *parliamentarism* itself, without examining the historical function of parliament in the class struggle.... It is not to be denied that trust in the possibility of social development under democracy is crumbling, and with it one of the strongest pillars of republican conviction.... The observer who has been won round to the world view of scientific socialism will see this crisis of democracy to be unavoidable.... The socialist does not believe, like the vulgar democrat, that *democracy itself* contains developmental forces, which drive society on beyond capitalism, but he recognizes it to be a valuable *form*, in which the transformation of the economic order can be completed without unnecessary sacrifices, and where class struggle, the struggle for political power, can be pursued with the certain clarity of a decision. In this recognition, he remains just as far from the utopia of a democracy which moves reform by reform to socialism as he does from its opposite pole of anarchist damnation of any political intervention whatever on the part of the proletariat.[221]

[217] Ibid., 15 Apr. 1898.   [218] Ibid., 4 Jan. 1902.   [219] Ibid., 26 Apr. 1914.
[220] Ibid., 9 Dec. 1913.   [221] Ibid., 3 Jan. 1909.

There were, of course, still some admirers of the French republic in the SPD, but the core of the party had turned against it definitively in the decade and a half before the First World War.[222]

5. Liberals

Both socialist and liberal publications were sometimes accused by conservatives of Francophilia. This was especially so during the Dreyfus affair, when the number of articles on France reached its peak. In fact, however, many of the reports which appeared in the liberal press between 1898 and 1900 questioned and challenged the Third Republic, rather than congratulating it. Although German liberal newspapers thereafter supported the ministries of Waldeck-Rousseau, Combes, Rouvier, and Clemenceau, their confidence in French republicanism had already been qualified, which in turn prepared the way for criticism of the republic after 1907.

The most obvious charge levelled against republican governments was that they had failed to maintain order. The cartoons of liberal satirical journals almost invariably depicted France in chaos during the Dreyfus affair, with common allusions to battlefield, zoo, and circus.[223] Still more popular were references to mob scenes. The *Lustige Blätter*, for example, envisaged 'Das Dreyfus-Theater', in which a tumultuous audience applauded as Dreyfus was brought onto stage in a small cage, with Drumont and Rochefort as his gaolers.[224] In similar fashion, *Ulk* portrayed the veiling of a statue of 'Die Wahrheit' in a Parisian gallery. An angry crowd was kept back by the police.[225] The serious picture reportage of the large circulation, weekly newspaper, the *Berliner Illustrierte Zeitung*, conveyed the same message. An article accompanying a front-page sketch of the 'Unruhen in Paris', which depicted the confusion of a 'Clash between police and demonstrators in the Avenue de l'Alma on 2 October', described how a Dreyfusard meeting at the Wagram hall had been stormed by

[222] Alsatians, in particular, continued to admire the Republic. See L. Strauss, 'Les Militants alsaciens et lorrains et les rapports entre les mouvements ouvriers français et allemands entre 1900 et 1923', *Revue d'Allemagne*, 4 (1972), and R. Stübling, '*Vive la France!' Der Sozialdemokrat Hermann Wendel 1884–1936* (Frankfurt a.M., 1983).

[223] 'Emile Zola, der neue Winkelried', *Lustige Blätter*, in anon., *Dreyfus-Bilderbuch*, 31. 'Aus dem Cirque Elysée', ibid. 87; 'Militarismus', ibid. 94, 112.

[224] 'Emile Zola', ibid. 38; 'Wehe den Wahrheitsforschern!', ibid. 55; 'Französischer Lumpenball', ibid. 86; 'Pariser Modelle', ibid. 99.

[225] *Ulk*, in anon., *Dreyfus–Bilderbuch*, 77.

anti-Dreyfusards. An attempt by the police, to ban the assembly of both sides had had no effect.[226] The judiciary, the police, and the army were in turmoil, it was suggested, and republican governments, deprived of the means of coercion, were left powerless. To liberal journals of all kinds, there seemed to be some truth in the *Lustige Blätter*'s cartoon, 'Die neue "Bourgogne" ', which compared France under the Third Republic to a recent maritime disaster. The Président du Conseil, Brisson, was characterized as a helpless captain at the helm, trying unsuccessfully to keep civilian passengers from attacking the military crew, who were rushing for lifeboats in order to save themselves: 'The French ship of state is in danger—and again it is the crew [the army] who knock everybody down just to save themselves', ran the caption.[227] The republic's response to the attempted *coup d'état* of Déroulède and to the Guérin siege in the rue de Chabrol betrayed a dangerous weakness in the opinion of most liberal newspapers.[228] The *National-Zeitung* was not even sure that republican governments would be able to guarantee the safety of foreign visitors to the World Exhibition in 1900.[229]

During the Dreyfus affair, French republicans were not only accused of impotence by German liberals, but also of immorality. The Third Republic, wrote the left-liberal journal *Die Nation* in November 1898, had been compromised by a spiral of legal improprieties: 'Violations of the law then mounted up and mounted up, and this picture of corruption in the army, amongst judges, in the press, in the ministries, this picture of parliament's weakness and lack of character betrayed the deep decay of French conditions.'[230] It appeared difficult to deny that republican ministries and deputies were implicated in miscarriages of justice when the Assembly had ordered by 572 votes to two that Cavaignac's affirmation of Dreyfus's guilt be posted on town hall doors throughout France.[231] To the *National-Zeitung*, Dreyfusards were those few intellectuals, 'who, in contrast to the government and parliament of France, stand up for justice and legality'.[232] Many of the republic's elder statesmen, it emerged, had colluded with the army. Ex-president Casimir-Périer was said, after refusing to answer

---

[226] *Berliner Illustrierte Zeitung*, 16 Oct. 1898.
[227] *Lustige Blätter*, in anon., *Dreyfus-Bilderbuch*, 81; *Kladderadatsch*, 25 Sept. 1898, no. 39.
[228] *National-Zeitung*, 21 Aug. 1899; ibid., 17 Aug. 1899, 22 Aug. 1899; *Freisinnige Zeitung*, 13 Aug. and 12 Dec. 1899, 16 June 1900.
[229] *National-Zeitung*, 19 Feb. 1899.   [230] *Nation*, 1898, no. 6.
[231] *National-Zeitung*, 31 Aug. 1898.
[232] Ibid., 31 Aug. 1898. Also, ibid., 26 Sept. 1898.

questions during the Zola trial, to have been informed of all the details of the Dreyfus case in 1894, but to have ignored them.[233] Méline was accused of informal collaboration with right-wing, anti-Dreyfusard parties: 'An actual formal alliance between himself and the right appears not to have existed, but it cannot be denied that there was a tacit agreement in their mutual interest.'[234] Dupuy—'who flirts with reaction', in the phrase of the *Freisinnige Zeitung*[235]—was seen to have done the same and Faure was alleged to have blocked revision in private, although he had not intervened formally in the affair.[236] The instincts of the republican establishment appeared, as *Kladderadatsch* spelled out, to be opportunist. Faure was depicted as Jupiter in a production of 'Orpheus in der Unterwelt', on stage with Dreyfus, whereas Brisson, portrayed as a military Pluto, reminded him from the margins of the set of his anti-Dreyfusard past: 'Do not look on so piously, / We know you Jupiter'.[237] This opportunism had pushed republican politicians to try to smother the Dreyfus affair, in deference to public opinion and from fear of revelations about their own corruption:

The defenders of truth and freedom constituted a small handful of good, clear-sighted, discerning republicans, whereas the great mass of the republican population did not see the danger to the state and was ready to buy peace in the country through the sacrifice of a miserable Jew; that was an act of moral nastiness and political short-sightedness, and it prevailed amongst millions of republicans, the republican ministries, and President Faure. . . . The masses wanted peace, other republicans in prominent positions could not take up the struggle with the insurrectionists because their own past was too tainted for them to expose themselves to the most ruthless revenge of the Caesarists. Thus, it came about that the republic seemed lost for a long time because of the blindness of the many and the lack of preparedness to fight, frivolity, petty, factional rivalries and indifference of the leading republicans all the way up to President Faure.[238]

German liberals never forgave the Third Republic completely for the injustices of the Dreyfus affair. Nonetheless, they did deflect criticism from the republican regime to an extent after 1898, first, by blaming anti-republican bugbears for some of the most heinous

[233] *National-Zeitung*, 8 Feb. 1898.
[234] Ibid., 17 June 1898. See also, ibid., 15 June 1898.
[235] *Freisinnige Zeitung*, 14 July 1906. Also *National-Zeitung*, 14 June 1899.
[236] *Nation*, 1899, no. 37. *National-Zeitung*, 26 Sept. 1898.
[237] *Kladderadatsch*, 9 Oct. 1898, no. 41.
[238] *Nation*, 1899, no. 37.

misdemeanours of the case and, second, by redefining the term 'republican' in order to exclude many right-wing and moderate supporters
of the republic, who were seen to have colluded with anti-
Dreyfusards. A good example of the former was a cartoon entitled
'Der Taucher', which appeared in *Kladderadatsch* in February 1899.
Loubet was shown diving into the murky waters beneath an outcrop
of land marked 'République Française'. Before collecting the presidential shell, he had to pass various hideous and dangerous fish, representing clerics, nationalist writers, and army officers.[239] This
perceived opposition between the French right, the church, and the
army, on the one hand, and the republic, on the other, was repeated
on many occasions by liberal newspapers in Germany. It was evident
to *Die Nation* in 1899 and to the *National-Zeitung* in 1900, for instance,
that the Dreyfus affair was a struggle between republic and church,
rather than a conflict which divided republican and Catholic ranks
internally: 'the struggle surrounding Dreyfus has become a wrestling
match between reactionary-clerical and republican forces in
France';[240] 'since the trial of Zola in January 1898, the clerical party
has shown itself more and more clearly to be the most irreconcilable
and dangerous enemy of the republic.'[241] To the *Freisinnige Zeitung*,
the same enmity existed between military and civilian—that is,
republican—jurisdictions: 'The great opposition between militarism
and citizenry, which, it should be noted, has assumed more and more
acute proportions in the French republic during the Dreyfus business, has now reached its high point.'[242] As has already been seen, this
'clerical-anti-Semitic-nationalist clique' was believed by German liberals to have threatened the very existence of the Third Republic
between 1898 and 1900.[243] At such moments, there was an obvious
distinction between those who were for the republican regime and
those who were against it.

The identification of true and false republicans, which took place
in the liberal press in Germany after 1898, inevitably redefined the
putative nature of French republicanism. With hindsight, this change
appeared self-evident to the *Vossische Zeitung* in 1910:

The general elections of 1898 made the Radicals the strongest group in the
chamber. In alliance with the socialists they constituted a majority. Both parties

---

[239] *Kladderadatsch*, 26 Feb. 1899, no. 9.   [240] *Nation*, 1899, no. 24.
[241] *National-Zeitung*, 28 Jan. 1900.   [242] *Freisinnige Zeitung*, 12 Sept. 1899.
[243] *Freisinnige Zeitung*, 14 July 1906.

concluded this alliance with great eagerness. The socialists tended at that time towards a relatively peaceful evolutionism and the Radicals were extremely willing to allow a socialist or at least social-reformist element into their programme; many of them were so much inclined to come to terms with the socialists that they called themselves Radical-Socialists. At that time, socialists and Radicals recognized unanimously their primary task to be the bitter struggle to the death against clericalism, with its links to monarchism, which they had got to know, fear, and abhor during the devastating, six-year domination of nationalism, especially during the Dreyfus affair.[244]

Redefinition of the Third Republic by German liberals occurred slowly and uncertainly. It was by no means clear from liberal newspapers that the election results of 1898 would precipitate political change, nor that Waldeck-Rousseau's ministry of republican defence—'the cabinet of improbabilities', according to the *Freisinnige Zeitung*— would be anything but ephemeral.[245] As the *Berliner Tageblatt* reminded its readers in 1909, the republic had experienced its first Radical ministry as late as 1895 and its first socialist minister in 1899.[246] Yet, between 1900 and 1906, most German liberal publications had redrawn the republican regime in France along Radical lines, so that it seemed to be founded on a unifying, secular policy of defence against the Catholic Church and on a shared manifesto of social and economic reform. The encomiums, which virtually all the major liberal newspapers bestowed upon Waldeck-Rousseau and Loubet in 1902, 1904, and 1906, revealed these new terms, on which, it was believed, the Third Republic had been secured: 'The summoning of a socialist into government was—Loubet could not be in any doubt about this...— the signal for a completely new grouping of parties, or rather: the two great parties, which had emerged during the Dreyfus affair, stood henceforth in clear and open conflict with one another.'[247] The *bloc*, it was well-known, consisted of Radicals, Radical-Socialists, and socialists, but the implications of this fact were less widely recognized by German liberals: moderate republicans had, effectively, been excluded from the republic proper. 'These people, who go as far as to call themselves progressive republicans, cannot be relied upon

[244] *Vossische Zeitung*, 3 Nov. 1910.

[245] *Freisinnige Zeitung*, 28 June 1899; *National-Zeitung*, 23 May 1898.

[246] *Berliner Tageblatt*, cited in *Freisinnige Zeitung*, 25 July 1909.

[247] *Münchner Neueste Nachrichten*, 1 Mar. 1906. See also *Freisinnige Zeitung*, 29 Apr. 1902, 20 Jan. and 14 July 1906; *Frankfurter Zeitung*, 31 Mar. 1902; *Berliner Tageblatt*, 11 Aug. 1904; *Hamburgischer Correspondent*, 11 Aug. 1904; *Berliner Börsenzeitung*, 19 Sept. 1906.

for a truly republican and progressive policy,' wrote the *Frankfurter Zeitung*.[248] As one of Germany's most famous journalists, Theodor Wolff, recalled in 1904, all masks had been removed during the Dreyfus affair and 'the "educated bourgeoisie"', which was represented, above all, by Méline and the *Journal des Débats*, had been exposed for what it was: cowardly and despicable.[249]

The election results of 1906 seemed to liberal newspapers in Germany to have confirmed the shift towards a Radical republic in France. For the first time, Radicals, Radical-Socialists, and left-wing republicans commanded an absolute majority in the Assembly.[250] If it were assumed that socialists would vote with Radical governments in most instances, the opposition counted only 96 reactionaries and 63 moderate republicans, observed the *Berliner Tageblatt*.[251] Now the Sarrien administration, which was dominated by Clemenceau, offered Radicals the opportunity to pursue positive policies. Previously, as the *Münchner Neueste Nachrichten* noted, governments had been obliged to concentrate on consolidating the Third Republic and on cementing new political alliances: 'During the last seven years, the Loubet years, the motto was: above all, consolidation of the republic, carrying out the ideas of the French Revolution, the realization of the secular state, an alliance of all convinced republicans, and alliance too with all those who dream of international democracy, of a republic of the proletariat.'[252] It was rarely doubted that both Waldeck-Rousseau and Combes would have enacted social and economic reforms, however, if they had had the opportunity. In this respect, the *Freisinnige Zeitung*'s assessment of the latter—'Social legislation remained piecemeal because the political-clerical struggle took up all the energy and attention of parliament'[253]—corresponded exactly with Theodor Wolff's obituary of the former: 'I think that he would have gladly provided France with new social-political legislation, and that these plans would have been realized, if he could have come to power again.'[254]

When Clemenceau, hitherto one of the most vociferous critics of government inefficacy, assumed office in 1906, backed by an absolute

[248] *Frankfurter Zeitung*, 5 May 1906; *Freisinnige Zeitung*, 29 Apr. 1902.
[249] *Berliner Tageblatt*, 11 Aug. 1904.
[250] Radicals had increased their number of seats from 103 to 115, Radical-Socialists from 119 to 132, and left-wing republicans from 76 to 90, to give a total of 337 seats.
[251] *Berliner Tageblatt*, 8 May 1907.
[252] *Münchner Neueste Nachrichten*, 16 Dec. 1905.
[253] *Freisinnige Zeitung*, 8 May 1906.   [254] *Berliner Tageblatt*, 11 Aug 1904.

Radical majority, it was no surprise that the expectations of German liberals were high. The promises of Radicals had been so frequent and so fulsome, it appeared, that the ministry would be forced to act, or be accused of hypocrisy. What was more, French socialists were seen to have become part of the political establishment, so that they would continue to influence government, even though they did not, as a party, participate in it: 'If the Radicals should forget about them [social reforms], then there are enough people there to remind them about them, more or less pressingly. Namely, the socialists.'[255] It will suffice here to examine the responses of two of the great liberal newspapers—the *Frankfurter Zeitung* and the *Berliner Tageblatt*—to Clemenceau's accession to office. Their starting-point was the same, summarized by the correspondent of the *Tageblatt*, who had just completed a twelve-year sojourn in Paris. France, he claimed, was still worthy of imitation:

One cannot turn energetically enough on the foolish and dangerous critics who, through conceited arrogance and complete ignorance, talk again and again of France's 'decadence'. There exists no *political* and no *economic* decline in a people, which in three decades, after defeat in war, has rebuilt its army, created an entire system of schools, won a powerful empire, playfully overcome gigantic financial catastrophes, and has annually increased its wealth by almost a billion francs.[256]

True, the Third Republic continued to lag behind monarchies such as those in Germany in the imposition of a redistributive income tax and in the introduction of social insurance, but this was because the republican regime had had to pass through conservative, liberal, and Opportunist phases in order to establish itself. Finally, concluded the *Frankfurter Zeitung*, the republic had entered a Radical-Socialist epoch, whose aims coincided more or less with those of social liberals in Germany: 'The Third Republic, which has been, consecutively, conservative, liberal, Opportunist, and Radical-Opportunist, has been transformed by Clemenceau's programme of government into a Radical-Socialist one, and from now on one will be able to say: the Third Republic will be social and political, or it will be nothing at all!'[257] Those measures already started, such as tax reform and old age pensions, would be passed immediately, continued the same newspaper, whereas other pledges, like decentralization, legal protection of

[255] *Frankfurter Zeitung*, 22 May 1906.   [256] *Berliner Tageblatt*, 17 Nov. 1906.
[257] *Frankfurter Zeitung*, 6 Nov. 1906.

individual rights, and regulation of work contracts, would be legislated over the longer term.[258] Neither publication questioned the imminence or the desirability of a social republic in France.

By 1909, however, it appeared that such expectations had been misplaced. Clemenceau's aggressive foreign policy and his inability to solve the labour issue were criticized widely in the German liberal press. Newspapers like the *Vossische Zeitung* and the *Münchner Neueste Nachrichten*, which had once approved of cooperation between Radicals and socialists, now depicted the government's difficulties with strikers as its nemesis.[259] The greatest disappointment for German liberals, however, was the failure of Clemenceau's ministry to fulfil its promises of reform. Even the most ardent erstwhile supporters of the Radical administration, such as the *Frankfurter Zeitung*, rebutted attempts to blame the unification and radicalization of French socialists for ministerial inaction: 'In truth, therefore, the socialists are guilty of breaking up the *bloc* majority. Whether they are also to blame for the stagnation of reform, however, is another question, to which one cannot give an affirmative answer. The Radicals are strong enough in number to form a government majority.'[260] By May 1907, the *Berliner Tageblatt* had already begun to despair of Clemenceau's government. Out of all the reforms promised by the ministry, new regulations for gambling-halls and a change in the law on the treatment of mental illness had alone been enacted: 'in fairness, one is forced to admit that no government period of office for a long time has been so unfruitful, so poor in terms of results'.[261] Two years later, the *Vossische Zeitung* came to the same conclusion: reform of the courts martial had not been completed, an income tax bill was about to be rejected by the Senate, and the nationalization of the railways had impaired rather than improved efficiency.[262] The verdict of the *National-Zeitung*, the *Hamburgischer Correspondent*, the *Frankfurter Zeitung*, the *Hannoverscher Courier*, the *Freisinnige Zeitung*, the *Weser Zeitung*, and the *Münchner Neueste Nachrichten* was similar: 'Radicalism gained unrestricted power. . . . Now, finally, the Radicals could carry out undisturbed all their great and splendid plans! And it was appropriate, therefore, that the most radical of the Radicals, *Clemenceau*, had at last become a

---

[258] Ibid.

[259] *Vossische Zeitung*, 20 Apr. 1907; *Münchner Neueste Nachrichten*, 18 July 1907.

[260] *Frankfurter Zeitung*, 24 May 1907.

[261] *Berliner Tageblatt*, 8 May 1907.

[262] *Vossische Zeitung*, 7 Apr. 1909.

minister.... The chamber which "could do everything that it wanted": what has it achieved? Nothing, absolutely nothing!"[263] As far as German liberals were concerned, the Clemenceau ministry had exploded the myth of progressive Radicalism.

The failure of the Radical republic was inferred from the perceived failure of French Radicalism. Between 1907 and 1909, a series of articles appeared in the German liberal press criticizing parliamentarism in France. The *Frankfurter Zeitung* was one of the few publications which did not lose faith completely in the Third Republic. Yet its critical evaluation of Clemenceau's achievement still led it to question France's parliamentary regime. Democratic reforms, which had been implemented after 1906, were insufficient, it seemed, if they were not followed by social and economic improvement: 'political freedom is not everything. Sincere and unselfish leaders of democracy, in France and elsewhere, have always realized and acknowledged that the political emancipation of a people, if it is to last and be worth anything, must go hand in hand with the intellectual and economic emancipation of the masses and, in particular, of the working classes... in economic and social spheres, the republic has still not fulfilled the expectations, which were placed on it by the masses.'[264] When the same newspaper went on to apportion blame, it not only mentioned Clemenceau and Radicalism, but also parliamentarism. The asking of the question was more significant than the fact that it found no answer: 'Now, is parliamentarism, the Radical Party, or the personality of Clemenceau to blame for this?'[265] In the preceding two years, articles appearing in the *Frankfurter Zeitung*, which had referred to the 'impotence of parliament' and 'a crisis of the republic', had already hinted that the parliamentary system of government itself bore some of the responsibility for the ministry's failure.[266] Other liberal newspapers were less reticent. The *Hamburgischer Correspondent*, for example, claimed that, since 1789, France had been in a state of structural crisis, which the Third Republic had been unable to resolve.[267] Alternating phases of parliamentary deadlock and dictatorship

---

[263] *Münchner Neueste Nachrichten*, 18 July 1907. *National-Zeitung*, 21 July 1909; *Hamburgischer Correspondent*, 20 Nov. 1908; *Frankfurter Zeitung*, 28 July 1909; *Hannoverscher Courier*, 23 Aug. 1907; *Freisinnige Zeitung*, 22 July 1909; *Weser Zeitung*, 15 Apr. 1910.

[264] *Frankfurter Zeitung*, 28 July 1909.

[265] Ibid.   [266] Ibid., 15 Apr. 1908 and 21 May 1909.

[267] *Hamburgischer Correspondent*, 20 Nov. 1908.

appeared to be the modern form of this crisis: both the *Vossische Zeitung* and the *Münchner Neueste Nachrichten* discussed how the self-interest of deputies and the inefficacy of government could push the populace towards Caesarism: 'they [dictators] could more easily break with all the dear traditions of parliamentarism—of parliamentary anarchy.'[268] Dictators became popular, it was held, after parliaments had failed, and in France, by 1909, it seemed that the 'decline of parliamentarism' was already well advanced: 'It is a fact that this parliament, and especially the chamber, has lost all of its prestige and does not impress the people in the slightest. The consequence of this, however, is that there is nothing between the moods and excitements of the mob and anarchy except a popular assembly without influence, power, and self-confidence, and that is one of the greatest dangers for the present internal predicament of France.'[269] Within three years, then, most German liberal newspapers had become disenchanted with parliamentary republicanism in France. The alacrity of their disenchantment is best explained by the exacting nature of their demands and by the chequered history of the Third Republic, as far as liberals were concerned, before 1899. Perhaps German liberals' expressed expectations of parliamentary republicanism were so high in 1906 precisely because the French republic was on probation, after the instability and scandal of its first three decades of existence.

The critical tone, which had been set by the German liberal press between 1907 and 1909, continued to characterize reports on France in the years before the First World War. The fragmentation of French parties, the corruption of the Radicals, and the stalemate of parliamentary government were the recurring themes of liberal correspondence.[270] Attempts to introduce proportional representation, which coincided with the period under discussion here, served to establish the constancy and conviction of such views. Not only did most liberal newspapers in Germany advocate electoral reform in France, in order to remove some of the defects of parliamentary republicanism, they also inculpated the Radicals as the principal opponents of that reform. The *Vossische Zeitung*, the *Frankfurter Zeitung*, and the *Freisinnige Zeitung* all concurred that Radical deputies profited most from the existing system of one-deputy

[268] *Vossische Zeitung*, 7 Apr. 1909; *Münchner Neueste Nachrichten*, 18 July 1907.
[269] *Vossische Zeitung*, 7 Apr. 1909. The article was entitled 'Der Niedergang des Parlamentarismus in Frankreich'.
[270] See Chs 1–3.

constituencies: it was to be expected that they would fight to preserve the electoral form through which they had, as a party, come to power.[271] Whereas, in the past, fear of Caesarism had constituted the main obstacle to the introduction of proportional representation, by 1912 the self-interest of Radicals appeared to block reform: 'Now that the reactionary menace has been banished, the system of Radical coteries has become all the more pronounced.'[272] Even a reputedly right-wing politician like Poincaré, who was one of the main proponents of the *scrutin de liste*, was preferable to nepotism, corruption, and inaction.[273] The *Berliner Tageblatt* went so far as to publish an article by the French president in support of proportional representation.[274] Of course, such advocacy expressed liberal hopes that the French parliamentary republic could be rescued. Yet it was marked most by distrust and uncertainty: electoral reform was, according to the *Berliner Börsen-Courrier*, untried and potentially dangerous; it was not, therefore, to be seen as a panacea.[275] 'Poincaré took it upon himself *to carry out electoral reform*, from which one hoped for a purging of domestic affairs, and which was meant to put a stop to nepotism.... That was no small risk for Poincaré, and it is still doubtful whether this long shot will come off', reported the *Freisinnige Zeitung* in 1912.[276] Thus, even if the Assembly could be induced to reform itself, it was by no means certain that proportional representation would remove most of the defects of the Third Republic—hence the use of indefinite verbs such as 'to hope' (*erhoffen*) and 'to be meant' (*machen sollen*). In 1906, some German liberal newspapers still depicted parliamentary republicanism in France as an archetypically modern form of government, capable of pioneering social and economic reform. Only six years later, they were to be found discussing the redundancy of the same political regime. If the speed of liberal disaffection is best explained by the supposition that French parliamentarism was, in effect, already on trial, then the longevity and consistency of that disaffection suggests that the French republic had been tried by all liberals, rejected by some, and passed by none.

---

[271] *Vossische Zeitung*, 26 June 1911; *Frankfurter Zeitung*, 28 Sept. 1909; *Freisinnige Zeitung*, 25 June 1911.

[272] *Freisinnige Zeitung*, 13 July 1912.

[273] *Berliner Tageblatt*, 19 Jan. 1913; *Frankfurter Zeitung*, 19 June 1912.

[274] *Berliner Tageblatt*, 18 Nov. 1913. The article was an extract from Poincaré's book *Wie Frankreich regiert wird*, which had just been published in Germany.

[275] *Berliner Börsen-Courrier*, 23 July 1912.

[276] *Freisinnige Zeitung*, 13 July 1912.

6

Conclusion

Politics and the German Nation-State

1. German Perceptions of France's Political Decline

This study began by asking certain fundamental questions about Wilhelmine politics and the German state. How was power to be ordered, regulated, and limited? Who had the right to exercise power and on what terms? How were the interests of individuals, groups, and the nation to be reconciled? How was ethical consensus to be achieved? What was politics, what was the state, and was a distinction to be made between them? The Third Republic provided new answers to such questions, but few were accepted unequivocally in Germany. As has been seen, the French state was described in different ways by Germans, yet it was widely agreed that its defining feature was the fusion of executive and legislative functions. It was this merger which had introduced political, social, and economic conflict into the state and which had, consequently, undermined neutral administration. Whereas a separation of competencies was perceived to have kept politics within reasonable bounds in Switzerland and the United States, their fusion in France seemed to have pushed the principles of political accountability and redress to extremes, at the expense of legality, justice, competence, honesty, and stability. With its revolutionary history, France was depicted in Germany as Europe's most radical example of a political, unhistorical, popularly sovereign state. In Britain, parliamentarism had emerged gradually and, as a result, had had to contend with ideas such as historical legitimacy and common law, it was held. The effects of parliamentarization were therefore mitigated, even if, over time, they became more pronounced. By contrast, in France, parliamentary ascendancy had been founded, after the French Revolution, on a priori theories of political legitimacy and on the notion of popular sovereignty. The covert proclivity of the British parliamentary regime towards democracy, despite its rhetoric of property, its tradition of inherited liberties, and its history of limited franchises, thus became an overt principle of the French regime.[1] The tendency of sovereign parliaments to override law in the name of the people had been made explicit in France, it was claimed. In short, politics had subsumed state and society: all areas of French life, it was believed, were subject to the intervention of political parties.

It is tempting to see German nationalism, whether implicit or explicit, as the principal cause of this rejection of French parliamentarism. Even in the 1900s and 1910s, Germans remained particularly sensitive to constitutional change of any kind because of the connection between national unification and the political settlement of 1871. Since national unity had only been achieved through political arrangement and compromise, reform of the Reich's constitution did not simply portend political dislocation, but appeared, to many observers, to endanger the nation-state itself. The possibility of returning to the supposed disorder and weakness of the seventeenth, eighteenth, and early nineteenth centuries was one of the commonest expressed fears of German political commentary. When such fears were added to the fact that parliamentarism was associated with France and Britain—that is, precisely those powers responsible for the historical disunity of the German nation—then the conditions seemed to be present for a national rejection of a foreign system of government. Germany, it could be contended, had united, conquered, and prospered against the wishes of its western neighbours and without political imitation: why should it copy France and Britain now that it had established itself? This mixture of political pride and sensitivity, on the one hand, and of national insecurity and contempt, on the other, might be expected to explain why German rejection of the French parliamentary regime crossed party lines.

The timing of Catholic, liberal, and socialist disenchantment with the Third Republic seems to contradict any thesis founded directly on German nationalism, however. At home, Germans were more willing, over time, to break taboos concerning constitutional reform, arguing that political amendments were in the national interest. Even

---

[1] A left-wing author like Hermann Fernau, *Die französische Demokratie*, 346, agreed about British democratization with right-wing counterparts such as Oskar Schmitz, in *Das Land der Wirklichkeit*, 102. On academics, see Schenk, *Die deutsch-englische Rivalität vor dem Ersten Weltkrieg in der Sicht deutscher Historiker*, 61.

Hintze implied as much, in an essay written in 1913.[2] Abroad, uninterrupted formal enmity between France and Germany, together with lingering memories of French oppression, should have precluded the notion of disillusionment altogether. National prejudices ought to have prevented support for French political institutions and practices throughout the period from 1870 to 1914. Yet, as has been shown, there was some sympathy for the Third Republic in four out of five of the main political parties in Germany. The junctures at which those parties rejected the French parliamentary regime, and the reasons which were given at the time for that rejection, did not coincide with party responses to international relations. Whilst liberal criticism surfaced in the wake of the first Moroccan crisis, from 1907 onwards, continuing calls in the liberal press for rapprochement between Paris and Berlin appeared to prove that the two events were not connected.[3] For their part, Catholic and socialist publications became disenchanted during an era of Franco-German détente, between 1898 and 1904. Investigation of Catholic, National-Liberal, left-liberal, and socialist newspaper reports shows that each party harboured certain expectations of the Third Republic, but found that these expectations had been misplaced. The arguments which were offered to explain parties' sudden disaffection concentrated almost exclusively on French domestic affairs.

Such evidence did not demonstrate that national biases had been removed from German accounts of French affairs, of course, but it did suggest that they existed, for the most part, on a deeper and more complex level, where they were inherent in preferences, values, principles, and arguments. These biases, if extant, were not expressed directly, in an outright rejection of French national institutions because they were French, but, rather, they were based on specific conceptions of ideal institutions. The former corresponded to stereotyping, the latter to analysis: France was not dismissed as a character but as a set of ideas. In discounting such ideas, Germans did not necessarily label them 'French'. Nor, in many instances, did they call those ideas 'German', which they could not discover abroad. There did, however, seem to be some commonly held German priorities, which were seen to have no place in France's

[2] Hintze, 'Machtpolitik und Regierungsverfassung', in *Staat und Verfassung*, 424–56.
[3] See, for instance, *Berliner Tageblatt*, 28 and 31 Mar. 1907, 21 Nov. 1908; *Hamburgischer Correspondent*, 27 June and 13 Nov. 1908, 23 Jan. 1909.

political regime and whose absence therefore occasioned criticism. Germans were able, it seemed, to find common priorities in rejecting other systems of government, even though they differed over the form of any ideal German polity. This, then, was the restricted sense in which a national political culture could be said to exist in Wilhelmine Germany: it was defined by criticism and it was not, in many cases, consciously national; it rested on the fact that German priorities were ignored in other countries or that foreign priorities were beyond the German pale, but it did not exclude the possibility of shared priorities across national borders.

In general, it was by German criteria of a strong state that the French parliamentary republic was adjudged to have failed. The enduring significance of national unification in Germany was unmistakable in such judgements of France. The criteria could be divided into two parts: those elements which were intended to protect the nation-state against external enemies and those which were expected to guard against internal collapse. Of the former, military power was perhaps the most important, but successful foreign policy, economic growth, and social stability were also requisite in modern states, it was postulated. On all these counts, the majority of German commentators found against French parliamentarism. Not only was France after the Dreyfus affair marked by social conflict, which manifested itself, amongst other things, in syndicalist extremism and the struggle between church and state, it was also beset by economic decline.[4] The amount of German

---

[4] H. Kaelble, 'Wahrnehmung der Industrialisierung. Die französische Gesellschaft im Bild der Deutschen zwischen 1891 und 1914', in W. Süß (ed.), *Übergänge. Zeitgeschichte zwischen Utopie und Machbarkeit* (Berlin, 1989). 123–38; id., *Nachbarn am Rhein* (Munich, 1991); R. Poidevin, 'La Puissance française face à l'Allemagne autour de 1900', in P. Milza and R. Poidevin (eds.), *La Puissance française à la belle époque* (Brussels, 1992), 227–39. J. B. Sägmüller, *Die Trennung von Kirche und Staat* (Mainz, 1907); M. Spahn, *Der Kampf um die Schule in Frankreich und Deutschland* (Kempten and Munich, 1907) and G. Weckmann, *Die Trennung von Kirche und Staat in Frankreich vom volkswirtschaftlichen Standpunkte aus* (Hamm, 1914); and liberals such as P. Müllendorff, *Staat und katholische Kirche in Frankreich und in Preußen* (Berlin, 1903). Some Germans backed the French state: for instance, R. Geigel, *Die Trennung von Staat und Kirche* (Munich, 1908) and W. Lüttge, *Die Trennung von Staat und Kirche in Frankreich und der französische Protestantismus* (Tübingen, 1912). On the question of French socialism and syndicalism, Werner Sombart, *Sozialismus und soziale Bewegung* (Jena, 1896), 223–33; W. Kulemann, *Die Berufsvereine*, 2nd revised edn. (Berlin, 1913), iv. 156–290; Anton Acht, *Der moderne französische Syndikalismus* (Jena, 1911). Verdicts on the state of the French economy were dictated above all by demography, J. Wolf, *Der Geburtenrückgang* (Jena, 1912); J. Goldstein, *Die vermeintlichen und die wirklichen Ursachen des Bevölkerungsstillstandes in Frankreich* (Munich, 1898); and id., *Bevölkerungsprobleme und Berufsgliederung in Frankreich* (Berlin, 1900). On French indebtedness, financial mismanagement, and industrial decline

press coverage devoted to events such as the post and rail strikes of 1909 and 1910 or the abolition of the concordat in 1905 spoke for itself. In one Catholic journal alone, there were at least thirty-six articles on the church issue between 1900 and 1914, with titles such as 'Declaration of War against the Church in France'.[5] Although reports on the French army and diplomacy often carried warnings against German complacency, they too were characterized by stories of political infighting, mutiny, technical incompetence, pacifism, and anti-militarism.[6] *Der wahre Jacob*, *Simplicissimus*, and *Kladderadatsch* all portrayed Marianne as the naive and harmless victim of Russian exploitation, pecuniary or otherwise.[7] Surprisingly, even French colonialism, which was acknowledged by many onlookers as one of the country's successes, barely reinforced the defences of the state, it was held. Whereas empire was viewed as potential power, metropolitan stability and efficiency were measured as real power. Although much attention was given to the question of colonial armies and imperial commerce in both the popular press and in official correspondence, French strength was gauged in terms of political decisiveness, public morale, financial reserves, military competence, technology, and man-power.[8] Externally, it appeared from a reading of the German press, France's power had waned under the Third Republic.

under parliamentary government, see Schmoller, *Skizze einer Finanzgeschichte von Frankreich, Österreich, England und Preußen*, 18–9, 63; W. Sombart, *Der Bourgeois* (Berlin. 1987), 139–42; E. Oberle, *Wird Frankreich aus der Reihe der leitenden Völker verschwinden?* (Strasbourg, 1905); and A. v. Brandt, *Beiträge zur Geschichte der französischen Handelspolitik von Colbert bis zur Gegenwart* (Leipzig, 1896).

[5] *Historisch-politische Blätter*, which was one of the principal Catholic publications and reported on diverse current affairs.

[6] G. Krumeich, 'La Puissance militaire française vue d'Allemagne autour de 1900', in Milza and Poidevin (eds.), *La Puissance française à la belle époque*, 199–210. M. Exner, *Die französische Armee in Krieg und Frieden*, 2nd edn. (Berlin, 1894), 3–5, and anon., *Deutschland und Frankreich. Politisch und militärisch verglichen* (Stuttgart, 1912), 15–27.

[7] 'Die Geheimnisse des Zweibundes', *Der wahre Jacob*, 11 July 1904, no. 730; 'Nach Baltischport', *Simplicissimus*, 26 Aug. 1912, no. 22; 'Iwans Weihnachtswunsch', *Kladderadatsch*, 7 Dec. 1913, no. 49. On the legend of French weakness in the conduct of foreign policy, see J. Bariéty and R. Poidevin, *Les Relations franco-allemandes, 1815–1975* (Paris, 1977), 150, 171, 174, 188–9, 194–7, 209, 213; Raulff, *Zwischen Machtpolitik und Imperialismus*, 126–44; P. Guillen, *L'Allemagne et le Maroc de 1870 à 1905* (Paris, 1967), 851–69; Oncken, *Panthersprung nach Agadir*, 46–63, 146–218.

[8] *Vossische Zeitung*, 20 May 1908 and 30 Dec. 1913; *Tag*, 17 July 1909 and 4 Dec. 1912; *Kölnische Zeitung*, 2 Apr. 1910; *Berliner Morgenpost*, 8 Dec. 1911; *Berliner Tageblatt*, 19 July 1913; *Berliner Illustrirte Zeitung*, 25 Nov. 1911; *Post*, 12 Sept. 1909 and 16 Aug. 1912; *Deutsche Tageszeitung*, 18 Sept. 1909, 25 Sept. 1909, and 23 Nov. 1911; *Deutsche Zeitung*, 19 Sept. 1909 and 9 July 1912; *Elsasser*, 20 Sept. 1909; *Neue Preußische Zeitung*, 18 Sept. 1909 and 23 Nov. 1911; *Berliner Neueste Nachrichten*, 2 Sept. 1911 and 26 June 1912;

Domestically, it was said, the signs were equally unambiguous. Broadly, German criteria of strong government, which were intended to prevent internal disintegration, rested on priniciples of corporate identity and social order. As has been demonstrated, many Germans came to believe that the French parliamentary republic had ignored or suppressed the mechanisms which guaranteed those priniciples: for historical legitimacy and respect for tradition, it had substituted rationalism and the supremacy of the majority; for law and legal liability, it had offered only politics and political account-ability; instead of groups, it had favoured the individual, and instead of party, faction; for expertise, it had substituted eloquence, and for honesty, money and power. The most obvious consequences, which French experience under the Third Republic appeared to have borne out, were political instability, government inaction, and social con-flict, to the point where anarchy and *coups d'état* appeared to be imminent. As was to be expected of principles which were designed to shore up a strong state, many of the charges in this German case against the Third Republic were conservative in nature. It was no coincidence that the right-wing critique of the French parliamentary regime changed least in the pre-war period, nor that that critique became, in the 1900s, the basis of cross-party criticism of France. Two qualifications need to be borne in mind, however.

First, each party had specific reasons for turning against the republic. This was especially true of the SPD, which was motivated above all by concern for the unity of French workers' parties and *syndicats*. Although they criticized the arbitrariness of legal process, the inconstancy of government, the venality of factions, and the injustice of administration in ways similar to those of their political rivals, socialists argued that such traits were typical of an oppressive bourgeois republic. Since, with the exception of some revisionists,

Reichsbote, 14 Nov. 1911; *Tägliche Rundschau*, 20 Nov. 1911; *Rheinisch-westfälische Zeitung*, 22 Aug. 1912; *Deutshe Volkswirtschaftliche Correspondenz*, 25 Feb. 1913. Judgement was mixed over the feasibility of a French colonial army. Helmuth von Moltke, Rosen, and oth-ers argued against the *Reichskanzlei's* view that a North African army was conceivable in the short or medium term. All saw such an army as a potential rather than a real power. Moltke, 25 Jan. 1910, AA R6751, A1539, and 2 Mar. 1910, AA R6751, A3775; *Reichskanzlei*, 22 Feb. 1910, AA R6751, A3337; Rosen, 1 Mar. 1910, AA R6751, A4253; König, 8 July 1911, AA R6752, A7951; Hardenberg, 14 May 1911, AA R6752, A7951. On colonial commerce, Friedrich Naumann, *Hilfe*, 9 Apr. 1905, no. 14, J. Wolf, *Tag*, 8 Sept. 1911; G. K. Anton, *Die Entwicklung des französischen Kolonialreiches* (Dresden, 1897); A. Zimmermann, *Die Kolonialpolitik Frankreichs von den Anfängen bis zur Gegenwart* (Berlin, 1901).

parliamentarism had never been an end in itself, but simply a stage to be superseded, the SPD actually felt duty-bound to expose its short-comings. Whilst the party was undoubtedly interested in the strength of the French regime, its priority was to prevent regression towards a feudal, authoritarian system of government, from which a transition to socialist society was, according to Marx, impossible. Despite the national premisses of some of their arguments, such as the claim that a militia would protect the nation-state more effect-ively than a professional army, socialists were driven more by the idea of social justice than by that of a strong state. Nevertheless, they agreed with the symptoms of parliamentary failure which were put forward by conservatives—unfairness, instability, corruption—even though they diagnosed a completely different illness. By contrast, the Centre and liberal parties added special symptoms of their own, such as the maltreatment of Catholics and lack of social reform, to a broader diagnosis of a weak state.

Second, cross-party principles such as corporate identity and social order, which were revealed through criticism of the parliamen-tary republic in France, did not imply a rejection of ideas such as political accountability and popular sovereignty, which were seen to underpin the French regime. One common criticism of the Third Republic, after all, was that it had detached government from popu-lar control. Thus, German parties' reactions against the French sys-tem were not directed at republican ideas themselves, but rather at a parliamentary state, which was based wholly on those ideas. It seemed as if the alleged one-sidedness of the French political order, with its actual, political, and individual bias, provoked German observers into defending contrary principles of legality, historical legitimacy, and collective identity. As has been shown, some onlook-ers went even further, distinguishing between 'French' and 'German' values and traditions. Yet most Germans did not arrive at such a stark antithesis, for they were challenged first, not by the principles of French parliamentarism, but by what they saw as its objective results, whether proven miscarriages of justice or incontrovertible cases of ministerial instability. Their immediate response was to crit-icize particular events, not to formulate general theories. Later, per-haps, some critics reflected on the causes of events in France, and adjusted their explanations of the French regime accordingly. But few of those felt obliged to reject 'French' principles completely, even though many came to reject France's parliamentary republic.

Rather, they sought to find a compromise between momentary individual preferences, popular sovereignty, and political accountability, on the one hand, and legal precedence, inherited values, corporate identities, and national interest, on the other. It seemed unlikely, however, that such a compromise would be achieved by a French-style parliamentary regime.

German depictions of the Third Republic appeared to warn of the dangers of parliamentarism. To an extent, academics, journalists, officials, and politicians had formed their views of France's polity in isolation from some of the pressures of domestic politics and before they had seriously considered the idea of a German parliamentary regime. Around the turn of the century, the Bismarckian state still appeared to be solid. Consequently, Wilhelmine observers contemplated French parliamentarism with a measure of disinterest, criticizing France's political institutions in similar ways to each other, despite disagreeing about the strengths and weaknesses of the German polity. During the late 1890s and early 1900s, therefore, through a common rejection of many aspects of the Third Republic, parties and presses unobtrusively established shared tenets of a German political culture. From 1908 onwards, the constitutional crisis of the *Kaiserreich* threatened to undermine that political culture by dividing Germany into two or more camps, for and against the existing regime. The emergence of parliamentarism as the principal alternative to the structure of the Bismarckian Empire made discussion of foreign parliamentary systems, especially those of France and Britain, a central part of German political debate. Now, the domestic significance of cross-party rejection of French parliamentarism was put to the test. The following three sections examine how perceptions of the Third Republic and other parliamentary regimes combined with political ideologies and calculations of interest to set the parameters and define the content of Germany's pre-war constitutional crisis. They show what role was played by national comparison in German political thought. The final section investigates the importance of a political component in German national identity.

2. Parliamentarism and Constitutionalism

The terms 'constitutionalism' and 'parliamentarism', which re-emerged during the late 1900s and 1910s, were part of an unprecedented debate in imperial Germany about different forms of political regime. The Reich was subjected, for the first time since its inception, to fundamental criticism and reassessment. In all political quarters after the turn of the century, questions were asked about the viability of German political institutions. During the next decade and a half, journalists, academics, politicians, and officials began to take sides in a controversy which had shifted its focus, almost imperceptibly, from particular institutions to Germany's entire polity. It was, wrote one correspondent in the *Deutsche Revue*, as if 'most of what has moved the German people in recent times is in some way an episode in this struggle'. The dispute over colonies in 1906, the *Daily Telegraph* affair, the reform of the Reich's finances, and the campaign for revision of Prussia's electoral laws could all be seen to be part of a broader political conflict, whose intensity and scope had surprised observers.[9] Looking back, in 1908, Friedrich Naumann was struck above all by the novelty of such a state of affairs:

In the last twenty years, one could regularly hear and read that the time of theoretical constitutional questions was over, for the constitution, as it was fashioned by Bismarck's hand, was to be accepted as the fixed property of the German people.... Almost every one of us who entered politics in the 1880s and 1890s has lived through a period in which he was rather indifferent to genuine constitutional questions.[10]

Thus, even Naumann, who had become one of the most voluble left-liberal critics of the Bismarckian state, had only a few years earlier ignored the possibility of thoroughgoing constitutional reform. As was to be expected, conservatives, Catholics, and National Liberals, most of whom rallied to the defence of the German Empire in the 1910s, had likewise ruled out significant changes to the political regime during the last decades of the nineteenth century.

Although many Wilhelmine observers, when forced to choose, decided to defend the German polity, most admitted at some point during the 1900s that the Reich was not functioning properly. Whereas the right tended to blame the self-interest, demagogy, or inefficacy of parliament and the parties, the left preferred to criticize the monarch, bureaucratic government, or the structure of the regime itself. Underlying such differences of interpretation, however, were common, domestic causes of disaffection, which crossed

---

[9] Anon., 'Gedanken über Parlamentarismus in Deutschland', *Deutsche Revue*, July 1910, vol. 35, no. 35, 2.

[10] F. Naumann, 'Die Umwandlung der deutschen Verfassung', *Patria*, 1908, 84.

party lines. First, all parties had become aware of the instability of their relationship with government, as their own shifting allegiances, together with the changing tactics of the administration, destroyed a succession of pro-government coalitions. After the collapse of Centre Party dominance in 1906, the fall of the Bülow bloc in 1909, the alienation of the conservatives by 1911, and the institution of Bethmann Hollweg's policy of diagonals, 'creating majorities from issue to issue',[11] in 1912, there was a larger pool of politicians who were prepared to challenge the workings of Germany's political system. Second, the growth of the German left, which was demonstrated by the SPD's success in the 1912 election, appeared to threaten the right-wing basis of government rule. By the 1910s, Bethmann Hollweg's administration seemed to be faced with the prospect of parliamentary and constitutional reform from the left, which according to Naumann and others would allow the necessary integration of 'proletarian liberals' in the SPD,[12] or with the possibility of reactionary measures from the right, which were motivated by the fear that the government would give in to socialist pressure. Third, most parties were convinced by the mid-1900s that the German Empire had evinced important technical shortcomings, which had encouraged political infighting between different organs of state and permitted errors in the conduct of foreign policy. In 1905–6, 1908, and 1910–13, conservatives, Catholics, liberals, and socialists had all raised questions, after conflict at home and failure abroad, about the malfunctioning of the German regime. Fourth, the connection in Germany between national and constitutional issues, although still pronounced in comparison with the rest of Europe, had become much more tenuous by 1900, as the integrity of the German nation began to seem self-evident. Politicians and publicists discussing a change of political system were now less likely to be branded traitors. Correspondingly, the number of critics of the German Empire increased.

Questions about the constitutional reform of the Reich, then, arose gradually from the daily round of domestic politics. The parameters of those questions, however, were often set by Germans' perceptions of foreign regimes. In general, politicians and officials made sense of demands for political change, which were frequently

---

[11] Bethmann Hollweg cited in Jarausch, *Enigmatic Chancellor*, 91.
[12] F. Naumann, 'Demokratie und Disziplin', *Hilfe*, 17 Apr. 1904, vol. 10, no. 16, 3; id., 'Die psychologischen Naturbedingungen des Sozialismus', *Zeit*, 1902, vol. 1, no. 7, 564–71.

motivated by calculations of party advantage, only within an international context. As a result, references to neighbouring states littered books, articles, and speeches during the principal constitutional crises of the *Kaiserreich*. Even in November and December 1908, at the high point of the *Daily Telegraph* affair, about half of the deputies speaking in the main Reichstag debates still found time to compare Germany's political system with those of other European countries.[13] Such comparisons were possible by that date because Wilhelmine commentators had, to a large extent, agreed on new typologies of modern political regimes. Consequently, parties were able to link their specific grievances to common, intelligible, and comparative analyses of the German polity. This had not always been the case. In the universities during the 1870s, 1880s, and 1890s, most academics had been content, as Georg Jellinek made clear in a review of Wilhelm Roscher's *Politik: Eine geschichtliche Naturlehre der Monarchie, Aristokratie und Demokratie*, merely to append their own theories to classical Greek schemes, ignoring critical distinctions between contemporary states.[14] In politics during the same period, typologies had been so uncertain that even left-liberal opponents of Bismarck such as Theodor Barth could argue, in 1902, that the influence of public opinion determined whether a regime was democratic, 'not the external form of government, be it republican or monarchical'.[15] In the growing corpus of writing on types of constitution, which appeared after 1900, authors flitted uneasily between diverse political labels: republic, monarchy, empire, dictatorship, despotism, autocracy, democracy, oligarchy, aristocracy, ochlocracy, parliamentarism, and constitutionalism were all used to describe turn-of-the-century systems of government. By the late 1900s and early 1910s, such confusion had been replaced by an increasingly unambiguous political classification of European, American, and Asian regimes. It was only against this background, on the eve of the First World War, that historians and publicists like Hans Delbrück and Otto Hintze

[13] *Verhandlungen des Reichstags: Stenographische Berichte* (Berlin, 1909), 10–11 Nov. and 2–3 Dec. 1908, vol. 233.

[14] G. Jellinek, *Ausgewählte Schriften und Reden* (Berlin, 1911), ii. 323. G. Hübinger, 'Staatstheorie und Politik als Wissenschaft im Kaiserreich: Georg Jellinek, Otto Hintze, und Max Weber', in H. Maier et al. (eds.), *Politik, Philosophie, Praxis* (Stuttgart, 1988), 143: Roscher intended to continue in the tradition of Dahlmann, Droysen, Waitz, and Treitschke.

[15] T. Barth, 'Prinz und Demokratie', *Nation*, 15 Mar. 1902, vol. 19, no. 24, 371.

could write, in terms which had become comprehensible to the Wilhelmine public, of a 'unique Prussian-German system'.[16]

The German polity was placed by observers in a typology together with parliamentarism and despotism, which were symbolized respectively by Western Europe and Asia. From such a broad, intercontinental spectrum, however, Europe and the United States alone were seen to belong to the civilized world of *Kulturstaaten*, which formed the basis of most political discussion in the *Kaiserreich*. Thus, to Delbrück and many of his contemporaries, it appeared that 'Germany constitutes the real, archetypal obverse of the parliamentary states'.[17] In other words, Britain and France, which were perceived to be archetypes of parliamentarism, were used more and more consistently in Wilhelmine debates about political reform in order to define, largely through a process of negation, the essence of the German regime. At the same time, older disputes about republicanism and democracy were adjusted, downgraded, or simply forgotten. By the early twentieth century, the distinction between republics and monarchies, which had characterized an age of revolutions, had been diminishing in importance for at least thirty years, since it obscured similarities between states such as Belgium and France, as well as dissimilarities between those like Britain and Germany. Accordingly, 'the dream of a German republic, which many of our best minds have dreamt about', had, as *Die Zukunft* rightly explained, 'disappeared into oblivion'.[18] During the *Daily Telegraph* affair, as almost all parties united in criticizing Wilhelm II after his public admission of German hatred of Britain, even the SPD had refrained from hoisting the republican flag, noted Naumann.[19] Despite occasional left-liberal warnings to the contrary, republicanism had become a side-issue by 1908. Similarly, democracy, although still a subject of discussion in the German press, appeared to have become less relevant in the classification of systems of government, partly because pure democracy was widely held to be unrealizable, partly because democratic institutions were compatible with a wide range of regimes. As the left-liberal journal *März* pointed out in 1907, 'democracy has individual mechanisms, such as universal

[16] Hintze, 'Das monarchische Prinzip und die konstitutionelle Verfassung' (1911), in *Staat und Verfassung*, 359; H. Delbrück, *Regierung und Volkswille* (Berlin, 1914), 126.

[17] Hintze, 'Das monarchische Prinzip' (1911), *Staat und Verfassung*, 359.

[18] E. Goldbeck, 'Der Landesvater', *Zukunft*, 17 Feb. 1906, vol. 54, 269.

[19] F. Naumann, 'Das Königtum', *Hilfe*, 10 Jan. 1910, vol. 15, no. 2, 15.

suffrage, freedom of association, assembly, and the press, in common
with other political systems: the mistaking of these means with ends
is responsible for the uncertainty which, for the most part, dominates
attempts to distinguish between different parties.'[20] During an era, in
Barth's opinion, of 'steady advancement towards more democratic
forms of public life in our old world', the term 'democracy' no longer
seemed specific enough to describe the diversity of European states.[21]

By contrast, 'parliamentary regime' and 'parliamentarism' had, in
the years before the First World War, become defining concepts of
German political thought. Between 1898 and 1914 more than seventy
major articles on *Parlamentarismus* had appeared in Wilhelmine journals.[22] Many others examined the same theme in newspapers and
under different titles. To an extent, such interest in parliamentary
practice was a consequence of the growing power of the Reichstag,
which was bolstered by the logic of democratization, a changing division of functions, and the ambition of parties to gain control of
government. 'We see', wrote the *Deutsche Revue*, 'two organs, government and parliament, which according to the German constitution
are not directly dependent on one another, locked in a struggle for
power.'[23] At the time of the article in 1910, however, the Wilhelmine
public had already begun to reinterpret the conflict between the
Reichstag and the Reich Chancellor. By that date, instead of treating
the growth of parliamentary power in isolation, academics, journalists, and politicians—and presumably their audiences—looked on it
from the perspective of a new typology of European states.
Increasingly, Germans asked themselves, as did the correspondent of
the *Deutsche Revue*, whether the Reich would become a parliamentary
regime like Britain and France, not merely whether the Reichstag
would acquire further competencies. Previously, earlier in the 1900s,
when authors had wondered, often idly, what type of regime would
replace the existing malfunctioning one, the choice had seemed less
clear-cut.[24] The label 'parliamentarism', as it was used in domestic

[20] D. Blumenthal, 'Die Zukunft der Demokratie in Deutschland', *März*, Mar. 1907, vol. 1,
no. 6, 485.

[21] T. Barth, 'Prinz und Demokratie', *Nation*, 15 Mar. 1902, vol. 19, no. 24, 371.

[22] *Internationale Bibliographie der Zeitschriftenliteratur.*

[23] Anon., 'Gedanken über Parlamentarismus in Deutschland', *Deutsche Revue*, July
1910, vol. 35, no. 35, 42.

[24] O. Mittelstaedt, 'Der Parlamentarismus, wie er geworden ist', *Zukunft*, 12 Feb.
1898, vol. 6, no. 20, 295; P. Ernst, 'Die reine Demokratie', *Gegenwart*, 11 June 1898,
vol. 53, no. 24, 372; anon., 'Parlamentarismus: Die tiefste Ursache seines Verfalls', *Wahrheit*,

political discourse, had often been defined broadly during this period to mean the conduct of parliamentary business. By the late 1900s and early 1910s, the same word, although never losing its old meaning completely, had come, less ambiguously than in the past, to denote a parliamentary system of government, in which ministries were appointed by popular assemblies. Such redefinition, which was adumbrated on both left and right before the *Daily Telegraph* affair, by means of qualifications such as 'pure' or 'genuine' parliamentarism,[25] was consolidated by Germany's constitutional crisis between 1908 and 1914. It was also at this time that the phrase 'parliamentary regime' passed back into everyday political language, after having virtually disappeared during the 1880s and 1890s.

The history of the term 'constitutionalism' was much more uneven, with left liberals and socialists continuing to challenge its usage throughout the pre-war era. Only a system where the 'leaders of the administration' were 'the representatives of the chamber or its majority... deserves the name "constitutional"', wrote Conrad Haußmann, leader of the German People's Party, in 1907. 'This connection is lacking in Germany', he went on: 'It is not only absent. The very necessity of it is denied and refused.'[26] In 1908 and 1913, left-wing deputies like Otto Wiemer and Paul Singer still referred to the Reich as 'sham' rather than 'real' constitutionalism.[27] Yet such politicians knew, as Haußmann hinted, that they were arguing against established terminology. Bismarck's regime, admitted Naumann, had successfully stood the test of time: 'The German Empire has become a solid political body. The danger that we shall again sink back into a confusion of small states [*Kleinstaaterei*] can be regarded as having been removed. The fear that this constitution would only be an interlude has not been borne out by events.'[28] From these assumptions, that the Reich constituted both a separate and

---

Apr. 1904, vol. 10, no. 4, 146; Outis, 'Der Parlamentarismus', *Preußische Jahrbücher*, June 1904, vol. 116, no. 3, 409–16; M. v. Brandt, 'Der Wert des Parlamentarismus', *Umschau*, 22 Dec. 1906, vol. 10, no. 52, 1023; F. Naumann, 'Die Umwandlung der deutschen Reichsverfassung', *Patria*, 1908, 84, 104; K. Kautsky, *Parlamentarismus und Demokratie*, 2nd revised edn. (Stuttgart, 1911), first published in 1893.

[25] C. Haußmann, 'Parlamentarismus', *März*, Mar. 1907, vol. 1, no. 5, 389–90; anon., 'Vierzig Jahre deutscher Parlamentarismus', *Grenzboten*, 1 Nov. 1906, vol. 65, no. 44, 229.

[26] Haußmann, 'Parlamentarismus', *März*, Mar. 1907, vol. 1, no. 5, 389–90.

[27] Otto Wiemer, Paul Singer, Conrad Haußmann, and Georg Lebedour, *Verhandlungen des Reichstags: Stenographische Berichte*, vol. 233, Nov.–Dec. 1908, 5375–93, 5916; Otto Wiemer, ibid., vol. 291, 6323.

[28] F. Naumann, 'Die Umwandlung des deutschen Reichsverfassung', *Patria*, 1908, 95.

enduring form of government, it was easier for Naumann to agree to the label 'constitutional monarchy'.[29] Even the most critical left-liberal newspapers, such as the *Berliner Tageblatt*, concurred. 'Our constitutionalism will continue to lead a sham existence', ran one of its articles on the Zabern incident, 'so long as the fully unconstitutional fusion of the upper house and the Reich ministry within the Bundesrat is maintained.' Thus, the German Empire had failed to fulfil the conditions of genuine constitutionalism only because of its inadequate separation of powers, since the executive was able to interfere in the affairs of the legislature through the Bundesrat. Constitutional and parliamentary regimes, it was implied, were two different types of government. Consequently, the same article concluded, the German people's immediate aim should be to perfect its constitutional system of government rather than to hope, in the short term at least, for a parliamentary one: 'And we, we who have not even managed to bring about an honestly conceived constitutionalism, are accused of wanting parliamentarism and, concealed behind this, "republicanism"!'[30] The word 'constitutional', it appeared, had finally begun to establish itself in popular political language, in reaction to the increased prominence of 'parliamentarism', to describe regimes which were neither parliamentary nor despotic. Arguably, only the direct challenge to the Reich which was issued between 1908 and 1914 made it necessary to define more precisely what had previously been assumed. The German regime, it was suggested, constituted a separate, perhaps unique system of government.

3. Lawyers, Parties, and Political Regimes

The distinction between parliamentarism and constitutionalism had first been made within the academic discipline of law. It was possible, as Georg Jellinek, Conrad Bornhak and others indicated, to trace the idea of two separate systems back to the writings of Friedrich Julius Stahl in the 1840s, the policies of the German states in the 1850s, and the machinations of Bismarck in the 1860s and 1870s.[31] Nevertheless, after the German Empire had been consolidated during the 1870s, it

---

[29] F. Naumann, 'Reichsverfassungsfragen', *Hilfe*, 7 Aug. 1913, vol. 19, no. 32, 499.

[30] *Berliner Tageblatt*, 15 Dec. 1913.

[31] G. Jellinek, 'Regierung und Parlament', *Vorträge der Gehe-Stiftung zu Dresden*, 13 Mar. 1909, no. 1, 3–36; C. Bornhak, 'Die weltgeschichtliche Entwicklung des Konstitutionalismus', *Internationale Monatsschrift für Wissenschaft, Kunst und Technik*, May 1912, vol. 6, no. 8, 1011–23.

was not until the late 1900s and early 1910s that historians, economists, politicians, and publicists began to adopt such a typology.
Although it dated back to the mid-nineteenth century, wrote Jellinek
in a 1911 addendum to an essay of 1883, 'the opposition between
constitutionalism and parliamentarism' could only 'now be counted
amongst the political catch-phrases of the day'.[32] Much earlier confusion, like later clarity, came from German readings of foreign politics. Here, despite their differing conclusions, which were drawn
from the same historical premises, Bornhak and Jellinek were in
agreement: both believed that the states of the German
Confederation, lacking adequate legal structures of their own, had
imported constitutional tenets, often out of context, from Britain and
France. As a result, constitutionalism was associated from the start in
Germany with misinterpreted British and French institutions,
including parliaments. Liberals of the 1840s such as Friedrich
Christoph Dahlmann had stressed the compatibility of full-blown
parliamentary and monarchical principles, ignoring the transfer of
the power of appointment from the king to the lower chamber in the
neighbouring states.[33] According to academic supporters of the Reich
like Otto Hintze and to critics like Walter Schücking, similar habits
of thought continued after 1848, with German elites routinely con-
flating parliamentary and constitutional regimes well into the imperial period. 'In educated and propertied circles,' recorded the latter, 'it
was not until the Bismarckian era that the older conception of genuine constitutionalism, which had been taken from foreign models,
began to be pushed aside by the idea of a specific "German constitutionalism".'[34] As has been seen, the old meaning of the term, which
had been founded, *inter alia*, on a misreading of French and British
parliamentarism, was not replaced definitively by a new notion of
German constitutionalism until the eve of the First World War.

By the late nineteenth century, Germany's law faculties already recognized the two distinct systems of government which were later
presented to a wider public by prominent *Staatsrechtler* such as
Bornhak. 'Following current terminology,' he declared in 1912,

---

[32] G. Jellinek, 'Die Entwicklung des Ministeriums in der konstitutionellen Monarchie',
in *Ausgewählte Schriften und Reden*, ii. 136.

[33] G. Jellinek, 'Regierung und Parlament', *Vorträge der Gehe-Stiftung zu Dresden*,
13 Mar. 1909, no 1, 13–14.

[34] W. Schücking, 'Der Übergang zum parlamentarischen Regierungsform', *März*, 1 Nov.
1910, vol. 4, no. 21, 177; O. Hintze, 'Das monarchische Prinzip und die konstitutionelle
Verfassung' (1911), in *Staat und Verfassung* ed. G. Oestreich, 2nd revised edn. (Göttingen,
1962), 366.

'parliamentary government, in contrast to its constitutional counter-part, is that in which ministries are formed out of the majority in the elected assembly from members of the majority party.'[35] A combination of legal argument and foreign example reinforced this typology, diminishing the probability in Germany of 'a gradual and almost unnoticed transition' from constitutionalism to parliamentarism.[36] In his analysis of the 'large legal obstacles to the parliamentary system', Bornhak repeated many of the points made three years earlier by Jellinek, his main opponent.[37] Both lawyers postulated that collegial government, ministerial responsibility, and parliament's power of appointment were incompatible with the federal basis of the Reich. In particular, executive reliance on the Bundesrat and on Prussia to initiate laws, make decrees, and nominate ministers would necessarily come to an end under full parliamentary government, as politically accountable ministries demanded competencies and powers to match their increased liability.[38] 'If one wanted to introduce parliamentarism in accordance with the Western model', wrote Jellinek, 'then this would only be possible with the marginalizing of the Bundesrat and, hence, with the repudiation of the federal structure of the Reich.'[39] It was evident from the experiences of foreign states, he continued, that the choice facing Germans was a stark one, involving a complete change of regime, not merely a readjustment of 'the mutual relationship of kaiser, chancellor, and Reichstag':

> One sees that the question of parliamentary or extra-parliamentary government also includes, as far as the German Reich is concerned, the question of a unitary or a federal state, unitarism or federalism. . . . In other federal states, too, parliamentary forms of government are ruled out. This is the case in the United States of America and the other American federal states which have copied it, just as it is true of the Swiss Confederation.[40]

Whereas Jellinek reluctantly concluded from such evidence that Germany would have to accept parliamentarism, since he believed that unitary pressures in the Reich were irresistible, Bornhak argued with renewed force in defence of constitutionalism, federalism, and monarchy. 'The constitutional foundations of Prussia and the Reich

---

[35] C. Bornhak, 'Parlamentarisches Regiment im Deutschen Reiche', *Internationale Monatsschrift für Wissenschaft, Kunst und Technik*, May 1912, vol. 6, no. 8, 1011–12.
[36] Ibid. 1013.   [37] Ibid. 1014.
[38] Ibid. 1014–18; G. Jellinek, 'Regierung und Parlament', *Vorträge der Gehe-Stiftung zu Dresden*, 13 Mar. 1909, no. 1, 27–31.
[39] Jellinek, 'Regierung und Parlament', *Vorträge der Gehe-Stiftung zu Dresden*, 13 Mar. 1909, no. 1, 31.   [40] Ibid. 32.

and their interdependent relationships with one another, on the one hand, and a parliamentary regime, on the other,' he warned, 'are as irreconcilable as fire and water.'[41] Other lawyers such as Karl von Stengel and Paul Laband agreed.[42]

Politicians and publicists were less dogmatic about the logic of federalism, preferring the argument of historians like Friedrich Meinecke that Bismarck's constitution was 'elastic and adaptable enough' to allow a 'transition from a Prussian to a German basis' without a change of regime.[43] Nonetheless, in the years after 1908, parties, newspapers, and journals adopted the same strict separation between constitutionalism and parliamentarism, which had been established in legal theory. Discussions about royal prerogatives, electoral laws, Reichstag procedures, and ministerial responsibility all began to take account of critical thresholds, which distinguished the two systems of government. Confronted by an increasing number of reforms, each of which provoked a flood of commentaries in the press, observers were left with the impression that the German parliament and constitution had entered 'a period of animated change'.[44] In general, supporters and opponents of constitutional and parliamentary regimes divided along party lines. Conservatives, most National Liberals, and the majority of the Centre Party defended the existing system; left liberals and socialists attacked it, albeit for different reasons. Broadly, journalists and correspondents, who interpreted and justified the actions of politicians, formed similar camps. Throughout the pre-war period, as left-liberal critics of the German Empire acknowledged, the defenders of constitutionalism dominated both the Reichstag and public opinion. According to the progressive historian Otto Harnack, writing in 1910, only the *Fortschrittliche Volkspartei* worked consistently towards a parliamentary regime, 'but it, alone, is too weak':

What could do more to make the Reichstag look like a non-entity against the one great ruler than this inability to recognize its own interests, to secure its own

---

[41] Bornhak, 'Parlamentarisches Regiment', 1024; also, C. Bornhak, 'Die weltgeschichtliche Entwicklung des Konstitutionalismus', *Internationale Wochenschrift für Wissenschaft, Kunst und Technik*, 4 Apr. 1908, vol. 2, no. 14, 427–38.

[42] K. v. Stengel, 'Konstitutionelle Monarchie und parlamentarische Regiurung', *Deutsche Monatsschrift für das gesamte Leben der Gegenwart*, Aug. 1904, vol. 3, no. 11, 736–47; P. Laband, 'Die geschichtliche Entwicklung der Reichsverfassung seit der Reichsgründung', *Jahrbuch des öffentlichen Rechts der Gegenwart*, 1907, vol. 1, 28–9; id., 'Der Staatsgerichtshof', *Deutsche Juristenzeitung*, 1 Apr. 1909, vol. 14, no. 7, 393–7.

[43] F. Meinecke, *Cosmopolitanism and the National State* (Princeton, 1970), 373.

[44] J. G. Weiß, 'Entwicklungstendenzen im Parlamentarismus', *Politisch-Anthropologische Revue*, Dec. 1908, vol. 7, no. 9, 486.

position?...But, to a great extent, public opinion in Germany, which has such a low opinion of the kaiser, bears much of the blame. For how many people are there in Germany, including those professing an interest in politics, who give any attention at all to these questions? And very many of them refrain from doing so, not only out of indolence, but also because they shy away from the very idea of 'parliamentarism' and the 'parliamentary system'.[45]

Conservative, National Liberal, and Catholic commentators, by recognizing parliament to be a pillar of the German regime, accepted the broad outline of a cross-party, international typology which distinguished the Bismarckian Empire, historically, from absolutism and, geographically, from eastern despotism. Nevertheless, right-wing and centrist typologies rested, above all, on comparisons which had been made between Germany and its western neighbours in the late nineteenth and early twentieth centuries. In the opinion of conservatives, the two principal domestic failings of the *Kaiserreich*—the corruption of parliament and fragmentation of parties—could be explained by reference to France and Britain. The former, which included incompetence, mediocrity, populism, bribery, embezzlement, and all manner of deception, appeared to the right and much of the centre to derive from the excesses of democracy. Such symptoms were widely believed to be present in the Reichstag by the turn of the century, after a long period of degeneration during the late 1870s, 1880s, and 1890s, although many still agreed with Maximilian Harden that conditions in Germany remained much better than those in other countries.[46] The Reich, it was held, had been shielded from the worst effects of democracy by its separation of powers. In order to envisage what might happen if these powers were merged, within a parliamentary regime, most authors looked to the Third Republic. Wilhelm Hasbach, who went on to write one of the main works on democracy in the pre-war era, evinced how right-wing publicists used France in order to discredit parliamentarism:

Experience shows that state bureaucracy and parliamentary government do not go together. Parliamentary ministers are dependent on the support of deputies, and the deputy relies on the backing of a large number of constituency support-ers. In order to tie these people to him, he must be able to distribute the posts

---

[45] O. Harnack, 'Aussichten des Parlamentarismus in Deutschland', *März*, Sept. 1910, vol. 4, no. 18, 430.

[46] M. Harden, 'Parlamentspolizei', *Zukunft*, 30 Apr. 1910, vol. 18, no. 31, 143. For Catholic agreement on this point, see anon., 'Parlamentarismus: die tiefste Ursache seines Verfalls', *Wahrheit*, Apr. 1904, vol. 10, no. 4, 147, 152.

which the government has at its disposal (these are numerous in France), he must have the power to force out uncooperative bureaucrats and create new posts for his own creatures, he must be in a position to promise rewards to his constituency in the shape of roads, canals, bridges and subsidies, if he were to be re-elected, and he must be able to remit fines and annul trials. All these means have been employed in France.[47]

Parliamentarism, claimed *Grenzboten*, was founded on a series of false assumptions, the consequences of which could be illustrated by the French case, amongst others: with democratic elections failing to select the best candidates and with elected candidates' own lack of responsibility to electors, parliament had come to represent self-interested political parties instead of the people; the majority, even if it could be represented, did not always choose the best course of action, as Treitschke's studies of the 'Terror' had proved; and deputies, whatever their feelings towards the electorate, could not expect to be technically competent in all areas yet they accepted all kinds of ministerial office and interfered in all parts of administration, effectively forming a 'second government' on a local level.[48] When these shortcomings were added, from the mid-nineteenth century onwards in France, to the stronger private interests of an industrial and capitalist society, argued another correspondent in *Die Zukunft*, then 'plutocracy must also come to dominate parliamentarism, which offers less and less and resistance to it'. A French plutocratic regime threatened, in turn, to be subsumed by 'a new period of Caesarism'. It would be 'more than reckless optimism', he concluded, 'to imagine that those events which we have seen in Vienna and Paris are abnormalities and contain nothing typical for the laws of development of modern parliamentarism.'[49]

Britain was the only case of a foreign regime which seemed to refute right-wing claims. Conservatives, National Liberals, and many Catholics were convinced, however, that the British parliamentary monarchy constituted an historical anomaly. Its two-party system could not be transferred to Germany, they argued, because of the regional, confessional, social, and political fragmentation of the

---

[47] W. Hasbach, 'Parlamentarismus', *Zukunft*, 18 Sept. 1909, vol. 68, 402. Id., *Die Demokratie* (Jena, 1912).

[48] Anon., 'Schwächen und Fiktionen des modernen Parlamentarismus', *Grenzboten*, 1904, no. 22, 490–5.

[49] O. Mittelstaedt, 'Der Parlamentarismus, wie er geworden ist', *Zukunft*, 12 Feb. 1898, vol. 6, no. 20, 288, 292–3.

Reich. It was not particularly perceptive, wrote Hasbach, 'to connect the undeniably lighter side of Britain's parliamentary government (not forgetting the dark sides stressed by Englishmen) to the existence in Westminster of only two parties, and it leaves an amusing impression to hear the friends of British parliamentarism declare all signs of *rapprochement* between fundamentally different parties in the Reichstag to be a harbinger of better times.' 'Here, too,' he continued, 'parliamentary government would probably create conditions akin to those in France; perhaps we would approach a "spoils system".'[50] In the conservative and National Liberal press, there was virtual consensus that Britain had been separated from continental Europe not merely by its geographical insularity, but also by its unique and successful opposition to absolutism in the early modern period, its small standing army, deep-rooted patriotism, self-government, and limited state intervention, as well as its early institution of parliamentary government, avoidance of universal suffrage, and maintenance of aristocratic parties.[51] Any residual inclination in the Wilhelmine era to compare British and German polities was seen to be the corollary of persisting myths of Britain as a model for European parliaments and constitutions. The idea of British parliamentary government had been passed on to Germany in misconstrued form through the works of French thinkers like Montesquieu, it was held, at the same time as French, not British, political institutions had been imitated by the states of the German Confederation.[52] From such different starting-points, contended one publicist, Britain had gone on to perfect its two-party system during the nineteenth century, whereas continental countries had continued to struggle against political splinter-groups and revolutionaries. By the early twentieth century, however, it appeared that London had succumbed to a European pattern rather than vice versa: 'The division of the British lower house into two great parties has in the

[50] W. Hasbach, 'Parlamentarismus', *Zukunft*, 18 Sept. 1909, vol. 68, 403.

[51] Ibid.; Freiherr von Nordenflycht, 'Der Parlamentarismus der Gegenwart', *Allgemeine konservative Monatsschrift für das christliche Deutschland*, May 1898, vol. 55, 470–8; anon., 'Schwächen und Fiktionen des Parlamentarismus', *Grenzboten*, 1904, no. 22, 485–6; anon., 'Vierzig Jahre deutscher Parlamentarismus', *Grenzboten*, 1 Nov. 1906, vol. 65, no. 44, 229; anon., 'Gedanken über Parlamentarismus in Deutschland', *Deutsche Revue*, July 1910, vol. 35, no. 35, 34–40; anon., 'Niedergang des Parlamentarismus', *Konservative Monatsschrift*, July 1912, vol. 69, no. 10, 982; W. von Massow, 'Zukunftsfragen des Parlamentarismus', *Grenzboten*, 11 Feb. 1914, vol. 73, no. 6, 294.

[52] *Grenzboten*, 1904, no. 22, 486–7.

meantime, during the last decades, been shattered.'[53] Commentators like Hans Plehn, who resurrected Lothar Bucher's allegedly neglected attempt to dispel myths about English parliamentarism during the 1850s, added to scepticism in the German centre and on the right about modern British politics.[54] With cabinet government, party rule, popular antipathy towards parliament, and an overly powerful press, Britain could no longer serve as a foreign prototype for German conservatives, it was implied.

Conservative, right-wing Catholic, and National Liberal academics, although deliberately staying aloof from the politics of the Reichstag, elucidated assumptions which were hidden in the shorter articles of political journals. The first and, arguably, most important set of ideas, explored by Otto Hintze in a seminal essay of 1911, concerned the role of the army. The German state, he contended, had evolved as a military organization, which brought absolute monarchy and bureaucratization in its wake, in contrast to Britain, where the 'historical pillars on which continental constitutional monarchy rests—absolutism, militarism, bureaucracy—have never come into being...since [England] enjoyed relative military security and early political centralization'.[55] Consequently, European monarchical constitutionalism, which had granted constitutions from above to regulate the affairs of a disunited civil society and to protect the relationship between monarch and army from the intrusion of civilians and public law, did 'not appear, precisely when compared to England, to be an incomplete stage of development on the way to parliamentarism, but rather a separate constitutional form,...which has an historical and political background quite different to that of the parliamentary system'.[56] A second set of questions, posed by Hans Delbrück in *Regierung und Volkswille* in 1914, re-examined the nature of parliamentary democracy. Which system of government (*Regierung*), he asked, best embodied the will of the people (*Volkswille*)? In order to answer this question, Delbrück pointed to the 'profound difference' between 'the system of parliamentarism', which rested on 'self-perpetuating oligarchies' produced by elite

[53] M. von Brandt, 'Der Wert des Parlamentarismus', *Umschau*, 22 Dec. 1906, vol. 10, no. 52, 1022.

[54] H. Plehn, 'Der englische Parlamentarismus, wie er heute ist', *Deutsche Monatsschrift für das gesamte Leben der Gegenwart*, Sept. 1906, vol. 10, no. 12, 736–50.

[55] Hintze, 'Das monarchische Prinzip und die konstitutionelle Verfassung' (1911), in *Staat und Verfassung*, 364–5.

[56] Ibid., 365.

revolutions 'against the masses' in Britain and France, and the system of 'constitutionalism' in Germany.[57] Party, which 'as such always
has its own interest', had come to dominate French and British parliaments, serving private economic ends before national ones.[58] By
contrast, contended Delbrück, the dual structure of the *Kaiserreich*
guaranteed state neutrality by balancing the 'historical power' and
'legitimate authority' of the monarch, army, and bureaucracy, on the
one hand, and the popular, critical sanction of the Reichstag, on
the other: 'We have a dualism in Germany, resting on the cooperation ... of an organized political intelligentsia [administration] with
broad strata of the people, which are represented in the
Reichstag. ... We have exploded the myth that, in France, America,
and England, the populace governs itself.'[59] A third series of assumptions, which were expounded by a Protestant economist like Gustav
Schmoller and a Catholic historian such as Martin Spahn, related to
the social question. Both authors assumed that the 'culture and education of individual strata of the populace is, in large peoples, much
too diverse, and the tension between actual social inequality and theoretical political equality too great, to allow a whole people to be
imbued overnight with democratic sentiments'. Instead, it was necessary to cajole, educate, and enrich the masses in order gradually to
raise the tone of politics. The attempts of parliamentary democracies
like France and Britain to grant political liberties before social
reform had led, it was argued, to unequal taxation, inferior schools,
unregulated industries, and inadequate social insurance.[60] Unlike
Western parliamentary regimes, propounded Schmoller, Spahn,
Delbrück, Hintze, and many other conservative, Catholic, and
National Liberal academics, Germany's constitutional system had
been fashioned from above to meet the social, political, and military
conditions of continental Europe.

The traditions of left-wing liberalism in Germany appeared to
provide ready-made arguments against conservative notions of elitist, bureaucratic government. During the crisis of the constitution in
the late 1900s and early 1910s, politicians like Conrad Haußmann
deliberately revived the memory of earlier struggles against 'court
and bureaucracy'.[61] Yet such calls to arms, although persisting until

[57] Delbrück, *Regierung und Volkswille*, 59, 68, 75, 86–7, 124.
[58] Ibid. 179.   [59] Ibid. 66, 178.
[60] G. Schmoller, 'Demokratie und soziale Zukunft', *Soziale Praxis*, 7 Nov. 1912, vol. 22,
no. 6, 78–9, 83; M. Spahn, 'Was ist Demokratie?', *Hochland*, 1913, vol. 11, no. 1, 69–72.
[61] C. Haußmann, 'Parlamentarismus', *März*, Mar. 1907, vol. 1, no. 5, 389–90.

1914, were increasingly obscured by newer political theories put forward by younger liberals after the death of Eugen Richter and much of the left-liberal old guard in the 1890s and early 1900s. Some commentators like Georg Jellinek openly began to challenge the claim of the Progressives that they had defended constitutionalism during the 1860s. If the liberals had defeated Bismarck over the Army Bill, he contended, 'their victory would probably not have meant a victory for the parliamentary system on the English or on the democratic, continental model.'[62] Other liberals like Theodor Barth, who was well-acquainted with European parliamentarism, chose to ignore foreign, parliamentary models and experimented with new political ideas around the turn of the century, partly because of a growing scepticism about the effects of democratization and the popularity of right-wing and socialist politics in the Reichstag and other continental assemblies.[63] Under the influence of party and press, the Houses of Parliamant in Britain and the Congress of the United States appeared to have become 'political stock exchanges, where powerful interests are played off one against the other'.[64] In 1902, Barth returned to the same theme in an article which compared the United States and Europe under the impact of mass-circulation newspapers, trusts, and party machines. His conclusion was that the polities of both continents were converging, as the New World became more aristocratic, with the appearance of economic and political elites, and as the Old World became more democratic, with the increasing significance of public opinion in policy making: 'From year to year, America becomes more European; Europe, and not least Germany, becomes yearly more American.'[65] Barth gave the impression that the institutional form which democracy would take, in a period of such flux, was uncertain. Only after 1906 did he argue unambiguously for British-style parliamentarism.[66]

Friedrich Naumann, who was perhaps Germany's foremost advocate of constitutional reform, followed a similar course to Barth, betraying in the process the new priorities of a younger generation of liberals who had reached adulthood under the Bismarckian Empire.

---

[62] G. Jellinek, 'Regierung und Parlament', *Vorträge der Gehe-Stiftung zu Dresden*, 13 Mar. 1909, no. 1, 25.
[63] K. Wegner, *Theodor Barth und die Freisinnige Vereinigung* (Tübingen, 1968), 59–66.
[64] T. Barth, in ibid. 65.
[65] T. Barth, 'Prinz und Demokratie', *Nation*, 15 Mar. 1902, vol. 19, no. 24, 371.
[66] Wegner, *Theodor Barth*, 61 n. 78.

During the 1890s and early 1900s, Naumann kept within the bounds of Germany's existing system of government and made few allusions to foreign polities. In *Demokratie und Kaisertum* and other essays, he acknowledged that the early 'decline of parliamentarism' in Germany made it difficult to envisage a transition to parliamentary rule.[67] More specifically, the Reichstag was 'far from the democratic ideal' of a 'full-blown two-party system', which existed in England and North America.[68] In outline, Naumann's alternative suggestion of democracy (*Demokratie*) and empire (*Kaisertum*), which deliberately juxtaposed a strong, Napoleonic emperor and an inexperienced, fragmented parliament, bore a close resemblance to 'the constitutional system'. The examples of France and Britain, whose erratic foreign policies rendered them barely 'capable of alliance', seemed, as far as they were considered at all, merely to underline the necessity of *Kaisertum*.[69] After 1907, however, the editor of *Die Hilfe* was forced to look abroad for a functioning model, as he was converted to the idea of a parliamentary regime. France was ruled out as a hierarchical and bureaucratic 'kingdom without a king', 'a country without population growth and without the violent transition to industrialism which we Germans have experienced.'[70] The Third Republic appeared to Naumann to have neither comparable social conditions to those of the Reich nor a genuine parliamentary system of government. Britain, on the other hand, seemed to have both. Abandoning his previous belief, Naumann now predicted that Germany could acquire a two-party system similar to that of the United Kingdom. Yet his conversion to British parliamentarism was founded on a theory of elites rather than democracy. The proclivity of the modern world as a whole, he contended, was towards a new form of monarchism, with 'kings of the banking system' and 'rulers of electricity companies'.[71] Germany was to effect the transition 'from absolutism to the English system',[72] which Delbrück 'half-correctly' characterized as a 'despotism of party caucuses', only because it seemed to have secured a more efficient selection of elites, administration of empire, and formulation of

---

[67] F. Naumann, 'Der Niedergang des Parlamentarismus', *Zeit*, 17 July 1902, no. 42, 487–9.
[68] F. Naumann, *Demokratie und Kaisertum*, 4th revised edn. (Berlin, 1905), 54.
[69] Ibid. 179.
[70] F. Naumann, 'Das Königtum', *Hilfe*, 10 Jan. 1910, vol. 15, no. 2, 18.
[71] Ibid. 17. W. Struve, *Elites against Democracy* (Princeton, 1973), 78–113.
[72] *Hilfe*, 17 Jan. 1910, vol. 15, no. 3, 31.

foreign policy.[73] Unsurprisingly, Naumann remained ambivalent about the core values of Britain's parliamentary regime. 'In our opinion', he wrote, 'we will have to seek our own procedure, just as the English have found theirs.'[74]

On the whole, the small minority of liberal academics who expressed public support for parliamentary regimes were even more ambivalent and reticent than politicians like Naumann. To many, such as the Weber brothers, the distinction between parliamentarism and constitutionalism had been eclipsed to a large degree by wider processes of disenchantment, rationalization, capitalism, and bureaucratization. Moreover, these insights into the transformation of the West continued to be interspersed with commonplace, national-minded criticism of parliamentary government. Even Alfred Weber, who had argued against Schmoller in 1907 that France was, 'at bottom, well-governed', conceded at the same time that this was 'in spite of its many changes of ministry'.[75] Two years later, when the dispute came to a head during the Vienna conference of the *Verein für Sozialpolitik*, the Webers, who were joined by a number of other liberal academics such as Lujo Brentano, referred to France only in mock support, with Alfred maintaining that French strikes demonstrated resistance to bureaucratization. Alternatively, they equated France with other supposedly 'corrupt' countries like Britain and the United States. Max Weber did not take issue with the internal defects of French and, to a lesser extent, British and American regimes because his priority was to expose the flaws of the German regime, particularly in the conduct of foreign policy:

I have the impression: yes, this 'corrupt' French bureaucracy, this corrupt American bureaucracy, this so widely despised nightwatchman government of England etc.—how are these countries doing then? How are they doing, for example, in the field of foreign policy? Is it us, then, who have progressed in this field, or is it someone else? Democratically governed countries, which in part, without doubt, have corrupt bureaucracies, have achieved far greater success in the world than our highly moral bureaucracy.[76]

Max Weber's reaction against German bureaucracy and Russian autocracy, which he had considered in detail in 1906, combined with

---

[73] F. Naumann, 'Der Volkswille', *Hilfe*, 18 Dec. 1913, no. 51.

[74] Ibid.

[75] Cited by F. Naumann, 'Können wir ein parlamentarisches Regiment haben?', *Hilfe*, 5 May 1907, vol. 13, no. 18, 275: the dispute took place in Vienna's *Neue Freie Presse*.

[76] *Verhandlungen des Vereins für Sozialpolitik in Wien, 1909* (Leipzig, 1910), 247, 286.

a long-standing preoccupation about the necessity of a forceful foreign policy to push him towards left-liberal supporters of parliamentarism. However, although in his private correspondence with Friedrich Naumann he recorded that 'the political structure was to blame' for the *Daily Telegraph* affair, which made *Weltpolitik* an 'impossibility', he was not sufficiently moved before the First World War to spell out, in the *Historische Zeitschrift* or elsewhere, as he had promised, exactly how the German system had evolved and how it was to be reformed. He realized that the '*parliamentarization of the Bundesrat* is the *practical* problem' but predicted that 'its solution would perhaps be consigned to the distant future', not least because Germany's most obvious point of reference was the United States, 'where likewise *because* of the federal character of the state there is *no* "parliamentarism"'.[77] Other liberal academics like Georg Jellinek, who had published reform proposals in the *Frankfurter Zeitung* in 1908, also stopped short, like Weber, of advocating a full parliamentary regime for Germany in the near future.[78]

Democratic Catholics adopted many of the themes of liberal intellectuals and politicians. Unlike left liberals, however, they remained uncertain until the eve of the First World War whether parliamentarism was desirable at all over the long or short term. The leader of the progressive wing of the Centre Party Matthias Erzberger, whose book *Politik und Völkerleben* appeared in 1914, was a case in point. A third of his chapter on 'The Power of Parliament' was devoted to Christensen's exposé of the Third Republic's failings, including incompetence, demagogy, careerism, over-regulation, superfluous bureaucratization, profligacy, and corruption. This, Erzberger believed, was 'an acute, not at all exaggerated depiction of the side-effects of the parliamentary regime in republics or half-toppled

---

[77] M. Weber to F. Naumann, 12 and 18 Nov. 1908, in M. Weber, *Gesamtausgabe*, ed. H. Baier, M. R. Lepsius, W. J. Mommsen, W. Schluchter, and J. Winckelmann (Tübingen, 1990), v. 693–8. Interpretation here is closer to that of Wolfgang Mommsen, *Max Weber and German Politics, 1890–1920* (Chicago, 1984), 21–189, which emphasizes the importance of elites and foreign policy in Weber's thinking, than to that of David Beetham, *Max Weber and the Theory of Modern Politics* (Cambridge, 1987), 36–118, which fails to make an adequate distinction between Weber's pre-war and wartime thought.

[78] G. Jellinek, 'Die Verantwortlichkeit des Reichskanzlers', *Ausgewählte Schriften und Reden*, ii. 431–8, first published in *Frankfurter Zeitung*, 1 Dec. 1908; id., 'Zur Verantwortlichkeit des Reichskanzlers: Ein Epilog', *Deutsche Juristenzeitung*, 1 May 1909, vol. 14, no. 9, 532–3.

monarchies, where the holders of state power constitute a puppet in the hands of parliament or the lodge'.[79] From his Catholic point of view, he needed little convincing of the degenerate nature of French and Italian parliamentarism, which was allegedly permeated by freemasonry and secular self-interest. Yet the failure of the German 'constitutional regime', which was perceived to be a euphemism for 'the rule of bureaucracy', eventually overrode Erzberger's earlier misgivings about parliamentary government.[80] His argument, like that of left liberals, was a mixture of party interest and a theory of elites. After Bülow had dispensed with the Centre Party as the fulcrum of German politics in 1906, the *Daily Telegraph* affair and the Zabern incident seemed to have proved that the Reich's administration, which required routine and stability on its lower levels, 'needed minds, not machines', in its upper echelons.[81] Responsible parties, which were nurtured by parliamentary government, appeared by 1914 to be the best mechanism for creating political elites to control Germany's unwieldy and oppressive bureaucracy: 'The number of political, statesmanlike, and diplomatic talents, which are developed in parliamentary countries, is far greater than in bureaucratic countries.'[82] Once again, as for old and new left liberals, the British example of parliamentarism seemed to furnish necessary proof from abroad that the system could operate effectively, in contrast to 'countries of autocracy' like Russia and Turkey or to a 'constitutional regime of bureaucracy' like the German Reich. Monarchy, Erzberger postulated, had provided a check in Britain and Belgium to the excesses, or 'dark sides', of the parliamentary regime.[83] This realization, though, which itself derived from admiration of German kingship during and before the Bismarckian era, was both tardy and precarious. For democratic Catholics and left-wing liberals, British parliamentarism was an antidote to German constitutionalism, not a panacea.

Between 1908 and 1914, it seemed as if socialists were Germany's most consistent and candid proponents of a parliamentary regime. Certainly, the SPD was the sole party to campaign unequivocally during those years for direct imitation of British-style parliamentarism. Yet it, too, like the left wing of the Centre Party and some of the younger generation of liberals, had only undergone a late and conditional

---

[79] M. Erzberger, *Politik und Völkerleben* (Paderborn, 1914), 26–7.
[80] Ibid. 22.   [81] Ibid. 23.   [82] Ibid. 28.   [83] Ibid. 27.

conversion to parliamentary government. Even Eduard Bernstein, Edmund Fischer, and other revisionists, who claimed that there was 'no reason to expect German development to take a different course to that of England',[84] remained circumspect about parliamentarism as a political goal. In *Parlamentarismus und Sozialdemokratie*, which was published in 1906, Bernstein argued that participation in bourgeois governments, which was to be restricted to countries 'where real parliamentarism prevailed',[85] was just a means to a socialist end and parliamentary government merely a transitory form of rule, which allowed the use of such means: a centralized parliament would 'inevitably' be replaced by a decentralized 'federal body', which was to be based on local and other kinds of self-government. 'With the continuation of this development,' he went on, 'political parties lose their purpose and, together with them, genuine parliamentarism dies out.'[86] Since a parliamentary regime depended on class struggle, which was already waning in Bernstein's opinion, its utility to Germany's working classes would be limited. Other, social-imperialist revisionists like Ludwig Quessel, Max Schippel, Gerhard Hildebrand, Karl Leuthner, Richard Calwer, and Max Maurenbrecher, all of whom were closely connected to the editor of the *Sozialistische Monatshefte* Joseph Bloch, were also sceptical about foreign models of parliamentarism, although they, too, preferred parliamentary government to a 'constitutional system of government'.[87] Like Naumann and the left-liberals, and unlike other socialists, who looked to parliamentarism as a step towards democracy, Bloch and many of his journalists had been impressed by the ruling elites, large empires, and powerful allies of parliamentary regimes. Like Bernstein, however, they saw parliamentarism as a temporary instrument to achieve anti-liberal, unparliamentary, socialist goals.[88] At best, Britain

---

[84] E. Fischer, 'Zur politischen Entwickelung Deutschlands', *Sozialistische Monatshefte*, 31 Dec. 1908, vol. 14, no. 26, 1638.

[85] E. Bernstein, *Parlamentarismus und Sozialdemokratie* (Berlin, 1906), 51. Id., 'Regierung und Sozialisten', *Sozialistische Monatshefte*, 24 July 1913, vol. 19, no. 14, 838–43; E. Fischer, 'Sozialdemokratie und Regierungsgewalt', ibid., 14 Mar. 1912, vol. 18, no. 5, 277.

[86] Bernstein, *Parlamentarismus und Sozialdemokratie*, 59–60.

[87] L. Quessel, 'Die ministerielle Abstinenz der Sozialdemokratie und ihre Folgen für die Demokratie', *Sozialistische Monatshefte*, 7 Aug. 1913, vol. 19, no. 15, 898; id., 'Sozialdemokratie und Monarchie', *Sozialistische Monatshefte*, 14 Mar. 1912, vol. 18, no. 5, 271–5.

[88] R. Fletcher, *Revisionism and Empire* (London, 1984), 50–65.

served as a transient, expendable paradigm. It was unwise, Leuthner declared, simply 'to transfer what had been said about English parties to continental ones'.[89]

Most Marxists within the SPD joined revisionists in calling for the introduction of a parliamentary regime, but nevertheless remained cautious.[90] By 1911, when a revised edition of *Parlamentarismus und Demokratie* was reissued, Karl Kautsky had concluded that 'the bourgeoisie eastwards of the Rhine' was too 'weak' and 'cowardly' to bring down 'the regime of bureaucrats and the sword':

> One thing is certain: in Germany as in Austria, indeed in most European countries, those preconditions which are needed for the favourable working of popular legislatures and, above all, necessary democratic institutions will not come into being *before* the victory of the proletariat. Popular legislatures can perhaps achieve a certain effect beforehand in the United States, in England and in the English colonies, and in some circumstances in France—for us eastern Europeans they belong to the inventory of the [socialist] 'state of the future'.[91]

In his historical references to parliamentary 'absolutism', 'party tyranny', corruption, and 'class rule' in Britain, Kautsky had already exposed the possible deficiencies of powerful parliaments in 1893.[92] Almost two decades later, the main ideologue of the SPD had been convinced that a parliamentary system of government could be achieved in central and eastern Europe only after the proletariat's rise to power. As a result, as Kautsky's disciples spelled out in the *Neue Zeit*, agitation on behalf of a class-bound Reichstag was to remain subordinate to the affairs of press, party, and unions.[93] This constituted a shift in the thinking of orthodox Marxists towards the arguments of Rosa Luxemburg and other radical, left-wing socialists, who eschewed parliamentary methods and discounted parliamentarism as one dispensable part of a much broader process of democratization and development of capitalism: 'Bourgeois parliamentarism

---

[89] K. Leuthner, 'Parlament und Demokratie', *Sozialistische Monatshefte*, 2 June 1910, vol. 16, no. 11, 683.

[90] For a detailed study of the SPD's attitude to parliamentarism, see E. Pracht, *Parlamentarismus und deutsche Sozialdemokratie, 1867–1914* (Pfaffenweiler, 1990).

[91] K. Kautsky, *Parlamentarismus und Demokratie*, 2nd revised edn. (Stuttgart, 1911), 140. The first edition appeared in 1893.

[92] Ibid. 53, 61–2, 114.

[93] F. Mehring, 'Regierung und Reichstag', *Neue Zeit*, 27 Sept. 1905, vol. 24, no. 1, 1–4; R. Breitscheid, 'Die Bedeutung des Parlaments', *Neue Zeit*, 24 Apr. 1914, vol. 32, no. 4, 157–60.

continues to exist only for the duration of the struggle between the bourgeoisie and feudalism.'[94] In the opinion of Luxemburg and other radical socialists, direct action was the sole, feasible alternative to discredited parliamentary tactics. The fact that methods such as the general strike found some support amongst SPD leaders like Kautsky demonstrated the depth of socialist unease by the 1910s with the whole idea of parliamentarism.[95] German Social Democrats shared with other left-wing politicians a tenuous and qualified attachment to parliamentary government on the British or French model. The ascendancy of parliament was perceived to be one means of achieving a diverse range of ends. It was not an end in itself. As such, it was likely to be sacrificed or compromised as the resistance of government, right-wing, and centrist parties became manifest.

4. National Comparison and Constitutional Crisis

Paradoxically, the constitutional crisis of the *Kaiserreich* between 1908 and 1914 demonstrated political parties' commitment to Germany's system of government. As has been seen, the terms of political debate were being redefined in an international context. The idea of a specific, German form of constitutionalism and the notion of a distinct type of foreign parliamentarism were widely disseminated and understood. Officials, politicians, and journalists became increasingly conscious of an unambiguous threshold, which most refused to cross, between Germany's political system and foreign parliamentary regimes. Their convictions were tested by a rapid succession of events, including the formation of the 'grand bloc' in Baden in 1909, reform of the Reich's finances, Prussian franchise agitation in 1910, discussion of an Alsatian constitution in 1911, Germany's failure during the second Moroccan crisis, the emergence of the SPD as the largest single Reichstag party in 1912, the imposition of a Centre Party government on the king of Bavaria, and the introduction of de facto votes of censure during Reichstag interpellations. Cursorily, such junctures could be seen to be signs of collapse or stages of parliamentarization. Yet these were precisely the points at which government and parties clarified their respective constitutional

---

[94] R. Luxemburg, 'Sozialdemokratie und Parlamentarismus', in id., *Gesammelte Werke* (Berlin, 1974), i. 449: the article was first published in the *Sächsische Arbeiter-Zeitung* on 5 and 7 Dec. 1904.

[95] Karl Kautsky, *Selected Political Writings*, ed. P. Goode (London, 1983), 81.

positions. In his speeches to the Reichstag, which were designed to allay any confusion created unintentionally by his predecessor Bülow, Bethmann Hollweg left no doubt in deputies' minds that he would defend the principles of neutral, elitist, bureaucratic, and constitutional government.[96] It was 'unconstitutional', he reminded the lower chamber in 1913, to attempt to 'exert pressure' on 'the free choice' of the kaiser in the appointment and dismissal of chancellors.[97] Confronted by such clear statements of government policy, German parties were compelled to draft unequivocal replies. Most of them opted, as conservative, liberal, and social-democratic observers acknowledged, to support the existing regime.[98] 'Great, enduring parties, filled with genuine constitutional life, are the necessary foundations of parliamentary government', lamented the *Vossische Zeitung*: 'The German people, not least, is responsible for their absence.'[99] This broad rejection of parliamentarism was evident even in November 1908 and December 1913, when the constitution of the Reich appeared to be close to its breaking-point.

The *Daily Telegraph* affair, which was provoked by Wilhelm II's unguarded interviews with a British officer about German foreign policy, united virtually all parties in criticism of the government. It did not, however, prompt a majority of deputies or editorial writers to call for a parliamentary regime. Conservatives and nationalists, although irritated by the incompetent and pro-British policy of the kaiser, quickly rallied to the defence of the *Kaiserreich*, applauding the assertion of Willy von Dircksen that the 'parliamentary and constitutional powers, which our parliament has, are—believe me!—significant enough'.[100] Notwithstanding warnings to a wayward monarch, journals and newspapers such as the *Reichsbote*, *Deutsche Tageszeitung*, and *Neue Preußische Zeitung* proclaimed that the constitutional system had been vindicated rather than discredited by the public debates of 1908.[101] It was 'pleasing', wrote one correspondent, to behold 'the serious, manly way, firm and true to monarchy,

---

[96] *Verhandlungen des Reichstages*, 9 Dec. 1909, vol. 258, 167–8; 19 Feb. 1910, vol. 259, 1410; 10 Dec. 1910, vol. 260, 3544; 16 Feb. 1912, vol. 283, 66–7; 22 May 1912, vol. 285, 2242.

[97] Ibid. 9 Dec. 1913, vol. 291, 6282.

[98] *Königsberger Allgemeine Zeitung*, 14 Dec. 1913; O. Harnack in *März*, Sept. 1910, vol. 4, no. 18, 429–32; *Vorwärts*, 11 Nov. 1908.

[99] *Vossische Zeitung*, 10 Nov. 1908.

[100] *Verhandlungen des Reichstags*, 2 Dec. 1908, vol. 233, 5935.

[101] *Reichsbote*, 12 Nov. 1908; *Deutsche Tageszeitung*, 11 Nov. 1908; *Neue Preußische Zeitung*, 11 Nov. 1908.

kaiser, and empire, in which this unity of national thinking found expression'.[102] The National Liberal and Centre Parties were less triumphant, but eventually adopted a similar strategy of complaint and inactivity. Peter Spahn, Georg Hertling, Ernst Bassermann, and Johannes Junck all agreed in the Reichstag that it was unnecessary 'to talk of a parliamentary government'.[103] Instead, parties were to limit themselves to a bill, which would not 'lead to a parliamentary regime', defining the legal responsibilities of the chancellor.[104] The principal sponsors of this initiative were left liberals and socialists. Amongst the former, some such as Otto Wiemer and Karl Schrader, who declared that 'we do not want a parliamentary regime', appeared to be both unsettled and undecided whilst others like Friedrich Naumann, Conrad Haußmann, and Friedrich von Payer recognized that the introduction of full-blown parliamentarism was impracticable in Germany over the short term: 'What we are fighting for today is not this form of parliamentary regime, but what the majority of the Reichstag wants is that we finally have constitutional conditions in the German Reich.'[105] Since parliamentarism was unrealizable, contended left liberals, an act specifying the legal liabilities of chancellors would at least guarantee genuine constitutionalism. Socialists alone went beyond this minimal programme to challenge the kaiser's exclusive power of appointment. The prevarication of bourgeois parties, which in the end withdrew their support for the bill, and an outcry in socialist and many left-liberal newspapers pushed the SPD to call for the political accountability of government. It was an act of self-delusion, argued the socialist lawyer and deputy Wolfgang Heine, for liberals and Catholics to believe that they could control ministers merely by means of juridical devices, for the question of control was a political one.[106] In the course of Reichstag discussions of the *Daily Telegraph* affair in 1908, the other political parties ignored such argument.

By the time of the Zabern incident in 1913, despite technical alterations in Reichstag procedures and five years of constitutional crisis, German parties had maintained, if not increased, their opposition to

[102] *Reichsbote*, 12 Nov. 1908.
[103] P. Spahn, in *Verhandlungen des Reichstags*, 2 Dec. 1912, vol. 233, 5914.
[104] Ibid.
[105] K. Schrader, in *Verhandlungen des Reichstags*, 11 Nov. 1908, vol. 233, 5415; F. v. Payer, ibid., 3 Dec. 1912, vol. 233, 5962.
[106] W. Heine, ibid., 3 Dec. 1908, vol. 233, 5968–9.

the introduction of a parliamentary regime in the near future. The main difference between 1913 and 1908 was the spectacle of right-wing panic, as conservatives were aroused from complacent constitutionalism. The Reichstag's vote of censure against Bethmann Hollweg, by 293 votes to 54, evinced an unexpected degree of cooperation between the SPD and centrist parties and adumbrated a new willingness to misuse constitutional mechanisms in order to impose a parliamentary system of government, warned newspapers such as the *Berliner Neueste Nachrichten* and the *Deutsche Tageszeitung*.[107] 'Attempts to institute pure parliamentarism, by means of incisive force,' recorded one journalist, 'have continuously gained ground.'[108] In fact, neither the liberal parties nor the Centre Party were prepared to treat an interpellation vote, which had been permitted by procedural changes in May 1912, as a vote of no confidence, designed to dismiss the chancellor and to create the basis of a parliamentary regime. In this respect, Erzberger was fully in agreement with Bassermann that an alteration of Reichstag standing orders should not be interpreted as a change in the constitution: 'What we have included in our procedures is not the vote of no confidence of a parliamentary system but disapproval of the handling of a single case; that is quite obvious.'[109] On the whole, the National Liberal press backed the views of the party's leader, with a few publications adding that parliamentarism could 'perhaps constitute a distant goal for us'.[110] Left-liberal newspapers and politicians adopted a similar stance: their aim, protested the *Berliner Tageblatt*, was genuine constitutionalism, not a parliamentary regime; only 'illusionists of the agrarian-conservative camp' claimed that measures like the Reichstag's vote of censure led 'irreversibly to parliamentarism'.[111] Contrary to the accusations of the German right, left-liberal deputies displayed greater caution after the Zabern incident than during the *Daily Telegraph* debates. It was true, declared Wiemer, that the *Fortschrittliche Volkspartei* wished to bolster the rights of parliament and held that parliamentarism was 'still better than sham constitutionalism,

---

[107] *Berliner Neueste Nachrichten*, 11 Dec. 1913.

[108] *Deutsche Tageszeitung*, 13 Dec. 1913.

[109] E. Bassermann and M. Erzberger, in *Verhandlungen des Reichstags*, 9 and 11 Dec. 1913, vol. 291, 6299 and 6363.

[110] *Münchner Neueste Nachrichten*, 16 Dec. 1913. Newspapers reiterating Bassermann's views included the *Kölnische Zeitung* and *Hannoversche Courier*, both cited in *Berliner Neueste Nachrichten*, 12 Dec. 1913.

[111] *Berliner Tageblatt*, 15 Dec. 1913.

as it today exists', but it did not believe that a vote of censure had signalled the commencement of an era of parliamentary rule in
Germany.[112] By its own admission and by the testimony of outsiders,
the SPD was the sole party in 1913 to direct public anger, which had
been provoked by the actions of army and government, towards the
introduction of parliamentarism.[113]

Many of the disputes about the constitution of the *Kaiserreich*
rested on an international typology of political regimes. As a consequence, during complicated and animated exchanges in the
Reichstag, deputies referred with unusual regularity to other nation-
states. From their speeches and interventions in the chamber, three
separate views of foreign polities—socialist, left-liberal, and conservative—could be discerned. The SPD alone made repeated use of
France as a political paradigm, but together with other 'advanced
cultural states' like Belgium and Denmark, and in a subordinate role
to Britain. Socialists required a list of such states to undermine
Germany's 'old system of feudal deference' and to justify theories of
political stages in which it was assumed, in Eduard David's words,
that 'modern peoples constitute a group with the closest intellectual
ties to each other'.[114] Although Paul Singer in 1908 and Philipp
Scheidemann in 1913 urged the Reichstag to 'take a look at England
and France', it was evident that the phrase was ordered hierarchic-
ally, meaning 'England then France'.[115] Revealingly, Social
Democrats like Heine, who tried to place Germany within a tradition
of 'continental states', felt compelled to explain during the *Daily
Telegraph* affair why the Reich should diverge from Britain rather
than why it ought to converge with France: his peroration that 'we
do not have to bind ourselves slavishly to England' followed an
extended analysis of the merits of British parliamentarism and complete neglect of the Third Republic.[116] For similar reasons, left-
liberal deputies focused almost exclusively on Britain, fearing that
reference to France, Italy, and other parliamentary regimes would
redound to their disadvantage. British parliamentarism was useful
not only because it was associated in many Germans' minds with
effective political leadership, domestic stability, and the world's

---

[112] O. Wiemer, in *Verhandlungen des Reichstags*, 10 Dec. 1913, vol. 291, 6323.
[113] *Vorwärts*, 15 Dec. 1913; *Leipziger Neueste Nachrichten*, 10 Dec. 1913.
[114] E. David, in *Verhandlungen des Reichstags*, 12 Dec. 1913, vol. 291, 6427.
[115] P. Singer, ibid., vol. 233, 5392; P. Scheidemann, ibid., vol. 291, 6278.
[116] W. Heine, ibid., 3 Dec. 1908, vol. 233, 5968–71.

largest empire, but also because it seemed to offer the possibility of gradual, unwritten adjustments to Germany's political system. Even so, Naumann spoke for many of his colleagues when, in December 1908, he advocated only cautious movement 'in the general direction of English development': 'English history', he declared, summarizing Schrader, was 'different to German history' and remained, as Sidney Low had proved, in a state of unpredictable flux.[117] Other left-liberals such as Payer continued to hold that the absence of a British-style two-party system in Germany meant that the question of parliamentarism could be 'left to the future'.[118] Conservative speakers in the Reichstag took up such qualifications in order to demonstrate that Britain should not be used as a 'model country' for Germany, since it lacked a democratic franchise, possessed a 'shocking' upper chamber and suffered high unemployment.[119] Instead, as Wolfgang Gans zu Putlitz proclaimed, Germans should examine the consequences of parliamentarism on the continent: 'in England circumstances are such that until recently parliamentarism was in the hands of two great aristocratic parties.... But the countries which we can imitate, in which there are not two great parties, are those where parliamentarism has had a disintegrative effect.'[120] It was no coincidence that Bethmann Hollweg singled out French constitutional conditions, allegedly favoured by Scheidemann and the SPD, against which to make his stand during the Zabern incident.[121] Overall, France was seen as a clear warning against parliamentarism, Britain as an ambiguous advertisement for it.

Progressives and socialists were forced to cite the case of Britain, which was a traditional liberal point of reference from the 1840s, 1860s, and 1870s, in order to refute allegations about a turn-of-the-century crisis of European parliamentarism. Indeed, in the years before the First World War, their allusions to British institutions had become stock-in-trade, provoking standard rejoinders from conservatives such as 'I thought England would come up' and 'You always want to present England to us as a worthy example.'[122] However, most well-known advocates of parliamentarism in Germany had been

---

[117] F. Naumann, *Verhandlungen des Reichstags*, 3 Dec. 1908, vol. 233, 5945–9.

[118] F. v. Payer, ibid. 5936.

[119] W. v. Dircksen, ibid., 26 Nov. 1910, vol. 262, 3196.

[120] W. Gans zu Putlitz, ibid., 19 Feb. 1912, vol. 283, 123.

[121] T. Bethmann Hollweg, ibid., 9 Dec. 1913, vol. 291, 6282.

[122] W. v. Dircksen and W. Gans zu Putlitz, ibid., 26 Nov. 1910 and 19 Feb. 1912, vols. 262 and 283, 3196 and 123.

converted by the imperatives of domestic politics and criticism of the German regime rather than by admiration of Britain. As has been shown, Naumann, Weber, Erzberger, Bloch, and Kautsky all wished to use particular elements of the British parliamentary system as means to other ends. If parliamentarism failed to produce successful elites or to prepare the way for socialist society, then it would quickly be abandoned. This was in keeping with the domestic causes of Germany's pre-war constitutional crisis, during which political parties had been compelled to recognize the failings of the Reich, particularly in the realm of foreign policy, and to rethink their relationship with government. The strength and breadth of party agitation was unprecedented: in 1908, spokesmen for all parties except the Free Conservatives criticized the actions of the kaiser in the Reichstag; in 1913, deputies passed their second successful vote of censure against the government by a ratio of almost six to one. Yet, although staid members of the National Liberal and Centre Parties had backed measures which extended the powers of parliament, such as permitting votes during interpellations, they did not seek to replace German constitutionalism. Between 1908 and 1914, only the SPD attempted to profit from the Reich's misfortune and introduce a British-style parliamentary regime. The Reichstag, wrote Otto Harnack, had, 'neither as a whole nor in its individual parties, demonstrated a will [to assert] its own parliamentary position of power'.[123]

By the late 1900s, the domestic bulwarks of the Bismarckian state were still strong but were starting to disintegrate. After the *Daily Telegraph* affair, conservative, National Liberal, and Centre Party politicians, who had previously defended the constitution unthinkingly, at various times threatened, in the words of the *Rheinisch-Westfälische Zeitung*, to work 'with all seriousness and haste' towards a 'change of constitution, which has already been talked about by different sides'.[124] Furthermore, parties had become estranged from government, with no group after 1909 acting as an intermediary between the executive and the Reichstag, and they had begun, with the exception of conservatives, to cooperate in an ad hoc manner with the SPD. Consequently, the advantages of governing coalitions within a parliamentary system, which according to socialists themselves would at first be conservative and Catholic, could be weighed up,

---

[123] O. Harnack, 'Aussichten des Parlamentarismus in Deutschland', *März*, Sept. 1910, vol. 4, no. 18, 430–1.

[124] *Rheinisch-Westfälische Zeitung*, 12 Nov. 1908.

sometimes favourably, against those of a government of bureaucrats, which sought to stand above sectional interests. Under such circumstances, with parties more receptive to change at home, arguments from abroad against parliamentarism helped to shore up the German regime. This occurred in two ways. First, national comparison set the parameters of the pre-war constitutional crisis of the *Kaiserreich*. Because of cross-party discussion of foreign polities, the introduction of parliamentarism would no longer be gradual and uncontroversial, as Naumann had hoped, but sudden, public, and contested, with resistance to the imitation of a British or French system of government. After a short interlude of experimentation in the 1890s and early 1900s, constitutional questions in Germany had become clear-cut and international. As a result, noted Harnack, defence of the constitution was interpreted by right-wing and centrist parties like the National Liberals as an act of patriotism, mixed with a sense of pride in Germany's economic and military power and with a feeling of isolation in Europe.[125] Second, German depictions of foreign parliamentary regimes during the late nineteenth and early twentieth centuries suggested a record of failure. France, Italy, and even Britain had been portrayed in the press as countries in decline. Parliamentarism, which according to one journal 'naturally has its weak sides', was perceived to have been connected, through excessive governmental corruption or populism, to poor administration and relative economic deterioration.[126] This spectre of parliamentary crisis was never fully exorcised from many Germans' minds, including those of supporters of parliamentarism such as Erzberger and Naumann, during the decade before the First World War.

Constitutional debate in Germany had come to rest, to a large extent, on comparative analysis of political regimes. Parliamentarism, which was associated with France and Britain, was the single most important concept in such debate, ensuring that the appointment and dismissal of ministers—that is, the merger or separation of executive and legislative competencies—became the critical threshold in German politics. Most parties were willing to countenance an increase in the powers of the Reichstag, often at the expense of federalism, so long as the Reich government, which had also acquired some of the functions of federal states, continued to be independent

---

[125] Harnack, 'Aussichten des Parlamentarismus', 431.

[126] Anon., 'Die bedeutendsten Parlamente der Welt', *Welt*, 4 Mar. 1906, vol. 12, no. 24, 490.

of the assembly. This independence was guaranteed, it was held, by the kaiser's power of appointment, which was usually exercised in conjunction with the government and federal states; it was threatened, according to evidence from France and other European countries, by an over-powerful parliament. The force of such an argument affected all German parties and helped to convince four out of five of the main groupings in the Reichstag not to introduce a parliamentary regime in Germany over the short term. Thus, Dieter Grosser's thesis of a 'stabilization of the constitutional monarchy' on the eve of the First World War seems more plausible than either Manfred Rauh's notion of a 'parliamentarization of the German Empire' or Hans-Ulrich Wehler's idea of stalemate within a semi-authoritarian, sham democracy.[127]

After the outbreak of war, the tradition of 'German constitutionalism' did not suddenly disappear. In 1918–19 and 1930–33, during the founding and the collapse of the Weimar Republic, anxieties about parliamentary government pervaded public debate about the new German regime. Many Germans continued to believe in the neutrality of the state and to fear the sectionalism of political parties. 'One finds suspicion everywhere', admitted Hugo Preuss, author of the Weimar constitution, in 1919: 'Germans cannot shake off their old political timidity and their deference to the authoritarian state.'[128] Although, with broad acceptance of the notion of popular

---

[127] For a good summary of the different positions, see K. v. Zwehl, 'Zum Verhältnis von Regierung und Reichstag im Kaiserreich 1871–1918', in G. A. Ritter (ed.), *Regierung, Bürokratie und Parlament in Preußen und Deutschland von 1848 bis zur Gegenwart* (Düsseldorf, 1983). Apart from D. Grosser, *Vom monarchischen Konstitutionalismus zur parlamentarischen Demokratie* (Den Haag, 1970), see E.-R. Huber, *Deutsche Verfassungsgeschichte*, iii (Stuttgart, 1988); H. Boldt, 'Parlamentarismustheorie. Bemerkungen zu ihrer Geschichte in Deutschland', *Der Staat*, 19 (1980), 385–412; H. Boldt, *Deutsche Verfassungsgeschichte*, ii (Munich, 1990). For views similar to those of H.-U. Wehler, *The German Empire* (Leamington Spa, 1985), see H. Boldt, 'Deutscher Konstitutionalismus und Bismarckreich', in M. Stürmer (ed.), *Das kaiserliche Deutschland* (Düsseldorf, 1970); M. Stürmer, *Regierung und Reichstag im Bismarckstaat 1871–1880* (Düsseldorf, 1974); H.-J. Puhle, *Agrarische Interessenpolitik und preußischer Konservatismus im wilhelminischen Reich, 1893–1914* (Hanover, 1966); P.-C. Witt, *Die Finanzpolitik des deutschen Reiches von 1903 bis 1914* (Lübeck and Hamburg, 1970). For theories of parliamentarization, see E.-W. Böckenförde, 'Der Verfassungstyp der deutschen konstitutionellen Monarchie im 19. Jahrhundert', in E.-W. Böckenförde (ed.), *Moderne deutsche Verfassungsgeschichte*, 2nd edn. (Königstein, 1981); M. Rauh, *Föderalismus und Parlamentarismus im Wilhelminischen Reich* (Düsseldorf, 1973); M. Rauh, *Die Parlamentarisierung des Deutschen Reiches* (Düsseldorf, 1977); H.-G. Zmarzlik, 'Das Kaiserreich in neuer Sicht?', *Historische Zeitschrift*, 222 (1976), 105–26.

[128] H. Preuss, cited in J. Hiden, *Republican and Fascist Germany* (London, 1996), 39.

sovereignty and a rejection of monarchy, there was no longer any doubt that power resided ultimately in the people, the old division between politics, parties, economic, and social interests, on the one hand, and the state, nation, and executive, on the other, continued to exist. The separate election of the president by universal suffrage, his position as commander-in-chief of the army, and his emergency powers under Article 48 of the constitution were all designed to give the new head of state, like the kaiser before him, a significant degree of independence from the alleged partiality and stalemate of what Max Weber called a ' "banausic" assembly'.[129] After defeat in 1918, it was widely agreed that 'constitutional monarchy' and 'German constitutionalism' had been discredited and needed to be replaced. Yet relatively few Germans, since they remained sceptical of French and British parliamentarism, could think what to replace it with.[130] The proclivity of pre-war political thought could not simply be reversed, even after the dislocation of the First World War.

5. Political Thought and National Identity

After revision of Fritz Fischer's assumptions—elaborated by his followers into theories—about a German *Sonderweg*, historians have begun to concentrate on national identity and nationalism in their own right, instead of treating them as by-products of late industrialization and unification. To date, despite agreeing with Wilhelmine observers such as Max Lehmann that 'the idea of nationality' dominated public life, affecting many areas of domestic and foreign policy, scholars have not yet established a new orthodoxy to replace that of the Hamburg and Bielefeld schools. Some like John Breuilly and Imanuel Geiss have depicted national identity and nationalism primarily as a reaction to state policy or to Germany's geopolitical predicament at the centre of Europe.[131] On the whole, their accounts show how calculations of power rather than national consciousness

---

[129] M. Weber, 'Politics as a Vocation' (1918), cited in Beetham, *Max Weber and the Theory of Modern Politics*, 235.

[130] Grosser, *Vom monarchischen Konstitutionalismus zur parlamentarischen Demokratie*, 135–9.

[131] J. Breuilly, *Nationalism and the State*, 2nd revised edn. (Manchester, 1993), 291–300; id. (ed.), *The State of Germany* (London, 1992), 1–15; id., *The Formation of the First German Nation-State, 1800–1871* (London, 1996); id., 'The National Idea in Modern German History' in M. Fulbrook (ed.), *German History since 1800* (London, 1997); I. Geiss, *The Question of German Unification, 1806-1996* (London, 1997).

dictated the course of German history before and after unification. Others such as Michael Hughes and Harold James have distinguished between the gradual construction of identity, by means of ideas and representations of *Deutschtum*, on the one hand, and the instrumentalization of competing versions of German culture by late nineteenth and early twentieth-century nationalist ideologies, on the other.[132] Their work draws on research into the continuities of national symbolism in Germany and on theoretical distinctions between Eastern and Western European types of nationalism.[133] All such historical interpretations—James, Breuilly, and Fischer—posit either that the cultural component of national identity was preponderant, becoming in turn the core of German nationalism, or that the idea of a strong state in Germany, often reinforced by fear of European encirclement and global exclusion, produced aggressive and expansionist types of nationalism. Few historians deny that the relationship between the nation and politics under the *Kaiserreich* was close, brittle, opaque, and frequently taboo, constituting a significant point of divergence between Germany and the Western powers.

This study, which has examined how a political component was added to German national identity as the Reich was compared favourably with other nation-states, does not seek to challenge the notion that both culture and state were unusually significant in the growth of national consciousness and nationalism in Germany. Such arguments, after all, were put forward at the time by Wilhelmine commentators themselves, many of whom attempted to link Idealist traditions of the state to Social Darwinist hierarchies of culture: only large and powerful states, Treitschke had declared, could produce great cultures; once powers such as Holland and Spain had ceased to compete with each other, they had experienced a cultural decline.[134] Because of the prominence of unification in Germany's history, most Wilhelmine observers accepted the necessity of a strong state, as

---

[132] M. Hughes, *Nationalism and Society: Germany, 1800–1945* (London, 1988), 1–174; H. James, *A German Identity, 1770–1990* (London, 1989), 1–110.

[133] On national symbolism, see D. Düding (ed.), *Öffentliche Festkultur: Politische Feste in Deutschland von der Aufklärung bis zum Ersten Weltkrieg* (Reinbek bei Hamburg, 1988); J. Link and W. Wülfung (eds.), *Nationale Mythen und Symbole in der zweiten Hälfte des 19. Jahrhunderts* (Stuttgart, 1991); G. L. Mosse, *The Nationalization of the Masses* (Ithaca, NY, 1975); M. Jeismann, *Das Vaterland der Feinde* (Stuttgart, 1992). On European typologies of nationalism, see esp. J. Plamenatz, 'Two Types of Nationalism', in E. Kamenka (ed.), *Nationalism* (New York, 1976), 22–36, and R. Brubaker, *Citizenship and Nationhood in France and Germany* (Cambridge, Mass., 1992), 1–138.

[134] H. v. Treitschke, *Selections from Treitschke's Lectures on Politics* (London, 1914), 16–20.

German reactions to the Third Republic had demonstrated. Even a liberal historian like Friedrich Meinecke, whatever his reservations about Bismarck's legacy, recognized that the Reich had had to be built on the foundations of the Prussian military monarchy. After 1871, he went on, this older type of 'state-nation' (*Staatsnation*) became a 'nation-state' (*Nationalstaat*), as the interdependence of government and the people increased.[135] During the nineteenth century, Meinecke concurred with Max Weber, nations came to be defined more and more in terms of the state: 'In fact, today, "nation-state" has become conceptually identical... with "state" '.[136] Throughout Europe since the French Revolution, it appeared, nations and states had striven to become coterminous. This did not mean, though, that the German nation, or culture, had been marginalized by the state or that its role was identical to that of French or British culture. Rather, contemporaries made a distinction, which Meinecke articulated and refined, between *Kulturnationen* such as Germany and Italy, in which national cultures preceded the institutions of a nation-state, and *Staatsnationen* like Britain and France, where administrations antedated—and often created—national languages and customs.[137] By the turn of the century, when most European cultural and state-nations had become nation-states, with a territorial monopoly of violence and extensive national government, Germany's history as a *Kulturnation* continued to have important ramifications, not least by making national culture appear primordial, self-evident and irreducible. 'In its common "ethnic" sense,' wrote Weber, albeit in disagreement, ' "nationality" normally shares with "people" at least the vague notion that a community of common descent must underpin it.'[138] To many Wilhelmine academics and publicists, defence of a national culture, which underpinned Germany's mission in the world, constituted the state's *raison d'être*. All such 'national affairs'—culture, state, and foreign policy—were to be protected from the damaging sectional conflicts of 'politics'.

From a reading of early twentieth-century German sources, it is evident that broad spheres of government in the Reich still enjoyed

---

[135] Meinecke, *Cosmopolitanism and the National State*, 9–22, 364–74.

[136] Weber, *Wirtschaft und Gesellschaft*, 242. The sections cited were written before the First World War.

[137] Meinecke, *Cosmopolitanism and the National State*, 10–12.

[138] Weber, *Wirtschaft und Gesellschaft*, 236–8, 242.

exemption from ordinary party politics, partly as a consequence of late unification and Prussian ascendancy. To a greater extent than in Britain or France, affairs of state and culture in Germany were perceived, respectively, to be matters of national interest and identity, standing above political controversy. By the late 1900s, however, the line between politics and the nation was less obvious. In this respect, it appeared, Germany was moving towards France and Britain on the eve of the First World War. Not only were national affairs discussed more freely by politicians, now that the survival of a German nation-state seemed more or less certain, but a political component had also been included in German national identity, as Germans had become reconciled to the institutional form of the *Kaiserreich* when compared to the inferior polities of other countries. Both of these processes ensured that political thought assumed a more prominent place in national affairs, which in turn brought national interest more clearly within the realm of national identity: as a result of more open political debate of all areas of policy, the question of what the German state should do was more visibly and fully subordinated to the question of what Germany was, which, by the early twentieth century, owed more to a set of political institutions and less to vaguely defined, frequently mystical notions of national character than had been the case during the second half of the nineteenth century. In other words, subject to many qualifications, Germany had begun to shift towards a Western model of political—rather than cultural and racial—national identity.

The addition of a significant, stabilizing political component to German identity took place against a background of increasing cultural instability. In part, such instability was intrinsic to national identity. Ideas and representations of German culture, from the philosophy of Herder and the architecture of Schinkel to the music of Wagner and the economics of Schmoller, were eighteenth- and nineteenth-century inventions of nationality, not timeless manifestations of German character.[139] Contrary to popular belief, wrote Weber, nations were not based on communities of descent: 'In reality, people who regard themselves as compatriots stand, not only occasionally but very often, much further from each other than those who are

---

[139] E. Hobsbawm and T. Ranger (eds.), *The Invention of Tradition* (Cambridge, 1983); E. Hobsbawm, *Nations and Nationalism since 1780* (Cambridge, 1990); B. Anderson, *Imagined Communities*, 2nd revised edn. (London, 1991).

counted amongst different and inimical nationalities.'[140] Because German identity was constructed deliberately by writers and academics, borrowing and rejecting various elements of French, British, Italian, Swiss, American, and ancient Greek cultures, it retained a claim to universality which appeared to contradict its own linguistic and ethnic foundations. In such circumstances, with this bewildering mixture of cultural precepts, Germany seemed to be caught between a threatening degree of diversity and openness, which supposedly presaged the collapse of identity altogether, and a necessary measure of cultural adaptability, which would guarantee the country's preeminence in the global struggle of great powers. 'Nothing is more unnational than national isolation', claimed Hans Delbrück in 1913.[141] By this time, the eclectic 'building blocks'[142] of German identity had been taken up and refashioned, in countless ways, by a diverse, mass-circulation press. As the range of newspapers and periodicals increased in the 1890s and 1900s, thousands of journalists set about reconstructing competing versions of German character, customs, and symbols. Simultaneously, hundreds of thousands of uninterpreted fragments of evidence, which seemed to prove or disprove the particularity of Germany's culture, were presented to the public. To some Wilhelmine observers, the cultural components of national identity appeared to be in danger of disintegrating as newspapers offered to readers a kaleidoscope of images of Germany and other nation-states. 'The press', postulated the sociologist Ferdinand Tönnies, 'was not confined to national borders but was, according to its proclivity and opportunity, thoroughly international.'[143] In this wider, more fragmented context, it was more difficult to distinguish the attributes of a German cultural identity.

By contrast, the political part of national identity rested on a set of concrete institutions—rather than intangible traits of character—which could be interpreted in a limited number of ways. As has been seen, by the late 1900s, only two types of regime—constitutional and parliamentary—were canvassed seriously in Germany. The very existence of the Bismarckian Reich gave it a legitimacy, which was

---

[140] Weber, *Wirtschaft und Gesellschaft*, 42.

[141] H. Delbrück, 'Was ist national?' (1913), in *Politische und historische Aufsätze, 1902–1925*, 380.

[142] James, *A German Identity*, 8–33. On writers and academics, B. Giesen, *Die Intellektuellen und die Nation* (Frankfurt a.M., 1993).

[143] F. Tönnies, *Gemeinschaft und Gesellschaft*, 8th edn. (Leipzig, 1935), 237. The first edition was published in 1887.

recognized by left-liberal opponents such as Naumann. Thus, the argument that German political institutions, many of which had been created between 1867 and 1878, were too newfangled to have gained deep, popular attachment loses much of its force. In an era of recent, invented traditions, in which all parts of national identity were constantly being renegotiated in the press, plausibility and success counted more than lineage. According to these criteria, the constitutional regime, which was seen by the majority of Wilhelmine onlookers to have performed at least as well as parliamentary systems, appeared to deserve a place in a broader German identity. What was more, during the course of the pre-war constitutional crisis of the *Kaiserreich*, the relationship between Germany's political system and the Bismarckian nation-state was reversed, giving to the former the latter's reputation of efficiency and historical legitimacy. Whereas, before 1908, the close association of polity and nation-state had precluded discussion of alternative political regimes, after that date, when such discussion became commonplace, the *Nationalstaat* was, in effect, politicized, despite a persisting myth of state neutrality. Now, the German nation-state was understood by many Wilhelmine commentators as a particular type of political system, with the bureaucracy and army, which had previously enjoyed a semi-autonomous status, having specific roles, beside the Reichstag, in a more clearly defined polity. As a result, Germany's political regime as a whole started to benefit from national histories of the state, which depicted the transition from Prussia's defeat in 1806 to Germany's pursuit of *Weltpolitik* after 1896 as an almost linear process of national consolidation, administrative progress, and military victory. As state intervention increased, the German political system was also associated with other components of national identity such as industrial growth and social insurance. In short, the stabilization of Germany's constitutional regime and the politicization of the German nation-state bestowed on the *Kaiserreich* the appearance of historical legitimacy and functional efficiency. All such impressions served to reinforce the political component of national identity.

In Germany, in particular, politics had been kept separate from the nation. In France and Britain, notwithstanding the state tradition of the former and the ambiguity of cultural identities in the latter, the sphere of politics was wider. Such a comparison would not have surprised the majority of Wilhelmine Germans who, as has been seen, had singled out the French regime as a cautionary example of a politicized nation-state. During the decades before the First World War, however, political and national spheres in Germany, too, were being redrawn: national identity was becoming broader, with the introduction of political elements, but it was also being discussed more frequently and less cautiously in public by politicians and journalists. The borderline between politics and national identity had become less pronounced and in some areas, such as that concerning constitutional questions, had disappeared altogether. Ironically, one of the main consequences of this fusion of spheres was the emergence of rival nationalisms, as competing versions of the nation and national identity were transformed, partly as a result of more open discussion in the press and the Reichstag, into political ideologies. 'In older nation-states,' noted Meinecke, 'there was, as a rule, no doubt about who was the head and who constituted the limbs which responded to it. Yet, in younger nation-states, where the most diverse individualities and social groups seize the idea of the nation and project themselves onto it, there is no end to the doubt and struggle over the issue.'[144] The fact that conflicting nationalisms were more strident and popular in Germany than in France or Britain demonstrated that the relationship between politics and the nation was still closer and more problematic under the *Kaiserreich* than under the Third Republic or the British monarchy. Nevertheless, from the point of view of German history, nationalist ideologies resulted, not from the nationalization of politics, but from the politicization of the nation-state, as national affairs were subjected for the first time since the 1870s to party-political and extra-parliamentary debate, and as the German nation-state came to be regarded, amongst other things, as a political system. Nationalism was a sign that a significant number of Germans were beginning to accept a British and French model of politics and national identity, even though they had rejected British and French paradigms of a parliamentary regime. Paradoxically, the Reich was coming to resemble the Third Republic, as a consequence of German discussion of national affairs, at the same time as many Wilhelmine Germans had come to reject France's system of government, as a result of cross-party scepticism of parliamentarism.

---

[144] Meinecke, *Weltbürgertum und Nationalstaat*, 13. See also R. vom Bruch, 'Massengesellschaft im Aufbruch', in A. Nitschke et al., *Jahrhundertwende. Der Aufbruch in die Moderne 1880–1930* (2 vols.; Reinbek b. Hamburg, 1990), i. 100–10.

In other words, whilst debates about political institutions in Germany continued to diverge from those in other Western European countries, discussion of national identity had started to converge with a Western European model. In this limited sense, Germany was moving towards the West.

SELECT BIBLIOGRAPHY

PRIMARY SOURCES

Archival Sources

Bundesarchiv I, Koblenz

Bernhard von Bülow papers, NL 16/151, 153–5, 179.
Philipp, Fürst zu Eulenburg und Hertefeld papers, NL 29/29, 53, 85.
Chlodwig, Fürst zu Hohenlohe-Schillingsfürst papers, NL/1368.
Oswald von Richthofen papers, NL 165/17.

Bundesarchiv II, Potsdam

Reichskanzlei, RK 11705–7.
Friedrich von Holstein papers, 90 Ho 5.
Ida von Stülpnagel-Dargitz papers, 90 Stu 1.

Politisches Archiv des Auswärtigen Amtes, Bonn

Die Finanzen Frankreichs, R6673–84.
Französische Finanzinstitute, R6689.
Die Militärangelegenheiten Frankreichs, R6740–56.
Die Marine-Angelegenheiten Frankreichs, R6678–788.
Die Kirchen und Schulangelegenheiten Frankreichs, R6821–30.
Französische Staatsmänner, R7019–42.
Präsidenten der französischen Republik, R7056–70.
Diverse Personalien, R7105–8.
Die französische Ministerien, R7125–35.
Das diplomatische Corps in Paris, R7160–2.
Parlamentarische Angelegenheiten Frankreichs, R7170–8.
Die Pariser Welt-Ausstellung im Jahre 1900, R7187–9.
Agenten und Spione in Frankreich, R7201–19.
Agent J. Hansen in Paris, R7220.
Die auswärtige Politik Frankreichs, R7282–3.
AA Botschaft Paris, 185a and b, Die Dreyfus-Sache 1899.

Printed Sources

Newspapers and Periodicals

Agrarpolitische   *Allgemeine konservative*
Wochenschrift   *Monatsschrift für*

*das christliche
   Deutschland*
Bayerischer Kurier
Berliner Blatt
Berliner Börsen-Courier
Berliner Börsenzeitung
Berliner Illustrirte Zeitung
Berliner Morgenpost
Berliner Neueste Nachrichten
Berliner Tageblatt
Berliner Volkszeitung
B.Z. am Mittag
Christliche Welt
Deutsche Juristenzeitung
Deutsche Kurier
*Deutsche Monatsschrift für
   das gesamte Leben der
   Gegenwart*
Deutsche Revue
Deutsche Tageszeitung
*Deutsche Volkswirtschaftliche
   Correspondenz*
Deutsche Zeitung
Dresdner Nachrichten
Dresdner Neueste Nachrichten
Fränkischer Kurier
Fränkischer Volksfreund
Frankfurter Zeitung
Freisinnige Zeitung
Gegenwart
Germania
Grenzboten
Hamburger Nachrichten
Hamburgischer Correspondent
Hannoverscher Courier
Die Hilfe
Historisch-politische Blätter
Hochland
*Internationale Monatsschrift
   für Wissenschaft, Kunst und
   Technik*
*Jahrbuch des öffentlichen
   Rechts der Gegenwart*
Kieler Neueste Nachrichten

Kladderadatsch
Kölnische Volkszeitung
Kölnische Zeitung
*Königsberger Allgemeine
   Zeitung*
Konservative Monatsschrift
Leipziger Neueste Nachrichten
Leipziger Volkszeitung
März
Münchner Allgemeine Zeitung
Münchner Neueste Nachrichten
Die Nation
National-Zeitung
Neue Preußische Zeitung
Die Neue Zeit
Norddeutsche Allgemeine Zeitung
Patria
Politisch-anthropologische Revue
Posener Tageblatt
Die Post
Preußische Jahrbücher
Der Reichsbote
Rheinisch-Westfälische Zeitung
Schlesische Volkszeitung
Schlesische Zeitung
Simplicissimus
Soziale Praxis
Sozialistische Monatshefte
Staatsbürger-Zeitung
Stimmen aus Maria Laach
Der Tag
Tägliche Rundschau
Ulk
Die Umschau
Vorwärts
Vossische Zeitung
Der Wahre Jacob
Die Wahrheit
Welt
Die Welt am Montag
Weser-Zeitung
Der Westfale
Die Zeit
Die Zukunft

Memoirs and Correspondence

Brandt, M. v., *Dreiunddreissig Jahre in Ostasien* (3 vols.; Leipzig, 1901).

Braun, M. v., *Von Ostpreußen bis Texas* (Stollhamm, Oldberg, 1955).

Bülow, B. v., *Deutsche Politik* (Berlin, 1916).

—— *Deutschland und die Mächte*, ii (Dresden, 1929).

—— *Denkwürdigkeiten* (4 vols.; Berlin, 1930–1).

Busch, M., *Tagebuchblätter*, ii and iii (Leipzig, 1899).

Bußmann, W. (ed.), *Staatssekretär Herbert von Bismarck. Aus seiner politischen Privatkorrespondenz* (Göttingen, 1964).

Curtius, F. (ed.), *Chlodwig, Fürst zu Hohenlohe-Schillingsfürst. Denkwürdigkeiten* (2 vols.; Stuttgart, 1906).

Die Deutschen Dokumente zum Kriegsausbruch, 1914, i (Berlin, 1921).

Dix, A. (ed.), *Ludwig Raschdau. Der Weg in die Weltkrise* (Berlin, 1934).

Eckardstein, H. v., *Lebenserinnerungen und politische Denkwürdigkeiten* (3 vols.; Leipzig, 1919).

Eulenburg-Hertenfeld, P. zu, *Erlebnisse an deutschen und fremden Höfen* (Leipzig, 1934).

Fisher, M. H., and Rich, N. (eds.), *Die Geheimen Papiere Friedrich von Holsteins* (4 vols.; Göttingen, 1956).

Franke, O., *Erinnerungen aus zwei Welten* (Berlin, 1954).

Goetz, W. v. (ed.), *Briefe Kaiser Wilhelms II an den Zaren 1894 bis 1914* (Leipzig, 1922).

Haller, J. (ed.), *Philipp zu Eulenburg-Hertenfeld. Aus 50 Jahren. Erinnerungen, Tagebücher und Briefe aus dem Nachlaß des Fürsten* (Berlin, 1923).

Hammann, O., *Der neue Kurs* (Berlin, 1918).

—— *Um den Kaiser. Erinnerungen aus den Jahren 1906–1909* (Berlin, 1919).

—— *Der missverstandene Bismarck* (Berlin, 1921).

—— *Bilder aus der letzten Kaiserzeit* (Berlin, 1922).

—— *Deutschlands Schicksalsjahre, 1870–1918. Diplomatische Vorgeschichte*, i (Berlin, 1925).

Hindenburg, H. v., *Am Rande zweier Jahrhunderte* (Berlin, 1938).

Hohenlohe, A. v., *Aus meinem Leben* (Frankfurt a.M., 1925).

Hohenlohe-Schillingsfürst, C. z., *Denkwürdigkeiten der Reichskanzlerzeit* (Stuttgart, 1931).

Holborn, H. (ed.), *Aufzeichnungen und Erinnerungen aus dem Leben des Botschafters Joseph Maria Radowitz* (2 vols.; Berlin, 1925).

Hutten–Czapski, B. v., *Sechzig Jahre Politik und Gesellschaft*, i (Berlin, 1936).

Jäckh, E. (ed.), *Kiderlen-Wächter. Der Staatsmann und Mensch. Briefwechsel und Nachlass* (2 vols.; Berlin, 1924).

Jagemann, E. v., *Fünfundsiebzig Jahre des Erlebens und Erfahrens* (Heidelberg, 1925).

Kühlmann, R. v., *Erinnerungen* (Heidelberg, 1948).

Lancken Wakenitz, O. v. der, *Meine dreissig Dienstjahre, 1888–1918* (Berlin, 1931).

Lepsius, J., and Mendelssohn-Bartholdy, A. (eds.), *Die Große Politik der europäischen Kabinette 1871–1914,* ix and xi (Berlin, 1922–7).

Lichnowsky, K. M. v., *Auf dem Wege zum Abgrund,* i (Dresden, 1927).

Mohl, O. v., *Fünfzig Jahre Reichsdienst* (Leipzig, 1920).

Monts, A. v., *Politische Aufsätze* (Berlin, 1916).

Müller, K. A. v. (ed.), *Fürsten Chlodwig zu Hohenlohe-Schillingsfürst. Denkwürdigkeiten der Reichskanzlerzeit* (Berlin, 1931).

Nowak, K. F., and Thimme, F. (eds.), *Erinnerungen und Gedanken des Botschafters Anton Graf Monts* (Berlin, 1932).

Penzler, J. (ed.), *Fürst Bülows Reden* (3 vols.; Berlin, 1907).

Pückler, K. v., *Aus meinem Diplomatenleben* (Schweidnitz, 1934).

Riezler, K., *Die Erforderlichkeit des Unmöglichen* (Munich, 1913).

—— [pseud. Ruedorffer, J. J.], *Grundzüge der Weltpolitik in der Gegenwart* (Berlin, 1913).

Rogge, H. (ed.), *Friedrich von Holstein. Lebensbekenntnis in Briefen an eine Frau* (Berlin, 1932).

—— (ed.), *Holstein und Harden* (Munich, 1959).

—— (ed.), *Holstein und Hohenlohe* (Stuttgart, 1957).

Röhl, J. C. G. (ed.), *Zwei deutsche Fürsten zur Kriegsschuldfrage* (Düsseldorf, 1971).

—— *Philipp Eulenburgs politische Korrespondenz* (3 vols.; Boppard, 1976).

Rosen, F., *Aus einem diplomatischen Wanderleben,* i (Berlin, 1931).

Schlözer, K. v., *Letzte römischer Briefe, 1882–1894* (Berlin, 1924).

—— *Briefe eines Diplomaten* (Stuttgart, 1957).

Schoen, W. E. v., *Erlebtes. Beiträge zur politischen Geschichte der neuesten Zeit* (Berlin, 1921).

Thimme, F. (ed.), 'Aus dem Nachlaß des Fürsten Radolin', *Berliner Monatshefte,* 15 (1937), 725–63, 844–902.

Vietsch, E. v. (ed.), *Gegen die Vernunft. Der Briefwechsel zwischen Paul Graf von Metternich und Wilhelm Solf, 1915–1918* (Bremen, 1964).

William II, *My Memoirs, 1878–1918* (London, 1922).

Zechlin, W., *Fröhliche Lebensfahrt. Diplomatische und undiplomatische Erinnerungen* (Berlin, 1936).

Treatises and Textbooks

Acht, A., *Der moderne französische Syndikalismus* (Jena, 1911).

Adler, J. B., *Die französische Revolutionund die Pariser Commune in sozialistischen Anschauungen* (Mainz, 1892).

Aichholz, C., *Mahnruf an die Franzosen* (Dresden, 1907).

Andler, M., *Die Städteschulden in Frankreich und Preußen und ihre wirtschaftliche Bedeutung* (Stuttgart, 1911).

Anon., *Das Dreyfus-Bilderbuch. Karikaturen aller Völker über die Dreyfus-Affaire* (Berlin, 1899).

—— *Das heutige Frankreich* (Hamm, 1903).

Anon., *Deutsche und französische Kunst. Eine Auseinandersetzung deutscher Künstler, Galerieleiter, Sammler und Schriftsteller*, 2nd edn. (Munich, 1912).

—— *Deutschland und Frankreich. Politisch und militärisch verglichen* (Stuttgart, 1912).

—— *Die französische Revolution im Spiegel deutscher Dichtung* (Berlin, 1889).

Anton, G. K., *Die Entwicklung des französischen Kolonialreiches* (Dresden, 1897).

Below, G. v., *Das parlamentarische Wahlrecht in Deutschland* (Berlin, 1909).

Bernstein, E., *Parlamentarismus und Sozialdemokratie* (Berlin, 1906).

Birch-Hirschfeld, A., and Suchier, H., *Geschichte der französischen Litteratur von den ältesten Zeiten bis zur Gegenwart* (Leipzig, 1900).

Blum, H., *Die Heiligen unserer Sozialdemokratie und die Pariser Kommune von 1871 in ihrer wahren Gestalt. Geschichtlichen Erinnerungen zur Warnung aller guten Deutschen* (Wurzen, 1898).

Boden, C. F., *Zur Psychologie der französischen Diplomatie* (Braunschweig, 1912).

Brandenburg, E., *Martin Luther's Anschauung vom Staate und der Gesellschaft* (Halle, 1901).

Brandt, A. v., *Beiträge zur Geschichte der französischen Handelspolitik von Colbert bis zur Gegenwart* (Leipzig, 1896).

Brentano, L., *Die Schrecken des überwiegenden Industriestaats* (Berlin, 1901).

—— *Konkrete Bedingungen der Volkswirtschaft* (Leipzig, 1924).

Brie, S., *Die gegenwärtige Verfassung Frankreichs. Staatsrechtliche Erörterungen* (Breslau, 1888).

Brüggemann, F., and Groppler, F., *Volk- und Fortbildungs-Schulwesen Frankreichs im Jahre 1900* (Berlin, 1901).

Bücher, K., *Die Entstehung der Volkswirtschaft*, i, 7th edn. (Tübingen, 1910).

Cartellieri, A., *Deutschland und Frankreich im Wandel der Jahrhunderte* (Jena, 1914).

Chamberlain, H. S., *Die Grundlagen des neunzehnten Jahrhunderts*, i, 10th edn. (Munich, 1912).

Cohn, G., *System der Nationalökonomie* (3 vols.; Stuttgart, 1885–98).

Dank, J., *Das französische Volksschulwesen am Ende des 19. Jahrhunderts* (Berlin, 1898).

Dannheisser, E., *Die Entwicklungsgeschichte der französischen Literatur* (Zweibrücken, 1901).

Delbrück, H., *Regierung und Volkswille* (Berlin, 1914).

—— *Vor und nach dem Weltkrieg. Historische und politische Aufsätze 1902–1925* (Berlin, 1926).

Deutsch, E. [pseud. Pudor, H.], *Studien und Skizzen aus der französischen Hauptstadt* (Dresden and Leipzig, 1890).

Dierks, O., *Die dramatische Bearbeitung nationaler Stoffe in Frankreich* (Münster, 1911).

Dilthey, W., *Einleitung in die Geisteswissenschaften* (Leipzig and Berlin, 1922).

Engel, E., *Psychologie der Französischen Literatur*, 4th edn. (Berlin, 1904).

Engels, F., *Einleitung* to Marx, K., *Der Bürgerkrieg in Frankreich*, 3rd edn. (Berlin, 1891).

Erzberger, M., *Politik und Völkerleben* (Paderborn, 1914).

Exner, M., *Die französische Armee in Krieg und Frieden*, 2nd edn. (Berlin, 1894).

Feld, W., *Die Kinder-Armenpflege in Elsaß-Lothringen und Frankreich* (Dresden, 1908).

Feldmann, S., *Paris gestern und heute. Kulturporträts* (Berlin, 1909).

Fernau, H., *Die französische Demokratie. Sozialpolitische Studien aus Frankreichs Kulturwerkstatt*, (Munich and Leipzig, 1914).

Franke, B., *Der Ausbau des heutigen Schutzzollsystems in Frankreich und seine Wirkungen im Lichte der Handelsstatistik* (Leipzig, 1903).

Fried, A., *Deutschland und Frankreich. Ein Wort über die Notwendigkeit und Möglichkeit einer deutsch-französischen Verständigung* (Berlin, 1905).

Friedrich, J. K. J., *Die Trennung von Staat und Kirche in Frankreich* (Giessen, 1907).

Geigel, R., *Die Trennung von Staat und Kirche* (Munich, 1908).

Gierke, O. v., *Die historische Rechtschule und die Germanisten* (Berlin, 1903).

Gloege, G., *Das höhere Schulwesen Frankreichs* (Berlin, 1913).

Gneist, R. v., *Der Rechtsstaat und die Verwaltungsgerichte in Deutschland*, 3rd edn. (Darmstadt, 1966).

Goldstein, J., *Die vermeintlichen und die wirklichen Ursachen des Bevölkerungsstillstandes in Frankreich* (Munich, 1898).

—— *Bevölkerungsprobleme und Berufsgliederung in Frankreich* (Berlin, 1900).

Gumplowicz, L., *Nationalismus und Internationalismus im 19. Jahrhundert* (Berlin, 1902).

Gundlach, F., *Französische Lyrik seit der Großen Revolution* (Leipzig, 1904).

Haas, J., *Frankreich. Land und Staat* (Heidelberg, 1910).

Hasbach, W., *Die Demokratie* (Jena, 1912).

Heckert, O., *Vergleich der deutschen und französischen Wehrverhältnisse, Landstreitkräfte und Heeresorganisationen* (Leipzig, 1912).

Hegemann, C., *Die Entwicklung des französischen Großbankbetriebes* (Münster i.W., 1908).

Heinzig, B., *Die Schule Frankreichs in ihrer historischen Entwicklung besonders seit dem deutsch-französischen Kriege von 1870–71* (Leipzig and Frankfurt a.M., 1891).

Heller, H. J., *Real-Encyclopädie des französischen Staats- und Gesellschaftslebens* (Oppeln and Leipzig, 1888).

Henger, H., *Die Kapitalsanlage der Franzosen in Wertpapieren mit besonderer Berücksichtigung der Kapitalsanlagein Handel und Industrie* (Stuttgart and Berlin, 1913).

Henrici, E., *Dreißig Jahre nachher. Betrachtungen über das Verhältnis zwischen Deutschland und Frankreich* (Berlin, 1901).

Hermann, K. H., *Das Besitzsteuerproblem in Deutschland und Frankreich in seiner heutigen Lösung* (Berlin, 1912).

Hillebrand, K., *Zeiten, Völker und Menschen*, i. *Frankreich und die Franzosen*, 4th edn. (Strasbourg, 1898).

Hintze, O., *Soziologie und Geschichte*, ed. G. Oestreich, 2nd revised edn. (Göttingen, 1962).

—— *Staat und Verfassung*, ed. G. Oestreich, 2nd revised edn. (Göttingen, 1962).

Hirschstein, H., *Die französische Revolution im deutschen Drama und Epos nach 1815* (Stuttgart, 1912).

Hübner, M., *Eine Pforte zum schwarzen Erdteil* (Halle a. Salle, 1904).

Immanuel, F., *Was man vom französischen Heere wissen muß* (Berlin, 1914).

Jellinek, G., 'Regierung und Parlament', *Vorträge der Gehe-Stiftung zu Dresden* (Dresden, 1909).

—— *Ausgewählte Schriften und Reden* (Berlin, 1911).

—— *Allgemeine Staatslehre*, 3rd edn. (Berlin, 1914).

Junker, H. P., *Grundriß der Geschichte der französischen Literatur von ihren Anfängen bis zur Gegenwart*, 6th edn. (Münster i.W., 1909).

Kautsky, K., *Parlamentarismus und Demokratie*, 2nd revised edn. (Stuttgart, 1911).

—— *Selected Political Writings*, ed. P. Goode (London, 1983).

Kirchhoff, A., *Was ist national?* (Halle, 1902).

Knies, K., *Die politische Oekonomie vom geschichtlichen Standpuncte*, 2nd revised edn. (Brunswick, 1883).

Koettschau, C., *Westeuropa kosakisch oder geeint. Die Notwendigkeit einer französisch-deutschen Versöhnung* (Strasbourg, 1890).

Kuhn, H. N., *Aus dem modernen Babylon. Pariser Bilder* (Cologne, 1892).

—— *Frankreich an der Zeitwende* (*Fin de Siècle*) (Hamburg, 1895).

Kulemann, W., *Die Berufsvereine*, iv, 2nd revised edn. (Berlin, 1913).

Landsberg, H., *Das galante Frankreich in Anekdoten*, 2nd edn. (Stuttgart, 1910).

Lapouge, G. V. de, 'Die Rassengeschichte der französischen Nation', *Politisch-anthropologische Revue*, 1 (1905), 16–35.

Lehmann, M., *Freiharr vom Stein* (Leipzig, 1903).

Lenz, M., *Martin Luther* (Berlin, 1883).

—— *Kleine historische Schriften* (Munich, 1910).

—— *Geschichte Bismarcks*, 4th edn. (Leipzig, 1913).

List, F., *Das nationale System der politischen Oekonomie*, 5th edn. (Jena, 1928).

Loewenthal, E., *Ein französisch-deutscher Ausgleich im Hinblick auf die Vorgänge in Rußland* (Berlin, 1891).

Lübke, W., *Grundriss der Kunstgeschichte*, v, 14th edn. (Esslingen a.N., 1909).

Lüttge, W., *Die Trennung von Staat und Kirche in Frankreich und der französische Protestantismus* (Tübingen, 1912).

Luxemburg, R., *Sozialreform oder Revolution?* (Leipzig, 1899).

—— *Gesammelte Werke* (Berlin, 1974).

Mahrenholtz, R., *Frankreich. Seine Geschichte, Verfassung und staatliche Einrichtungen* (Leipzig, 1897).

Mann-Tiechler, K. H. v., *Deutschland und Frankreich. Politische und militärische Betrachtungen am Anfang des zwanzigsten Jahrhunderts* (Berlin and Leipzig, 1903).

Marcks, E., *Kaiser Wilhelm I* (Berlin, 1897).

Marx, A., *Die französische Handelsgesetzgebung* (Bonn, 1911).

Mehrens, B., *Die Entstehung und Entwicklung der grossen französischen Kreditinstitute mit Berücksichtigung ihres Einflusses auf die wirtschaftliche Entwicklung Frankreichs* (Stuttgart and Berlin, 1911).

Meinecke, F., *Weltbürgertum und Nationalstaat*, 7th edn. (Berlin, 1927).

—— *Cosmopolitanism and the National State* (Princeton, 1970).

Mey, O., *Die Schulen und der organische Bau der Volksschule in Frankreich mit Berücksichtigung der neuesten Reformen* (Berlin, 1893).

Meyer, E., *Die Entwicklung der französischen Literatur seit 1830* (Gotha, 1898).

Meyer, H., *Die Einkommensteuerprojekte in Frankreich bis 1887* (Berlin, 1905).

Müllendorff, P., *Staat und katholische Kirche in Frankreich und Preußen* (Berlin, 1903).

Mutermilch, L., *Crédit foncier de France und seine Bedeutung für den land-wirtschaftlichen Grundkredit in Frankreich* (Leipzig, 1893).

Muther, R., *Geschichte der Malerei*, iii, 4th edn. (Berlin, 1922).

Naumann, F., *Demokratie und Kaisertum*, 4th revised edn. (Berlin, 1905).

Neumann, F., *Volk und Nation* (Leipzig, 1888).

Nordau, M., *Paris unter der dritten Republik. Neue Bilder aus dem wahren Milliardenlande*, 2nd edn. (Leipzig, 1881).

Oberle, E., *Wird Frankreich aus der Reihe der leitenden Völker verschwinden?* (Strasbourg, 1905).

Oncken, H., *Der Kaiser und die Nation* (Heidelberg, 1913).

Osten, M. v. der, *Die Fachvereine und die sociale Bewegung in Frankreich* (Leipzig, 1891).

Ostwold, W., *Frankreich als Friedensbringer. Eine deutsch-französische Erörterung* (Berlin, 1911).

Raif, A. F., *Die Urteile der Deutschen über die französische Nationalität im Zeitalter der Revolution und der deutschen Erhebung* (Berlin and Leipzig, 1911).

Reber, J., *Ein Blick auf Frankreichs Schulwesen. Eine pädagogische Skizze* (Aschaffenburg, 1897).

Reichenbach, R., *Revanche! Die friedensgefährlichen Tendenzen der französischen Volkserziehung in Schule und Heer* (Leipzig, 1911).

Reuter, W., *Das kaufmännische Unterrichtswesen in Frankreich* (Leipzig, 1909).

Richter, J. P., *Das französische Volksschulwesen* (Halle a.G., 1891).

Roscher, W., *Grundlagen der Nationalökonomie*, 20th edn. (Stuttgart, 1892).

—— *Politik* (Stuttgart, 1892).

Rühlmann, P., *Der staatsbürgerliche Unterricht in Frankreich (instruction morale et civique)* (Leipzig, 1912).

Sägmüller, J. B., *Die Trennung von Kirche und Staat. Eine kanonistisch-dogmatische Studie* (Mainz, 1907).

Samosch, S., *Pariser Feste und Streifzüge in die Normandie, Bretagne und Vendée* (Minden i. W, 1897).

Sarrazin, J., *Kreyssigs Geschichte der französischen Nationalliteratur*, ii, 6th edn. (Berlin, 1889).

Sarrazin, J., *Das moderne Drama der Franzosen in seinen Hauptvertretern*, 2nd edn. (Stuttgart, 1893).

Schäffle, A., *Deutsche Kern- und Zeitfragen* (Berlin, 1894).

Schermann, J. E., *Von Paris zurück. Kunstbetrachtungen und französisches Unterrichtswesen nach der Weltausstellung 1900* (Ravensburg, 1901).

Schirmacher, K., *Deutschland und Frankreich seit 35 Jahren* (Berlin, 1906).

—— *Die Trennung von Staat und Kirche in Frankreich* (Leipzig, 1908).

—— *Was ist national?* (Posen, 1912).

Schmidt, G., *Der Einfluß der Bank- und Geldverfassung auf die Diskontopolitik im Deutschen Reich, in England, Frankreich, Österreich-Ungarn, Belgien und den Niederlanden* (Leipzig, 1910).

Schmidt, K. E., *Im Lande der Freiheit, Gleichheit und Brüderlichkeit* (Berlin and Stuttgart, 1908).

Schmitz, O. A. H., *Das Land der Wirklichkeit. Der französischen Gesellschafts-probleme*, 5th edn. (Munich, 1914).

Schmoller, G., *Zur Geschichte der deutschen Kleingewerbe im 19. Jahrhundert* (Halle, 1870).

—— *Grundriß der allgemeinen Volkswirtschaftslehre* (2 vols.; Leipzig, 1900–4).

—— *Skizze einer Finanzgeschichte von Frankreich, Österreich, England und Preußen (1500–1900). Historische Betrachtungen über Staatenbildungen und Finanzentwicklung* (Leipzig, 1909).

Schnitzer, J., *Trennung von Kirche und Staat in Frankreich* (Bern, 1912).

Schomann, E., *Französische Utopisten und ihr Frauenideal* (Berlin, 1911).

Schultz, K., *Die französische Volksschule* (Bielefeld, 1905).

Schwander, R., *Armenpolitik Frankreichs während der großen Revolution und die Weiterentwicklung der französischen Armengesetzgebung bis zur Gegenwart* (Strasbourg, 1904).

Schwemer, R., *Das höhere Schulwesen in Frankreich. Eine pädagogische Skizze* (Frankfurt a.M., 1895).

Semmig, H., *Czar, Empereur und Republik, oder Frankreich vor dem Richterstuhl des gesunden Menschenverstandes* (Leipzig, 1894).

Simmel, G., *Schriften zur Soziologie*, ed. H.-J. Dahme and O. Rammstedt (Frankfurt a.M., 1983).

Soltau, O., *Die französischen Kolonialbanken* (Strasbourg, 1907).

Sombart, W., *Der Bourgeois* (Berlin, 1987).

—— *Sozialismus und die soziale Bewegung*, 9th edn. (Jena, 1896).

Sommerfeld, A., *Frankreichs Ende im Jahre 19??. Ein Zukunftsbild* (Berlin, 1912).

Spahn, M., *Der Kampf um die Schule in Frankreich und Deutschland* (Kempten and Munich, 1907).

Springer, A., *Handbuch der Kunstgeschichte*, 5th revised edn. (Leipzig, 1909).

Steinhauser, A., *Neustes aus Frankreich. Christliche Demokratie* (Cologne, 1899).

Sternfeld, R., *Französische Geschichte*, 2nd edn. (Leipzig, 1908).

Stoklossa, P., 'Der Inhalt der Zeitung. Eine statistische Untersuchung', *Zeitschrift für die gesamte Staatswissenschaft*, 66 (1910), 555–65.

Sturmhoefel, K., *Deutsches Nationalgefühl und Einheitsstreben im 19. Jahrhundert* (Leipzig, 1904).

Süpfle, T., *Geschichte des deutschen Kultureinflusses auf Frankreich mit besonderer Berücksichtigung der literarischen Einwirkung* (2 vols.; Gotha, 1886–90).

Sybel, H. v., *Was wir von Frankreich lernen können* (Bonn, 1872).

—— *Geschichte der Revolutionszeit von 1789–1800*, 4th edn. (Frankfort a.M., 1882).

Tecklenburg, A., *Die Entwicklung des Wahlrechts in Frankreich seit 1789* (Tübingen, 1911).

Tönnies, F., *Gemeinschaft und Gesellschaft*, 8th edn. (Leipzig, 1935).

Treitschke, H. v., 'Die Aufgabe des Geschichtsschreibers', *Historische Zeitschrift*, 76 (1896).

—— *Politik* (Leipzig, 1898).

—— *Historische und politische Aufsätze*, iii, 6th edn. (Leipzig, 1903).

—— *Selections from Treitschke's Lectures on Politics* (London, 1914).

Treuherz, W., *Die zollpolitische Assimilationsgesetzgebung Frankreichs und ihre Wirkung auf die Kolonien* (Jena, 1913).

Tyszka, C. v., *Löhne und Lebenskosten in Westeuropa im 19. Jahrhundert. Nebst einem Anhang: Lebenskosten deutscher und westeuropäischer Arbeiter früher und jetzt* (Munich and Leipzig, 1914).

Unruh, F., *Das patriotische Drama im heutigen dem Frankreich* (Königsberg, 1891).

Verhandlungen des Vereins für Sozialpolitik in Wien, 1909 (Leipzig, 1910).

Vogel, K., *Die dritte französische Republik bis 1895* (Berlin, 1895).

Wagner, A., *Die akademische Nationalökonomie und der Socialismus* (Berlin, 1895).

—— *Vom Territorialstaat zur Weltmacht* (Berlin, 1900).

—— *Agrar- und Industriestaat* (Jena, 1901).

—— *Theoretische Sozialökonomik* (Leipzig, 1907).

Weber, M., *Verhandlungen des Vereins für Sozialpolitik in Wien, 1909* (Leipzig, 1910).

—— *Gesammelte politische Schriften*, 2nd revised edn. (Tübingen, 1958).

—— *Max Weber on Charisma and Institution Building*, ed. S. N. Eisenstadt (Chicago, 1968).

—— *Wirtschaft und Gesellschaft*, 5th edn. (Tübingen, 1972).

—— *The Protestant Ethic and the Spirit of Capitalism* (London, 1987).

—— *Max Weber: Gesamtausgabe*, v, ed. M. Baier, M. R. Lepsius, W. J. Mommsen, W. Schluchter, and J. Winckelmann (Tübingen, 1990).

Weckmann, G., *Die Trennung von Kirche und Staat in Frankreich vom volkswirtschaftlichen Standpunkte aus* (Hamm, 1914).

Weigert, M., *Die Volksschule und der gewerbliche Unterricht in Frankreich* (Berlin, 1890).

Wiegler, P., *Französische Rebellen. Abriß einer Geschichte des Enthusiasmus in Frankreich* (Berlin, 1903).

Wolf, J., *System der Sozialpolitik*, i (Stuttgart, 1892).

—— *Der Geburtenrückgang. Die Rationalisierung des Sexuallebens in unserer Zeit* (Jena, 1912).

—— *Die Volkswirtschaft der Gegenwart und Zukunft* (Leipzig, 1912).

Woltmann, L., *Die Germanen und die Renaissance in Italien* (Leipzig, 1905).
—— *Die Germanen in Frankreich* (Leipzig, 1907).
Zimmermann, A., *Die Kolonialpolitik Frankreichs von den Anfängen bis zur Gegenwart* (Berlin, 1901).
Zwicker, A., *Im Raubstaat der Jakobiner und daneben. Französisches und spanisches aus Europas wildem Westen* (Spaichingen, 1910).

SECONDARY SOURCES

Abelein, M., and Bondy, F., *Deutschland und Frankreich. Geschichte einer wechselvollen Beziehung* (Düsseldorf, 1973).
Abraham, R., *Rosa Luxemburg* (Oxford, 1989).
Alter, P., *Nationalismus* (Frankfurt a.M., 1985).
Anderson, B., *Imagined Communities*, 2nd revised edn. (London, 1991).
Anderson, M. L., *Windthorst: A Political Biography* (Oxford, 1981).
—— 'The Kulturkampf and the Course of German History', *Central European History*, 19 (1986), 82–115.
Anderson, P. R., *The Background of Anti-English Feeling in Germany, 1890–1902* (Washington, 1939).
Applegate, C., *A Nation of Provincials: The German Idea of Heimat* (Oxford, 1990).
Bariéty, J., and Poidevin, R., *Les Relations franco-allemandes, 1815–1975* (Paris, 1977).
Barlow, I. M., *The Agadir Crisis* (Durham, NC, 1940).
Barraclough, G., *From Agadir to Armageddon: Anatomy of a Crisis* (London, 1982).
Bärsch, C.-E., *Der Staatsbegriff in der neueren deutschen Staatslehre und seine theoretischen Implikationen* (Berlin, 1974).
Bauer, R., *Das Bild des Deutschen in der französischen und das Bild des Französen in der deutschen Literatur* (Düsseldorf, 1965).
Becker, W. (ed.), *Die Minderheit als Mitte. Die deutsche Zentrumspartei in der Innenpolitik des Reiches, 1871–1933* (Paderborn, 1986).
Beetham, D., *Max Weber and the Theory of Modern Politics* (Cambridge, 1987).
Bendikat, E., 'Deutschland und Frankreich in der Wahlkampfagitation der Parteien 1884–1889', *Francia*, 17 (1990), 15–30.
Benz, W., and Graml, H. (eds.), *Aspekte deutscher Außenpolitik im 20. Jahrhundert* (Stuttgart, 1976).
Berghahn, V. R., *Der Tirpitz-Plan* (Düsseldorf, 1971).
—— *Germany and the Approach of War in 1914* (London, 1973).
—— *Rüstung und Machtpolitik. Zur Anatomie des 'Kalten Krieges' vor 1914* (Düsseldorf, 1973).
—— *Imperial Germany, 1871–1914* (Oxford, 1994).
Bisdorff, E., *Thomas Mann und Frankreich* (Luxemburg, 1980).
Blackbourn, D., *Class, Religion and Local Politics in Wilhelmine Germany: The Centre Party in Württemburg before 1914* (London, 1980).

—— *Germany, 1780–1918* (London, 1997).

—— and Eley, G., *The Peculiarities of German History: Bourgeois Society and Politics in Nineteenth-Century Germany* (Oxford, 1984).

—— and Evans, R. J. (eds.), *The German Bourgeoisie* (London, 1991).

Böckenförde, E. W., *Gesetz und gesetzgebende Gewalt* (Berlin, 1958).

—— 'Der verfassung styp der deutschen konstitutionellen Monarchie im 19. Jahrhundert', in E.-W. Böckenförde (ed.), *Moderne deutsche Verfassungsgeschichte*, 2nd edn. (Königstein, 1981).

Boldt, H., 'Parlamentarismustheorie. Bemerkungen zu ihrer Geschichte in Deutschland', *Der Staat*, 19 (1980), 385–412.

—— *Deutsche Verfassungsgeschichte*, ii (Munich, 1990).

Bott, G., *Deutsche Frankreichkunde 1900–1933* (Rheinfelden, 1982).

Brandt, P., and Groh, D., *Vaterlandslose Gesellen. Sozialdemokratie und Nation, 1860–1990* (Munich, 1992).

Breuilly, J. (ed.), *The State of Germany* (London, 1992).

—— *Nationalism and the State*, 2nd revised edn. (Manchester, 1993).

—— *The Formation of the First German Nation-State, 1800–1871* (London, 1996).

Brocke, B. vom (ed.), *Sombarts 'Moderner Kapitalismus'* (Munich, 1987).

Brubaker, R., *Citizenship and Nationhood in France and Germany* (Cambridge, Mass., 1992).

Bruch, R. vom, *Wissenschaft, Politik und öffentliche Meinung. Gelehrtenpolitik im wilhelminischen Deutschland* (Husum, 1980).

—— 'Massengesellschaft im Aufbruch', in A. Nitschke et al., *Jahrhundertwende. Der Aufbruch in die Moderne 1880–1930* (2 vols, Reinbek b. Hamburg, 1990).

—— Graf, F. W., and Hübinger, G. (eds.), *Kultur und Kulturwissenschaften um 1900. Krise der Moderne und Glaube an die Wissenschaft* (Stuttgart, 1988).

Buchner, R., *Die deutsch-französische Tragödie 1848–1864. Politische Beziehungen und psychologisches Verhältnis* (Würzburg, 1965).

—— *Die elsässische Frage und das deutsch-französische Verhältnis im 19. Jahrhundert* (Darmstadt, 1969).

Büsch, O., and Erbe, M. (eds.), *Otto Hintze und die moderne Geschichtswissenschaft* (Berlin, 1983).

—— and Sheehan, J. J. (eds.), *Die Rolle der Nation in der deutschen Geschichte und Gegenwart* (Berlin, 1985).

Bullock, N., and Read, J., *The Movement for Housing Reform in Germany and France, 1840–1914* (Cambridge, 1985).

Burgelin, H., 'Le Mythe de l'ennemi héréditaire dans les relations franco-allemandes', in *Documents. Revues des questions allemandes* (Paris, 1979), 76–88.

Bußmann, W., *Treitschke. Sein Welt- und Geschichtsbild* (Göttingen, 1952).

Calleo, D., *The German Problem Reconsidered* (Cambridge, 1978).

Carroll, E. M., *Germany and the Great Powers, 1860–1914: A Study in Public Opinion and Foreign Policy* (New York, 1938).

Carsten, F. L., *August Bebel und die Organisation der Massen* (Berlin, 1991).

Cecil, L., *The German Diplomatic Service, 1871–1914* (Princeton, 1976).

Chapman, B., *Police state* (London, 1970).

Cheval, R., 'L'Imagerie franco-allemande. Naissance et cheminement des représentations', *Revue d'Allemagne*, 2 (1973), 224–34.

Chickering, R., *'We Men Who Feel Most German': A Cultural Study of the Pan-German League, 1886–1914* (London, 1984).

Christadler, M., *Kriegserziehung im Jugendbuch. Literarische Mobilmachung in Deutschland und Frankreich vor 1914* (Frankfurt a.M., 1978).

—— (ed.), *Deutschland-Frankreich. Alte Klischees. Neue Bilder* (Duisburg, 1981).

Coetzee, M. S., *The German Army League: Popular Nationalism in Wilhelmine Germany* (Oxford, 1990).

Cohen, Y., and Manfrass, K. (eds.), *Frankreich und Deutschland: Forschung, Technologie und industrielle Entwicklung* (Munich, 1990).

Conze, W., and Groh, D., *Die Arbeiterbewegung in der nationalen Bewegung. Die deutsche Sozialdemokratie vor, während und nach der Reichsgründung* (Stuttgart, 1966).

Craig, G. A., *The Politics of the Prussian Army* (Oxford, 1955).

—— *From Bismarck to Adenauer: Aspects of German Statecraft* (Baltimore, 1958).

Czempiel, E.-O., *Das deutsche Dreyfus-Geheimnis. Eine Studie über den Einfluß des monarchischen Regierungssystems auf die Frankreichpolitik des Wilhelminischen Reiches* (Munich, 1966).

Dahrendorf, R., *Society and Democracy in Germany* (New York, 1967).

Dann, O., *Nation und Nationalismus in Deutschland* (Munich, 1993).

—— *Die deutsche Nation* (Vierow bei Greifswald, 1994).

Dehio, L., *Germany and World Politics in the Twentieth Century* (New York, 1959).

Demeter, K., *The German Officer Corps in Society and State, 1650–1945* (London, 1965).

Deutsch, K. W., *Nationalism and Social Communication* (Cambridge, Mass., 1953).

—— *Nationalism and its Alternatives* (New York, 1969).

Deutsch-Französisches Institut, Ludwigsburg, *Deutschland-Frankreich. Ludwigsburger Beiträge zum Problem der deutsch-französischen Beziehungen* (4 vols.; Stuttgart, 1954–66).

Deutsch-Französisches Kulturzentrum, Essen, *Deutschland-Frankreich. Höhen und Tiefen einer Zweierbeziehung* (Essen, 1988).

Dominick, R. H., *Wilhelm Liebknecht and German Social Democracy, 1869–1900* (Chapel Hill, NC, 1973).

Droz, J., *L'Allemagne et la révolution française* (Paris, 1949).

—— *Einfluß der deutschen Sozialdemokratie auf den französischen Sozialismus 1871–1914* (Opladen, 1973).

Ducatel, P., *Histoire de la IIIᵉ République vue à travers l'imagerie populaire et la presse satirique*, iii and iv (Paris, 1976).

Düding, D., *Der Nationalsoziale Verein 1896–1903* (Munich, 1972).

—— (ed.), *Öffentliche Festkultur: Politische Feste in Deutschland von der Aufklärung bis zum Ersten Weltkrieg* (Reinbek bei Hamburg, 1988).

Dumont, L., *L'Idéologie allemande: France-Allemagne et retour* (Paris, 1991).

Dyson, K. H. F., *The State Tradition in Western Europe* (Oxford, 1980).

Eksteins, M., *Rites of Spring* (London, 1989).

Eley, G., *Reshaping the German Right* (New Haven, 1980).

—— *From Unification to Nazism* (London, 1986).

Elm, L., *Zwischen Fortschritt und Reaktion. Geschichte der Parteien der liberalen Bourgeoisie in Deutschland 1893–1918* (Mainz, 1973).

Engelsing, R., *Analphabetentum und Lektüre. Zur Sozialgeschichte des Lesens in Deutschland zwischen feudaler und industrieller Gesellschaft* (Stuttgart, 1973).

Epstein, K., *Matthias Erzberger and the Dilemma of German Democracy* (Princeton, 1959).

Erbe, M. (ed.), *Friedrich Meinecke heute* (Berlin, 1981).

Espagne, M., and Werner, M. (eds.), *Transferts. Les Relations interculturelles dans l'espace franco-allemand* (Paris, 1988).

Evans, E. L., *The German Centre Party, 1870–1933* (Carbondale, Ill., 1981).

Evans, R. J., *The German Peasantry* (London, 1986).

—— *Rethinking German History* (London, 1987).

—— and Strandmann, H. Pogge v. (eds.), *The Coming of the First World War* (Oxford, 1988).

Farrar, L. L., Jr., *Arrogance and Anxiety: The Ambivalence of German Power, 1848–1914* (Iowa City, 1981).

Faulenbach, B. (ed.), *Geschichtswissenschaft in Deutschland* (Munich, 1974).

Fehrenbach, E., *Wandlungen des deutschen Kaisergedankens 1871–1918* (Munich, 1969).

—— 'Rankerenaissance und Imperialismus in der wilhelminischen Zeit', in B. Faulenbach, (ed.), *Geschichtswissenschaft in Deutschland* (Munich, 1974), 54–65.

Fink, C., Hull, I. V., and Knox, M. (eds.), *German Nationalism and the European Response, 1890–1945* (Norman, Okla., 1985).

Fischer, F., 'Das Bild Frankreichs in Deutschland in den Jahren vor dem ersten Weltkrieg', *Revue d'Allemagne*, 4 (1972), 505–19.

—— *Griff nach der Weltmacht. Die Kriegspolitik des kaiserlichen Deutschland 1914–1918* (Düsseldorf, 1961).

—— *Krieg der Illusionen. Die deutsche Politik von 1911 bis 1911* (Düsseldorf, 1969).

Fischer, H.-D., *Handbuch der politischen Presse in Deutschland 1480–1980* (Düsseldorf, 1981).

Fletcher, R., *Revisionism and Empire: Socialist Imperialism in Germany, 1897–1914* (London, 1984).

—— (ed.), *Bernstein to Brandt* (London, 1987).

Forum für Philosophie Bad Homburg, *Die Ideen von 1789 in der deutschen Rezeption* (Frankfurt a.M., 1989).

Fromm, H., *Bibliographie deutscher Übersetzungen aus dem französischen, 1700–1948* (Baden-Baden, 1948).

Fulbrook, M. (ed.), *German History since 1800* (London, 1997).

Gall, L., 'Bismarck und der Bonapartismus', *Historische Zeitschrift*, 223 (1976), 618–37.

—— (ed.), *Liberalismus* (Königstein, 1985).

Gasman, D., *The Scientific Origins of National Socialism: Social Darwinism in Ernst Haeckel and the German Monist League* (London, 1971).

Gay, P., *The Dilemma of Democratic Socialism: Eduard Bernstein's Challenge to Marx* (New York, 1972).

Geiss, I., *German Foreign Policy, 1871–1914* (London, 1976).

—— *Geschichte des Rassismus* (Frankfurt a.M., 1988).

—— *The Question of German Unification, 1806–1996* (London, 1997).

—— and Wendt, B.-J. (eds.), *Deutschland in der Weltpolitik des 19. und 20. Jahrhunderts* (Düsseldorf, 1973).

Gellner, E., *Nations and Nationalism* (Oxford, 1983).

Giddens, A., *Capitalism and Modern Social Theory: An Analysis of the Writings of Marx, Durkheim and Max Weber* (Cambridge, 1971).

Giesen, B., *Die Intellektuellen und die Nation* (Frankfurt a.M., 1993).

—— (ed.), *Nationale und kulturelle Identität* (Frankfurt a.M., 1991).

Gilcher-Holtey, I., *Das Mandat des Intellektuellen. Karl Kautsky und die Sozialdemokratie* (Berlin, 1986).

Gilg, P., *Die Erneuerung des demokratischen Denkens im wilhelminischen Deutschland* (Wiesbaden, 1965).

Glaser, H., *Bildungsbürgertum und Nationalismus* (Munich, 1993).

Gollwitzer, H., 'Der Cäsarismus Napoleons III. im Widerhall der öffentlichen Meinung Deutschlands', *Historische Zeitschrift*, 173 (1952), 23–75.

Gooch, G. P., *Franco-German Relations, 1871–1914* (London, 1923).

Gorges, I., *Sozialforschung in Deutschland, 1872–1914. Gesellschaftliche Einflüsse auf Themen und Methodenwahl des Vereins für Sozialpolitik* (Königstein, 1980).

Goubard, D., *Das Frankreichbild in der Zeitschrift 'Der Türmer' 1898–1920. Ein Beitrag zur komparatistischen Imagologie*, D.Phil. thesis (Aachen, 1977).

Grebing, H., *A History of the German Labour Movement* (London, 1969).

—— *Arbeiterbewegung, sozialer Protest und kollektive Interessenvertretung bis 1914* (Munich, 1985).

Greenfield, L., *Nationalism: Five Roads to Modernity* (Cambridge, Mass., 1993).

Greiffenhagen, M., *Das Dilemma des Konservatismus in Deutschland* (Munich, 1971).

Grimm, D., *Recht und Staat der bürgerlichen Gesellschaft* (Frankfurt a.M., 1987).

Groh, D., *Negative Integration und revolutionärer Attentismus. Die deutsche Sozialdemokratie am Vorabend des ersten Weltkrieges* (Frankfurt a.M. and Berlin, 1973).

—— *Rußland im Blick Europas. 300 Jahre historische Perspektiven*, 2nd revised edn. (Frankfurt a.M., 1988).

Grosser, A. (ed.), *Frankreich und Deutschland. Elemente der Neuorientierung in der kulturellen und politischen Begegnung de beiden Nachbarvölker* (Wurzburg, 1963).

Grosser, D., *Vom monarchischen Konstitutionalismus zur parlamentarischen Demokratie* (Den Haag, 1970).

Groth, O., *Die Zeitung. Ein System der Zeitungskunde* (4 vols.; Berlin, 1928–30).

Grupp, P., *Deutschland, Frankreich und die Kolonien. Der französische 'Parti colonial' und Deutschland von 1880 bis 1914* (Tübingen, 1980).

Guillen, P., *L'Allemagne et le Maroc de 1870 à 1905* (Paris, 1967).

Guttsmann, W. L., *The German Social Democratic Party, 1875–1933* (London, 1981).

Hall, A., *Scandal, Sensation and Social Democracy* (Cambridge, 1977).

Haller, J., *Tausend Jahre deutsch-französische Beziehungen* (Stuttgart, 1936).

Hammerstein, N. (ed.), *Deutsche Geschichtswissenschaft um 1900* (Stuttgart, 1988).

Happ, W., *Das Staatsdenken Friedrich Naumanns* (Bonn, 1968).

Hardtwig, W., *Geschichtskultur und Wissenschaft* (Munich, 1990).

Hartmann, V., *Repräsentation in der politischen Theorie und Staatslehre in Deutschland* (Berlin, 1979).

Hauck, G., *Geschichte der soziologischen Theorie. Eine ideologiekritische Einführung* (Reinbek b. Hamburg, 1984).

Hausenstein, W., 'Kulturelle Beziehungen Zwischen Frankreich und Deutschland', in Deutsch-Französisches Institut, Ludwigsburg, *Deutschland-Frankreich* (Stuttgart, 1954–66).

Heckart, B. A., *From Bassermann to Bebel: The Grand Bloc's Quest for Reform in the Kaiserreich, 1900–1914* (New Haven and London, 1974).

Hepp, C., *Avantgarde. Moderne Kunst, Kulturkritik und Reformbewegungen nach der Jahrhundertwende* (Munich, 1987).

Herre, F., *Deutsche und Franzosen. Der lange Weg zur Freundschaft* (Lübbe, 1983).

Herwig, H. H., *The German Naval Officer Corps: A Social and Political History, 1890–1918* (Oxford, 1973).

Hiden, J., *Republican and Fascist Germany* (London, 1996).

Hildebrand, K., *Deutsche Aussenpolitik, 1871–1918* (Munich, 1989).

Hillgruber, A., *Germany and the Two World Wars* (Cambridge, Mass., 1981).

Hobsbawm, E. J., and Ranger T. (eds.), *The Invention of Tradition* (Cambridge, 1983).

—— *Nations and Nationalism since 1780* (Cambridge, 1990).

Hofer, W., *Geschichtsschreibung und Weltanschauung* (Munich, 1950).

Hoffmann, J., *Stereotypen–Vorurteile–Völkerbilder in Ost und West–in Wissenschaft und Unterricht. Eine Bibliographie* (Dortmund, 1986).

Holl, J., and List, G. (eds.), *Liberalismus und imperialistischer Staat* (Göttingen, 1975).

—— Trautmann, G., and Vorländer, H. (eds.), *Sozialer Liberalismus* (Göttingen, 1986).

Holl, K., *Pazifismus in Deutschland* (Frankfurt a.M., 1988).

Hroch, M., *Social Preconditions of National Revival in Europe* (Cambridge, 1985).

Huber, E.-R., *Deutsche Verfassungsgeschichte*, iii (Stuttgart, 1988).

Hübinger, G., 'Staatstheorie und Politik als Wissenschaft im Kaiserreich: Georg Jellinek, Otto Hintze und Max Weber', in H. Maier *et al.* (eds.), *Politik, Philosophie, Praxis. Festschrift für Wilhelm Hennis* (Stuttgart, 1988), 143–61.

—— and Mommsen, W. J. (eds.), *Intellektuelle im Deutschen Kaiserreich* (Frankfurt a.M., 1993).

Hübner, K., *Das Nationale* (Graz, 1991).

Hucko, E. (ed.), *The Democratic Tradition* (Oxford, 1987).

Hughes, M., *Nationalism and Society: Germany, 1800–1945* (London, 1988).

Hull, I. V., *The Entourage of Kaiser Wilhelm II, 1888–1918* (Cambridge, 1982).

Igelmund, C. M., *Frankreich und das Staatslexikon von Rotteck und Welcker* (Frankfurt a.M., 1987).

Iggers, G. G., *The German Conception of History: The National Tradition of Historical Thought from Herder to the Present* (Hanover, NH, 1983).

James, H., *A German Identity, 1770–1990* (London, 1989).

Jarausch, K., *The Enigmatic Chancellor* (London, 1973).

—— *Students, Society and Politics in Imperial Germany: The Rise of Academic Illiberalism* (Princeton, 1982).

Jeismann, M., *Das Vaterland der Feinde* (Stuttgart, 1992).

John, M., *Politics and the Law in late Nineteenth-Century Germany: The Origins of the Civil Code* (Oxford, 1989).

Joll, J., *The Origins of the First World War* (London, 1984).

Jones, L. E., and Retallack, J. (eds.), *Elections, Mass Politics and Social Change in Modern Germany* (Cambridge, 1992).

Jordan, L. (ed.), *Interferenzen. Deutschland und Frankreich. Literatur-Wissenschaft-Sprache* (Düsseldorf, 1983).

Kaelble, H., 'Wahrnehmung der Industrialisierung. Die französische Gesellschaft im Bild der Deutschen zwischen 1891 und 1914', in W. Süß (ed.), *Übergänge. Zeitgeschichte zwischen Utopie und Machbarkeit* (Berlin, 1989).

—— *Nachbarn am Rhein* (Munich, 1991).

—— and Winckler. H. A. (eds.), *Nationalismus, Nationalitäten und Supernationalität* (Stuttgart, 1993).

Kahane, M., and Wild, N., *Wagner et la France* (Paris, 1983).

Kamenka, E. (ed.), *Nationalism* (New York, 1976).

Kautz, K., *Das deutsche Frankreichbild im ersten Hälfte des 19. Jahrhunderts*, D.Phil. thesis (Cologne, 1957).

Keane, J. (ed.), *Civil Society and the State* (London, 1988).

Kelly, A., *The Descent of Darwin: The Popularization of Darwin in Germany, 1860–1914* (Chapel Hill, NC, 1981).

Kennedy, P. M., *The Rise of the Anglo-German Rivalry, 1860–1914* (London, 1980).

—— (ed.), *The War Plans of the Great Powers, 1880–1914* (London, 1979).

—— and Nicholls, A. J. (eds.), *Nationalist and Racialist Movements in Britain and Germany before 1914* (London, 1981).

Kirchner, J., *Das deutsche Zeitschriftenwesen*, ii (Wiesbaden, 1962).

Kitchen, M., *The German Officer Corps, 1890–1914* (Oxford, 1968).

Knipping, F., and Weisenfeld, E. (eds.), *Eine ungewöhnliche Geschichte. Deutschland-Frankreich seit 1870* (Bonn, 1970).

Koch, H. W., *Der Sozialdarwinismus. Seine Genese und sein Einfluß auf das imperialistische Denken* (Munich, 1973).

—— (ed.), *The Origins of the War of 1914: Great Power Rivalry and German War Aims* (London, 1972).

Koch, U. E., *Voisins et ennemis* (Munich, 1990).

Kocka, J., 'Otto Hintze, Max Weber und das Problem der Bürokratie', *Historische Zeitschrift*, 233 (1981), 65–105.

—— (ed.), *Bürgertum im 19. Jahrhundert. Deutschland im europäischen Vergleich* (3 vols.; Munich, 1988).

—— (ed.), *Bildungsbürgertum im 19. Jahrhundert* (4 vols.; Stuttgart, 1989).

Koepping, K.-P., *Adolf Bastian and the Psychic Unity of Mankind: The Foundations of Anthropology in Nineteenth-Century Germany* (St Lucia, 1983).

Kohn, H., *The Mind of Germany* (London, 1965).

—— *Prelude to Nation-States: The French and German Experience, 1789–1815* (Princeton, 1967).

Kolboom, I., 'Zur Rezeption der französischen Gewerkschaftsbewegung im Deutschen Reich und in der Bundesrepublik. Eine bibliographische Skizze', *Lendemains*, 7 and 8 (1977), 5–30.

Kornberg, J., 'Dilthey's Introduction to the Social Sciences: Liberal Social Thought in the Second Reich', in M. Eksteins and H. Hammerschmidt (eds.), *Nineteenth-Century Germany* (Tübingen, 1983).

Kornbichler, T., *Deutsche Geschichtsschreibung im 19. Jahrhundert. Wilhelm Dilthey und die Begründung der modernen Geschichtswissenschaft* (Pfaffenweiler, 1984).

Kortländer, B., and Nies, F. (eds.), *Französische Literatur in deutscher Sprache* (Düsseldorf, 1986).

Koszyk, K., *Deutsche Presse im 19. Jahrhundert* (Berlin, 1966).

—— 'Sozialdemokratie und Antisemitismus zur Zeit der Dreyfus-Affäre', in L. Heid and A. Paucker (eds.), *Juden und deutsche Arbeiterbewegung bis 1933* (Tübingen, 1992).

Krieger, L., *The German Idea of Freedom* (Boston, 1957).

Krill, H.-H., *Die Rankerenaissance. Max Lenz und Erick Marcks. Ein Beitrag zum historisch-politischen Denken in Deutschland, 1880–1935* (Berlin, 1962).

Krüger, D., *Nationalökonomen im wilhelminischen Deutschland* (Göttingen, 1983).

Krumeich, G., 'Die Resonanz der Dreyfus-Affare im Deutschen Reich', in G. Hübinger and W. J. Mommsen (eds.), *Intellektuelle im Deutschen Kaiserreich* (Frankfurt a.M., 1993).

Lambi, I. N., *The Navy and German Power Politics, 1862–1914* (Boston, 1984).

Langewiesche, D., 'Das Deutsche Kaiserreich—Bemerkungen zur Diskussion über Parlamentarisierung und Demokratisierung Deutschlands', *Archiv für Sozialgeschichte*, 19 (1979), 628–42.

—— *Liberalismus in Deutschland* (Frankfurt a.M., 1988).

—— (ed.), *Liberalismus im 19. Jahrhundert. Deutschland im europäischen Vergleich* (Göttingen, 1988).

Langhorne, R., *The Collapse of the Concert of Europe: International Politics, 1890–1914* (London, 1981).

Lauren, P. G., *Diplomats and Bureaucrats* (Stanford, Calif., 1976).

Lauret, R., *Notre voisin l'allemand. Deux peuples s'affrontent* (Paris, 1960).

Leenhardt, J., and Picht, R. (eds.), *Esprit/Geist. 100 Schlüsselbegriffe für Deutschen und Franzosen* (Munich, 1989).

Lehner, H., *Auf der Suche nach Frankreich. Der Nachbar im Westen und die deutsche Kultur* (Herrenalb, 1966).

Leiner, W., *Das Deutschlandbild in der französischen Literatur* (Darmstadt, 1989).

Lepenies, W., *Between Literature and Science: The Rise of Sociology* (Cambridge, 1988).

Lerman, K. A., *The Chancellor as Courtier: Bernhard von Bülow and the Governance of Germany, 1900–1909* (Cambridge, 1990).

Levine, N., 'Engels, England and the English Working-Class', in G. Niedhart (ed.), *Großbritannien als Gast- und Exilland für Deutsche im 19. und 20. Jahrhundert* (Bochum, 1985), 58–88

Lidtke, V. L., *The Outlawed Party: Social Democracy in Germany, 1878–1890* (Princeton, 1966).

—— *The Alternative Culture: Socialist Labour in Imperial Germany* (Oxford, 1985).

Lindenlaub, D., *Richtungskämpfe im Verein für Sozialpolitik: Wissenschaft und Sozialpolitik im Kaiserreich vornehmlich vom Beginn des 'Neuen Kurses' bis zum Ausbruch des ersten Weltkrieges* (Wiesbaden, 1967).

Link, J., and Wülfung, W. (eds.), *Nationale Mythen und Symbole in der zweiten Hälfte des 19. Jahrhunderts. Strukturen und Funktionen nationaler Identität* (Stuttgart, 1991).

Loebel, H. (ed.), *Frankreich und Deutschland. Zur Geschichte einer produktiven Nachbarschaft* (Bonn, 1986).

Lorenz, I. S., *Eugen Richter* (Husum, 1981).

Loth, W., *Katholiken im Kaiserreich. Der politische Katholozismus in der Krise des wilhelminischen Deutschlands* (Düsseldorf, 1984).

Lüsebrink, H.-J., and Riesz, J. (eds.), *Feindbild und Faszination* (Frankfurt a.M., 1984).

Magnou, J., *Die Dreyfus-Affäre im Spiegel der Wiener Presse. Eine ideologische Studie* (Siegen, 1983).

Maier, H., Matz, U., Sontheimer, K., and Weinacht, P.-L. (eds.), *Politische Wissenschaft in Deutschland* (Munich, 1969).

—— *Die ältere deutsche Staats- und Verwaltungslehre*, 2nd revised edn. (Munich, 1980).

Malettke, K., 'La Révolution française dans l'historiographie allemande du XIX siècle: Le Cas de Heinrich von Sybel', *Francia*, 16 (1989), 100–19.

Malhotra, R., *Horror-Galérie. Ein Bestiarium der Dritten Französischen Republik* (Dortmund, 1980).

Mann, G. (ed.), *Biologismus im 19. Jahrhundert* (Stuttgart, 1973).

Mayer, A. J., *The Persistence of the Old Regime* (Princeton, 1981).

Metz, K. H., *Grundformen historiographischen Denkens. Wissenschaftsgeschichte als Metholodogie* (Munich, 1979).

Miller, S., *Das Problem der Freiheit im Sozialismus*, 2nd edn. (Frankfurt a.M., 1964).

—— and Potthoff, H., *A History of German Social Democracy* (Leamington Spa, 1986).

Milza, P., and Poidevin, R. (eds.), *La Puissance française à la belle époque* (Brussels, 1992).

Mitzman, A., *Sociology and Estrangement: Three Sociologists of Imperial Germany* (Oxford, 1987).

Moltmann, G., 'Deutsch-amerikanische Wanderungen und deutsch-amerikanische Beziehungen', *Zeitschrift für Kulturaustausch*, 4 (1982), 446–9.

Mommsen, H., *Arbeiterbewegung und nationale Frage* (Göttingen, 1979).

Mommsen, W. J., *Max Weber and German Politics, 1890–1920* (Chicago, 1984).

—— 'Ranke and the Neo-Rankean School in Imperial Germany', in J. M. Powell (ed.), *Ranke and the Shaping of the Historical Discipline* (Syracuse, 1988), 124–40.

—— *Grossmachtstellung und Weltpolitik 1870–1914* (Frankfurt a.M., 1993).

—— *Imperial Germany, 1867–1918* (London, 1995).

—— and Osterhammel, J. (eds.), *Max Weber and his Contemporaries* (London, 1987).

Mosse, G. L., *The Nationalization of the Masses* (Ithaca, NY, 1975).

—— *Nationalismus und Sexualität. Bürgerliche Moral und sexuelle Normen* (Munich, 1985).

—— *Die Geschichte des Rassismus in Europa* (Frankfurt a.M., 1990).

Nerlich, M. (ed.), *Kritik der Frankreichforschung, 1871–1975* (Berlin, 1977).

Nipperdey, T., *Die Organisation der deutschen Parteien vor 1918* (Düsseldorf, 1961).

—— *Nachdenken über die deutsche Geschichte* (Munich, 1986).

—— *Deutsche Geschichte 1866–1918* (2 vols.; Munich, 1993).

Nitschke, A., Ritter, G. A., Peukert, D. J. K., and Bruch, R. vom (eds.), *Jahrhundertwende. Der Aufbruch in die Moderne 1880–1930* (2 vols.; Reinbek b. Hamburg, 1990).

Nolte, E., 'Deutscher Scheinkonstitutionalismus?', *Historische Zeitschrift*, 228 (1979), 529–50.

Nurdin, J., 'Images de la France en Allemagne 1870–1970', *Ethno-psychologie*, 26 (1971), 389–414.

—— 'Karl Hillebrand. Un émigré au carrefour des cultures', *Francia*, 14 (1986), 381–8.

Oberschall, A., *Empirical Social Research in Germany, 1848–1914* (The Hague, 1965).

Ody, H. J., *Begegnung zwischen Deutschland, England und Frankreich im höheren Schulwesen seit Beginn des 19. Jahrhunderts* (Saarbrücken, 1959).

Oncken, E., *Panthersprung nach Agadir. Die deutsche Politik während der Zweiten Marokkokrise 1911* (Düsseldorf, 1981).

Pabst, W., and Werner, K.-F., *Das Jahrhundert der deutsch-französischen Konfrontation* (Hanover, 1983).

Paret, P., *Die Berliner Secession* (Frankfurt a.M., 1983).

Picht, P. (ed.), *Deutschland, Frankreich, Europa. Bilanz einer schwierigen Partnerschaft* (Munich, 1978).

Picht, R. (ed.), *Das Bündnis im Bündnis. Deutsch-französische Beziehungen im internationalen Spannungsfeld* (Berlin, 1982).

Poggi, G., *The Development of the Modern State* (London, 1978).

Poidevin, R., *Les Relations économiques et financières entre la France et l'Allemagne de 1891 à 1914* (Paris, 1969).

Pois, R. A., *Friedrich Meinecke and German Politics in the Twentieth Century* (Berkeley, 1972).

Poliakov, L., *Le Mythe aryen*, 2nd edn. (Brussels, 1987).

—— Delacampagne, C., and Girard, P. (eds.), *Über den Rassismus* (Stuttgart, 1979).

Pommerin, R., *Der Kaiser und Amerika. Die USA in der Politik der Reichsleitung 1890–1917* (Cologne, 1986).

Pracht, E., *Parlamentarismus und deutsche Sozialdemokratie, 1867–1914* (Pfaffenweiler, 1990).

Pross, H., *Literatur und Politik. Geschichte und Programme der politisch-literarischen Zeitschriften im deutschen Sprachgebiet seit 1870* (Freiburg i.B., 1963).

Puhle, H.-J., *Agrarische Interessenpolitik und preußischer Konservatismus im wilhelminischen Reich, 1893–1914* (Hanover, 1966).

Quaritsch, H., *Staat und Souveränität*, i (Frankfurt a.M., 1970).

Raddatz, V., *Konzeptionen einer Englandkunde für höhere Schulen im Wandel deutscher Erziehungsziele 1886–1945* (Saarbrücken, 1974).

Rauh, M., *Föderalismus und Parlamentarismus im Wilhelminischen Reich* (Düsseldorf, 1973).

—— *Die Parlamentarisierung des Deutschen Reiches* (Düsseldorf, 1977).

Raulff, H., *Zwischen Machtpolitik und Imperialismus. Die deutsche Frankreichpolitik 1904–1905* (Düsseldorf, 1976).

Renouvin, P. (ed.), *Histoire des relations internationales*, vi (Paris, 1955).

Retallack, J., *Notables of the Right: The Conservative Party and Political Mobilisation in Germany, 1876–1918* (Boston, 1988).

Reynaud, L., *Histoire générale de l'influence française en Allemagne* (Paris, 1914).

Rich, N., *Friedrich von Holstein: Politics and Diplomacy in the Era of Bismarck and Wilhelm II* (2 vols.; Cambridge, 1965).

Richterling, G., *Deutschland-Frankreich. Mythen und Bilder im Wandel* (Münster, 1989).

Riedel, M., 'Der Staatsbegriff der deutschen Geschichtsschreibung des 19. Jahrhunderts in seinem Verhältnis zur klassisch-politischen Philosophie', *Der Staat*, 2 (1963), 41–63.

Ringer, F., *The Decline of the German Mandarins: The German Academic Community, 1890–1933* (Cambridge, Mass., 1969).

Ritter, A. (ed.), *Deutschlands literarisches Amerikabild* (New York, 1977).

Ritter, G., *The Schlieffen Plan* (New York, 1956).

Ritter, G. A. (ed.), *Gesellschaft, Parlament und Regierung* (Düsseldorf, 1974).

—— (ed.), *Regierung, Bürokratie und Parlament in Preußen und Deutschland von 1848 bis zur Gegenwart* (Düsseldorf, 1983).

Rohe, K., *Elections, Parties and Political Traditions in Germany, 1867–1987* (Oxford, 1990).

Röhl, J. C. G., *Germany without Bismarck: The Crisis of Government in the Second Reich, 1890–1900* (London, 1967).

Roth, G., *The Social Democrats in Imperial Germany* (Totowa, NJ, 1963).

Rüther, G. (ed.), *Geschichte der christlich-demokratischen und christlich-sozialen Bewegung in Deutschland* (2 vols.; Bonn, 1989).

Sagave, P.-P., *Berlin und Frankreich 1685–1871* (Berlin, 1980).

Schenk, W., *Die deutsch-englische Rivalität vor dem Ersten Weltkrieg in der Sicht deutscher Historiker*, D.Phil. thesis (Zürich; published Aarau, 1967).

Schieder, T., Dann, O., and Wehler, H.-U. (eds.), *Nationalismus und Nationalstaat* (Göttingen, 1991).

Schlobach, J. (ed.), *Médiations: Aspects des relations franco-allemandes du XVIIᵉ siècle à nos jours* (Berne, 1992).

Schmidt, H., 'Napoleon in der deutschen Geschichtsschreibung', *Francia*, 14 (1986), 530–60.

—— 'Die französische Revolution in der deutschen Geschichtsschreibung', *Francia*, 17 (1990), 181–206.

Schniedewind, K., 'Soziale Sicherung im Alter. Nationale Stereotypen und unterschiedliche Lösungen in Deutschland und Frankreich in der ersten Hälfte des 20. Jahrhunderts', *Francia*, 21 (1994), 29–49.

Schoenbaum, D., *Zabern 1913: Consensus Politics in Imperial Germany* (London, 1982).

Schöllgen, G. (ed.), *Flucht in den Krieg? Die Außenpolitik des kaiserlichen Deutschlands* (Darmstadt, 1991).

Schorn-Schütte, L., *Karl Lamprecht. Kulturgeschichtsschreibung zwischen Wissenschaft und Politik* (Göttingen, 1984).

Schorske, C. E., *German Social Democracy, 1905–1917* (New York, 1955).

Schröder, H.-C., *Sozialismus und Imperialismus* (Bonn, 1975).

Schulte, B. F., *Die deutsche Armee 1900–1914* (Düsseldorf, 1977).

Schulz, W. (ed.), *Der Inhalt der Zeitungen* (Düsseldorf, 1970).

Schulze, H., *States, Nations and Nationalism* (Oxford, 1996).

Schumann, H.-G. (ed.), *Konservatismus* (Königstein, 1984).

Schwabe, K. (ed.), *Deutsche Hochschullehrer als Elite 1815–1845* (Boppard, 1988).

Sheehan, J. J., *German Liberalism in the Nineteenth Century* (London and Chicago, 1978).

Sieburg, H.-O., *Deutschland und Frankreich in der Geschichtsschreibung des 19. Jahrhunderts* (2 vols.; Wiesbaden, 1954–8).

—— 'Die französische Revolution in der deutschen Geschichtsschreibung 1789–1989', in *Relazioni Congresso Associazione degli Storici Europei maggio 1989* (Rome, 1991), 67–76.

Simon, J., 'Wilhelm Liebknecht und Frankreich 1863–1865', in H.-P. Harstick (ed.), *Arbeiterbewegung und Geschichte* (Trier, 1983).
—— *Das Frankreichbild der deutschen Arbeiterbewegung 1859–1865* (Gerlingen, 1984).
Singer, P., *Hegel* (Oxford, 1983).
Smith, A. D., *National Identity* (London, 1991).
Smith, H. W., *German Nationalism and Religious Conflict: Culture, Ideology, Politics, 1870–1914* (Princeton, 1995).
Smith, W. D., *The Ideological Origins of Nazi Imperialism* (Oxford, 1986).
—— *Politics and the Sciences of Culture* (Oxford, 1991).
Sperber, J., 'The Shaping of Political Catholicism in the Ruhr Basin, 1848–1881', *Central European History*, 16 (1983), 347–67.
—— *Popular Catholicism in Nineteenth-Century Germany* (Princeton, 1984).
Spies, W. (ed.), *Paris–Berlin. 1900–1933* (Munich, 1979).
Stegmann, D., Wendt, B.-J., and Witt, P.-C. (eds.), *Deutscher Konservatismus im 19. und 20. Jahrhundert* (Bonn, 1983).
Stern, F., *The Politics of Cultural Despair* (Los Angeles, 1963).
Stolleis, M., 'Verwaltungsrechtswissenschaft und Verwaltungslehre 1866–1914', *Die Verwaltung*, 15 (1982), 45–77.
Struve, W., *Elites against Democracy: Leadership Ideals in Bourgeois Political Thought in Germany, 1890–1933* (Princeton, 1973).
Stuart Hughes, H., *Consciousness and Society: The Reorientation of European Social Thought, 1890–1930* (Brighton, 1979).
Stübling, R., *'Vive la France!' Der Sozialdemokrat Hermann Wendel, 1884–1936* (Frankfurt a.M., 1983).
Stürmer, M., *Regierung und Reichstag im Bismarckstaat 1871–1880* (Düsseldorf, 1974).
—— (ed.), *Das kaiserliche Deutschland* (Düsseldorf, 1970).
Tavel, H. C. v. (ed.), *Le Cavalier bleu* (Berne, 1986).
Thadden, R. v., *Nicht Vaterland, nicht Fremde: Essays zur Geschichte und Gegenwart* (Munich, 1989).
Theiner, P., *Sozialer Liberalismus und deutsche Weltpolitik. Friedrich Naumann im wilhelminischen Deutschland 1860–1919* (Baden-Baden, 1983).
Trommler, F. (ed.), *Amerika und die Deutschen. Bestandsaufnahme einer 300 jährigen Geschichte* (Opladen, 1986).
Trouillet, B., *Das deutsch-französische Verhältnis im Spiegel von Kultur und Sprache* (Weinheim, 1987).
Uthmann, J., *Le Diable est-il allemand? 200 ans de préjugés franco-allemands* (Paris, 1984).
Vagts, A., *Deutschland und die Vereinigten Staaten in der Weltpolitik*, i (London, 1935).
Vincent, A., *Theories of the State* (Oxford, 1987).
Weber, W., *Priester der Clio. Historisch-sozialwissenschaftliche Studien zur Herkunft und Karriere deutscher Historiker und zur Geschichte des Geschichtswissenschaft, 1800–1970* (Frankfurt a.M., 1984).

Wegner, K., *Theodor Barth und die freisinnige Vereinigung* (Tübingen, 1968).

Wehler, H.-U., *Sozialdemokratie und Nationalstaat* (Würzburg, 1962).

—— *The German Empire* (Leamington Spa, 1985).

—— (ed.), *Deutsche Historiker* (9 vols.; Göttingen, 1971–82).

Weindling, P., *Health, Race and German Politics between National Unification and Nazism, 1870–1945* (Cambridge, 1989).

Weiner, R., *Das Amerikabild von Karl Marx* (Bonn, 1982).

Weingart, P., Kroll, J., and Bayertz, K., *Rasse, Blut und Gene. Geschichte der Eugenik und Rassenhygiene in Deutschland* (Frankfurt a.M., 1988).

Weiss, S. F., *Race Hygiene and National Efficiency: The Eugenics of Wilhelm Schallmayer* (Los Angeles, 1987).

Wernecke, K., *Der Wille zur Weltgeltung. Außenpolitik und Öffentlichkeit im Kaiserreich am Vorabend des Ersten Weltkrieges* (Düsseldorf, 1970).

White, D. S., *The Splintered Party: National Liberalism in Hessen and the Reich, 1867–1918* (Cambridge, Mass., 1976).

Winkel, H., *Die deutsche Nationalökonomie im 19. Jahrhundert* (Darmstadt, 1977).

Winkler, H.-A., *Liberalismus und Antiliberalismus* (Göttingen, 1979).

—— *Nationalismus* (Königstein, 1985).

Winzen, P., *Bülows Weltmachtkonzept. Untersuchungen zur Frühphase seiner Außenpolitik, 1897–1901* (Boppard, 1977).

Witt, P.-C., *Die Finanzpolitik des deutschen Reiches von 1903 bis 1914* (Lübeck and Hamburg, 1970).

Zmarzlik, H.-G., *Bethmann Hollweg als Reichskanzler* (Düsseldorf, 1957).

—— 'Das Kaiserreich in neuer Sicht?', *Historische Zeitschrift*, 222 (1976), 105–26.

INDEX